A *New* HARMONY OF THE GOSPELS

Other Books by A. C. Wieand

THE GOSPEL OF PRAYER - ITS PRACTICE AND PSYCHOLOGY
STUDIES IN THE GOSPEL OF MATTHEW
STUDIES IN THE GOSPEL OF MARK
STUDIES IN THE GOSPEL OF JOHN
etc.

A *New* HARMONY OF THE GOSPELS

THE GOSPEL RECORDS OF THE MESSAGE AND MISSION OF JESUS CHRIST

Based on the Revised Standard Version

by Albert Cassel Wieand

Founder, Bethany Biblical Seminary, Chicago

WM. B. EERDMANS PUBLISHING CO.

Grand Rapids Michigan

Sixth printing, January, 1961

PHOTOLITHOPRINTED BY CUSHING - MALLOY, INC.
ANN ARBOR, MICHIGAN, UNITED STATES OF AMERICA

The Message and Mission

WHAT THE GOSPELS PROPOSE TO TELL US

"The beginning of the Good-News of Jesus Christ,
the Son of God." - Mark 1:1.

"A narrative of the things which have been accomplished among us,
just as they were delivered to us
by those who from the beginning were eyewitnesses
and ministers of the word." - Luke 1:1-2.

"Immanuel-Jesus," which means, "God-with-us-to-save-us." - Mt.1:21,23.
(Cp. "God was in Christ, reconciling the world to himself." - II Cor.5:19)

"No One has ever seen God; the only Son has made Him known." - Jn.1:18.

HOW JESUS HIMSELF SUMMED UP HIS MESSAGE AND MISSION AT THE END OF HIS PUBLIC MINISTRY, AS REPORTED IN Jn.12:44-50

The Message

And Jesus cried out and said:

"He who believes in me,
believes not in me
but in Him who sent me.

"And He who sees me,
sees Him who sent me.

"For I have not spoken on my own authority;
The Father who sent me
has himself given me commandment
what to say and what to speak.

"And I know that His commandment
is eternal life.

"What I say, therefore,
I say as the Father has bidden me."

The Mission

"I have come as light into the world,
that whoever believes in me
may not remain in darkness.

"I did not come to judge the world but to save the world."

"He who rejects me and does not receive my sayings
has a judge;

"The word that I have spoken
will be his judge
on the last day."

(See § 181, *p.195)*

PREFACE AND INTRODUCTION

There is a perennial freshness and a dynamic appeal about the Gospels that will never grow old, and the steady and insistent popular demand for a simple and ordered Life of Christ which began in apostolic times (Lk.1:1,3.) will never run out.

More books have been written about the Life and Teachings of Christ than about any other human event. And yet almost the only authentic and realistic records we have of Christ's Life and Teachings are our four Gospels, first bound together about A.D. 150.

The church has taken almost infinite pains to preserve these Gospels in the most perfect possible form. Scholars have used every means to sift and purify them. They are still substantially the same. Our translators have done their utmost to give them to us in the best possible form in our own language and in the idiom of our own time. Here these records are presented probably in the best translation it has as yet been possible to produce.

A "Harmony" of the Gospels is essentially a pedagogical device. It is not so much intended to "harmonize" the Gospels as it is a parallel arrangement in order to facilitate all kinds of comparative study of them.

This book is a more analytic and detailed parallel arrangement than is usually attempted. Its major purpose is to "appeal to the creative historical imagination," as Horace Bushnell somewhere says. It aims to "remove the remoteness" of the Biblical events; to bring out with greater force the inherent dramatic power of each incident, and of the life of Christ as a whole; and to make them seem more real to us.

In these days when visual education is so greatly exploited, is it not highly important that we give historically accurate and pedagogically sound guidance to the eager feet of those who seek to give realistic and dynamic expression to the message and mission of Jesus?

It is of course impossible to write a complete and historically authentic biography of Jesus from the slender records we have of only a few years of His life. Still it is imperative that we set down such records as we have, in the best order known to New Testament scholarship and in the best arrangement that can be devised by pedagogical wisdom. And New Testament scholars of all kinds are always doing it in some form or other.

Our Gospels, however, are not history or biography, so much as they are four unique portraits of the greatest life ever lived, the only perfect life ever portrayed. And when we put the four together for comparative study it is in order that we may form a composite portrait of Him whom the Gospels present and to visualize as realistically as possible every incident in the unique life He lived, the works He wrought, and the message He brought from the Father.

Essential Features

1. The text is that of the Revised Standard Version. It is used by special permission.
2. The Gospels are here presented in complete parallel arrangement to facilitate the fullest comparison.
3. All incidents of the Life of Christ are printed separately and in historical sequence, so far as that is possible in the present state of our knowledge. Each incident has an appropriate title and sectional number.
4. These sections are fully co-ordinated in an overall Analytic Outline. A complete Diagram or chart of all the Gospel materials should enable students to remember the entire Life of Christ, or any part of it, in orderly fashion.
5. There are Sectional Detailed Outlines of all Principal Divisions.
6. There are Sketch Maps corresponding to these Outlines, so as to locate events as far as possible geographically, from the Biblical allusions. This should help the memory, as well as the creative historical imagination.
7. Each story is scenically analyzed and divided into paragraphs.
8. There are paragraph titles in the margin, so formulated in associated sequence as to form a graphic story-outline of each incident. This should prove especially valuable in Story-Analysis, Visualization, Dramatic Presentation, or Pictorial Illustration.
9. Paragraphs are analyzed into their essential ideas; each is printed in a line by itself; and each directly parallels the same idea in the other Gospels. This, it is hoped, will save the student hours of time and much annoyance, and will exhibit to him many similarities and contrasts, especially unique colorful details, which he might otherwise have overlooked. This should help greatly in graphic life-like Visualization.
10. The paging also is arranged with great care, so as to present incidents as a whole to the eye, wherever that seemed practicable.

Acknowledgments

During thirty years of studying and teaching the *LIFE OF CHRIST*, inevitably one's obligations to others become very great. Scores of commentaries and "Harmonies" of the Gospels, old and new, and unified and interwoven stories of the Life of Christ have been helpful: a few especially so.

Collaboration with a group of primary teachers in publishing a textbook of graded lessons, entitled "The Child's Life of Christ", in 1917-18, imposed upon me the necessity of being clear about an ordered sequence of events, so far as that can be reasonably assured.

Then it was I found that my first task was to harmonize the "Harmonies", so as to conserve, if possible, the valuable points of all.

Some divide by passovers, some by geographical subdivision, some by logical terms, some mix these all up. This tends to confuse the memory, not to say the understanding. In this book chronological terms are co-ordinated with chronological; geographical with geographical, logical with logical. So far as possible co-ordinate points are carefully associated. This greatly aids the memory, as witness pages 4, 8, 9 and 10, or any of the sectional outlines.

Through years of teaching the Gospels my students of College and Seminary grade were my greatest inspiration and my best critics and helpers.

My deep gratitude is due to my teacher, colleague and long-time friend, Dr. Edward Frantz, sometime College President and Professor, whose long years as editor of the *GOSPEL MESSENGER* made his help in proofreading and his cordial encouragement a very great service to me.

Profoundest of all is my obligation to my wife's selfless and constant devotion and cooperation, without which this volume could not have been begun, nor continued.

"THE ORDER OF EVENTS AND MAIN DIVISIONS OF THE LIFE OF CHRIST"

These are rather definitely indicated by the Gospels themselves. Mark follows a historical order of sequence and has seemingly no other outline or structure. LUKE follows the same order, with slight variations and large additions. The structure of MATTHEW and JOHN vary rather widely from this. Matthew is topically organized; John is supplementary and theological. So it is usual to follow the historical order of MARK-LUKE, rearranging MATTHEW where necessary to fit into this order and filling in JOHN where it belongs, so as to make all of them parallel. This can be seen at a glance by studying the diagrams and the INDEX on pages 265-268.

So far as the Major Divisions are concerned, they are all indicated by crisis events, as pointed out at the bottom of each column of the diagram on page 9, as discussed on page 259. These "Crisis events" seem to determine the movements of Jesus as to time and place.

For the main chronological structure, we are almost entirely dependent on the GOSPEL OF JOHN, who alone locates events in reference to the "set feasts" of Israel, as is clearly shown in both diagrams.

The Geographical locations are indicated by all the Gospels, very simply but with remarkable clarity and definiteness. The sketch maps show at a glance where the events took place.

DIAGRAM OF THE FOUR GOSPELS AS RELATED TO EACH OTHER

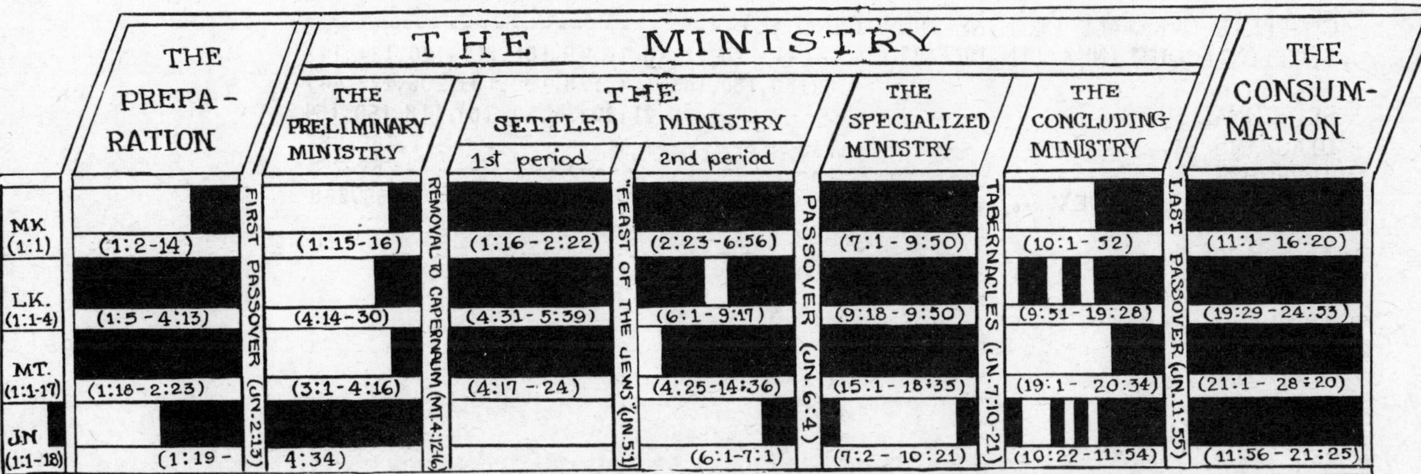

For a separate diagram of the thought structure of each of the Gospels individually see pp.260 and 261.

CONTENTS

YOU CAN REMEMBER
THE LIFE OF CHRIST

[Try in ten minutes to commit The Main Outline on this page]

There are two main headings:
"Introduction"

"The Life of Christ"
In the "Introduction" there are four points,
"Mark's Title,"
" Luke's Preface,"
" John's Prologue,"
" Matthew's Genealogy."

In "The Life of Christ" itself there are Three Parts:

"Part One: The Preparation,"
"Part Two: The Ministry,"
"Part Three: The Consummation."

In "The Preparation" there are four points.
Note how they fit together.
Close your eyes and repeat them.
Then Write Them.
Now speak them aloud.

In "The Ministry," there are four divisions. Commit them in the same way.

In "The Consummation" there are three parts. In the same way commit them.

Now read the whole outline as one unit.
Now write it.
Then repeat it with eyes shut.
Repeat it tonight when you go to bed.
Then in the morning test yourself.
You will remember it.
Review a few times, until it is your permanent possession.

INTRODUCTORY NOTES BY THE GOSPEL WRITERS*

1. MARK'S TITLE § 1

Mk. 1:1

God's Good News (Mk.1:14)
Concerning
His Son (Ro.1:1-4)

1 The beginning of the Gospel**
of Jesus Christ,
the Son of God. ***

2. LUKE'S PREFACE § 2

Lk. 1:1-4

What Others
Have Written

1 Inasmuch as many have undertaken
to compile a narrative
of the things which have been accomplished among us,
2 just as they were delivered to us
by those who from the beginning were eyewitnesses *(II Pet.1:16-18;*
and ministers of the word, *I Jn.1:1-2; Ac.1:21-22)*

What Luke
Proposes
To Write

3 it seemed good to me also,
having followed all things closely[b]
for sometime past,
to write an orderly account
for you, most excellent Theophilus,

What
His Purpose
Is

4 that you may know the truth
concerning the things of which you have been informed.

....

NOTE: *Lettered footnotes are part of the Revised Standard Version text.*
Starred footnotes are the author's comments.

[a]*Some ancient authorities omit* the Son of God. [****But cf.Lk.1:32,35;4:3,9; Mt.4:3,5; Mk.1:24;14:61,62; Lk.22:69-70)*
[b]*Or* accurately.
**These "Notes by the Gospel Writers" are not properly a part of the story of Christ's Life itself, but introductory to it.*
***Or* The good news.

HOW TO USE THIS BOOK

1. *To find the passage you wish to study turn to the index, pp,263-266. Gospel references are at the right side of the page.*
2. *Read the title or subject of the incident, e.g. "Luke's Preface"*
3. *Read the marginal titles on left of page.*
4. *Note that the ideas are grouped into paragraphs.*
5. *See how the "Marginal Titles" sum up the paragraphs.*
6. *See the relation and sequence of the paragraphs.*
7. *Consider how the "Marginal Titles" form a complete outline of the story.*
8. *Visualize each scene and see it merge into the next, like a moving picture.*
9. *Consider what the main message of the whole story is, and the truth it teaches.*
10. *Think out its application to life today, in yourself, in others, and in society.*
11. *Do this for every incident in the book, then you will "see Christ openly set forth before your eyes," and He and His message will be much more real to you.*

(For the underlying Pedagogy, Psychology, see discussion in the Appendix, "HOW TO STUDY THE BIBLE", on page 261, and also especially p. 262. Study these pages many times, until you have mastered them and they have become your habits of thought and conduct).

[***YOU CAN REMEMBER** the Outlines of "Mark's Title" and of "Luke's Preface," by noting how the Marginal Titles of the paragraphs are related to each other. Try it.*

Jn. 1:1-18

THE WORD

(1) His Essential Nature and Relationships (1-5)

His Pre-Existence	1 In the beginning* was the Word,
His Relation to God	and the Word was with God, and the Word was God.
His Relation to Things	2 He was in the beginning * with God; 3 all things were made through him, (Col.1:16) and without him was not anything made that was made.
His Relation to Men	4 In him was life,[a] and the life was the light of men (v.9,14) 5 The light shines in the darkness, and the darkness has not overcome** it.

(2) His Historical Manifestation and How He was Received (6-13)

John Comes To Testify Concerning Him	6 There was a man sent from God, whose name was John. 7 He came for testimony, to bear witness to the light, that all might believe through him. 8 He was not the light, but came to bear witness to the light.
The True Light Of All Men Was Coming	9 The true light that enlightens every man was coming into the world;
He had been In The World Since its Creation Through Him.	10 he was in the world, and the world was made through him, yet the world knew him not;
His Own People Had not Received Him	11 he came to his own home, and his own people received him not.
Some Had Believed and So Had Received Him	12 But to all who received him, who believed in his name, he gave power to become children of God;
They Became Children of God, By Being Born of God (Jn.3:3-5,p.32)	13 who were born, not of blood nor of the will of the flesh nor of the will of man, but of God.

[*YOU CAN REMEMBER* the Outline of John's Prologue.
The Title is "The Word".
There are three Main Divisions.
See how they fit together.
Next note how the paragraph titles in the margin are associated.
Then repeat them aloud with eyes shut.
Then write them.
Proceed with the second and third main points in the same way.
Do this again just before retiring.
Repeat next morning.*

(3) His Unique Character and Mission (14-18)

He Became The Incarnate Word Full of Gracious Truth	14 And the Word became flesh (Phil.2:6-8) and dwelt among us, full of grace and truth; (Col.1:15-20)
He Manifests God's Unique Glory	we have beheld his glory, (Jn.2:11; II Cor.4:6) glory as of the only Son from the Father.
He Is Incomparably Greater Than John	(15 John bore witness to him, and cried, "This was he of whom I said, 'He who comes after me ranks before me, for he was before me.'") (Jn.1:30, p.27)
He Is Greater Than Moses	16 And from his fullness have we all received, (v.14) grace upon grace. 17 For the law was given through Moses; grace and truth came through Jesus Christ.
He Only Adequately Reveals The Father	18 No one has ever seen God; ***(Jn.6:46,p.99; 1 Jn.4:12; Col.1:15; Ex.33:20) the only Son, who is in the bosom of the Father, he has made him known.

....

[a] *Or was not anything made.* That which has been made was life in him.

*1 Jn.1:1; 2:13,14; Gen.1:1; Isa. 40:21.

**Or understood it.

***Bodily senses cannot perceive spiritual realities.

*(Compared With Luke's)**

THE HUMAN ANCESTRY OF THE MESSIAH

Mt. 1:1-17

1The book
of the genealogy of Jesus Christ,
the son of David,
the son of Abraham.

From Abraham to David

2Abraham was the father of Isaac,
and Isaac the father of Jacob,
and Jacob the father of Judah and his brothers,
3and Judah the father of Per´ez
and Ze´rah by Ta´mar,
and Per´ez the father of Hez´ron,
and Hez´ron the father of Ram,[a]
4and Ram[a] the father of Am-min´a-dab,
and Am-min´a-dab the father of Nah´shon,
and Nah´shon the father of Sal´mon,
5and Sal´mon the father of Bo´az by Ra´hab,
and Bo´az the father of O´bed by Ruth,
and O´bed the father of Jesse,
6and Jesse the father of David the king.

From David to the Captivity

And David was the father of Solomon
by the wife of U-ri´ah,
7and Solomon the father of Re-ho-bo´am,
and Re-ho-bo´am the father of A-bi´jah,
and A-bi´jah the father of Asa,[b]
8and Asa[b] the father of Je-hosh´a-phat,
and Je-hosh´a-phat the father of Jo´ram,
and Jo´ram the father of Uz-zi´ah,
9and Uz-zi´ah the father of Jo´tham,
and Jo´tham the father of A´haz,
and A´haz the father of Hez-e-ki´ah,
10and Hez-e-ki´ah the father of Ma-nas´seh,
and Ma-nas´seh the father of Amon,[c]
and Amon[c] the father of Jo-si´ah,
11and Jo-si´ah the father of Jech-o-ni´ah
and his brothers,
at the time of the deportation to Babylon.

From the Captivity to Christ

12And after the deportation to Babylon:
Jech-o-ni´ah was the father of She-al´ti-el,[d]
and She-al´ti-el[d] the father of Ze-rub´ba-bel,
13and Ze-rub´ba-bel the father of A-bi´ud,
and A-bi´ud the father of E-li´a-kim,
and E-li´a-kim the father of A´zor,
14and A´zor the father of Za´dok,
and Za´dok the father of A´chim,
and A´chim the father of E-li´ud,
15and E-li´ud the father of E-le-a´zar,
and E-le-a´zar the father of Matthan,
and Matthan the father of Jacob,
16and Jacob the father of Joseph
the husband of Mary,
of whom Jesus was born,
who is called Christ.

Summary

17So all the generations
from Abraham to David
were fourteen generations,
and from David to the deportation to Babylon
fourteen generations,
and from the deportation to Babylon to the Christ
fourteen generations.

Lk. 3:23-38

(Luke tells the genealogy in reverse order and differs in some items. We lack data to make a complete comparison because neither gives all the facts.)

From Joseph and Mary Back to David

being the son (as was supposed) of Joseph,
the son of He´li,
24the son of Matthat,
the son of Levi,
the son of Mel´chi,
the son of Jan´na-i,
the son of Joseph,
25the son of Mat-ta-thi´as,
the son of Amos,
the son of Na´hum,
the son of Es´li,
the son of Nag´ga-i,
26the son of Ma´ath,
the son of Mat-ta-thi´as,
the son of Sem´e-in,
the son of Jo´sech,
the son of Joda,
27the son of Jo-an´an,
the son of Rhesa,
the son of Ze-rub´ba-bel,
the son of She-al´ti-el,[d]
the son of Ne´ri,
28the son of Mel´chi,
the son of Addi,
the son of Cosam,
the son of El-ma´dam,
the son of Er,
29the son of Jesus,
the son of E-li-e´zer,
the son of Jorim,
the son of Matthat,
the son of Levi,
30the son of Symeon,
the son of Judas,
the son of Joseph,
the son of Jonam,
the son of E-li´a-kim,
31the son of Me´le-a,
the son of Men´na,
the son of Mat´ta-tha,
the son of Nathan,
the son of David,

From David Back to Abraham

32the son of Jesse,
the son of O´bed,
the son of Bo´az,
the son of Sal´mon,[e]
the son of Nah´shon,
33the son of Am-min´a-dab,[f]
the son of Ar´ni,[g]
the son of Hez´ron,
the son of Pe´rez,
the son of Judah,
34the son of Jacob,
the son of Issac,
the son of Abraham,

From Abraham back to Adam

the son of Te´rah,
the son of Na´hor,
35the son of Se´rug,
the son of Re´u,
the son of Pe´leg,
the son of Eber,
the son of She´lah,
36the son of Ca-i´nan,
the son of Ar-pha´xad,
the son of Shem,
the son of Noah,
the son of Lamech,
37the son of Methuselah,
the son of Enoch,
the son of Ja´red,
the son of Ma-ha´la-le-el,
the son of Ca-i´nan,
38the son of Enos,
the son of Seth,
the son of Adam,
the son of God.

**The Talmud hints that Matthew gives* Joseph's *descent and Luke* Mary's. *Luke calls Joseph the son of Heli. By marrying Mary, the daughter of Heli, he became his son or as we would say son-in-law. These genealogies connect the Old Testament with the New Testament and indicate the fulfillment of the prophecy. The Old Testament says the Messiah will be a descendant of David and also of Abraham.*

[a]*Greek* Aram. [b]*Greek* Asaph. [c]*Some authorities read* Amos. [d]*Greek* Salathiel. [e]*Some ancient authorities read* Sala. [f]*Many ancient authorities insert* son of Admin *or* son of Aram. [g]*Some ancient authorities write* Aram.

PART ONE: THE PREPARATION *(Learning God's Message in The Laboratory of Life)*

(From His Birth, B.C. 5; To the Beginning of His Public Ministry, A.D.27)

I. THE INFANCY OF JESUS
II. THE CHILDHOOD OF JESUS
III. THE YOUTH OF JESUS
IV. THE YOUNG MANHOOD OF JESUS

THE FIRST PASSOVER (Jn.2:13)

PART TWO: THE MINISTRY *(Giving God's Message to The People)*

(From His First Public Appearance in Jerusalem at the First Passover, A.D.27)
To His Final Return to Jerusalem to Die, at the Passover, A.D. 30)

I. THE PRELIMINARY MINISTRY *(Heralding the Messianic Kingdom In all Parts of Palestine)*

(From His First Public Appearance in Jerusalem, Passover A.D. 27;
To His Settlement in Capernaum, 6 or 8 months later)

(I) IN JUDEA
(II) IN SAMARIA
(III) IN GALILEE

THE REMOVAL TO CAPERNAUM (Mt.4:12-16)

II. THE SETTLED MINISTRY *(Systematic and Intensive Evangelization) (In Galilee)*

(A) THE FIRST PERIOD, or THE EARLIER GALILEAN MINISTRY (4 to 6 months)
(From the Settlement in Galilee to the "Second" Passover)

(I) AT CAPERNAUM
(II) THROUGHOUT GALILEE
(III) BACK AGAIN AT CAPERNAUM

THE SECOND (?) PASSOVER, or THE FEAST OF PURIM (Jn.5:1)

(B) THE SECOND PERIOD, or THE LATER GALILEAN MINISTRY (One Year)
(From the "Second" Passover, April, A.D. 28; To the "Third", April, A.D. 29)

(I) TO THE PASSOVER AND RETURN
(II) TO THE MOUNT OF BEATITUDES AND RETURN
(III) THROUGH SOUTHERN GALILEE AND RETURN
(IV) TO THE GERASENES AND RETURN
(V) IN CAPERNAUM
(VI) THE TWELVE SENT THROUGHOUT ALL GALILEE
(VII) TO BETHSAIDA AND RETURN THROUGH GENNESARET TO CAPERNAUM

THE THIRD (?) PASSOVER (Jn.6:4)

III. THE SPECIALIZED MINISTRY *(Special Training of the Twelve)*

(In Foreign Parts; Mostly Outside Galilee)
(From The Great Crisis *in Galilee, April A.D. 29)*
To The Final Departure *from Galilee, October A.D. 29)*
(6 months: From the Passover to the Feast of Tabernacles)

(I) IN CAPERNAUM AND PHOENICIA
(II) IN DECAPOLIS
(III) IN DALMANUTHA (MAGADAN)
(IV) NEAR BETHSAIDA
(V) NEAR CAESAREA-PHILIPPI
(VI) THROUGH GALILEE
(VII) IN CAPERNAUM
(VIII) FINAL DEPARTURE FROM GALILEE

THE FEAST OF TABERNACLES (Jn.7:2)

IV. THE CONCLUDING MINISTRY *(Intensive Evangelization of Judea and Perea)*

(Controversies in Jerusalem, and Evangelizing in Judea and Perea)
(From the Feast of Tabernacles, Oct.29; To the Feast of the Passover, April A.D.30)

(I) FROM GALILEE TO JUDEA *(THE LATER JUDEAN MINISTRY)*
(II) FROM JUDEA TO PEREA *(FIRST PART OF THE PEREAN MINISTRY)*
(III) FROM PEREA TO BETHANY AND EPHRAIM *(INTERRUPTION OF THE PEREAN MINISTRY)*
(IV) FROM EPHRAIM TO BETHANY *(SECOND PART OF THE PEREAN MINISTRY)*

PART THREE: THE CONSUMMATION *(Pressing for the Final Showdown)*

(From Palm Sunday to Pentecost, 57 days; Spring of A.D. 30)

THE FOURTH (?) PASSOVER (Jn.11:55)

I. CONFLICTS AND WARNINGS *(Invading the Camp of His Enemies) (Sunday to Wednesday)*

(I) THE FINAL CONTROVERSIES AND WARNINGS
(II) THE FINAL DEPARTURE

II. SUFFERINGS AND DEATH *(Outward Triumph of His Enemies) (Thursday to Saturday)*

(I) PREPARATION FOR HIS DEATH
  (1) By Jewish Rulers
  (2) By Jesus
(II) EVENTS LEADING TO HIS DEATH
  (1) Betrayal and Arrest
  (2) Trials and Crucifixion
  (3) Death and Burial

III. TRIUMPH AND GLORY *(His Own Real Triumph) (Fifty Days)*

(I) THE RESURRECTION AND APPEARANCES *(Forty Days)*
(II) THE FINAL COMMISSION AND ASCENSION
(III) THE GLORIFICATION OF JESUS AND THE COMING OF THE HOLY SPIRIT *(Cf.p.178)*

THE LIFE AND TEACHINGS OF CHRIST (in Diagram Form)

PART ONE THE PREPARATION *(30 Years)*		PART TWO THE MINISTRY *(Three Years*										PART THREE THE CONSUMMATION *(57 Days)*
	THE FIRST PASSOVER (Jn. 2:13)	I THE PRELIMINARY MINISTRY *(4-6 months)*	*THE REMOVAL TO CAPERNAUM (Mt. 4:12-16)*	II THE SETTLED MINISTRY *(A Year and a Half)*			*THE THIRD (?) PASSOVER (Jn.6:4)*	III THE SPECIALIZED MINISTRY *(6 months)*	*THE FEAST OF TABERNACLES (Jn. 7:2)*	IV THE CONCLUDING MINISTRY *(6 months)*	*THE FOURTH (?) PASSOVER (Jn. 11:55)*	
I THE INFANCY OF JESUS II THE CHILDHOOD OF JESUS III THE YOUTH OF JESUS IV THE YOUNG MANHOOD OF JESUS		(I) IN JUDEA (II) IN SAMARIA (III) IN GALILEE		*(6-8 months)* *First Period* *(A) THE EARLIER* *GALILEAN MINISTRY* (I) AT CAPERNAUM (II) THROUGHOUT GALILEE (III) BACK AGAIN AT CAPERNAUM	*THE SECOND (?) PASSOVER or THE FEAST OF PURIM (Jn.5:1)*	*(One Year)* *Second Period* *(B) THE LATER* *GALILEAN MINISTRY* (I) TO JERUSALEM TO THE PASSOVER AND RETURN (II) TO THE MOUNT OF BEATITUDES AND RETURN (III) THROUGH SOUTHERN GALILEE AND RETURN (IV) TO THE GERASENES AND RETURN (V) IN CAPERNAUM (VI) THE TWELVE SENT THROUGHOUT GALILEE (VII) TO BETHSAIDA AND RETURN THROUGH GENNESARET TO CAPERNAUM		(I) IN CAPERNAUM AND PHOENICIA (II) IN DECAPOLIS (III) IN DALMANUTHA (MAGADAN) (IV) NEAR BETHSAIDA (V) NEAR CESAREA- PHILIPPI (VI) THROUGH GALILEE (VII) IN CAPERNAUM (VIII) FINAL DEPARTURE FROM GALILEE		(I) FROM GALILEE TO JUDEA *(THE LATER* *JUDEAN MINISTRY)* (II) FROM JUDEA TO PEREA *(FIRST PART* *OF THE* *PEREAN MINISTRY)* (III) FROM PEREA TO BETHANY AND EPHRAIM *(INTERRUPTION* *OF THE* *PEREAN MINISTRY)* 1.The Resurrection of Lazarus 2.The Retirement in Ephraim (IV) FROM EPHRAIM BACK TO BETHANY *(SECOND PART* *OF THE* *PEREAN MINISTRY)*		I CONTROVERSIES AND WARNINGS (I) FINAL APPEALS (II) FINAL DEPARTURE II SUFFERINGS AND DEATH (I) PREPARATIONS FOR HIS DEATH (II) EVENTS LEADING TO HIS DEATH III TRIUMPH AND GLORY (I) THE RESURRECTION and APPEARANCES (II) THE FINAL COMMISSION and ASCENSION (III) THE GLORIFICATION OF JESUS AND THE COMING OF THE HOLY SPIRIT
(The First *Cleansing* *of the Temple* *Jn. 2:15)*		*(The Rejection* *at Nazareth* *Lk. 4:29)*		*(Determined* *Opposition* *By Scribes and* *Pharisees* *Mt. 12:14* *Jn. 5:16,18)*		*(The Great* *Galilean Crisis* *Jn.6:66)*		*(Setting His* *Face to Go* *to Jerusalem* *Lk. 9:51)*		*(The* *Triumphal Entry* *Jesus Offers* *Himself as* *Messianic King* *Mk. 11)*		*(Pentecost* *Lk. 24:49;* *Ac. 1 and 2)*

THE LIFE OF CHRIST

PART ONE

A. THE PREPARATION [*In Detailed Outline*] *(Learning The Father's Message in the Laboratory of Life - Heb.5:8-9)*

(From His Birth, B.C. 5;
To the Beginning of His Public Ministry, A.D. 27)

I. THE INFANCY OF JESUS *(B.C. 6 or 5)* (p.11) *(Ancient Promises and Prophecies Coming True in His Divine--Human Infancy)*

1. The Annunciation to Zechariah and Elizabeth (Lk. 1:5-25) [1]
2. The Annunciation to Mary (Lk. 1:26-38), and Her Visit to Elizabeth (Lk.1:39-56) [2]
3. The Annunciation to Joseph (Mt. 1:18-25) [2]
4. The Birth and Early Life of John the Baptist (Lk.1:57-80) [3]
5. The Birth of Jesus (Lk. 2:1-20) [4]
6. The Circumcision and Naming of Jesus (Mt.1:25b; Lk.2:21) [4]
7. The Consecration of Jesus (Lk. 2:22-39a) [1]
8. The Visit of the Magi (Mt. 2:1-12) [5,1,4,5]
9. The Flight into Egypt (Mt. 2:13-18) [6]

II. THE CHILDHOOD OF JESUS *(B.C. 4 to A.D. 7)* (p.19) [7,2] *(Ideal Childhood)*

1. His Nazareth Home (Mt.2:19-23; Lk.2:39b) [7]
2. His Normal Growth (Lk. 2:40) [2]
   (1) His Physical Growth
      a. In Size -- "And the child grew"
      b. In Strength -- "and waxed strong"
   (2) His Mental Growth
      a. The Increase -- "Becoming" (Gk.)
      b. The Fulness -- "full of wisdom"
   (3) His Spiritual Growth
      a. The Source -- "The grace of God"
      b. The Use -- "was upon him"

III. THE YOUTH OF JESUS *(A.D. 8 to 25)* (p.20) *(Ideal Youth)*

1. The Inquiring Boy (Lk. 2:41-50) [1]
2. The Obedient Son (Lk. 2:51) [2]
3. The Developing Youth (Lk. 2:52) [2]
   (1) In Wisdom
   (2) In Stature
   (3) In Grace
      a. With God
      b. With Men

[IV. THE YOUNG MANHOOD OF JESUS]
(See page 21ff.)

[***YOU CAN REMEMBER***

Try committing this outline.
First Note Its Subject, "The Preparation".
Then Note its Three Main Points and how they naturally follow each other.
Now take the details under Point I. There are 9 of them. See how the first three are related; Then the next two; Circumcision was 8 days after birth and consecration was at 40 days. Then follow "Magi," and "Flight to Egypt."
Locate each story on map.
Review night and morning.

Sketch Map for
THE PERIOD OF PREPARATION

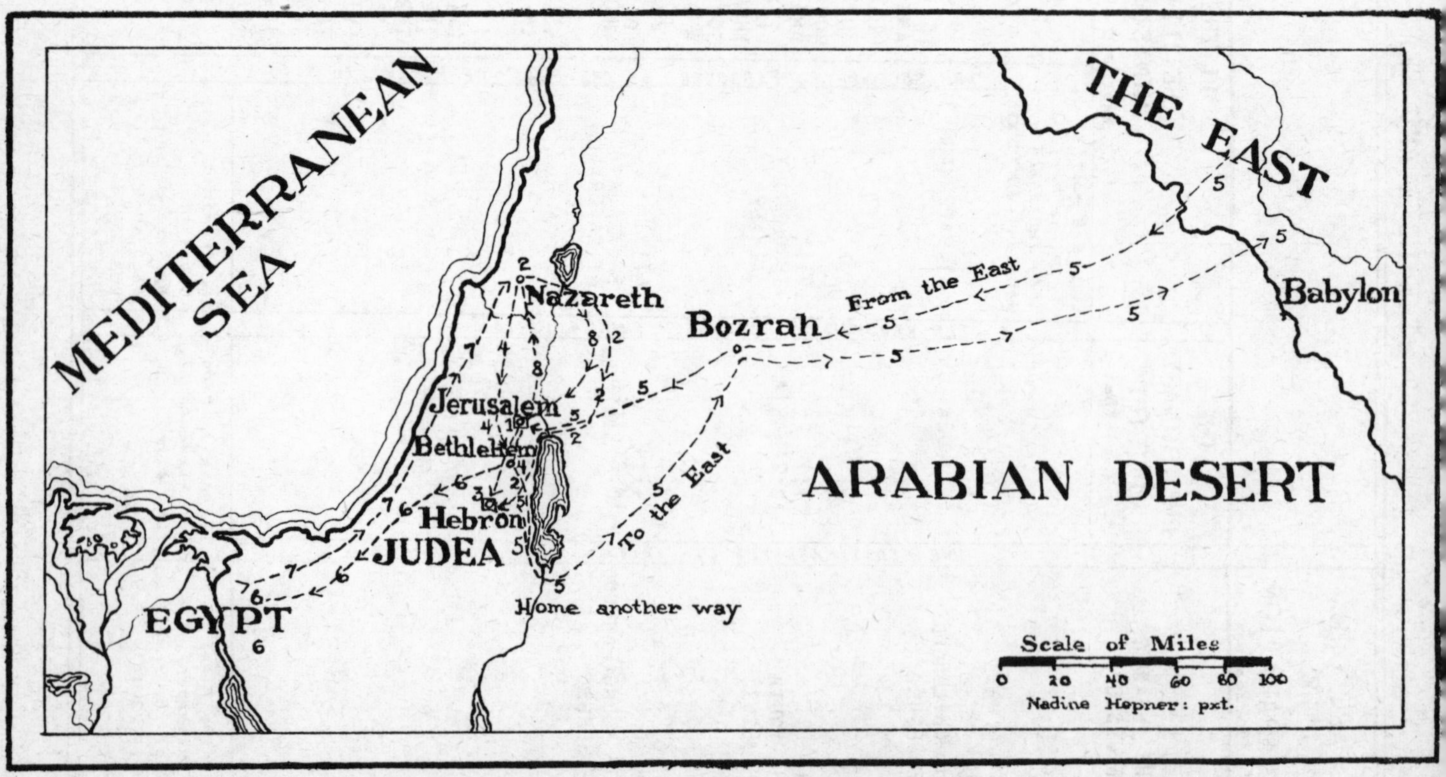

**Bracketed numbers [1] refer to places on the map.*

PART ONE

A. THE PREPARATION* (for The Ministry of Jesus)

I. THE INFANCY OF JESUS (B.C. 6-4)

1. The Annunciation to Zechariah and Elizabeth. § 5

Lk.1:5-25

The Introduction

The Time, place, and persons

5 In the days of Herod, king of Judea,

The King
The Parents of John are Characterized
Their Priestly Descent

there was a priest named Zech-a-ri´ah,[a]
of the division of A-bi´jah; *(Cf. I Chron. 24:1-10)*
and he had a wife of the daughters of Aaron,
and her name was Elizabeth.

Their Names
Their Character

6 And they were both righteous before God,
walking in all the commandments and ordinances of the Lord blameless.

Their One Great Sorrow,

7 But they had no child, because Elizabeth was barren,
and both were advanced in years.

The Story

In the Priests' Quarters
The One Who Is To Offer Incense Is Chosen By Lot

8 Now while he was serving as priest before God
when his division was on duty,
9 according to the custom of the priesthood,
it fell to him by lot to enter the temple of the Lord and burn incense.

The People are Praying Outside The Temple

10 And the whole multitude of the people were praying outside
at the hour of incense.

Inside The Holy Place
At the Altar of Incense
An Angel Appears To Zechariah

11 And there appeared to him an angel of the Lord
standing on the right side of the altar of incense. *(Ex.30:1-10; Rev.8:3-5)*

Zechariah is Overawed

12 And Zech-a-ri´ah was troubled when he saw him,
and fear fell upon him.

The Angel Tells His Message:

A Son Is Promised

13 But the angel said to him,
"Do not be afraid, Zech-a-ri´ah,
for your prayer is heard,
and your wife Elizabeth will bear you a son,
and you shall call his name John. *(v.60,63, p.14)*

He Will Bring Joy to Many,

14 "And you will have joy and gladness,
and many will rejoice at his birth;
15 for he will be great before the Lord,

He Will Be Spirit-Filled,

"And he shall drink no wine nor strong drink,
and he will be filled with the Holy Spirit,
even from his mother's womb.

He Will Bring Israel to Repentance.

16 And he will turn many of the sons of Israel
to the Lord their God,
17 and he will go before him in the spirit and power of Elijah, *(Mal.4:5-6)*
to turn the hearts of the fathers to the children,
and the disobedient to the wisdom of the just,
to make ready for the Lord a people prepared."

Zechariah Asks for Assurance

18 And Zech-a-ri´ah said to the angel,
"How shall I know this?
For I am an old man,
and my wife is advanced in years."

The Angel Replies I Am Gabriel

19 And the angel answered him,
"I am Gabriel, who stand in the presence of God; *(v.26)*

God Has Sent Me To Tell You This Message,

And I was sent to speak to you,
and to bring you this good news.

And You Will Be Dumb

20 "And behold, you will be silent and unable to speak
until the day that these things come to pass, *(v.64, p.14)*
because you did not believe my words,
which will be fulfilled in their time."

---

[a] *Greek* Zacharias.

* *For the complete outline of the life of Christ, see preceding pages. It will greatly help you if you refer to it often, pp.8,9.*

The People Outside Wonder at the Delay:

21And the people were waiting for Zech-a-ri´ah,
and they wondered at his delay in the temple.

Zechariah Comes Out, and Dismisses The Service In Silence

22And when he came out, he could not speak to them,
and they perceived that he had seen a vision in the temple;
and he made signs to them and remained dumb.

The Conclusion

Zechariah Returns Home

23And when his time of service was ended,
he went to his home.

The Angel's Promise Comes True

24After these days his wife Elizabeth conceived,
and for five months she hid herself, saying,
25"Thus the Lord has done to me
in the days when he looked on me,
to take away my reproach among men."

2. The Annunciation to Mary, And Her Visit to Elizabeth. § 6

Lk. 1:26-56

The Angel's Visit to Mary (26-38)

The Angel's Coming:

He Is Sent To Nazareth To Mary

26In the sixth month *(v.19)*
the angel Gabriel was sent from God
to a city of Galilee named Nazareth,
27to a virgin betrothed to a man whose name was Joseph,
of the house of David;
and the virgin's name was Mary.

He Comes To Mary and Greets Her

28And he came to her and said,
"Hail, O favored one,
the Lord is with you!"[a]

She Is Startled

29But she was greatly troubled at the saying,
and considered in her mind what sort of greeting this might be.

The Angel's Message Is A Wonderful Promise

30And the angel said to her,
"Do not be afraid, Mary, for you have found favor with God.

Mary Is To Be Mother of The Messiah, His Greatness and Fame His Kingdom Will Never End

31"And behold, you will conceive in your womb and bear a son,
and you shall call his name Jesus. *(Mt.1:21;* § 10*)*

32"He will be great, and will be called the Son of the Most High. *(v.35)*

"And the Lord God will give to him the throne of his father David,
33and he will reign over the house of Jacob forever;
and of his kingdom there will be no end." *(Is.9:6-7; Zech.9:9-10)*

Mary Wonders How It Can Be

34And Mary said to the angel,
"How can this be, since I have no husband?" Cf. Nicodemus

The Angel Explains

35And the angel said to her,
"The Holy Spirit will come upon you,
and the power of the Most High will overshadow you;
therefore the child to be born[b]
will be called holy, the Son of God. *(v.32)*

He Gives A Thoughtful Suggestion

36"And behold, your kinswoman Elizabeth
in her old age has also conceived a son;
and this is the sixth month with her who was called barren.

37"For with God nothing will be impossible." *(Mk.14:36, p.222)*

Mary Vows Obedience

38And Mary said,
"Behold I am the handmaid of the Lord;
let it be to me according to your word."

The Angel Departs

And the angel departed from her.

---

[a]*Some ancient authorities add* "Blessed are you among women!"
[b]*Some ancient authorities add* of you.

Mary's Visit to Elizabeth (39-56)

Lk. 1:26-56

Mary's Coming and Greeting

39 In those days Mary arose
and went with haste into the hill country,
to a city of Judah,
40 and she entered the house of Zech-a-ri´ah
and greeted Elizabeth.

Elizabeth's Response

41 And when Elizabeth heard the greeting of Mary,
the babe leaped in her womb;

What She Said

and Elizabeth was filled with the Holy Spirit *(v.67,p.15)*
42 and she exclaimed with a loud cry,

She Blesses Mary And Her Child
She Rejoices and Prophesies.

"Blessed are you among women,
and blessed is the fruit of your womb!
43 And why is this granted me,
that the mother of my Lord should come to me?
44 For behold, when the voice of your greeting came to my ears,
the babe in my womb leaped for joy.
45 And blessed is she who believed
that there would be[a] a fulfillment
of what was spoken to her from the Lord."

Mary's Song of Praise:
For God's Blessing to Her

46 And Mary said,
"My soul magnifies the Lord,
47 and my spirit rejoices in God my Savior,
48 for he has regarded the low estate of his handmaiden.
For behold, henceforth all generations will call me blessed;
49 for he who is mighty has done great things for me,
and holy is his name.

For God's Mercy and Judgment Upon All

50 "And his mercy is on those who fear him
from generation to generation.
51 He has shown strength with his arm,
he has scattered the proud in the imagination of their hearts,
52 he has put down the mighty from their thrones,
and exalted those of low degree;
53 he has filled the hungry with good things,
and the rich he has sent empty away.

For God's Blessing to Israel

54 "He has helped his servant Israel,
in remembrance of his mercy,
55 as he spoke to our fathers,
to Abraham and to his posterity forever." *(Gen.12:1-3)*

Mary's Prolonged Stay

56 And Mary remained with her about three months,

Her Return Home

and returned to her home.

---

[a]Or Believed, for there will be.

3. The Annunciation to Joseph. §7

Mt. 1:18-25

The Betrothal and the Discovery

18Now the birth of Jesus Christ[a] took place in this way.
When his mother Mary had been betrothed to Joseph,
before they came together
she was found with child of the Holy Spirit. *(Lk.1:35,p.12)*

Joseph's Perplexity

19And her husband Joseph,
being a just man
and unwilling to put her to shame,
resolved to divorce her quietly.

An Angel's Explanation And Instructions

20But as he considered this, behold,
an angel of the Lord appeared to him in a dream, saying,
"Joseph, son of David,
do not fear to take Mary your wife,
for that which is conceived in her is of the Holy Spirit; *(v.18)*
21she will bear a son,
and you shall call his name **Jesus**, (§10)
for he will save his people from their sins."

An Ancient Prophecy Fulfilled

22All this took place to fulfill
what the Lord had spoken by the prophet: *(Is.7:14)*
23"Behold, a virgin shall conceive and bear a son,
and his name shall be called Em-man'u-el"
(which means, God with us).

Joseph's Obedience

24When Joseph woke from sleep,
he did as the angel of the Lord commanded him;
he took his wife,
25but knew her not until she had borne a son;
and he called his name **Jesus**. [*see* §10]

4. The Birth of John the Baptist. §8

Lk. 1:57-80

John Is Born

57Now the time came for Elizabeth to be delivered,
and she gave birth to a son.

The Friends Rejoice

58And her neighbors and kinsfolk heard
that the Lord had shown great mercy to her,
and they rejoiced with her.

He Is Circumcised

59And on the eighth day
they came to circumcise the child;

He Is Named

and they would have named him Zech-a-ri'ah
after his father,

60but his mother said,
"Not so;
he shall be called John." *(v.63)*

61And they said to her,
"None of your kindred is called by this name."

62And they made signs to his father,
inquiring what he would have him called.

As The Angel Had Commanded

63And he asked for a writing tablet,
and wrote,
"His name is John." *(v.13,p.11)*

And they all marveled.

Zechariah's Speech Is Restored

64And immediately his mouth was opened
and his tongue loosed, *(v.20,p.11)*
and he spoke, blessing God.

The People Are Awed

65And fear came on all their neighbors.
And all these things were talked about
through all the hill country of Judea;

---

[a]*Some ancient authorities read* of the Christ

66 and all who heard them laid them up in their hearts,
saying,
"What then will this child be?"
For the hand of the Lord was with him.

Zechariah's Hymn of Praise For God's Great Salvation Is at Hand.

67 And his father Zech-a-ri´ah was filled with the Holy Spirit, *(v.41,p.13)*
and prophesied, saying,
68 "Blessed be the Lord God of Israel,
for he has visited and redeemed his people,
69 and has raised up a horn of salvation for us
in the house of his servant David,
70 as he spoke by the mouth of his holy prophets from of old,

It Fulfills Ancient Prophecies

71 that we should be saved from our enemies,
and from the hand of all who hate us;
72 to perform the mercy promised to our fathers,
and to remember his holy covenant,
73 the oath which he swore to our father Abraham, *(v.55)*

It Will enable us to Serve God More Fully

74 " to grant us that we, being delivered from the hand of our enemies,
might serve him without fear,
75 in holiness and righteousness before him all the days of our life.

This Child Will Prepare The Way For The Messiah And His Great Salvation.

76 " And thou, child, shalt be called the prophet of the Most High; *(Mt.11:10)*
for thou shalt go before the Lord to prepare his ways,
77 to give knowledge of salvation to his people
in the forgiveness of their sins,
78 through the tender mercy of our God,
when the day shall dawn upon[a] us from on high
79 to give light to those who sit in darkness and in the shadow of death, *(Mt.4:16)*
to guide our feet into the way of peace."

The Early Life of John

He Develops Normally In Body and Spirit

80 And the child grew
and became strong in spirit.

He Lives In Obscurity

And he was in the wilderness
till the day of his manifestation to Israel. *(Lk.3:2)*

5. The Birth of Jesus. § 9

Lk. 2:1-20

(1) The Introduction

Caesar Decrees an Enrollment

1 In those days
a decree went out from Caesar Augustus
that all the world should be enrolled.

It was The First

* 2 This was the first enrollment,
when Qui-rin´i-us was governor of Syria.

The People Everywhere Respond

3 And all went to be enrolled,
each to his own city.

(2) The Birth

*Joseph and Mary Go to Bethlehem Their Ancestral Home, To Be Enrolled**

4 And Joseph also went up from Galilee,
from the city of Nazareth, to Judea,
to the city of David, which is called Bethlehem,
because he was of the house and lineage of David,
5 to be enrolled
with Mary, his betrothed,
who was with child.

*Jesus is Born in Bethlehem He Is Dressed In Baby Clothes Then Laid In a Manger***

6 And while they were there,
the time came for her to be delivered.
7 And she gave birth to her first-born son
and wrapped him in swaddling clothes,
and laid him in a manger,**
because there was no place for them in the inn.

---

[a] Or whereby the dayspring will visit us. *Many ancient authorities read* since the dayspring has visited.

* *This was what we call a "census". We take them every ten years, the Romans took them every fourteen years. Some of the census blanks used in Egypt have been found, all filled in, including women and children; and they were taken according to tribal descent, as here. A second enrollment is mentioned in Ac.5:37.*

** *" manger" in Palstine is a feeding trough about 30 inches long and half that wide. Half filled with chaff or cut straw and lined with some baby things, it made a fine bassinette. It stood on the ground at the head of a stall.*

(3) The Angels and The Shepherds

While Shepherds Are Keeping Watch Over Their Flocks	8And in that region there were shepherds out in the field, keeping watch over their flock by night.
An Angel Appears To Them *They Are Overawed*	9And an angel of the Lord appeared to them, and the glory of the Lord shone around them, and they were filled with fear.
The Angel Speaks: I bring You Good News, The Messiah Is Born.	10And the angel said to them, "Be not afraid; for behold, I bring you good news of a great joy which will come to all the people; 11for to you is born this day in the city of David a Savior, who is Christ the Lord.
This is The Sign.	12"And this will be a sign for you: you will find a babe wrapped in swaddling cloths* and lying in a manger."
Many Angels Come Singing In Heaven - Glory On Earth - Peace When Men please God	13And suddenly there was with the angel a multitude of the heavenly host *(Cf. Heb.1:6)* praising God and saying, 14"Glory to God in the highest, and on earth peace among men with whom he is pleased!" [a]
The Angels Return to Heaven	15When the angels went away from them into heaven,
The Shepherds Decide to Go And See The Child	the shepherds said to one another, "Let us go over to Bethlehem and see this thing that has happened, which the Lord has made known to us."

(4) The Shepherds and The Child

They Go Eagerly *They Find The Babe*	16And they went with haste, and found Mary and Joseph, and the babe lying in a manger.
They Tell What the Angels had told them	17And when they saw it they made known the saying which had been told them concerning this child;
Everyone Marvels	18and all who heard it wondered at what the shepherds told them.
Mary Meditates Reverently	19But Mary kept all these things, pondering them in her heart.
As The Shepherds Return They Are Praising God	20And the shepherds returned, glorifying and praising God for all they had heard and seen, as it had been told them.

6. The Circumcision and Naming of Jesus. § 10

	Mt. 1:25b	*Lk. 2:21*
On The Eighth Day, Jesus Is Circumcised And Named	25bAnd he called his name Jesus. *(Mt.1:21,p.14;Lk.1:31,p.12)*	21And at the end of eight days, when he was circumcised, he was called Jesus, the name given by the angel before he was conceived in the womb.

---

[a] *Some ancient authorities read* "peace, goodwill among men."
* *Or* baby clothes.

7. The Consecration of Jesus. § 11

Lk. 2:22-39a

(1) He Is Dedicated

When He Was 40 Days Old They Brought Him To Jerusalem	22 And when the time came for their purification according to the law of Moses, *(Lev. 12:1-8)* they brought him up to Jerusalem to present him to the Lord
a. To Consecrate Him and	23 (as it is written in the law of the Lord, *(Ex.13:2-16)* "Every male that opens the womb shall be called holy to the Lord")
b. To Remove Ceremonial Uncleanness from the Mother	24 and to offer a sacrifice according to what is said in the law of the Lord, "a pair of turtledoves, or two young pigeons." *(Lev.12:1-8)*

(2) He Is Received by Simeon, A Prophet

Simeon Is Characterized As Righteous, Expectant, Spiritual	25 Now there was a man in Jerusalem, whose name was Simeon, and this man was righteous and devout, *(Lk.1:6,p.11)* looking for the consolation of Israel, and the Holy Spirit was upon him.
He Had A Revelation	26 And it had been revealed to him by the Holy Spirit[a] that he should not see death before he had seen the Lord's Christ.
He Comes To The Temple The Parents Bring Jesus In	27 And inspired by the Spirit[a] he came into the temple; and when the parents brought in the child Jesus, to do for him according to the custom of the law,
Simeon Sees Him He Takes the Child in His Arms He Praises God For His Great Salvation Which Will Be World-Wide	28 he took him up in his arms and blessed God and said, 29 "Lord, now lettest thou thy servant depart in peace, according to thy word; 30 For mine eyes have seen thy salvation *(v.26)* 31 which thou hast prepared in the presence of all peoples, 32 a light for revelation to the Gentiles, *(Ac.13:47; Isa.49:6)* and for glory to thy people Israel."
The Parents Marvel	33 And his father and his mother marveled at what was said about him;
Simeon Blesses Them	34 and Simeon blessed them and said to Mary his mother,
He Prophesies About The Child	"Behold, this child is set for the fall and rising of many in Israel, and for a sign that is spoken against
He Forewarns The Mother of Piercing Sorrow	35 (and a sword will pierce through your own soul also), that thoughts out of many hearts may be revealed."

(3) He Is Received by Anna, A Prophetess

Anna Is Described	36 And there was a prophetess, Anna, the daughter of Phanu-el, of the tribe of Asher;
She Is Old	she was of a great age,
Was married 7 Years	having lived with her husband seven years from her virginity,
Is a Widow	37 and as a widow till she was eighty-four.
Worshiped Constantly In The Temple	She did not depart from the temple, worshipping with fasting and prayer night and day.
She Comes Up Just Then. She Gives Thanks She Prophecies About The Child	38 And coming up at that very hour she gave thanks to God, and spoke of him to all who were looking for the redemption of Jerusalem.

(4) The Parents Go Home

*The Parents Return to Bethlehem And *Later to Nazareth*	39 And when they had performed everything according to the law of the Lord, they returned [into Galilee, to their own city, Nazareth.]*

*For this return to Nazareth, see § 14, p. 19. It took place after the residence in Egypt.

[a]Or in the Spirit.

8. The Visit of the Magi.* § 12

Mt. 2:1-12

When Jesus Is Born
*Magi in the East**
See His Star (v.2)
They Come to Jerusalem

1 Now when Jesus was born in Bethlehem of Judea
in the days of Herod the king,

behold, wise men* from the East** came to Jerusalem,

[At The Eastern Gate]
They Inquire For
the New-born King
of the Jews

saying,
2 " Where is he who has been born king of the Jews?
For we have seen his star in the East**,
and have come to worship him."

The News Is Brought
To Herod the King
He and Jerusalem
Are Worried

3 When Herod the king heard this,
he was troubled,
and all Jerusalem with him;

Herod Assembles
the Jewish Rulers
He Inquires of Them

4 and assembling
all the chief priests and scribes of the people,
he inquired of them where the Christ was to be born.

In Reply
They Quote
A Startling Prophecy,
The Messiah
Is To Be Born
In Bethlehem
He Will Be The Ruler
of God's People

5 They told him,
" In Bethlehem of Judea;
for so it is written by the prophet: (*See Micah 5:2*)

6 'And thou Bethlehem, in the land of Judah,
art by no means least among the rulers of Judah;
for from thee shall come a ruler
who will govern my people Israel.' "

Then Herod
Confers Secretly
With the Magi

7 Then Herod summoned the wise men secretly
and ascertained from them what time the star appeared;

He Sends Them
In Search of
The Child

8 and he sent them to Bethlehem, saying,
" Go and search diligently for the child,
and when you have found him
bring me word,
that I too may come and worship him."

The Magi Leave,
They Go On
to Bethlehem

9 When they had heard the king
they went their way;

When They Near That City
The Star Reappears
to Guide Them

and lo, the star which they had seen in the East**
went before them,
till it came to rest over the place where the child was.

Then They Rejoice
Exceedingly.

10 When they saw the star,
they rejoiced exceedingly with great joy;

Following The Star,
They Go On.
They Find the Child

11 and going into the house
they saw the child with Mary his mother,

They Worship Him

and they fell down and worshiped him.

They Present
Their Royal Gifts

Then, opening their treasurers,
they offered him gifts,
gold and frankincense and myrrh.

At Night
God Warns Them
Of Herod's Treachery
So They Go Home
Another Way

12 And being warned in a dream
not to return to Herod,

they departed to their own country by another way.

[YOU CAN REMEMBER
How to remember a story.
First divide it into scenes.
Then see how scene one merges into scene two and that into the next. In other words make a moving picture of your story.
Note how the story is printed in scenes. Then see how the marginal titles label the scenes.
Then visualize each scene and see it move on into the next.
With a little reviewing, both oral and written, you can repeat the story either forward or backward. In this way memorize this story.]

*For this use of "Wise Men" see Dan. 5:7b-8a.
**"The East" is a geographical term in the Bible, designating Mesopotamia (i.e., Babylonia and Assyria)

9. The Flight Into Egypt. § 13

Mt. 2:13-18

After The Magi Are Gone

13 Now when they had departed,

An Angel Warns Joseph of Herod's Plot, And Tells Him To Flee to Egypt

behold, an angel of the Lord appeared to Joseph in a dream and said,
"Rise, take the child and his mother,
and flee to Egypt,
and remain there till I tell you;
for Herod is about to search for the child, to destroy him."

Joseph Obeys They Go to Egypt

14 And he rose and took the child and his mother by night,
and departed to Egypt,

They Stay in Egypt Till Herod's Death

15 and remained there until the death of Herod. *(4 B.C.)*
This was to fulfill what the Lord had spoken by the prophet,
"Out of Egypt have I called my son." *(Hos.11:1; Ex.4:22)*

But When The Magi Fail to Return to Jerusalem Herod Is Furious He Sends Soldiers and Massacres The Children of Bethlehem And Its Environs

16 Then Herod, when he saw that he had been tricked by the wise men,
was in a furious rage,
and he sent
and killed all the male children in Bethlehem
and in all that region
who were two years old or under,
according to the time which he had ascertained from the wise men.

In This Way An Ancient Prophecy Comes True

17 Then was fulfilled what was spoken by the prophet Jeremiah: *(Jer. 31:15)*
18 "A voice was heard in Ra'mah,
wailing and loud lamentation,
Rachel weeping for her children;
she refused to be consoled, because they were no more."

II. THE CHILDHOOD OF JESUS (B.C. 4 to A.D. 7)

1. His Nazareth Home. § 14

(The Return from Egypt to Nazareth)

Mt. 2:19-23; Lk. 2:39b

An Angel Comes to Joseph In a Dream He Tells Him To Return Home For Herod Is Dead

19 But when Herod died,
behold, an angel of the Lord appeared in a dream to Joseph in Egypt,
saying,
20 "Rise, take the child and his mother,
and go to the land of Israel,
for those who sought the child's life are dead."

Joseph obeys, Returning To Palestine, And There Hears That Herod's Son Is Reigning There He is Afraid

21 And he rose and took the child and his mother,
and went to the land of Israel.

22 But when he heard
that Ar-che-la'us reigned over Judea in place of his father Herod,
he was afraid to go there,

Then, Instructed by God, He Returns to Nazareth.

Mt.	*Lk. 2:39b*
and being warned in a dream	
he withdrew to the district of Galilee.	They returned into Galilee,*
23 And he went and dwelt in a city called Nazareth,	to their own city, Nazareth.

In This Way Another Prophecy Comes True

that what was spoken by the prophets
might be fulfilled,
"He shall be called a Nazarene." *(Is.11:1,Heb.; Mk.1:24)*

Heb. pr. 17 →

2. His Normal Growth. § 15

Lk. 2:40

Throughout Childhood

He Develops Normally

Physical Growth

40 And the child grew and became strong,

Mental Growth

filled with wisdom;

Spiritual Growth

and the favor of God was upon him.

**Cf. Footnote p. 17*

III. THE YOUTH OF JESUS

Lk. 2:41-52

1. The Inquiring Boy. § 16

Lk. 2:41-50

They Go to Passover Annually;

41Now his parents went to Jerusalem
every year at the feast of the Passover. *(Dt.16:1 and 16)*

When Jesus is Twelve He Goes Along.

42And when he was twelve years old,
they went up according to custom.

After The Festival, When They Leave Jerusalem Jesus Unwittingly Is Left Behind

43And when the feast was ended,
as they were returning,
the boy Jesus stayed behind in Jerusalem.
His parents did not know it,
44but supposing him to be in the company
they went a day's journey,

His Parents Hunt for The Lost Boy

and they sought him among their kinsfolk and acquaintances;
45and when they did not find him,
they returned to Jerusalem, seeking him.

They Find Him

46After three days
they found him in the temple,

*He Was In The Temple School**

sitting among the teachers,
listening to them
and asking them questions;
47and all who heard him were amazed
at his understanding
and his answers.

The Parents Are Surprised

48And when they saw him
they were astonished;

They Rebuke Him

and his mother said to him,
"Son, why have you treated us so?
Behold, your father and I have been looking for you anxiously."

He Replies, Naturally Enough, But

49And he said to them,
"How is it that you sought me?**
Did you not know that I must be in my Father's house?"

They Do Not Understand

50And they did not understand the saying which he spoke to them.

2. The Obedient Son. § 17

Lk. 2:51

51And he went down with them
and came to Nazareth,

He Returns Home

He Is Obedient

and was obedient to them;

His Mother Ponders Events

and his mother kept all these things in her heart.

3. The Developing Youth. § 18

Lk. 2:52

Throughout Adolescence

His Normal Development

52And Jesus increased

Mentally — in wisdom

Physically — and in stature,[a]

Spiritually — and in favor

and Socially — with God and man.

YOU CAN REMEMBER

Any story in the Gospels accurately, and confidently for teaching or story telling, for expository preaching, or writing.
Now try memorizing this story, Then the first story in the N.T., that of the Annunciation to Zechariah and Elizabeth.
First note the division into scenes.
Then visualize the first scene, and the second, and see each scene merge into the next, to the end of the story.
Review occasionally.

....

aOr years.

**At this temple School the Rabbis were educated. It was the Jewish "Theological Seminary." Its great teachers were famous as far as Jews were scattered. Here Paul had been sent from Tarsus to be "brought up at the feet of Gamaliel." Before him had been the Great Hillel and Shammi. No wonder that Jesus was fascinated, for during the Passover festival, these great Rabbis taught all who were interested, from the temple steps.*

***These are the very first words of Jesus which have come down to us. Do they mean, "Didn't you know that, I would be here--in my Father's house--in this temple school where His Word is taught?"*

IV. THE YOUNG MANHOOD OF JESUS (A.D. 26 to 27), pp22-29.

(The Messiah Is Consecrated and Initiated).

1. John Is Preaching and Baptizing *(Mt. 3:1-12; Mk. 1:2-8; Lk. 3:1-18; Cf. Jn. 1:33)* [1]** pp.23-24
2. Jesus Is Baptized by John *(Mt. 3:13-17; Mk. 1:9-11; Lk. 3:21-23a)* [2] p.25
3. Jesus Is Tempted by the Devil *(Mt. 4:1-11; Mk. 1:12-13; Lk. 4:1-13)* [3] pp.25-26
*4. John Testifies Concerning Jesus *(Jn. 1:19-34)* [4 & 5] p.27
5. Jesus Wins His First Disciples *(Jn. 1:35-51)* [4] p.28
6. Jesus Attends a Wedding *(Jn. 2:1-11)* [5 and 6] p.29
7. Jesus Visits Capernaum *(Jn. 2:12)* [7] p.29

....

**These last four points may be classified as the opening events of His "Ministry". They are in fact introductory and transitional events of a semi-private nature. However, the real "Public" Ministry was launched at Jerusalem, at Passover time, as is shown in the next section.*

***These numbers refer to the journeys traced on the accompanying map.*

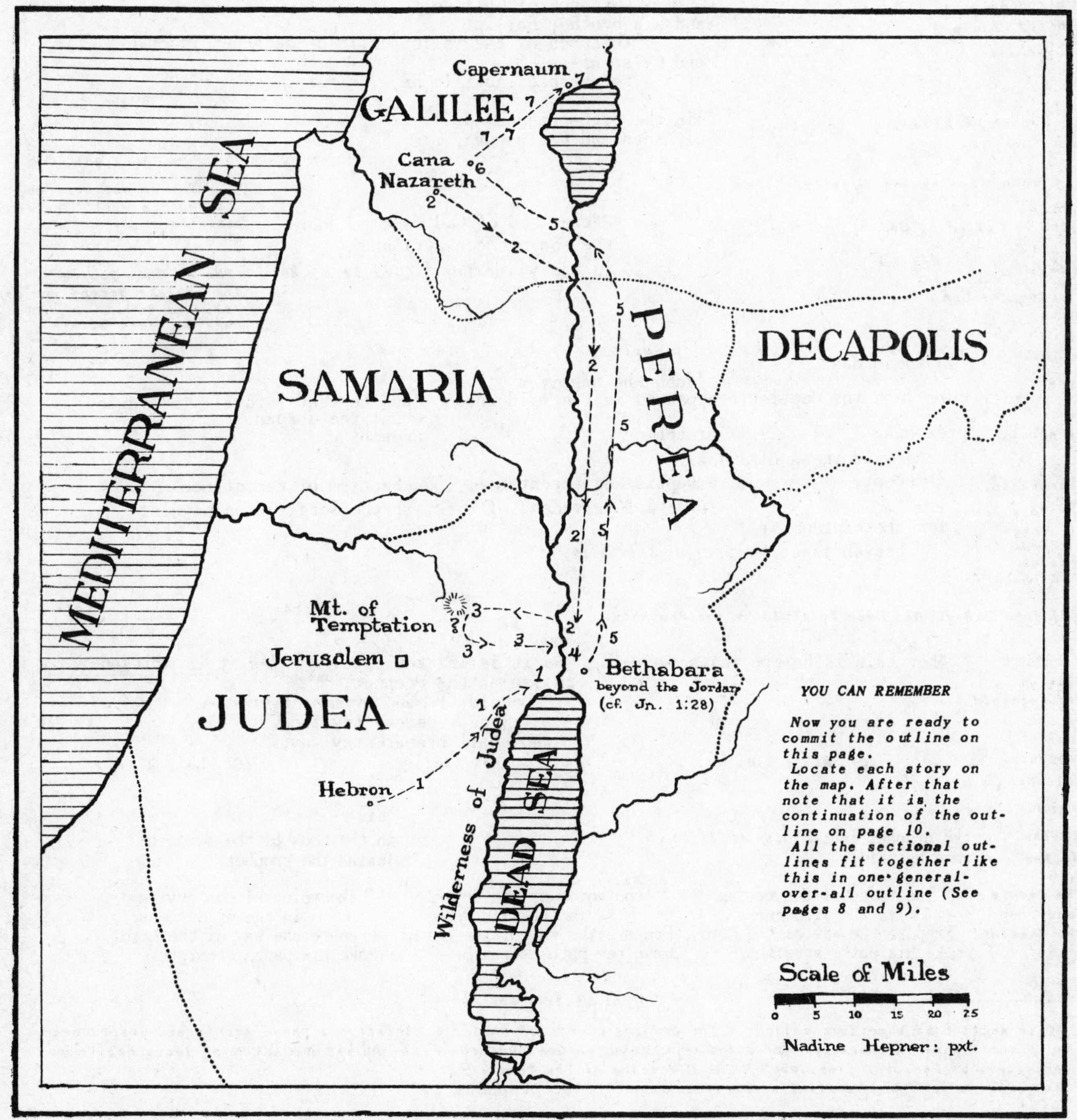

YOU CAN REMEMBER

Now you are ready to commit the outline on this page.
Locate each story on the map. After that note that it is the continuation of the outline on page 10.
All the sectional outlines fit together like this in one general-over-all outline (See pages 8 and 9).

IV. THE YOUNG MANHOOD OF JESUS (A.D. 25-27)

(The Messiah is Consecrated and Initiated)

I. John Is Preaching and Baptizing. § 19

Mt. 3:1-12 | Mk. 1:2-8 | Lk. 3:1-18 | [Cf. Jn.1:33b]

(1) The Time of John's Coming and The Rulers of That Time

The Date	[1]In the fifteenth year of the reign
The Rulers	
The Roman Emperor	of Tiberius Caesar,
The Roman Governor of Judea-Samaria	Pontius Pilate being governor of Judea,
The Tetrarchs	
Herod Antipas	and Herod being tetrarch of Galilee,
Herod Philip	and his brother Philip tetrarch of the region of It-u-rae´a and Trach-o-ni´tis,
Lysanias	and Ly-sa´ni-as tetrarch of Ab-i-le´ne,
The Jewish High Priests	[2]in the high-priesthood of Annas and Ca ia-phas,

(2) John's Coming and Mission

	Lk.	Cf. Jn.1:33b.
John Is Called by God and A Sign Is Promised Him	[2b]the word of God came to John the son of Zech-a-ri´ah in the wilderness; *(Lk 1:5f.,57,80)*	[[33]" *But he who sent me to baptize with** water said to me, 'He on Whom you see the Spirit decend and remai this is he who baptizes with** the Holy Spirit'.* "]

	Mt.	Mk.	Lk.
John	[1]In those days came John the Baptist,	[4]John the baptizer appeared in the wilderness,	[3]and he went into all the region about the Jordan,
Preaches	preaching in the wilderness of Judea,	preaching	preaching
Repentance, and Forgive-ness and That The Messiah Is At Hand	[2]"Repent, for the kingdom of heaven is at hand." *(Cf.Mt.4:17,p.40)*	a baptism of repentance for the forgiveness of sins.	a baptism of repentance for the forgiveness of sin.

(3) John's Work Had Been Foretold by the Prophets.

	Mt.	Mk.	Lk.
John's Mission Was Foretold by the Ancient Prophets Malachi	[3]For this is he who was spoken of *(Cf. Mt. 11:10)*	[2]As it is written in Isaiah the Prophet, a*** "Behold, I send my messenger before thy face, who shall prepare thy way; *(Mal. 3:1)*	[4]As it is written *(Cf. Lk.7:27)*
and Isaiah He Was To Get The People Ready for The Messiah	by the prophet Isaiah *(Isa.40:3ff.)* when he said, "The voice of one crying in the wilderness: Prepare the way of the Lord, make his paths straight."	[3]"the voice of one crying in the wilderness: Prepare the way of the Lord, make his paths straight--"	in the book of the words of Isaiah the prophet, "The voice of one crying in the wilderness: Prepare the way of the Lord, make his paths straight.

[For Mk.1:4, see above]

....

**This section is sometimes called, "The Opening Events of Christ's Ministry". These events are introductory and transitional in character--of a* semi-private *nature. But the real* public ministry *of Jesus begins at Jerusalem, at Passover time, with "The Cleansing of The Temple".*

Greek in. aSome ancient authorities read* in the prophets.

The Messiah Will Bring God's Great Salvation To All Mankind

Lk.

5" Every valley shall be filled,
and every mountain and hill shall be brought low,
and the crooked shall be made straight,
and the rough ways shall be made smooth;

6" and all flesh shall see the salvation of God."

(4) John's Dress and Personal Habits were Like That of The Prophets.

John Wore Prophetic Dress And Ate Desert Food*

Mt.

4Now John wore a garment of camel's hair,
and a leather girdle around his waist;*
and his food was locusts and wild honey.

Mk.

6Now John was clothed with camel's hair,
and had a leather girdle around his waist,
and ate locusts and wild honey.

(5) The Enormous Effectiveness of John's Preaching

John Was Most Effective Stirring The Country From Circumference To Center

Mt.

5Then went out to him
Jerusalem
and all Judea
and all the region
about the Jordan,

John Deals Uncompromisingly With Sin

6and they were baptized by him
in the river Jordan,
confessing their sins.

Mk.

5And there went out to him
all the country of Judea,
and all the people of Jerusalem;
(Cf. vs. 3 above)
and they were baptized by him *(Cf. Lk. 3:21)*
in the river Jordan,
confessing their sins.

(6) Concrete Illustrations of John's Preaching

(For Mk.1:6 see above)

Rulers And The Crowds Alike

7But when he saw many of the
Pharisees and Sadducees
coming for baptism,
he said to them,
" You brood of vipers! *(Mt.12:34,p.72)*

He Warned Of Judgment

Who warned you to flee
from the wrath to come?

He Urged True Repentance

8Bear fruit
that befits repentance,
9and do not presume

He Demolished Excuses

to say to yourselves,
'We have Abraham as our father';
for I tell you,
God is able from these stones
to raise up children to Abraham.

He Insisted That Every Individual Must Either Repent or Perish

10Even now the ax
is laid to the root of the trees;
every tree therefore
that does not bear good fruit
is cut down
and thrown into the fire.

Lk.

7He said therefore to the multitudes
that came out to be baptized by him,
" You brood of vipers!
Who warned you to flee
from the wrath to come?
8Bear fruits
that befit repentance,
and do not begin
to say to yourselves,
'We have Abraham as our father'; *(Cf.Jn.8:39-40)*
for I tell you,
God is able from these stones
to raise up children to Abraham.
9Even now the ax *(Cf.Mal.3:1-6; Jn.5:22,27; Ac.17:31)*
is laid to the root of the trees;
every tree therefore
that does not bear good fruit
is cut down
and thrown into the fire."

....

**John wore the regular Prophetic dress.*
See 2K.1:8, Zech.13:4 speaks of false prophets who wore the prophetic dress so as to deceive people.
See also Christ's allusion to John's stern habits, Lk.7:25 & 26, p. 69.

(7) John's Personal Dealing with Inquirers

	Lk.
Dealing Personally	10 And the multitudes asked him, "What then shall we do?"
a. With the Multitudes	11 And he answered them, "He who has two coats, let him share with him who has none; and he who has food, let him do likewise."
b. With the Publicans	12 Tax collectors also came to be baptized, and said to him, "Teacher, what shall we do?" 13 And he said to them, "Collect no more than is appointed you."
c. With the Soldiers	14 Soldiers also asked him, "And we, what shall we do?" And he said to them, "Rob no one by violence or by false accusation, and be content with your wages."

(8) John's Message About the Messiah's Coming

	Mt.	Mk.	Lk.
The Great Expectancy. When The Psychologic Moment Had Come He Announced The Messiah's Coming.			15 As the people were in expectation, and all men questioned in their hearts concerning John, whether perhaps he were the Christ,
		7 And he preached, saying, *(Cf. vs.8 below)*	16 John answered them all,
The Messiah's Incomparable Greatness	11 "I baptize you with* water for repentance, but he who is coming after me is mightier than I, whose sandals I am not worthy to carry;	"After me comes he who is mightier than I, the thong of whose sandals I am not worthy to stoop down and untie.	"I baptize you with** water; but he who is mightier than I is coming, the thong of whose sandals I am not worthy to untie;
His Unique Work	*(Cf. vs. 11a)* he will baptize you with* the Holy Spirit and with fire.	8 "I have baptized you with** water; but he will baptize you with** the Holy Spirit."	*(Cf. vs. 16b)* he will baptize you with* the Holy Spirit and with fire.
His Cleansing Judgment	12 His winnowing fork is in his hand, and he will clear his threshing floor and gather his wheat into the granary, but the chaff he will burn with unquenchable fire."		17 His winnowing fork is in his hand, to clear his threshing-floor, and to gather the wheat into his granary, but the chaff he will burn with unquenchable fire."
A Concluding General Statement			18 So, with many other exhortations, he preached good news to the people.

(For vs. 19-20 see page 33, § 32)

---

*Greek (En) in. **Or in (dative)

2. Jesus Is Baptized by John. § 20

Jesus Comes To Be Baptized

Mt. 3:13-17

13Then
Jesus came
from Galilee to the Jordan
to John,
to be baptized by him.

He Overcomes John's Hesitation

14John would have prevented him,
saying,
"I need to be baptized by you,
and do you come to me?"

15But Jesus answered him,*
"Let it be so now;
for thus it is fitting for us
to fulfill all righteousness."

John Consents He baptizes Jesus

Then he consented.

(Cf. Mt. 3:6)

16And when Jesus
was baptized,

Then

he went up immediately
from the water,

As Jesus Is Praying, He Sees Heaven Opened, And the Spirit Descending

and behold,
the heavens were opened[a]

and he saw the Spirit of Cod
descending
like a dove
and alighting on him;

A Voice Also Speaks From Heaven

17And lo, a voice
from heaven, saying,
"This is my beloved son[b],
with whom I am well pleased."

[After the 40 days,
Jesus returned again
to John at the Jordan (See § 23, p.28)]

Mk. 1:9-11

9In those days
Jesus came
from Nazareth of Galilee

and was baptized by John
in the Jordan.

(Cf. Mk. 1:5)

10And when
he came up out of the water,

immediately he saw
the heavens opened

and the Spirit
descending upon him
like a dove;

11and a voice came
from heaven,
"Thou art my beloved Son[b];
with thee I am well pleased."

(Ps. 2:7b; Is. 42:1)

Lk. 3:21-23a

21Now when all the people
were baptized,
and when Jesus also
had been baptized

and was praying,

the heaven was opened,

22and the Holy Spirit
descended upon him
in bodily form, as a dove,

and a voice came
from heaven, (See §104, v.7; Jn. 12:28, p.194)
"Thou art my beloved Son[b];
with thee I am well pleased."[c]

Jesus Is Thirty Years Old

23Jesus,
when he began his ministry,
was about thirty years of age.
[For vs. 23b-38 see § 4]

3. Jesus Is Tempted by the Devil.** § 21

The Occasion

Immediately After His Baptism

1) Jesus Is Led By The Spirit into the Wilderness

Mt. 4:1-11

1Then Jesus was

led up
by the Spirit

into the wilderness
to be tempted by the devil.

(Heb. 2:18; 4:15-16)

[After the 40 days,
Jesus returned Again
....

Mk. 1:12-13

12The Spirit
immediately drove him
out into the wilderness.

13And he was

in the wilderness
forty days,

Lk. 4:1-13

1And Jesus,
full of the Holy Spirit,
returned from the Jordan,
and was led
by the Spirit

2for forty days
in the wilderness,

[a]Some ancient authorities add to him. [b]Or my Son, my (or the) Beloved. [c]Some ancient authorities read today have I begotten thee.

*This is the second authentically recorded utterance of Jesus. Does it mean, as Principal James Denny explains in "The Death of Christ", that His baptism here as always elsewhere, signifies His death for the sins of the world?

**Since, when Jesus had this experience, He was alone in the wilderness, "with the wild beasts." He only could have reported this incident.
It is interesting to observe how Jesus had nurtured His spirit on the Old Testament scriptures, and on what He now relies as the acid test of temptations, and how He dealt with His own inner conflicts.

2) He Is Tempted By The Devil

Mk. tempted by Satan;

Lk. tempted by the devil.
And he ate nothing
in those days;

(1) To Indulge Himself [Or To Win By Compromise]

a. The Situation

2And he fasted
forty days and forty nights,
and afterward
he was hungry.

Mk. and he was with the
wild beasts;

Lk. and when they were ended,
he was hungry.

b. The Enticement

3And the tempter came and said to him,
"If you are the Son of God,
command these stones to become loaves of bread."

Lk. 3The devil said unto him,
"If you are the Son of God,
command this stone to become bread."

c. The Answer

4But he answered,
"It is written, *(Dt.8:3)*
'Man shall not live by bread alone,
but by every word that proceeds
from the mouth of God.'"

Lk. 4And Jesus answered him,
"It is written,
'Man shall not live by bread alone.'"
(For verses 5-8 see below)

(2) To Put God To the Test

a. The Situation

5Then the devil took him to the holy city,
and he set him on the pinnacle of the temple,

Lk. 9And he took him to Jerusalem,
and set him on the pinnacle of the temple,

b. The Enticement

6and said to him,
"If you are the Son of God,
throw yourself down;
for it is written, *(Dt.6:13)*
'He will give his angels charge of you,'
and *(Ps.91:12)*
'On their hands they will bear you up,
lest you strike your foot against a stone.'"

Lk. and said to him,
"If you are the Son of God,
throw yourself down from here;
10for it is written,
'He will give his angels charge of you,
to guard you,' *(Ps.91:11)*
11and
'On their hands they will bear you up,
lest you strike your foot against a stone.'"

c. The Answer

7Jesus said to him,
"Again it is written, *(Dt.6:16)*
'You shall not tempt the Lord your God.'"

Lk. 12And Jesus answered him,
"It is said,
'You shall not tempt the Lord your God.'"

(3) To Worship The Devil [Or To Conquer By Military Force]

a. The Situation

8Again,
the devil took him to a very high mountain,
and showed him all the kingdoms of the world
and the glory of them;

Lk. 5And the devil took him up,
and showed him all the kingdoms of the world
in a moment of time,

b. The Enticement

9and he said to him,
"All these I will give you,
if you will fall down and worship me."

Lk. 6and said to him
"To you I will give all this authority
and their glory;
for it has been delivered to me,
and I give it to whom I will.
7If you, then, will worship me,
it shall all be yours."

c. The Answer

10Then Jesus said to him,
"Begone, Satan!
for it is written, *(Dt.6:13)*
'You shall worship the Lord your God,
and him only shall you serve.'"

Lk. 8And Jesus answered him,
"It is written,
'You shall worship the Lord your God
and him only shall you serve.'"

3) He Is Victorious

11Then the devil
left him,
and behold, angels came
and ministered to him.

Mk. and the angels
ministered to him.

Lk. 13And when the devil had ended every temptation,
he departed from him
until an opportune time.

NOTE: The three temptations correspond to the three politico-religious parties among the Jews, and the three ways advocated by them for the bringing in of the kingdom of God. The first were the Chief Priests and Sadducees (the worldly wise men) who advocated compromise and cooperation with Rome. The second were the Zealots who advocated military revolution. The third were the Pharisees who were expecting great signs from heaven *to establish Jewish independence and usher in the kingdom of God as an earthly kingdom.*

There was also a fourth party among the Jews, the devout spiritually-minded people who "were righteous before God", such as Zechariah and Elizabeth (Lk. 1:5-6), Joseph and Mary, Simeon and Anna, who expected the kingdom to come by spiritual means and who gave Jesus a wholehearted welcome.

4. John Testifies Concerning Jesus. § 22

Jn. 1:19-34

(1) HIS TESTIMONY TO THE OFFICIAL COMMITTEE FROM JERUSALEM

a. Who John Is

The Pharisees Send a Committee to Investigate John

19 And this is the testimony of John,
when the Jews sent priests and Levites from Jerusalem
to ask him,
"Who are you?"

Their Questions and John s Denials

20 He confessed,
he did not deny, but confessed,

Is He the Messiah?

"I am not the Christ." *(Cf.Lk.3:15-16,p.24)*

21 And they asked him,

Is He Elijah?

"What then? Are you Elijah?" *(Cf.Mt.17:10-13,p.110)*
He said,
"I am not."

Is He "The Prophet?"

"Are you the prophet?" *(Ac.7:37; Dt.18:15).*
And he answered,
"No."

Well then Who Is He?

22 They said to him then,
"Who are you?
Let us have an answer for those who sent us.
What do you say about yourself?"

John's Own Answer

23 He said,
"I am the voice of one crying in the wilderness,
'Make straight the way of the Lord,'
as the prophet Isaiah said." *(Is.40:3; Mt.3:3, p.22)*

b. Why John Baptizes

24 Now they had been sent from the Pharisees.*

(a) Their Question

25 They asked him,
"Then why are you baptizing, *(v.33)*
if you are neither the Christ,
nor Elijah, nor the prophet?"

(b) John's Reply

26 John answered them,
"I baptize with ** water; *(Mt.3:11,p.24)*
but among you stands one whom you do not know,
27 even he who comes after me,
the thong of whose sandal I am not worthy to untie."

28 This took place in Bethany beyond the Jordan,
where John was baptizing.

(2) HIS TESTIMONY TO THE MULTITUDES

John Identifies Jesus As The Messiah

(See § 20 for How John had found out)

29 The next day he saw Jesus coming toward him, and said,
"Behold, the Lamb of God, who takes away the sin of the world! *(v.35-36)*
30 This is he of whom I said,
'After me comes a man who ranks before me, *(Jn.1:15,p.6)*
for he was before me.' *(Mk.1:7,p.24)*

(John himself had not known Jesus was Messish until Mt.3:16-17)

31 "I myself did not know him;
but for this I came baptizing with** water,
that he might be revealed to Israel."

c. How John Knows that Jesus is the Messiah

32 And John bore witness,

He Saw the Spirit Descend and Remain

"I saw the Spirit descend as a dove from heaven,
and it remained on him. *(See § 20)*

33 "I myself did not know him;

When God Sent Him This Sign Had Been Promised

but he who sent me to baptize with ** water said to me,
'He on whom you see the Spirit descend and remain,
this is he who baptizes with ** the Holy Spirit.'

This He Saw And So He Testifies

34 "And I have seen and have borne witness
that this is the Son of God." ***

*The Pharisees specialized in the study and the teachings of the Law, and were considered to be the responsible guardians of orthodox teaching and authorized teachers. ***"The Son of God" was one of the Jew's names for the Messiah. So also was "Son of Man." **Greek in.

5. Jesus Wins His First Disciples. § 23

Jn. 1:35-51

John Points Out Jesus Who Now Returns From The Temptation (§ 21)

35 The next day again
John was standing with two of his disciples;
36 and he looked at Jesus as he walked, and said,
"Behold, the Lamb of God!" *(See vs.29-34)*

Two of John's Disciples Follow Jesus

37 The two disciples heard him say this,
and they followed Jesus.

He Turns and Asks a friendly Question

38 Jesus turned, and saw them following, and said to them,
"What do you seek?"

Their Embarrassed Reply

And they said to him,
"Rabbi (which means Teacher),
Where are you staying?"

He Invites Them

39 He said to them,
"Come and see."

They Visit With Jesus and Come to Faith in Him As Messiah (v.41)

They came and saw where he was staying;
and they stayed with him that day,
for it was about the tenth hour.*

40 One of the two who had heard John speak, and followed him,
was Andrew, Simon Peter's brother.

Then Andrew Brings Peter

41 He first** found his brother Simon, and said to him,
"We have found the Messiah" (which means Christ).

42 He brought him to Jesus.

Jesus Wins Peter

Jesus looked at him, and said,
"So you are Simon the son of John?
You shall be called Ce´phas" (which means Rock[a]).

Next Day. Jesus Calls Philip

43 The next day Jesus decided to go to Galilee.
And he found Philip and said to him,
"Follow me."

He is Won To the Faith (v.45)

44 Now Philip was from Beth-sa´i-da, the city of Andrew and Peter.

Then Philip Confesses His Faith To Nathanael

45 Philip found Na-than´a-el, and said to him,
"We have found him of whom Moses in the law and also the prophets wrote,
Jesus of Nazareth, the son of Joseph."

He Responds Doubtingly

46 Na-than´a-el said to him,
"Can anything good come out of Nazareth?"

Philip Tells Him To See for Himself

Philip said to him,
"Come and see."

Nathanael Meets Jesus And Questions Him

47 Jesus saw Na-than´a-el coming to him, and said of him,
"Behold, an Israelite indeed, in whom is no guile!"

48 Na-than´a-el said to him,
"How do you know me?"

Jesus Answers Him

Jesus answered him,
"Before Philip called you,
when you were under the fig tree, I saw you."

He Confesses Faith in Jesus As Son of God And Messiah

49 Na-than´a-el answered him,
"Rabbi, you are the Son of God! ***
You are the King of Israel!"

Jesus Promises Greater Things

50 Jesus answered him,
"Because I said to you,
I saw you under the fig tree, do you believe?
You shall see greater things than these."

You shall have Experiences like Those of Jacob (Genesis 28:12)

51 And he said to him,
"Truly, truly, I say to you,
you will see heaven opened, *(Cf. Jn.12:29,p.219;Lk.22:43,p.222)*
and the angels of God ascending and descending upon the Son of Man." ***

....

[a]*Greek* Peter. ****See footnote on previous page.*

**Reckoned by Roman time in Ephesus, where John wrote, "the tenth hour" would mean 10 A.M.*

** "First" *here implies that the modest author then also found his brother James.*

***[*See note on bottom of next page*]

6. Jesus Attends a Wedding With His Disciples.* § 24

Jn. 2:1-11

The Wedding Guests

1On the third day
there was a marriage at Cana in Galilee,
and the mother of Jesus was there;
2Jesus also was invited to the marriage, with his disciples.

Jesus' Mother Appeals to Him

3When the wine failed,
the mother of Jesus said to him,
"They have no wine."

His Pregnant Answer

4And Jesus said to her,
"O woman, what have you to do with me?
My hour has not yet come." *(Jn.7:6,8,30; 8:20,* §112, §115, §119: *Cf. Lk.22:53,p.226)*

Her Command to the Servants

5His mother said to the servants,
"Do whatever he tells you."

6Now six stone jars were standing there,
for the Jewish rites of purification,
each holding two or three measures.[a]

The Miracle "Fill the Jars", and They Did.

7Jesus said to them,
"Fill the jars with water."

"Now Draw Some Out"; and They Did.

And they filled them up to the brim.

"Take Some to the Steward"; and They did.

8He said to them,
"Now draw some out,
and take it to the steward of the feast."

So they took it.

The Ruler's Unconscious Testimony to its Genuineness

He Samples It and Is So Impressed that He Calls the Groom and Compliments Him

9When the steward of the feast tasted the water now become wine,
and did not know where it came from
(though the servants who had drawn the water knew),
the steward of the feast called the bridegroom
10and said to him,
"Every man serves the good wine first;
and when men have drunk freely, then the poor wine;
but you have kept the good wine until now."

The Resultant Deepening of the Faith of the Disciples

11This, the first of his signs,
Jesus did at Cana in Galilee,
and manifested his glory. *(Jn.1:14; II.Cor.4:6)*

And his disciples believed in him.

7. Jesus Visits Capernaum. § 25

Jn. 2:12

12After this he went down to Ca-per´na-um

with his mother

and his brothers

and his disciples;

and there they stayed for a few days.

[a]That is, about twenty or thirty gallons. **Whenever Jesus touches life there is something unique in that touch. This is of course Christ's first miracle, but it is so quietly and fittingly done as to seem almost an essential part of the circumstances. The author's purpose in relating the incident is of course in conformity to his major purpose in writing his gospel (Jn.20:30-31). It does as the last verse tells us strengthen the essential but elementary faith of His disciples, by manifesting His glory.*

Note for p.28.

****In this incident we have the first recorded dealing of Jesus with persons, and of His unique power over men. Note how each man through his own personal contact with Jesus gets a unique experience, elementary faith to be sure; nevertheless an essential faith in Jesus As the Messiah. Andrew tells Peter he has found the Messiah; Philip identifies Him as the one Moses wrote about; Nathaniel calls Him not only Rabbi, but Son of God (A term for the Messiah) and then King of Israel. Jesus assures them that their faith will grow henceforth.*

PART TWO

B. THE MINISTRY

30 I. THE PRELIMINARY MINISTRY (6 or 8 months) [*In Detail*] *Jesus Launches His Public Ministry*
(From His Public Appearance at Jerusalem, April A.D. 27;
To His Settlement at Capernaum, Autumn, A D. 27)

(I) IN JUDEA (pp. 31-34)

1. *AT JERUSALEM* [1] *He Begins in the Nation's Capital, at the Great Passover Festival*
   (1) Jesus Cleanses the Temple (Jn. 2:13-22)
   (2) Through His Signs Many Believe (Jn. 2:23-25) p.31
   (3) Nicodemus Is an Example of these (Jn. 3:1-21) pp.31-32
2. *IN THE COUNTRY He Merges His Campaign with John's*
   (1) Jesus Is Baptizing Disciples in Judea (Jn. 3:22) [2] p.33
   (2) John also Is Baptizing at Aenon (Jn. 3:23,24) [3] p.33
   (3) John Testifies Concerning Jesus, at Ænon (Jn. 3:25-36) [3] p.33
   (4) John Is Imprisoned by Herod (Lk. 3:19,20; Cf. Mt. 4:12) [4] p.33
   (5) Jesus Leaves Judea for Galilee, via Samaria (Jn. 4:1-4; Mt. 4:12; Mk. 1:14a; Lk. 4:14a; Cf. Mt. 14:3-5; Mk. 6:17-20) [5] p.34

(II) IN SAMARIA [6] (pp. 34-36) *He Is Recognized as "The Savior of the World."*

(1) Jesus Talks With a Samaritan Woman at Jacob's Well.(Jn.4:5-26 [5] pp.34-35
(2) The Woman Appeals to Her People (Jn.4:27-30) [6] p.35
(3) Jesus Appeals to His Disciples (Jn.4:31-38) [6] p.36
(4) The Revival in Sychar (Jn. 4:39-42) [6] p.36

(III) IN GALILEE (pp. 37-38) *He Settles in Galilee for Intensive Evangelizing.*

(1) Jesus Returns to Galilee (Jn. 4:43-45) [7] p.37
(2) Jesus Teaches in the Synagogues of Galilee (Lk.4:14-15)
(3) Jesus Heals A Nobleman's Son At Cana (Jn.4:46-54) [8] p.37
(4) Jesus Is Rejected at Nazareth (Lk.4:16-30) [9] p.38

[II. THE SETTLED MINISTRY
III. THE SPECIALIZED MINISTRY
IV. THE CONCLUDING MINISTRY]

YOU CAN REMEMBER

Now is the time to begin to fit all these Divisional Outlines into the general diagram of the entire life of Christ (pp.8 and 9.) Make repeated references to this diagram until it becomes very familiar, and soon you can remember the whole Life of Christ.

Sketch Map for THE PRELIMINARY MINISTRY

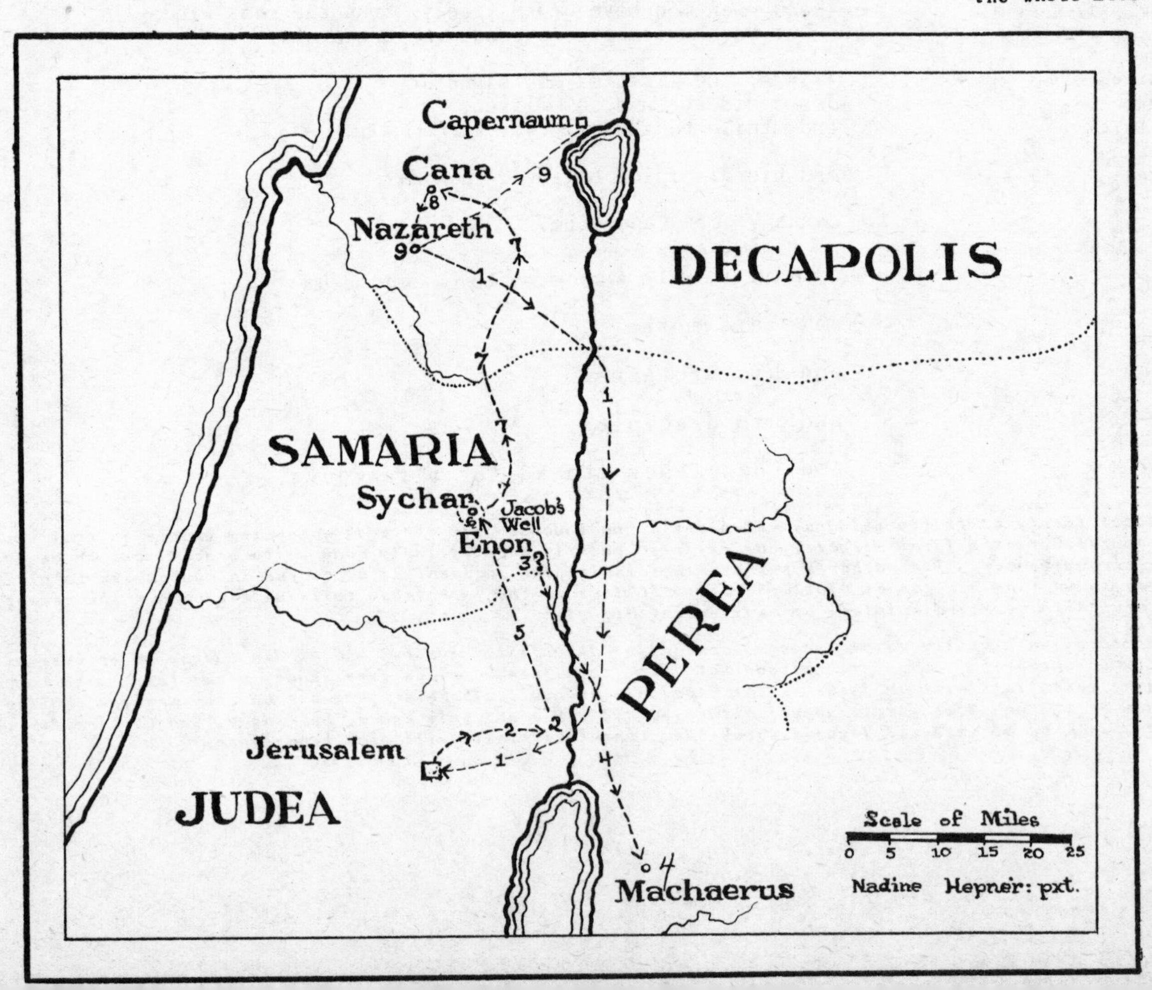

(I) IN JUDEA

1. AT JERUSALEM

(1) Jesus Cleanses the Temple . § 26 *(Cf.* § 165* *)*

Jn. 2:13-22

The Passover Comes

13 The Passover of the Jews was at hand,

Jesus Attends

and Jesus went up to Jerusalem.

He Finds the Temple Desecrated

14 In the temple he found
those who were selling oxen and sheep and pigeons,
and the money-changers at their business.

He Cleanses It
He drives Out
(a The Animals and Their Keepers Follow

15 And making a whip of cords,
he drove them all, with** the sheep and oxen, out of the temple;

(b)He puts Out The Money-Changers

and he poured out the coins of the money-changers
and overturned their tables.

(c) He Orders The Dove Cages Carried Out

16 And he told those who sold the pigeons,
"Take these things away;

He Explains Why

you shall not make my Father's house a house of trade."

The Disciples Are Astonished

17 His disciples remembered that it was written,
"Zeal for thy house will consume me."

The Jewish Officials Challenge Christ's Authority

18 The Jews then said to him,
"What sign have you to show us for doing this?" *(Mt.12:38ff.,p.72;* § 99*; Lk.11:29ff.,p.140)*

He Answers Them

19 Jesus answered them, *(Cf.Mt.26:61, p.229)*
"Destroy this temple,
and in three days I will raise it up."

They Are Mystified

20 The Jews then said,
"It has taken forty-six years to build this temple,
and will you raise it up in three days?"

What He Meant

21 But he spoke of the temple of his body.

Later His Disciples Remember and Understand

22 When therefore he was raised from the dead,
his disciples remembered that he had said this;
and they believed the scripture
and the word which Jesus had spoken.

(2) Through His Signs Many Believe. § 27 *(Jn. 2:23-25)*

Jesus Does Many Signs: Many Believe

23 Now when he was in Jerusalem at the Passover feast,
many believed in his name
when they saw his signs which he did;

Jesus Does Not Entrust Himself To Them For Their Faith Is Superficial

24 but Jesus did not trust himself to them,

25 because he knew all men
and needed no one to bear witness of man;
for he himself knew what was in man.***

(3) Nicodemus is an Example of These. *(Jn. 3:1-21)* § 28 ****

Nicodemus Comes to Enquire of Jesus
He Accepts Jesus As A Teacher But Not as Messiah

1 Now there was a man of the Pharisees, named Nic-o-de´mus, *(Jn.7:50;19:39)*
a ruler of the Jews.
2 This man came to Jesus[a] by night and said to him,
"Rabbi, we know that you are a teacher come from God;
for no one can do these signs that you do, unless God is with him."

**The Synoptic Gospels also report a Cleansing of the Temple, but at the close of His Ministry (See p.181, § 165). Some would identify them, but that would be doing violence to the records without objective evidence. The abuses were so grave and so deeply intrenched that it is not improbable that Jesus struck twice at such monstrous abuses as even the Jewish writings record. (Cf. § 165 and footnote, p.181)*

***Literal translation* both the sheep and the oxen. *He used the whip on the animals, not on the men. Note that he* "poured out", *not* "threw away", *or* "scattered about". He *did this before he overturned the tables.*

****Their belief in Jesus was superficial, and not an all-out faith in Him as the Messiah or Savior. As the story of Nicodemus illustrates, they accepted Him only as a great* Teacher. *(See 3:2). Jesus was never satisfied with faith short of accepting Him as Messiah, or Savior. Only such faith is saving faith.*

[a] *Greek* him.

*****Note: In this incident* (§ 28), *we have the first extended record of Jesus' teaching. It deals with the foundations of the Christian life,--vital faith in Christ as Savior and a life regenerated and controlled and guided by the Holy Spirit within.*

a. Christ's Testimony About Earthly Things (Cf.v.12).

*Jesus Goes At Once to the Root of His Trouble**

[3]Jesus answered him,
"Truly, truly, I say to you,
unless one is born anew, *(Jn.1:13,p.6)*
he cannot see the kingdom of God.*"

Nicodemus Is Puzzled

[4]Nic-o-de′mus said to him,
"How can a man be born when he is old?
Can he enter a second time into his mother's womb and be born?"

Why A New Birth Is Necessary

(See p.6, Jn.1:12-13 and Marginal titles)

[5]Jesus answered,
"Truly, truly, I say to you,
unless one is born of water and the Spirit,
he cannot enter the kingdom of God.
[6]That which is born of the flesh is flesh,
and that which is born of the Spirit is spirit.[a]
[7]Do not marvel that I said to you,
'You must be born anew.'

What A Man Born of God Is Like

[8]"The wind[a] blows where it wills,
and you hear the sound of it,
but you do not know whence it comes or whither it goes;
so it is with every one who is born of the Spirit."

Nicodemus is Bewildered and Keeps Still.

[9]Nic-o-de′mus said to him,
"How can this be?"

Jesus Rebukes a Teacher's Ignorance

[10]Jesus answered him,
"Are you a teacher of Israel, and yet you do not understand this?

The Certainty of Christian Knowledge and The Folly of Disbelieving Christ's Testimony

[11]"Truly, truly, I say to you,
we speak of what we know, and bear witness to what we have seen;
but you do not receive our testimony. *(v.32)*

[12]"If I have told you earthly things and you do not believe,
how can you believe if I tell you heavenly things?

He Is The Only Competent Witness

[13]"No one has ascended into heaven *(See v.31 and ref.)*
but he who descended from heaven, the Son of man.[b]"

b. Christ's Testimony About "Heavenly Things" (Cf. v.12)

The Messiah Must Die That Men May Live

[14]"And as Moses lifted up the serpent in the wilderness, *(Jn.8:28,p.127;*
so must the Son of man be lifted up, *12:32-34,p. 194)*
[15]that whoever believes in him may have eternal life."

Eternal Life Comes Only Through Believing on the Messiah

[16] For God so loved the world
that he gave his only Son,
that whoever believes in him should not perish *(v.36)*
but have eternal life.

God's Purpose Is to Save, Not Judge

[17] For God sent the Son into the world, not to condemn the world,
but that the world might be saved through him.

Judgment Comes Through Disbelief

[18] He who believes in him is not condemned;
he who does not believe is condemned already,
because he has not believed
in the name of the only Son of God.

Disbelief and Refusal Are Due to Love of Evil

[19] And this is the judgment,
that the light has come into the world, *(Jn.1:4,9; 8:12;9:5; 12:35,46)*
and men loved darkness rather than light,
because their deeds were evil.

Evil Men Hate the Light

[20] For every one who does evil hates the light,
and does not come to the light, *(1 Jn.1:5-7; 2:8-11)*
lest his deeds should be exposed.

Good Men Seek the Light

[21] But he who does what is true comes to the light,
that it may be clearly seen
that his deeds have been wrought in God.

[a]*The same Greek word means both* wind *and* spirit. [b]*Some ancient authorities add* who is in heaven.

**Because of the preaching of John and of Jesus (See Mt.3:1-3;4:17), "The Coming of The Kingdom of God" was the most talked about topic in Jerusalem at that time. Just how was the Messiah's Kingdom to Be Ushered in?(See the Four Conflicting views, footnote, p.25).*

(1) Jesus Baptizes Disciples in Judea. § 29
Jn. 3:22

Jesus Is Baptizing At the Jordan

22 After this
Jesus and his disciples went into the land of Judea;
there he remained with them and baptized.

(2) John Also Baptizes, At Aenon. § 30
Jn. 3:23-24

John Is Baptizing At Aenon
(See map, p.30)

23 John also was baptizing
at Ae´non near Salim,
because there was much water there;
and people came and were baptized.

24 For John had not yet been put in prison.

(3) John Testifies Concerning Jesus at Aenon. § 31
Jn. 3:25-36
A Petty Dispute and a Magnanimous Testimony

A Dispute Arises

25 Now a discussion arose
between John's disciples and a Jew
over purifying.

John's Disciples Complain About Jesus' Popularity

26 And they came to John, and said to him,
"Rabbi, he who was with you beyond the Jordan,
to whom you bore witness,
here he is, baptizing, and all are going to him."

*John's Testimony * About Jesus*

27 John answered,
"No one can receive anything except what is given him from heaven. *(Jn.19:11,p.237)*

He Is The Bridegroom

28 "You yourselves bear me witness, that I said, *
I am not the Christ, but
I have been sent before him.

I'm Only 'Friend of the Bridegroom.'

29 "He who has the bride is the bridegroom; **
the friend of the bridegroom, who stands and hears him,
rejoices greatly at the bridegroom's voice; *(Mt.9:14-15,p.48)*
therefore this joy of mine is now full.

30 "He must increase, but I must decrease."

He Comes From Heaven and

31 He who comes from above is above all; *(Jn.8:23; 3:13,p.32; Jn.6:32,33,38,42,62,p.98)*
he who is of the earth belongs to the earth, and of the earth he speaks;
he who comes from heaven is above all.

Tells About Heavenly Things

32 He bears witness to what he has seen and heard,
yet no one receives his testimony; *(v.11)*

We Must Believe Him

33 he who receives his testimony sets his seal to this,
that God is true.

For God Sent Him And
He Speaks God's Message
He Has The Full Spirit
He Has All Authority

34 For he whom God has sent utters the words of God,
for it is not by measure that he gives the Spirit;
35 the Father loves the Son,
and has given all things into his hand. *(Mt.11:27,p.147; Mt.28:18,p.258; Jn.5:20,p.52;17:2, p.220)*

Faith in Him Brings Life Eternal

36 He who believes in the Son has eternal life; *(v.14-18)*

Disobedience of Him Brings Judgment

he who does not obey the Son shall not see life,
but the wrath of God rests upon him. *(v.18-19)*

(4) John Is Imprisoned by Herod. § 32
Lk. 3:19-20

John Rebukes Herod

19 But Herod the tetrarch,
who had been reproved by him for He-ro´di-as, his brother's wife,
and for all the evil things that Herod had done,

Herod Imprisons John

20 added this to them all, *(Cf. & §33 ;Mk.6:17-19,p.91)*
that he shut up John in prison.

**How clean-cut is the Baptist's conviction and how ringing his testimony, here as in Jn.1:19-34. For the root of such a faith, see Jn.1:33 and then verses 31 and 32.*
***In this incident Christ is called "the Christ, the bridegroom, the one coming from heaven, the Son." Belief in Him as the Son of God brings eternal life. I Jn.4:15;5:5,10-12.*

(5) Jesus Leaves Judea for Galilee, via Samaria. § 33

	Mt. 4:12	*Mk. 1:14a*	*Lk. 4:14a*	*Jn. 4:1-4*
After John Was Arrested		14 Now after John was arrested,		
Jesus Hears of John's Imprisonment By Herod (§ 32)	12 Now when he heard that John had been arrested,	*(Cf. § 32 ref.)*		
He Also Hears that The Pharisees Are Suspicious of Jesus' Great Success				1 Now when the Lord knew *(Cf. § 31)* that the Pharisees had heard that Jesus was making and baptizing more disciples than John 2 (although Jesus himself did not baptize, but only his disciples),
	he withdrew			3 he left Judea and departed again
So He Leaves Judea		Jesus came	14 And Jesus returned in the power of the Spirit	
For Galilee	into Galilee;	into Galilee.	into Galilee.	to Galilee.
Via Samaria				4 He had to pass through Sa-ma′ria.

(II) IN SAMARIA ***

1. AT THE WELL

(1) Jesus Talks With a Samaritan Woman at Jacob's Well.* § 34

Jn. 4:5-26

Jesus Arrives at Jacob's Well

5 So he came to a city of Sa-ma′ri-a, called Sy′char,*
near the field that Jacob gave to his son Joseph. *(See v.12)*

After the Day's Journey He is Tired And Is Seated On The Well-curb

6 Jacob's well was there,*
and so Jesus, wearied as he was with his journey,
sat down beside the well.
It was about the sixth hour. *(6 p.m.)*

A Water Carrier Comes Jesus Requests a Drink

7 There came a woman of Sa-ma′ri-a to draw water.
Jesus said to her,
"Give me a drink."
8 For his disciples had gone away into the city to buy food.

The Woman Replies Curtly and Voices an Ancient Prejudice

9 The Samaritan woman said to him,
"How is it that you, a Jew,
ask a drink of me, a woman of Samaria?"

For Jews have no dealings with Samaritans.

By Way of Reply Jesus Suggests How Her Spiritual Thirst May Be Satisfied

10 Jesus answered her,
"If you knew the gift of God,**
and who it is that is saying to you,
'Give me to drink',
you would have asked him,
and he would have given you living water."

Her Astonishment Deepens As She Ponders And Tries To Puzzle Out The Answers

11 The woman said to him,
"Sir, you have nothing to draw with,
and the well is deep;
where do you get that living water?
12 Are you greater than our father Jacob,
who gave us the well, *(See Gen.33:18-20; Cf.Jn.4:5 above)*
and drank from it himself,
and his sons, and his cattle?"

Jesus Replies that Spiritual Thirst May Be Perennially Quenched From Eternal Springs

13 Jesus said to her,
"Every one who drinks of this water will thirst again,
14 but whoever drinks of the water that I shall give him
will never thirst; *(Jn.6:35,p.98; 7:37-38,p.124)*
the water that I shall give him
will become in him
a spring of water
welling up to eternal life."

Confused Desires Are awakening in the Woman's Heart

15 The woman said to him,
"Sir, give me this water,
that I may not thirst,
nor come here to draw."

....

*, **, *** - *For These Footnotes see Page 36.*

Her Hidden Sin Is Uncovered

16Jesus said to her,
"Go, call your husband,
and come here."

She Tries Vainly to Deny Her Guilt

17The woman answered him,
"I have no husband."

Jesus said to her,
"You are right in saying, 'I have no husband';

Jesus Probes Deeper

18for you have had five husbands,
and he whom you now have is not your husband;
this you said truly."

She Hedges and Changes The Subject

19The woman said to him,
"Sir, I perceive that you are a prophet.

*She Raises A Disputed Question About The Place To Worship**

20"Our fathers worshiped on this mountain; *
and you say
that in Jerusalem is the place where men ought to worship." *

Jesus Explains The Essential Nature Of True Worship

21Jesus said to her,
"Woman, believe me, the hour is coming
when neither on this mountain
nor in Jerusalem
will you worship the Father.

A True Conception of God Inspires Real Worship

22You worship what you do not know;
we worship what we know,
for salvation is from the Jews.

Real Worship Is Energizing On The Spiritual Level

23"But the hour is coming, and now is,
when the true worshipers
will worship the Father in spirit and truth,
for such the Father seeks to worship him.

Because God Is Spirit, Only So Can We Contact God

24"God is Spirit,
and those who worship him
must worship in spirit and truth."

The Woman Begins to Wonder About the Messiah's Coming

25The woman said to him,
"I know that Messiah** is coming
(he who is called Christ);**
when he comes,
he will show us all things."

Jesus Declares Himself to Be The Messiah,

26Jesus said to her,
"I who speak to you am he."

(2) The Woman Appeals to Her People. § 35

Jn. 4:27-30

But Then They Are Interrupted, The Disciples Return to Jesus, They Are Surprized That He Is Talking To A Woman

27Just then his disciples came.
They marveled that he was talking with a woman,
but none said,
"What do you wish?" or
"Why are you talking with her?"

The Woman Leaves She Goes to Sychar She Invites Others To Hear Jesus

28So the woman left her water jar,
and went away into the city,
and said to the people,
29"Come, see a man who told me all that I ever did.
Can this be the Christ?"

Jesus Sees The Crowd Coming Thru The Wheatfields

30They went out of the city
and were coming to him.

*, ** - For These Footnotes see Page 36.

(3) Jesus Appeals to His Disciples. § 36

Jn. 4:31-38

The Disciples Beg Jesus to Eat

31 Meanwhile the disciples besought him, saying,
"Rabbi, eat."

He Tells of Other Food

32 But he said to them,
"I have food to eat of which you do not know."

They Wonder

33 So the disciples said to one another,
"Has any one brought him food?"

Jesus Explains That To Do God's Will Is Spiritual Food

34 Jesus said to them,
"My food is to do the will of him who sent me,
and to accomplish his work. (Cf. Heb. 10:5-10)

Then He Points to the Samaritans Coming To Inquire About The Messiah

35 "Do you not say,
'There are yet four months
and then comes the harvest'?
I tell you,
Lift up your eyes, and see how the fields*
are already white for harvest.

He Speaks of Spiritual Harvests In That Grain Field Which They Must Reap Now

36 "He who reaps receives wages,
and gathers fruit for eternal life,
so that sower and reaper may rejoice together.
37 For here the saying holds true,
'One sows and another reaps.'
38 I sent you to reap that for which you did not labor;
others have labored,
and you have entered into their labor."

2. THE REVIVAL IN SYCHAR. § 37

Jn. 4:39-42

In Sychar

Many Samaritans Believe In Jesus

39 Many Samaritans from that city believed in him
because of the woman's testimony,
"He told me all that I ever did."

They Invite Him to Stay Longer

40 So when the Samaritans came to him,
they asked him to stay with them;

He Does, And Many More Believe

and he stayed there two days.
41 And many more believed because of his word.

They Confess Their Faith In Jesus As the Savior of The World

42 They said to the woman,
"It is no longer
because of your words that we believe,
for we have heard for ourselves,
and we know that this is indeed the Savior of the world." **

....

**Jesus is sitting on the well-curb looking north, across a mile of wheat fields, towards Sychar. There, coming along the road, diagonally through the grain field, He sees all that crowd of Samaritans coming, led by the woman (v.29). The disciples, having just come from there, have their backs to them; so Jesus bids them turn and see the eager crowd coming to see the Messiah. (Consider again verses 25,26 and 29 and see how ripe the fields are).*

***Compare 1 John 2:2. Isn't it strange at first that these half-heathen Samaritans should be the first to grasp this truth of the universality of Christ's salvation. Of course, on second thought it isn't so strange after all, for only on this basis could they have any hope in Him; if He were Savior of Jews only, why then of course they, the Samaritans (and indeed we also) would be "without hope and without God in the world," as Paul says.*

FOOTNOTES FOR PAGE 34

**See Map, p.30. "One of the best certified spots in Palestine." He sat on the well curb.*
***In everyday talk water was called "the gift of God," because it was so rare and precious.*
****While Herod took John from Enon, across the Jordan, to Machaerus, his own winter capital (as Josephus tells us), at the same time Jesus goes to Enon and Sychar--perhaps to gather up the remanents of John's disheartened disciples.*

FOOTNOTES FOR PAGE 35

**See Deut., Chs.12 and 13-14. In order to prevent idolatry, the Jews were to destroy all altars and were to offer sacrifices only in Jerusalem, not "in every place." The Samaritans were not allowed to worship with them (Ezra.4; Neh.13:4-9). So the Samaritans grew hostile and built a temple of their own in Samaria, and offered sacrifices there.*
***Both these words (the first Hebrew, the second Greek) mean literally* anointed *and really, as v.4 shows, mean* Savior.

1. Jesus Returns to Galilee. § 38 *(Cf. § 33)*

	Mt. 4:12	*Mk. 1:14a*	*Lk. 4:14a*	*Jn. 4:43-45*
Jesus Leaves Samaria, and Arrives In Galilee	[He withdrew into Galilee.]	[Jesus came into Galilee,]	[14 And Jesus returned in the power of the Spirit into Galilee.]	43 After the two days he departed to Galilee.
In spite of Natural Prejudice,				44 For Jesus himself testified that a prophet has no honor in his own country. *(Lk.4:24)*
He Is Welcomed In Galilee Because of What They Had Witnessed At Jerusalem				45 So when he came to Galilee, the Galileans welcomed him, having seen all that he had done in Jerusalem at the feast, *(Jos.2:23-25)* for they too had gone to the feast.

2. Jesus Teaches In the Synagogues of Galilee. § 39

Lk. 4:14b-15

His Fame Spreads Far and Wide

14b And a report concerning him
went out through all the surrounding country.

He Is Teaching in Their Synagogues

15 And he taught* in their synagogues,
being glorified by all.

3. Jesus Heals A Nobleman's Son At Cana. § 40

Jn. 4:46-54

Jesus Arrives at Cana

46 So he came again to Cana in Galilee,
where he had made the water wine. (§ 24)

A Nobleman At Capernaum Whose Son Is Sick,

And at Ca-per ′na-um there was an official
whose son was ill.

Hearing of Jesus, Comes to Cana He Appeals For Help

47 When he heard that Jesus had come from Judea to Galilee,
he went and begged him
to come down and heal his son,
for he was at the point of death.

Jesus "Puts Him Off"

48 Jesus therefore said to him,
"Unless you see signs and wonders you will not believe." *(Cf.Jn.2:23+3:2)*

The Request Is Urged Again

49 The official said to him,
"Sir, come down before my child dies."

It Is Granted

50 Jesus said to him,
"Go; your son will live."

The Man Believes The Word of Jesus

The man believed the word** that Jesus spoke to him
and went his way.

His Son is Healed

51 As he was going down,
his servants met him and told him that his son was living.

The Proof Is Given.

52 So he asked them the hour when he began to mend.

And they said to him,
"Yesterday at the seventh*** hour the fever left him."

The Man and His Household Are Won to Faith in Jesus As Messiah

53 The father knew that was the hour when Jesus had said to him,
"Your son will live."

And he himself believed,
and all his household.

The Author's Footnote.

54 This was now the second sign that Jesus did
when he had come from Judea to Galilee.

---

*was teaching *(continuous action)*.

***In v.50 he now believes Jesus can heal; in v.53 he believes in Jesus as the Messiah-Savior, and so becomes a disciple.*

****Seven, P.M.*

4. Jesus Is Rejected at Nazareth. § 41 *(Cf. § 81,p.87)*

Lk. 4:16-30

Jesus Preaches in the Synagogue At His Boyhood Home

16And he came to Nazareth, where he had been brought up;
and he went to the synagogue, as his custom was, on the sabbath day.

And he stood up to read;

17and there was given to him the book of the prophet Isaiah.

The Opening Service
Jesus Unrolls The Scroll
He finds His Text (Is.61:1-2a)
He Reads.

He opened the book,
and found the place where it was written,
18" The Spirit of the Lord is upon me,
because he has anointed me to preach good news to the poor.
He has sent me to proclaim release to the captives
and recovering of sight to the blind,
to set at liberty those who are oppressed,
19to proclaim the acceptable year of the Lord."

He Rolls Up The Scroll

20And he closed the book,

He Hands It To The Caretaker

and gave it back to the attendant,

He Sits Down

and sat down;

He Gets Everyone's Attention

and the eyes of all in the synagogue were fixed on him.

Then He Preaches.

21And he began to say to them,
" Today this scripture has been fulfilled in your hearing."

The People Respond They Are Favorable at first

22And all spoke well of him,
and wondered at the gracious words which proceeded out of his mouth;

Then They Become Resentful

and they said,
" Is not this Joseph's son?"

So Jesus Rebukes Them

23And he said to them,
" Doubtless you will quote to me this proverb,
'Physician, heal yourself;

(a) Their Attitude

what we have heard you did at Ca-per ′na-um, [*See* §§ 25 and 40]
do here also in your own country.'"

(b) The Reason for it

24And he said,
" Truly, I say to you,
no prophet is acceptable in his own country. *(Jn.4:44)*

(c) Two Illustrations

25" But in truth, I tell you,
there were many widows in Israel in the days of Elijah,
when the heaven was shut up three years and six months,
when there came a great famine over all the land;

Elijah in Sidon

26and Elijah was sent to none of them
but only to Zar′e-phath, in the land of Sidon,
to a woman who was a widow. *(1 K.17:8-24)*

Elisha and Naaman

27" And there were many lepers in Israel
in the time of the prophet Elisha;
and none of them was cleansed,
but only Na′a-man the Syrian."*(2 K.5:1-14)*

They Become Enraged

28When they heard this,
all in the synagogue were filled with wrath.

They Attempt To Kill Him.

29And they rose up
and put him out of the city,
and led him to the brow of the hill on which their city was built,
that they might throw him down headlong.

Jesus Escapes.

30But passing through the midst of them he went away. *(Jn.8:59;12:36)*

II. THE SETTLED MINISTRY *(In Galilee), pp.39-48. His Unprecedented Popularity.*

(A) THE FIRST PERIOD, or THE EARLIER GALILEAN MINISTRY (4 to 6 months)
(From the Settlement at Capernaum, Autumn, A.D. 27;
To The Second Passover, April, A.D. 28)

(I) AT CAPERNAUM (pp. 40-43)

1. The Settlement at Capernaum (Mt. 4:13-17; Mk.1:14[b]-15: Lk.4:31[a]) [1]* p.40.
2. The Call of the Four to Learn Evangelism (Mt. 4:18-22; Mk. 1:16-20; Lk. 5:1-11) [2] p.40-41.
3. The Day of Miracles (Mt. 8:14-17; Mk. 1:21-34; Lk. 4:31-41) [2] p.42.
   (a) Forenoon--At the Synagogue: A Demoniac Healed p.42.
   (b) Afternoon--At Peter's House--Peter's Mother-in-law Healed p.42.
   (c) Evening--At the Street Door: Many Healed p.43.

(II) THROUGHOUT GALILEE (p.44) [3]
1. A Morning of Prayer and
   Breaking Away from the People (Mk. 1:35-38; Lk. 4:42 -43) p.43.
2. Preaching Throughout Galilee (Mt.4:23-24; Mk.1:39; Lk. 4:44) p.44.
3. Healing a Leper (Mt. 8:2-4; Mk. 1:40-45; Lk. 5:12-16) p.44.

(III) BACK AGAIN AT CAPERNAUM (pp. 45-48) [2]

1. Jesus Returns and Teaches (Mk. 2:1,2; Lk. 5:17) p.45.
2. Jesus Forgives and Heals a Paralytic (Mt. 9:2-8; Mk. 2:3-12; Lk. 5:18-26) p.45-46.
3. Jesus is Teaching by the Lake (Mk. 2:13) p.47.
4. Jesus Calls Matthew (Mt. 9:9; Mk. 2:14; Lk. 5:27,28) p.47.
5. Matthew Invites His Friends to Meet Jesus (Mt. 9:10-13; Mk. 2:15-17; Lk. 5:29-32) p.47.
6. Jesus Discusses Fasting with the Disciples of John (Mt. 9:14-17; Mk. 2:18-22; Lk.5:33-39) p.48.

[*(B) The Second Period, or "The Later Galilean Ministry." pp.49-100*]

Sketch Map for

THE FIRST PERIOD OF THE GALILEAN MINISTRY

**Numbers in square brackets [1] refer to places on the map.*

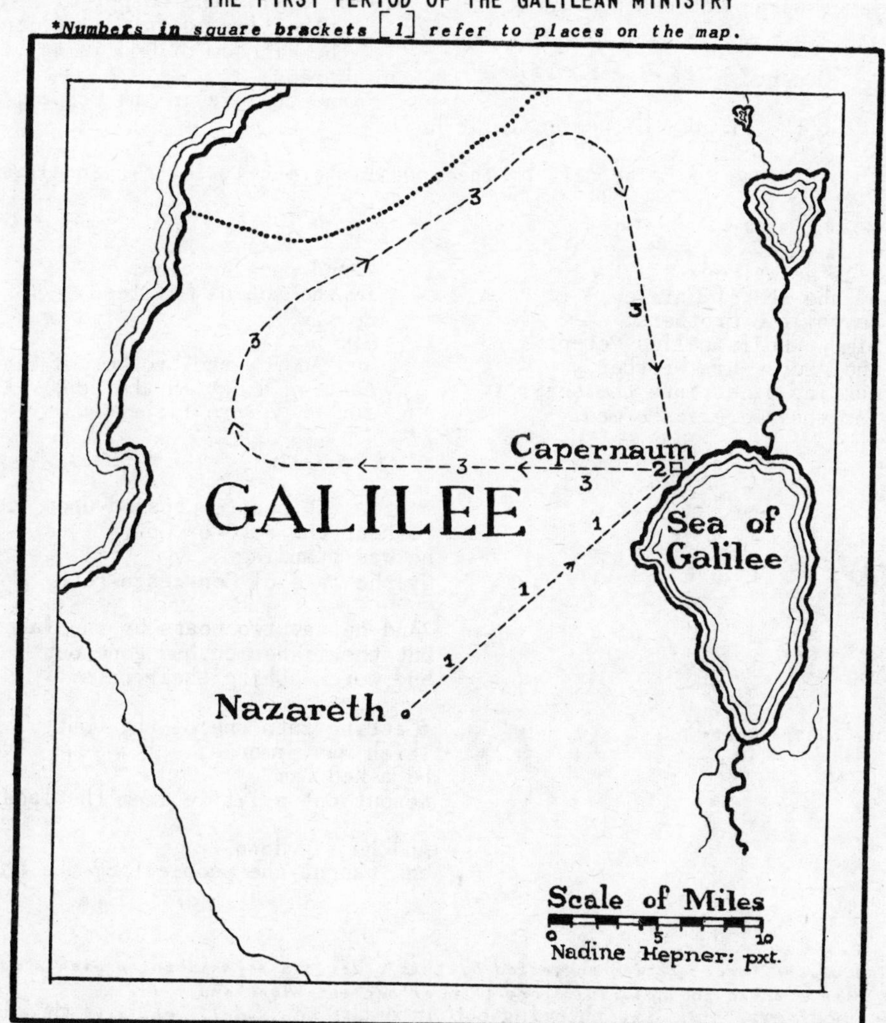

II. THE SETTLED MINISTRY

(A) THE FIRST PERIOD, or "THE EARLIER GALILEAN MINISTRY"

(Four to Six Months: Autumn A.D. 27 to April 28)

(I) AT CAPERNAUM

I. The Settlement at Capernaum. § 42

Mt. 4:13-17 — *Mk. 1:14b-15* — *Lk. 4:31a*

Jesus Moves to Capernaum

Mt.:

13 And leaving Nazareth
he went

Lk.:

31 And he went down
to Ca-per´na-um,
a city of Galilee.

Mt.:

and dwelt in Ca-per´na-um by the sea,
in the territory
of Zeb´u-lun and Naph´ta-li,

And So An Ancient Prophecy Comes True

14 that what was spoken by the prophet Isaiah might be fulfilled:
15 " The land of Zeb´u-lun and the land of Naph´ta-li,
toward the sea, across the Jordan,
Galilee of the Gentiles--
16 the people who sat in darkness
have seen a great light,
and for those who sat in the region and shadow of death
light has dawned." *(Is.9:1-7)*

General Statement of Christ's Preaching in Galilee

Jesus Proclaims The Kingdom of God, And Preaches Repentance and Faith

Mt.:

17 From that time
Jesus began to preach, saying,

" Repent, *(Cf.Mt.3:2,p.22)*

for the kingdom of heaven is at hand."

Mk. 1:14b-15

14 preaching the Gospel of God,** 15 and saying,
" The time is fulfilled, and
the kingdom of God is at hand;
Repent,
and believe in the Gospel.**"

2. The Call of the Four Fisherman to Learn Evangelism.**** § 43*

Mt. 4:18-22 — *Mk. 1:16-20* — *Lk. 5:1-11*

Very Early Jesus Is Walking By The Lake. Jesus Sees Four Failing Fishermen.

Mt.:

18 As he walked
by the sea of Galilee,
he saw two brothers,
Simon who is called Peter
and Andrew his brother,
casting a net into the sea; ***
for they were fishermen.

Mk.:

16 And passing along
by the sea of Galilee,
he saw
Simon
and Andrew the brother of Simon
casting a net in the sea; ***
for they were fishermen.

Lk. 5:1-11

As Jesus Returns Near The City Gate, A Crowd Gathers Round Jesus, and He Is Teaching Them

1 While the people pressed upon him
to hear the word of God,
he was standing
by the lake of Gen-nes´a-ret.

The Fishermen Bring Their Boats to the Shore.

2 And he saw two boats by the lake;
but the fishermen had gone out of them
and were washing their nets.

Jesus Gets Into One of The Boats He Sits Down He Preaches To The Crowd On The Shore.

3 Getting into one of the boats,
which was Simon's,
he asked him
to put out a little from the land.

And he sat down
and taught the people from the boat.

....

*The combination of the three stories suggested by this order and arrangement presents no difficulties, and makes a far more graphic and colorful story than either one alone would do.

**That is the good news. ***Mt. has throwing out into the sea, while Mk. says throwing around in the sea.

****They had already been called to discipleship; see § 23, p.28. Hence, this is a call to studentship for the ministry. Later they are ordained to apostleship (p.57, § 60), especially Lk.6:12-13.

	Lk.
Then He Stops Preaching *And Plans* *an Object Lesson* *He Asks* *To Go Fishing*	4 And when he had ceased speaking, he said to Simon, "Put out into the deep and let down your nets for a catch."
Peter Objects At First *Then Consents*	5 And Simon answered, "Master, we toiled all night and took nothing! But at your word I will let down the nets."
The Fishermen *Are Outdone* *At Their Own Game*	6 And when they had done this, they enclosed a great shoal of fish;
The Nets Are Filled *To The Breaking Point* *They Call For Help*	and as their nets were breaking, 7 they beckoned to their partners in the other boat to come and help them.
Their Partners (v.10) Come	And they came
They Fill Both Boats	and filled both the boats,
To The Sinking Point.	so that they began to sink.
Peter is *Overwhelmed*	8 But when Simon Peter saw it, he fell down at Jesus' knees, saying, "Depart from me, for I am a sinful man, O Lord."
All Are Overawed *At The Miracle.*	9 For he was astonished, and all that were with him, at the catch of fish which they had taken;
	10 and so also were James and John, sons of Zebedee, who were partners with Simon.
Jesus Calms *Their Fears*	And Jesus said to Simon, "Do not be afraid; henceforth you will be catching men."
They Come To Shore.	11 And when they had brought their boats to land,

	Mt.	Mk.	Lk.
Jesus Calls *Peter* *and Andrew*	19 And he said to them, "Follow me, and I will make you fishers of men."	17 And Jesus said to them, "Follow me and I will make you become fishers of men."	
They Follow Him *Instantly,*	20 Immediately	18 And immediately	
Leaving Things *To Their* *Partners (See v.9)*	they left their nets and followed him.	they left their nets and followed him.	
Jesus Goes On	21 And going on from there	19 And going on	
To James *and John* *At Their* *Mooring Place*	he saw two other brothers, James the son of Zeb'e-dee and John his brother, in the boat with Zeb'e-dee their father, mending their nets;	a little further, he saw James the son of Zeb'e-dee and John his brother, who were in their boat mending the nets.	
He Calls *Them*	and he called them.	20 And immediately he called them:	
They, Also, *Follow Jesus* *Instantly* *Leaving Things* *To Others*	22 Immediately they left the boat and their father,	and they left their father Zeb'e-dee in the boat with the hired servants,	they left everything
....	and followed him.	and followed him.	and followed him.

(1) A Demoniac Healed. § 44

(In the Forenoon, at the Synagogue)

	Mk. 1:21-28	*Lk. 4:31b-37*
Jesus Goes To Church	21 And they went into Ca-per´na-um; and immediately on the sabbath he entered the synagogue *	31 And
He Is Preaching	and taught.	he was teaching them on the sabbath;
*He Speaks With Authority***	22 And they were astonished at his teaching, for he taught them as one who had authority, and not as the scribes.**	32 and they were astonished at his teaching, for his word was with authority.
He is Interrupted by a Demoniac's Ravings.	23 And immediately there was in their synagogue a man with an unclean spirit; 24 and he cried out, "What have you to do with us, Jesus of Nazareth? Have you come to destroy us? I know who you are, the Holy One of God." *(Jn.6:69)*	33 And in the synagogue there was a man who had the spirit of an unclean demon; and he cried out with a loud voice, 34 "Ah! [a] what have you to do with us, Jesus of Nazareth? Have you come to destroy us? I know who you are, the Holy One of God."
Jesus Rebukes Him.	25 But Jesus rebuked him, saying, "Be silent, and come out of him!"	35 But Jesus rebuked him, saying, "Be silent, and come out of him!"
He Cures the Man.	26 And the unclean spirit, convulsing him and crying with a loud voice, came out of him.	And when the demon had thrown him down in the midst, he came out of him, having done him no harm.
The People Are Amazed. They Discuss The Case.	27 And they were all amazed, so that they questioned among themselves, saying, "What is this? A new teaching! With authority he commands even the unclean spirits, and they obey him." *(Cf.Mk.4:41;also § 73)*	36 And they were all amazed and said to one another, "What is this word? For with authority and power he commands the unclean spirits, and they come out."
The News Spreads Everywhere.	28 And at once his fame spread everywhere throughout all the surrounding region of Galilee.	37 And reports of him went out into every place in the surrounding region.

(2) Jesus Heals Peter's Wife's Mother. § 45

(In the Afternoon, at Peter's House)

	Mt. 8:14-15	*Mk. 1:29-31*	*Lk. 4:38-39*
From Church They Go To Peter's House	14 And	29 And immediately, he[b] left the synagogue, and entered the house of Simon and Andrew, with James and John.	38 And he arose and left the synagogue, and entered Simon's house.
They Find a Very Sick Grandmother.	when Jesus entered Peter's house, he saw his mother-in-law lying sick with a fever,	30 Now Simon's mother-in-law lay sick with a fever; and immediately they told him of her.	Now Simon's mother-in-law was ill with a high fever, and they besought him for her.
Jesus Heals Her	15 and he touched her hand,	31 And he came and took her by the hand and lifted her up,	39 And he stood over her and rebuked the fever,
She Gets Lunch For Them	and the fever left her, and she rose and served him.	and the fever left her; and she served them.	and it left her; and immediately she rose and served them.

[a] Or let us alone. [b] *Many ancient authorities read* they.

**We shall visit this Synagogue of Capernaum frequently. It's ruins are thought by some to be still there. It was a gift to the city by a Roman Captain § 62,p.66,v.4-5). It was a spacious and noble structure.*

***The Rabbis quoted others as authority.*

(3) Many Are Healed. § 46

(In the Evening, at the Street Door)

	Mt. 8:16-17	*Mk. 1:32-34*	*Lk. 4:40-41*
*When the Sabbath is Past**	16 That evening	32 That evening, at sundown,*	40 Now when the sun was setting,* all those who had any that were sick with various diseases
	they brought to him many who were possessed with demons;	they brought to him all who were sick or possessed with demons.	brought them to him;
A Whole City is At His Door		33 And the whole city was gathered together about the door.	
			and he laid his hands on every one of them
All the Sick are Healed	and he cast out the spirits with a word, and healed all who were sick.	34 And he healed many who were sick with various diseases, and cast out many demons;	(v,41) and healed them.
Many Demoniacs (or crazy people) also are Healed.		and he would not permit the demons to speak, because they knew him.	41 And demons also came out of many, crying, "You are the Son of God!" But he rebuked them, and would not allow them to speak, because they knew that he was the Christ.
As Isaiah Foretold About The Messiah,	17 This was to fulfill what was spoken by the prophet Isaiah, ** "He took our infirmities and bore our diseases."		

(4) A Morning of Prayer. § 47

	Mk. 1:35	*Lk. 4:42a*
Before Daylight Jesus slips Out To Pray in Solitude, Seeking Guidance.	35 And in the morning, a great while before day, he rose and went out to a lonely place, and there he prayed.	42 And when it was day he departed and went into a lonely place.

Breaking Away From the People.

	Mk. 1:36-38	*Lk. 4:42b-43*
The Disciples and The Crowds Hunt Him Up	36 And Simon and those who were with him followed him,	And the people sought him
They Find Him	37 and they found him and said to him, "Everyone is searching for you."	and came to him,
They Want To Keep Him There		and would have kept him from leaving them;
But Jesus Leaves to go Elsewhere	38 And he said to them,	43 but he said to them, "I must preach the good news of the kingdom of God to the other cities also;
For A Tour Through Galilee	"Let us go on to the next towns, that I may preach there also; for that is why I came out."	for I was sent for this purpose."

*The Jewish Sabbath began at sunset, on Friday evening, and ended at sunset, on Saturday evening. The rabbis forbad healing on the sabbath unless the sick one could not live till the sabbath was over at sundown.

**Isa.53:12, "Surely He has born our sicknesses and carried our sorrows" (R.V. margin. See also vv.6 and 12c. Then see I.Pet.2:24).

***Some demoniacs at least were lunatics. (Mt.4:24), epileptic (Mt.17:15), raving maniacs (Mk.5:2-6,p.80). Jesus brought the cure for physical, mental, and spiritual ailments.

(1) Preaching Throughout Galilee. § 48

	Mt. 4:23-24	*Mk. 1:39*	*Lk. 4:44*
Jesus Preaches and Heals Throughout All Galilee	23And he went about all Galilee, teaching in their synagogues and preaching the gospel of the Kingdom and healing every disease and every infirmity	39And he went throughout all Galilee, preaching in their synagogues	44And he was preaching in the synagogues of Judea.*[a]
(Josephus says there were over 200 towns and villages in Galilee)	among the people.	and casting out demons.	
His Fame Spreads	24So his fame spread throughout all Syria,		
All The Sick Are Healed	and they brought him all the sick, those afflicted with various diseases and pains, demoniacs, epileptics, and paralytics, and he healed them.		

(2) Healing a Leper. § 49

	Mt. 8:2-4	*Mk. 1:40-45*	*Lk. 5:12-16*
A Leper Appeals to Jesus	2And behold a leper came to him	40And a leper came to him	12While he was in one of the cities, there came a man full of leprosy; and when he saw Jesus,
Kneeling Before Him He Expresses His Faith	and knelt before him, saying, "Lord, if you will, you can make me clean." *(Cf. "Make whole" 4:34)*	beseeching him, and kneeling said to him, "If you will, you can make me clean."	he fell on his face and besought him, "Lord, if you will, you can make me clean."
Jesus Touches Him and Heals Him	3And he stretched out his hand and touched him, saying, "I will; be clean."	41And being moved with pity, he stretched out his hand and touched him, and said to him, "I will; be clean."	13And he stretched out his hand, and touched him, saying, "I will; be clean."
The Cure Is Instantanous.	And immediately his leprosy was cleansed.	42And immediately the leprosy left him, and he was made clean.**	And immediately the leprosy left him.

	Mt.	*Mk.*	*Lk.*
Jesus Charges Him Not To Tell Anyone,	4And Jesus said to him, "See that you say nothing to any one;	43and he sternly charged him, and sent him away at once, 44and said to him, "See that you say nothing to any one;	14And he charged him to tell no one;
But to Offer the Customary Sacrifice as Evidence Of His Cleansing.	but go, show yourself to the priest, and offer *(Cf. § 147)* the gift that Moses commanded, for a proof to the people."[b]	but go, show yourself to the priest, and offer for your cleansing what Moses commanded *(Lev. 14)* for a proof to the people."[b]	but "Go and show yourself to the priest, and make an offering for your cleansing, as Moses commanded, for a proof to the people."[b]

(3) The Result

	Mk.	*Lk.*
The Charge Is Disregarded; So The Tour is Forced to Close.	45But he went out and began to talk freely about it, and to spread the news, so that Jesus[c] could no longer openly [enter a town, but was out in the country; and people came to him from every quarter.	15But so much the more the report went abroad concerning him; and great multitudes gathered to hear and to be healed of their infirmities.
Jesus Again Retires For Prayer		16But he withdrew to the wilderness and prayed.

*[a] *Some ancient authorities read* Galilee. *This reading is preferable.* [b]*Greek* to them. [c]*Greek* he.

***For Footnote see page 45.*

(1) Jesus Returns and Teaches. § 50

	Mk. 2:1-2	Lk. 5:17
Jesus' Return Home Is Noised About	1And when he returned to Ca-per´na-um after some days, it was reported that he was at home.	17On one of those days,
Crowds Gather	2And many were gathered together, so that there was no longer room for them, not even about the door;*	
He Is Teaching Them*	and he was preaching* the word to them.	as he was teaching,*
Pharisees and Theologians Are Present		there were Pharisees and teachers of the law* sitting by, who had come from every town of Galilee and Judea and from Jerusalem;
Jesus Is Conscious of Power to Heal	(Mk.5:30)	and the power of the Lord was with him to heal.[a]

(2) Jesus Forgives and Heals a Paralytic.* § 51

	Mt. 9:2-8	Mk. 2:3-12	Lk. 5:18-26
Four Men Bring a Paralyzed Man On a Mattress	2And behold, they brought to him a paralytic lying on his bed;	3And they came, bringing to him a paralytic carried by four men.	18And behold, men were bringing on a bed a man who was paralyzed,
They Try To Find Some Way To Get Him to Jesus			and they sought to bring him in and lay him before Jesus;[b]
But They Fail Because of the Crowd		4And when they could not get near him because of the crowd,	19but finding no way to bring him in, because of the crowd,
Then They Get an Idea They Go Up on the Roof They Take Up the Roof Tiles		they removed the roof above him; and when they had made an opening,	they went up on the roof
The Man, On His Bed, Is Let Down Through The Roof Before Jesus		they let down the pallet on which the paralytic lay.	and let him down with his bed
In the Midst Of the Crowd Inside, Right Before Jesus.			through the tiles into the midst before Jesus.
Jesus Forgives the Man's Sins	and when Jesus saw their faith he said to the paralytic, "Take heart, my son; your sins are forgiven."	5And when Jesus saw their faith, he said to the paralytic, "My son, your sins are forgiven."	20And when he saw their faith he said, "Man, your sins are forgiven you."

....

[a] *Some ancient authorities read* was present to heal them. [b] *Greek* him.

**Probably in the Synagogue (Note, p.42). Even this largest auditorium in Capernaum was not large enough, so in (Mk.2:13) they go to the spacious lake beach.*

FOOTNOTE FOR PAGE 44.

*** Lepers are always said to be "made clean," instead of "made whole," used in other cures. The inspection by the priest and the offering (v.4) removed the quarantine against them.*

	Mt.	*Mk.*	*Lk.*
The Scribes Charge Jesus with Blasphemy	3 And behold, some of the scribes said to themselves,	6 Now some of the scribes were sitting there, questioning in their hearts, 7 "Why does this man speak thus?	21 And the scribes and the Pharisees began to question, saying, "Who is this
For Only God Can Forgive Sins	"This man is blaspheming."	It is blasphemy! Who can forgive sins but God alone?"	that speaks blasphemies? Who can forgive sins but God only?"
Jesus Reads Their Thot's and Explains	4 But Jesus knowing[a] their thoughts, said,	8 And immediately Jesus, perceiving in his spirit that they thus questioned within themselves, said to them,	22 When Jesus perceived their questionings, he answered them,
He Proposes A Test	"Why do you think evil in your hearts?	"Why do you question thus in your hearts?	"Why do you question in your hearts?
He Asks Them a Question.	5 For which is easier, to say, 'Your sins are forgiven,' or to say, 'Rise and walk'?	9 Which is easier, to say to the paralytic, 'Your sins are forgiven'; or to say, 'Rise, take up your pallet and walk'?	23 Which is easier, to say, 'Your sins are forgiven you', or to say, 'Rise and walk'?
The Healing Will Demonstrate God's Approval.	6 "But that you may know that the Son of man* has authority on earth to forgive sins" -- *(1 Jn.2:2;Ro.3:23-25)*	10 But that you may know that the Son of man* has authority on earth to forgive sins"--	24 But that you may know that the Son of man* has authority on earth to forgive sins" --
Then He Commands	he then said to the paralytic--	he said to the paralytic--	he said to the man who was paralyzed--
The Man To Get Up.	"Rise, take up your bed, and go home."	11 "I say to you, Rise, take up your pallet and go home."	"I say to you, Rise, take up your bed and go home."
The Man Is Healed Instantly, And Walks Out Carrying His Bed.	7 And he rose and went home.	12 And he rose, and immediately took up the pallet and went out before them all;	25 And immediately he rose up before them, and took up that on which he lay, and went home, glorifying God.
Everybody Is Overawed	8 When the crowds saw it, they were afraid,	so that they were all amazed	26 And amazement seized them all,
And They Give Praise To God	and they glorified God, who had given such authority to men.	and glorified God, saying, "We never saw anything like this!"	and they glorified God and were filled with awe, saying, "We have seen strange things today."

[a] *Many authorities read* seeing.

**"The Son of man" is identified with "the Christ" in Lk.22:67-69,p.231. and "Christ" is used as the Greek transalation of "Messiah", in Jn.4:25, and as "the Savior of the world" in Jn.4:42. (See also p.165)*

(3) Jesus is Teaching by the Lake. § 52

		Mk. 2:13	Lk. 5:27[a]
They Go out to the Lake-side. There Jesus Teaches Them		13 He went out again beside the sea; and all the crowd gathered about him, and he taught them.	27 After this he went out,

(4) Jesus Calls Matthew. § 53

(Cf. § 43, p.40)

	Mt. 9:9	Mk. 2:14	Lk. 5:27b-28
Returning, Jesus Passes the Customs Booth.	9 And as Jesus passed on from there, he saw a man called Matthew	14 And as he passed on, he saw Levi the son of Alphaeus	and saw a tax collector,* named Levi,
He Sees Matthew. He Calls Him to Studentship	sitting at the tax office; and he said to him, "Follow me."	sitting at the tax office, and he said to him, "Follow me."	sitting at the tax office; and he said to him, "Follow me."
	And he rose and followed him.	And he rose and followed him.	28 And he left everything, and rose and followed him.

(5) Matthew Invites His Friends to Meet Jesus. § 54

(Cf. § 141, p.155)

	Mt. 9:10-13	Mk. 2:15-17	Lk. 5:29-32
The Grateful Convert Invites His Pals to Meet Jesus.	10 And as he sat at table[a] in the house, behold, many tax collectors ** and sinners came and sat down with Jesus and his disciples.	15 And as he sat at table in his house, many tax collectors and sinners were sitting with Jesus and his disciples; for there were many who followed him.	29 And Levi made him a great feast in his house; and there was a large company of tax collectors and others sitting at table[b] * with them.
The Supercilious Pharisees Are Contemptuous.	11 And when the Pharisees saw this, they said to his disciples,	16 And the scribes of[c] the Pharisees, when they saw that he was eating with the sinners and tax collectors,* said to his disciples,	30 And the Pharisees and their scribes murmured against his disciples, saying,
(Cf.Lk.19:7)	"Why does your teacher eat with tax collectors and sinners?"	"Why does he eat and drink[d] with tax collectors ** and sinners?"	"Why do you eat and drink with tax collectors and sinners?"
Christ's Compassionate Heart Gives a Sublime Answer	12 But when he heard it, he said, "Those who are well have no need of a physician, but those who are sick. 13 Go and learn what this means, 'I desire mercy, and not sacrifice.' (Hos.6:6) for I came not to call the righteous, but sinners."	17 And when Jesus heard it, he said to them, "Those who are well have no need of a physician, but those who are sick; I came not to call the righteous, but sinners."	31 And Jesus answered them, "Those who are well have no need of a physician, but those who are sick; 32 I have come not to call the righteous, but sinners to repentance."

....

[a] *Greek* reclined. [b] *Greek* reclining. [c] *Some ancient authorities read* and. [d] *Some ancient authorities omit* and drink. **Tables were only 12 to 18 inches high;so the only way to get up close to them was to "recline" on a mat or on a couch (or else sit on one's folded legs).*

*** The "Publicans", or tax-collectors, were despised by the Pharisees, and no attempt was made to convert them: so they were outcasts, even forbidden to come to the Synagogue.*

(6) Jesus Discusses Fasting with the Disciples of John.* § 55

	Mt. 9:14-17	*Mk. 2:18-22*	*Lk. 5:33-39*
(1) Why Christ's Disciples Do Not Fast.			
John's Disciples were Fasting		18 Now John's disciples and the Pharisees were fasting; and people came	
Jesus' Disciples Did Not Fast.	14 Then the disciples of John came to him, saying, "Why do we	and said to him, "Why do John's disciples	33 And they said to him, "The disciples of John fast often and offer prayers,
The Pharisees Ask Why	and the Pharisees fast,[a] but your disciples do not fast?"	and the disciples of the Pharisees fast, but your disciples do not fast?"	and so do the disciples of the Pharisees, but yours eat and drink."
In His Reply Jesus Alludes to John's Teaching (Cf. Jn. 3:29)	15 And Jesus said to them, "Can the wedding guests mourn as long as the bridegroom is with them?	19 And Jesus said to them, "Can the wedding guests fast while the bridegroom is with them? As long as they have the bridegroom with them, they cannot fast.	34 And Jesus said to them, "Can you make wedding guests fast while the bridegroom is with them?
(2) They Will Fast Some Day			
But There Will Come a Time to Fast	"The days will come, when the bridegroom is taken away from them, and then they will fast.	20 "The days will come, when the bridegroom is taken away from them and then they will fast on that day.	35 "The days will come, when the bridegroom is taken away from them, and then they will fast in those days."
(3) Christ's Teaching Is No Mere Patchwork.			36 He told them a parable also:
Jesus is Not Just Patching up the Old Religion; That Would Make It Worse.	16 "And no one puts a piece of unshrunk cloth on an old garment, for the patch tears away from the garment, and a worse tear is made.	21 "No one sews a piece of unshrunk cloth on an old garment; if he does, the patch tears away from it, the new from the old, and a worse tear is made.	"No one tears a piece from a new garment and puts it on an old garment; if he does, he will tear the new, and the piece from the new will not match the old.
(4) The New Teaching Will Have New Forms			
The New Religion Must Have New Forms To Express it Adequately.	17 Neither is new wine put into old wineskins; if it is, the skins burst, and the wine is spilled, and the skins are destroyed; but new wine is put into fresh wineskins, and so both are preserved."	22 And no one puts new wine into old wineskins; if he does, the wine will burst the skins, and the wine is lost, and so are the skins."[b]	37 And no man puts new wine into old wineskines; if he does, the new wine will burst the skins and it will be spilled, and the skins will be destroyed. 38 But new wine must be put into fresh wineskins.
(5) But Old Tastes Dislike New Forms			
Pharisees Do Not Like Jesus' Teaching			39 And no one after drinking old wine desires new; for he says 'The old is good.'"

....

[a] *Many ancient authorities add* much *or* often. [b] *Some ancient authorities add* but new wine is for fresh skins.

**For the sake of simplicity of arrangement, the sequence of Mk. 2:13-22, of Mt. 9:9-10, and of Lk. 5:27-38 is followed, rather than the implication of the wording of Mt. 9:18.*
But this section might also be placed between § 75 and § 76.

[*(A) THE FIRST PERIOD, or "THE EARLIER GALILEAN MINISTRY" (pp.39-48)*].
(B) THE SECOND PERIOD or "THE LATER GALILEAN MINISTRY" * *(Pp.49-100)*
(One Year: From the Passover, A.D. 28, to the Passover, or Purim, A.D.29).
(From the Sabbath Controversies, to the Great Galilean Crisis)

(I) TO JERUSALEM AND RETURN (pp. 51-55) [1]*
(Jn. 5:1-47; Mt. 12:1-14; Mk. 2:23-3:6; Lk. 6:1-11)

(1) Healing an Impotent Man on the Sabbath (Jn. 5) p.51-53.
(2) Plucking Grain on the Sabbath (Mt. 12:1-8; Mk. 2:23-28; Lk. 6:1-5) p.53-54.
(3) Healing a Withered Hand on the Sabbath (Mt. 12:9-14; Mk. 3:1-6; Lk. 6:6-11) p.54-55.

(II) TO THE MOUNT OF BEATITUDES AND RETURN (pp. 56-67) [2]
(Mt. 4:24-8:1,5-13, 12:15-21; Mk. 3:7-19a; Lk. 6:12-7:10)

(1) Jesus is Followed by Great Crowds (Mt.4:24-25, 12:15-21; Mk. 3:7-12) p.56.
(2) He Spends the Night in Prayer (Mk. 3:13a; Lk. 6:12) p.57.
(3) He Ordains the Twelve Apostles (Mt. 10:2-4; Mk. 3:12-19a; Lk. 6:13-16) p.57.
(4) He Preaches the Ordination Sermon (Mt. 5,6,7; Lk. 6:17-49) p.58-66.
(5) He Returns to Capernaum and Heals the Centurion's Servant (Mt.8:1,5-13; Lk.7:1-10) p.66-67.

(III) THROUGH SOUTHERN GALILEE AND RETURN (Lk.7:11-8:3; Mt.11:2-30)(pp. 68-70) [3]

(1) Jesus Restores a Widow's Son to Life (Lk. 7:11-17) p.68.
(2) John Sends an Inquiry to Jesus (Mt. 11:2-6; Lk. 7:18-23) p.68.
(3) Jesus Evaluates John and Laments His Rejection (Mt.11:7-19; Lk.7:24-35) p.69.
(4) Jesus is Anointed by a Sinful Woman (Lk. 7:36-50) p.70.
(5) Jesus Has Women Helpers in His Work (Lk. 8:1-3) p.70.
(6) Jesus Returns Home to Capernaum (Mk. 3:19b) p.71.

(IV) TO THE GERASENES AND RETURN (Mk.3:19b-5:20; Mt.12:22-13:53;8:28-34; Lk.8:4-39) (pp.71-82) [4]

(1) Jesus' Friends Say He is Beside Himself (Mk. 3:19b-21) p.71.
(2) Scribes and Pharisees Say He is a Demoniac, and that His Power is From the Devil (Mt. 12:22-45; Mk.3:22-30) p.71-73.
(3) His Relatives Interfere (Mt. 12:46-50; Mk. 3:31-35; Lk. 8:19-21) p.73.
(4) Jesus Teaches by Parables (Mt. 13:1-53; Mk. 4:1-34; Lk. 8:4-18) p.74-79.
(5) Jesus Stills a Tempest (Mt.8:18,23-27;Mk.4:35-41; Lk. 8:22-25) p.79-80.
(6) Jesus Cures Two Demoniacs (Mt.8:28-34;Mk. 5:1-16; Lk. 8:26-36) p.80-82.
(7) Jesus Leaves Their Country (Mt. 8:34; Mk. 5:17-20; Lk. 8:37-39)p.82.

(V) HEALING IN CAPERNAUM AGAIN (Mt. 9:1,18-34; Mk. 5:21-43; Lk. 8:40-56) (pp.83-86) [5]

(1) Jesus Returns to Capernaum and Is Welcomed by the Multitudes (Mt.9:1; Mk.5:21; Lk.8:40)p.83.
(2) Jairus Pleads With Jesus for His Daughter (Mt. 9:18-19; Mk.5:22-24; Lk.8:41-42) p.83.
(3) A Woman Touches His Garment and is Healed (Mt. 9:20-22; Mk. 5:25-34; Lk. 8:43-48) p.83-84.
(4) Jesus Raises Jairus' Daughter (Mt. 9:23-26; Mk. 5:35-43; Lk. 8:49-56) p.85.
(5) Jesus Cures Two Blind Men (Mt. 9:27-31) p.86.
(6) Jesus Cures A Dumb Demoniac (Mt. 9:32-34) p.86.

(VI) THE TWELVE SENT THROUGHOUT ALL GALILEE (pp. 87-92) [6]
(Mt. 9:35-11:1; Mk. 6:1-30; Lk. 9:1-10)

(1) Jesus' Last Visit to Nazareth (Mt. 13:54-58; Mk. 6:1-6a) p.87.
(2) Jesus' Last Tour Through Galilee (Mt. 9:35-38; Mk. 6:6b) p.87.
(3) Jesus Sends Out the Twelve (Mt. 10:1,5-42; Mk. 6:7-13; Lk. 9:1-6) p.88-90.
(4) Jesus Goes Out Also (Mt. 11:1) p.90.
(5) Herod Kills John the Baptist (Mt. 14:1-12; Mk. 6:14-29; Lk. 9:7-9) p.91-92.
(6) The Apostles Return and Report to Jesus (Mk. 6:30; Lk. 9:10) p.92.

(VII) TO BETHSAIDA AND THE RETURN THROUGH GENNESARET (pp. 93-100) [7]
(Mt. 14:13-36; Mk. 6:31-56; Lk. 9:11-17; Jn. 6:1-71)

(1) Jesus Feeds Five Thousand (Mt. 14:13-21; Mk. 6:31-44; Lk. 9:11-17; Jn. 6:1-14) p.93-95.
(2) Jesus Spends the Night in Prayer (Mt. 14:22-23; Mk. 6:45-46; Jn. 6:15) p.95.
(3) Jesus Walks on the Water (Mt.14:23b-33; Mk. 6:47-52; Jn. 6:16-21) p.96-97.
(4) Jesus Heals Many in Gennesaret (Mt. 14:34-36; Mk. 6:53-56) p.97.
(5) The Spiritual Nature of the Messiah's Work (Jn. 6:22-59) p.97-99.
(6) Many Disciples Forsake Jesus (Jn. 6:60-71) p.100.

(The Great Galilean Crisis)

**These numerous events are best associated, visualized, and remembered by noting that they are grouped (by the Gospels) in these several journeys, and then drawing the journeys on a map. See next page.*
Certainly there are enough activities here to fill out a very full year.

***YOU CAN REMEMBER** even this most difficult section of all--if you will follow Jesus around on these journeys as indicated on the map (p.50)--These journeys too are definitely indicated in the Gospels.*

Sketch Map for

THE LATER GALILEAN MINISTRY

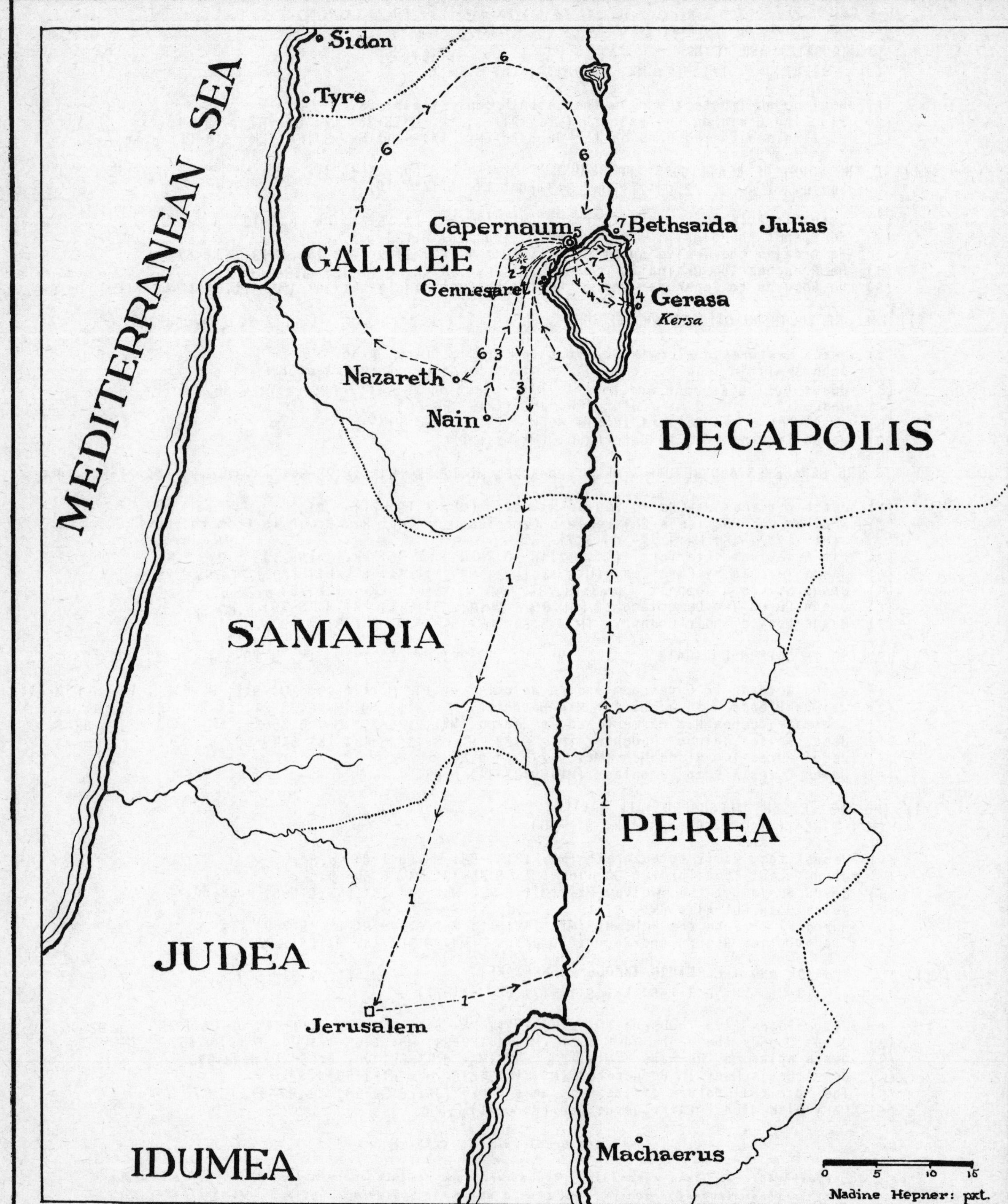

Numbers on the map refer to bracketed [1] *in the outline.*

(I) TO JERUSALEM AND RETURN:

(Jn. 5:1-47; Mt. 12:1-14; Mk. 2:23-3:6; Lk. 6:1-11)

(1) Healing a Sick Man on the Sabbath, and the Controversy that Grew Out of it. § 56

Jn. 5:1-47 ((Cf. Jn.7:21-25,p.123)

a. THE MIRACLE

(a) The Situation

Jesus Goes Up to the Feast at Jerusalem

1 After this *(See Jn.4:46-54. John omits all the events of pp.38-48).*
there was a feast of the Jews,*
and Jesus went up to Jerusalem.

He Sees Many Sick At the Pool of Bethesda

2 Now there is in Jerusalem by the sheep gate
a pool, in Hebrew called Beth-za'tha,[a] which has five porticoes.
3 In these lay a multitude of invalids, blind, lame, paralyzed.

(b) The Preparation

4 **

One Sick Man Is Singled Out,

5 One man was there,
who had been ill for thirty-eight years.

Jesus Arouses

6 When Jesus saw him
and knew that he had been lying there a long time,
he said to him,
"Do you want to be healed?"

His Profound Desire,

His Daring Faith, and His Full Cooperation.

7 The sick man answered him,
"Sir, I have no man to put me into the pool when the water is troubled,
and while I am going another steps down before me."

(c) The Healing

8 Jesus said to him,
"Rise, take up your pallet, and walk."

He is Healed and Walks Off Carrying His Bed.

9 And at once the man was healed,
and he took up his pallet and walked.

(d) The Criticism by the Rulers

The Jewish Rulers Censure Him

Now that day was the sabbath.
10 So the Jews said to the man who was cured,
"It is the sabbath,
it is not lawful for you to carry your pallet."

He Defends His Action

11 But he answered them,
"The man who healed me said to me,
'Take up your pallet, and walk.'"

They Ask Who Had Healed Him

12 They asked him,
"Who is the man who said to you,
'Take up your pallet, and walk?'"

**Was this feast a Passover? Or the feast of Purim, or of Pentecost, or Tabernacles, or Dedication? Each one has been advocated. In fact, no one really knows: we have not sufficient evidence to decide once for all. It makes no essential difference which it is. It does have a bearing on the length of Christ's ministry. If this feast was the Passover, then four Passovers are mentioned by John (2:13; 5:1; 6:4; 11:55). This would make three years from the First Passover (Jn. 2:13) to the last (Jn. 11:55). The time occupied by the introductory events of Christ's ministry, reported in Jn. 1:19-2:12 and in Mt. 3:1-4:11 would have to be added to the three years. The usual theory is here followed, as being more likely. It also gives a better basis for the division of the Life of Christ, as shown in the general outline and Diagram on pp. 8 and 9 The feast of Purim fell in March.*

***The best ancient authorities omit verse 4. It is a marginal note, inserted in the manuscript later, to explain why these people were there, waiting for the water to be moved,* 4 for an angel of the Lord went down at certain seasons into the pool, and troubled the water: whosoever then first after the troubling of the water stepped in was made whole, with whatsoever disease he was holden. *(Copied from American Standard Version)*

[a] *Some ancient authorities read* Bethesda, *others* Bethsaida.

He Doesn't Know For Jesus had Slipped Away From The Crowd

13 Now the man who had been healed did not know who it was,
for Jesus had withdrawn,
as there was a crowd in the place.

Later, Jesus Finds The Man And Warns Him.

14 Afterward, Jesus found him in the temple, and said to him,
"See, you are well!
Sin no more, that nothing worse befall you." *(Jn.8:11,p.126)*

*The Man Reports to the Rulers that it Was Jesus Who Had Healed Him Then They Persecute Jesus for Breaking the Sabbath**

15 The man went away
and told the Jews
that it was Jesus who had healed him.

16 And this was why the Jews persecuted Jesus,
because he did this on the sabbath.*

He Replies that God Himself Had Done The Healing

17 But Jesus answered them,
"My Father is working still,
and I am working."

They Accuse Jesus of Blasphemy By Thus Putting Himself on The Same Basis as God.

18 This was why the Jews sought all the more to kill him, *(Mt.12:14,p.55;Jn.7:7)*
because he not only broke the sabbath
but also called God his Father,
making himself equal with God.

b. THE CONTROVERSY

This Point Jesus Discusses Further

(a) About Making Himself Equal With God (v. 18f)

The Mutual Interdependence and Equality of the Father and the Son

The Father Does His Work Through the Son

19 Jesus said to them,
"Truly, truly, I say to you,
the Son can do nothing of his own accord,
but only what he sees the Father doing;

for whatever he does,
that the Son does likewise.

The Father Entrusts All Things To The Son

20 "For the Father loves the Son,
and shows him all that he himself is doing; *(Jn.3:25;Mt.11:27,p.47;Mt.28:18)*

He Gives Spiritual **Life** *Through The Son*

and greater works than these will he show him,
that you may marvel.
21 For as the Father raises the dead and gives them life,
so also the Son gives life to whom he will.

So Also The Father **Judges** *Only Through The Son*

22 "The Father judges no one,
but has given all judgment to the Son, *(Mt.16:27;25:31-32; Ac.17:31)*
23 that all may honor the Son, even as they honor the Father.
He who does not honor the Son does not honor the Father who sent him.

Eternal Life Comes, By Believing God's Message, Through the Son

24 "Truly, truly, I say to you,
he who hears my word and believes him who sent me;
has eternal life; he does not come into judgment,
but has passed from death to life.

The Hour Is Here For The Spiritually Dead to Live

25 "Truly, truly, I say to you,
the hour is coming, and now is,
when the dead will hear the voice of the Son of God,
and those who hear will live.

Because God Gave This Authority and Power to The Son

26 "For as the Father has life in himself,
so he has granted the Son also to have life in himself,
27 and has given him authority to execute judgment,
because he is the Son of man.

Final Resurrection and Final Judgment Also Come Through the Son

28 "Do not marvel at this;
for the hour is coming
when all who are in the tombs *(Rev.20:11-15)*
will hear his voice, 29 and come forth,
those who have done good, to the resurrection of life,
and those who have done evil, to the resurrection of judgment.

**The Rabbis had a rule that it was breaking the Sabbath to heal on that holy day, unless there was danger that the patient would die before sundown, when the Sabbath ended. Jesus had, of course, plainly ignored such trifling casuistry.*

(b) About The Reason Why The Jewish Rulers Disbelieve

Their Disbelief is Not *because of Insufficient Evidence:*

30" I can do nothing on my own authority; *(Jn.7:16-18,p.123)*
as I hear, I judge;
and my judgment is just,
because I seek not my own will but the will of Him who sent me.

The Testimony Is Adequate

31" If I bear witness to myself, my testimony is not true;
32there is another who bears witness to me,
and I know that the testimony which he bears to me is true.

(a) They Have John's Testimony *(But Have Disobeyed it)*

33" You sent to John, and he has borne witness to the truth.
34Not that the testimony which I receive is from man;
but I say this that you may be saved.
35He was a burning and shining lamp, *(Cf.Jn.1:6-9,*§3 *)*
and you were willing to rejoice for a while in his light.*(Lk.3:15,p.24)*

(b) And the Father's Testimony Through Christ's Works *(This,too, They Have Resisted and violently Misconstrued)*

36" But the testimony which I have is greater than that of John;
for the works which the Father has granted me.to accomplish,
these very works which I am doing, bear me witness
that the Father has sent me. *(v.17ff.;Jn.10:32-38,p.149)*
37And the Father who sent me has himself borne witness to me.
His voice you have never heard, his form you have never seen;
38and you do not have his word abiding in you,
for you do not believe him whom he has sent.

(c) And the Father's Testimony, Through the Scriptures *(These They Have Disobeyed and Nullified)*

39" You search the scriptures,
because you think that in them you have eternal life;
and it is they that bear witness to me;
40yet you refuse to come to me that you may have life.

But *They Disbelieve:*
(a) Because They Seek Glory From Men; On This Account They Are Incapacitated for Believing,

41" I do not receive glory from men. *(Jn.8:49,50,54,p.128; 12:43)*
42But I know that you have not the love of God within you.
43I have come in my Father's name, and you do not receive me;
if another comes in his own name, him you will receive.
44How can you believe, who receive glory from one another *(v.41 and ref.)*
and do not seek the glory that comes from the only God?

(b) Because They Have Been Unfaithful to Previous Light Through The Scriptures.

45" Do not think that I shall accuse you to the Father;
it is Moses who accuses you,
on whom you set your hope.
46If you believed Moses, you would believe me,
for he wrote of me.
47But if you do not believe his writings, how will you believe my words?"

(2) Plucking and Eating Ears of Grain on a Sabbath and the Resulting Controversy. § 57

	Mt. 12:1-8	*Mk. 2:23-28*	*Lk. 6:1-5*
A Second Sabbath Controversy	1At that time	23One sabbath	1On a sabbath,[a]
a. The Occasion	Jesus went	he was going	while he was going
	through the grainfields on the sabbath;	through the grainfields;	through the grainfields,
		and as they made their way	
	his disciples were hungry, and they began	his disciples began	his disciples
	to pluck ears of grain and to eat.	to pluck* ears of grain.	plucked and ate some ears of grain,
			rubbing them in their hands.*

[a]*Many ancient authorities read* on the second first sabbath *(on the second sabbath after the first).*
"Plucking", the Pharisees said, was reaping; *and "rubbing the ears in their hands" was* threshing: *therefore it was* work; *and consequently it was wrong to do these things on the sabbath.*

	Matthew	Mark	Luke
b. The Dispute	2 But when the Pharisees saw it, they said to him,	24 And the Pharisees said to him,	2 But some of the Pharisees said,
Their Accusations	"Look, your disciples are doing what is not lawful to do on the sabbath."	"Look, why are they doing what is not lawful on the sabbath?"	"Why are you doing what is not lawful to do on the sabbath?"
The Reply of Jesus	3 He said to them, "Have you not read what David did,	25 And he said to them, "Have you never read what David did, when he was in need	3 And Jesus answered, "Have you not read what David did
The Example of David	when he was hungry, and those who were with him:	and was hungry, he and those who were with him:	when he was hungry, he and those who were with him:
Eating The Holy Bread	4 "how he entered the house of God, and ate the bread of the Presence, which it was not lawful for him to eat nor for those who were with him, but only for the priests?	26 "how he entered the house of God, when A-bi´a-thar was high priest, and ate the bread of the Presence, which it is not lawful for any but the priests to eat, and also gave it to those who were with him?"	4 how he entered the house of God, and took and ate the bread of the Presence, which it is not lawful for any but the priests to eat, and also gave it to those with him?"
A Second Argument from Scripture	5 "Or have you not read in the law how on the sabbath the priests in the temple profane the sabbath,* and are guiltless?		
	6 "I tell you, something greater than the temple is here.	27 And he said to them,	5 And he said to them,
A Third Deduction From Scripture	7 "And if you had known what this means, 'I desire mercy, and not sacrifice,' you would not have condemned the guiltless.		
A Twofold Conclusion: *(a) The Sabbath and man.*		"The sabbath was made for man, not man for the sabbath;	
(b) The Sabbath and the Son of man.	8 "For the Son of man is lord of the sabbath."	28 so the Son of Man is lord even of the sabbath."	"The Son of man is lord of the sabbath."

(3) Healing a Withered Hand on the Sabbath. § 58

*The Resulting Controversy*** *and Their Conspiracy To Destroy Him*

	Mt. 12:9-14	*Mk. 3:1-6*	*Lk. 6:6-11*
A Third Sabbath Controversy *a. The Occasion:* *Jesus is Teaching in the Synagogue,*	9 And he went on from there, and entered their synagogue.	1 Again he entered the synagogue,	6 On another sabbath, when he entered the synagogue and taught,
An Unfortunate Man Is Present.	10 And behold, there was a man with a withered hand.	and a man was there who had a withered hand.	a man was there whose right hand was withered.

*By building fires and butchering animals for the sacrifices.

**"Healing" was forbidden by their rules of sabbath observance, unless there was danger the sick one could not live till sundown, when the sabbath ended.

On three later occasions (Jn. 9:1-34; Lk. 13:10-21; Lk. 14:1-6; cf. Jn. 7:20-24) controversies arose about Sabbath observance. Jesus' teaching on Sabbath observance may be summarized as follows: (1) The Sabbath was made for man's welfare. (2) It is designed for rest and worship. (3) Deeds of mercy and acts of worship justify necessary work on the Sabbath. (4) It is lawful to do good on the Sabbath. (5) The Messiah is lord of the Sabbath.

Topic	Matthew	Mark	Luke
Jesus' Wily Enemies Are Present Also, And Watching Him	*(Lk.14:1,p.153)*	2 And they watched him, to see* whether he would heal him on the sabbath,	7 And the scribes and the Pharisees watched him, to see whether he would heal on the sabbath,
They Question Him	And they asked him, " Is it lawful to heal on the sabbath?" so that they might accuse him.	so that they might accuse him.	so that they might find an accusation against him. 8 But he knew their thoughts,
Jesus Calls The Man Out To Stand In Front.		3 And he said to the man who had the withered hand, " Come here."	and he said to the man who had the withered hand, " Come and stand here." And he rose and stood there.
Jesus Raises the Moral Issue.		4 And he said to them, " Is it lawful on the sabbath to do good or to do harm, to save life or to kill?"	9 And Jesus said to them, "I ask you, Is it lawful on the sabbath to do good or to do harm, to save life or to destroy it?"
They Are Silent.		But they were silent.	
He Illustrates From Their Own Practices	11 He said to them, " What man of you, if he has one sheep and it falls into a pit on the sabbath, will not lay hold of it and lift it out? 12 " Of how much more value is a man than a sheep!		
He Draws A Conclusion.	So it is lawful to do good on the sabbath."	*(Mk.3:4 above)*	
He looks Around Reproachfully.		5 And he looked around at them with anger, grieved at their hardness of heart,	10 And he looked around on them all,
He Heals the Man.	13 Then he said to the man, " Stretch out your hand." And the man stretched it out, and it was restored, whole like the other.	and said to the man, " Stretch out your hand." He stretched it out, and his hand was restored.	and said to him, " Stretch out your hand." And he did so, and his hand was restored. 11 But they were filled with fury **
The Religious Authorities Plot With The Political How To Destroy Jesus	14 But the Pharisees went out and took counsel against him how to destroy him. ** *(Jn.5:18; Jn.7:1 and footnote)*	6 The Pharisees went out, and immediately held counsel with the Herodians, ** against him how to destroy him.	and discussed with one another what they might do to Jesus.

***They " are" filled with fury" ; (b) They " held counsel with one another" ; (c) They hatched a conspiracy with the politicians (" the Herodians") and plotted to kill Him. This purpose has already emerged at Jerusalem at the Passover (Jn.5:18) but they had not been able to accomplish it there, so they are hounding Him about now from place to place. (See* §§ 56,57,58*). Their grievances had been accumulating: first, He had claimed to forgive sins, (they called it blasphemy,* § 51*); then (* § 53 *) He had mingled freely with untouchables; next He had ignored their fastings (* § 55 *); and worst of all, He had repeatedly violated their rules of Sabbath keeping (pp.50-55); so they are filled with fury and are determined to do away with Him by plotting with the political rulers.*

(Mt. 4:25-8:1; 8:5-13; Mk. 3:7-10a; Lk. 6:12-7:10)

(I) Jesus Is Followed by Great Crowds. § 59

	Mt. 12:15 4:24-25,12:16-21	Mk. 3:7-12
Jesus, Knowing Their Plot, Goes Out Of the Synagogue, To The Lakeside	15 Jesus, aware of this,* withdrew from there.	7 And Jesus with his disciples withdrew* to the sea,
Great Crowds Go Along.	And many followed him, and he healed them all,	and a great multitude from Galilee followed;
	Mt. 4:24-25	
His Fame Has Spread Far and Wide.	24 So his fame spread throughout all Syria,	*(Cf. vs. 8 below)*
They Come Bringing Their Sick.	and they brought him all the sick, those afflicted with various diseases and pains, demoniacs, epileptics, and paralytics, and he healed them.	
And The Crowds Come From Everywhere. (Locate These Places On the Map p. 50)	25 And great crowds followed him from Galilee and the De-cap´o-lis and Jerusalem and Judea and from beyond the Jordan. *(Cf. vs. 24 above)*	also from Judea 8 and Jerusalem and Id-u-me´a and from beyond the Jordan *(See Map, p. 50)* and from about Tyre and Sidon a great multitude, hearing all that he did, came to him.
To Avoid The Jam and Confusion Jesus Gets Into A Boat To Teach.		9 And he told his disciples to have a boat ready for him because of the crowd, lest they should crush him;
Multitudes Had Been Healed		10 for he had healed many, so that all who had diseases pressed upon him to touch him.
Demoniacs too Do Homage Before Him		11 And whenever the unclean spirits beheld him, they fell down before him and cried out, "You are the Son of God."
	Mt. 12:16-21	
*He Sternly Charges Secrecy.**	16 and ordered them not to make him known.	12 And he strictly ordered them not to make him known.
Thus Prophecy About the Messiah Is fulfilled	17 This was to fulfill what was spoken by the prophet Isaiah: *(Isa. 42:1ff.)*	

18 "Behold, my servant whom I have chosen,
my beloved with whom my soul is well pleased.

"I will put my Spirit upon him,
and he shall proclaim justice to the Gentiles.

19 "He will not wrangle or cry aloud,
nor will any one hear his voice in the streets;

20 "he will not break a bruised reed
or quench a smoldering wick,
till he brings justice to victory;

21 "and in his name will the Gentiles hope."

**Because of the hostility of the rulers (See previous section). They are envious ('jealous') of hisgreat power over the people (See Pilate's shrewd observation, Mt. 27:18, p. 235). The envy that then reached its fatal climax was already working here. This is the first time the religious leaders and the political rulers (Herodians) ganged together against Jesus. The Jewish leaders had hounded him from the Passover at Jerusalem with evil intent (Jn. 5:18, p. 52). They accuse Him of Sabbath breaking and blasphemy; but their real motive is envy.*

	Mt. 5:1a 10:2-4	*Mk. 3:13-19a*	*Lk. 6:12-16*
			[12]In these days
Jesus Goes to the Mountain and Prays All Night	[1]Seeing the crowds, he went up on the mountain.	[13]And he went up into the hills,	he went out into the hills to pray; and all night he continued in prayer to God.*
			[13]And when it was day,
He chooses and Ordains Twelve Apostles		and called to him those whom he desired; and they came to him.	he called his disciples,
			and chose from them twelve,
		[14]And he appointed twelve,[a] to be with him, and to be sent out to preach [15]and have authority to cast out demons:	whom he named apostles;
	s	*(Cf. Also the list in Ac.1:13)*	
	r;	[16]Simon whom he surnamed Peter;	[14]Simon, whom he named Peter, and Andrew his brother,
	ee,	[17]James the son of Zebedee and John the brother of James, whom he surnamed Bo-a-ner´ges, that is, sons of thunder; [18]Andrew,	and James and John,
	ew;	and Philip, and Bartholomew, and Matthew, and Thomas,	and Philip, and Bartholomew, [15]and Matthew, and Thomas,
	aeus,	and James the son of Alphaeus,	and James the son of Alphaeus,
of Four.	and Thaddaeus;[b] [4]Simon the Cananaean,	and Thaddaeus,*** and Simon the Cananaean,	and Simon who was called the Zealot,** [16]and Judas*** the son[c] of James;***
	and Judas Iscariot, who betrayed him.	[19]and Judas Iscariot, who betrayed him.	and Judas Iscariot, who became a traitor.

....

**Evidently, this was preparatory to the next day's far-reaching responsibilities.*

***Zealots were revolutionists.*

****This Judas then is the same as Thaddaeus.*

[a]*Some ancient authorities add* whom also he named apostles.

[b]*Some ancient authorities read* Lebbaeus, or Lebbaeus called Thaddaeus.

[c]*Or* brother.

(3) Jesus Preaches the Ordination Sermon. § 61*

	Mt. 5:1b-7:29	*Lk. 6: 17-49*
Great Multitudes; The Twelve, The People, Gather on a Level Place From Everywhere. (Lk. 6:17)		17And he came down with them and stood on a level place, with a great crowd of his disciples and a great multitude of people from all Judea and Jerusalem and the seacoast of Tyre and Sidon, who came to hear him and to be healed of their diseases; 18and those who were troubled with unclean spirits were cured.
	Mt. 5:1	19And all the crowd sought to touch him, for power came forth from him and healed them all.
Jesus Gets Ready to Preach to Them.	1And when he sat down his disciples came to him.	20And he lifted up his eyes on his disciples,
	2And he opened his mouth and taught them, saying:	and said:

A. THE RIGHTEOUSNESS OF THE SONS OF THE KINGDOM OF GOD,

Or CHRISTIAN CHARACTER PORTRAYED

(Mt. 5; Lk. 6:20-36)

1. In Its Inner Essential Nature

The Inner Essence of Righteousness *(a) Negatively: Right Attitude Towards Sin*	3"Blessed are the poor in spirit, *(11:29)* for theirs is the kingdom of heaven.	20b"Blessed are you poor, for yours is the kingdom of God.
(Humility, v.3 and Repentance, v.4)	4"Blessed are those who mourn, for they shall be comforted.	*(Cf. v. 21b)*
(b) Positively: Right Attitude Towards Righteousness	5"Blessed are the meek, *(Ps.37:11)* for they shall inherit the earth.	
(Obedience, v.5, and Aspiration, v.6)	6"Blessed are those who hunger and thirst for righteousness, for they shall be satisfied.	21"Blessed are you that hunger now, for you shall be satisfied.
	(Cf. v. 4)	"Blessed are you that weep now, for you shall laugh.
(c) Right Attitude Towards Others (Unselfish Love)	7"Blessed are the merciful, for they shall obtain mercy.	
(d) Right Attitude Towards Self (A Clean Conscience, Heb.9:14b)	8"Blessed are the pure in heart, for they shall see God	
(e) Right Attitude Towards God (Peace with God, Peace with Self, Peace with All)	9"Blessed are the peacemakers, *(v.45)* for they shall be called sons of God.	

**Since this was the occasion of the ordaining of the Apostles, it is not unlikely that Jesus Himself may have summarized the fundamental principles of the Righteousness of the Kingdom as a sort of constitution. Whether He did it or some one else, it is most helpful to see the logical relations of these principles to each other.*

2. In Its Outer Relationships

(a) The World's Persecution of the Righteous

10 "Blessed are those who are
persecuted for righteousness' sake,
for theirs is the kingdom of heaven. *(Jn.15:18-25;p.217)*

11 "Blessed are you when men
revile you
and persecute you
and utter all kinds of evil
against you falsely
on my account.

(Mt.10:34-39)

22 "Blessed are you when men hate you,
and when they exclude you
and revile you,
and cast out your name as evil, *(Jn.15:18-25,p.217)*
on account of the Son of man!

(b) How To Meet such Persecution.

12 "Rejoice, and be glad,
for your reward is great in heaven,
for so men persecuted
the prophets
who were before you.

23 "Rejoice in that day, and leap for joy,
for behold, your reward is great in heaven;
for so their fathers did
to the prophets.

The Opposite Character Brings "woe" Instead of Blessing

24 "But woe to you that are rich,
for you have received your consolation.

25 "Woe to you that are full now,
for you shall hunger.

"Woe to you that laugh now,
for you shall mourn and weep.

26 "Woe to you, when all men speak well of you,
for so their fathers did
to the false prophets.

The Christian's Relation to the World

(a) Like Salt

13 "You are the salt of the earth; *(Lk.14:34-35,p.155; Mk.9:50,p.116)*
but if salt has lost its taste,
how can its saltness be restored?
It is no longer good for anything
except to be thrown out and trodden under foot by men.

(b) Like Light.

14 "You are the light of the world.
A city set on a hill cannot be hid.

Shining So That Men May Be Led to Glorify God

15 "Nor do men light a lamp *(Lk.11:33-36;8:16)*
and put it under a bushel,
but on a stand,
and it gives light to all in the house.
16 Let your light so shine before men,
that they may see your good works
and give glory to your Father who is in heaven.

3. Christian Righteousness versus The Righteousness of the Law

(1) General Statement

Jesus Will Not Destroy but Fulfill the Law
For Moral Law Is More Inviolable Than Physical Law

17 "Think not that I have come to abolish the law and the prophets;
I have come not to abolish them but to fulfill them.
18 For truly, I say to you,
Till heaven and earth pass away, *(Mt.24:35,p.201; Lk.16:17)*
not an iota, not a dot, will pass from the law
until all is accomplished.

Strict Obedience Indicates True Greatness (As in Science)

19 "Whoever then relaxes one of the least of these commandments
and teaches men so,
shall be called least in the kingdom of heaven;
but he who does them and teaches them
shall be called great in the kingdom of heaven. *(Mt.18:1,4,p.114; § 156,p.172)*

Their Most Approved Examples Fall Far Short Of Kingdom Demands

20 "For I tell you,
unless your righteousness exceeds that of the scribes and Pharisees,
you will never enter the kingdom of heaven.

(2) Specific Examples

(a) Murder

Murder in Its Deepest Significance

21 "You have heard that it was said to the men of old, *(Ex.20:13; Dt.5:17)*
'You shall not kill;
and whoever kills shall be liable to judgment.'

The Right Attitude Toward a Brother

22 "But I say to you
that every one who is angry with his brother[a] shall be liable to judgment;
whoever insults[b] his brother shall be liable to the council,
and whoever says, 'You fool!' shall be liable to the hell[c] of fire.

23 "So if you are offering your gift at the altar, *(Lk.12:57-59,p.145)*
and there remember that your brother has something against you,
24 leave your gift there before the altar and go;
first be reconciled to your brother,
and then come and offer your gift.

The Right Attitude Toward An Adversary-at-law and Why

25 "Make friends quickly with your accuser,
while you are going with him to court,
lest your accuser hand you over to the judge,
and the judge to the guard,
and you be put in prison;
26 truly, I say to you,
you will never get out till you have paid the last penny.

(b) Adultery

Adultery:- In Its Deepest Motive

27 "You have heard that it was said, *(Ex.20:14; Dt.5:18)*
'You shall not commit adultery.'
28 But I say to you
that every one who looks at a woman lustfully
has already committed adultery with her in his heart.

How to Deal With An Adulterous Look, or Touch,

29 "If your right eye causes you to sin,
pluck it out and throw it away;
it is better that you lose one of your members
than that your whole body be thrown into hell.[c]
30 "And if your right hand causes you to sin,
cut it off
and throw it away;
it is better that you lose one of your members
than that your whole body go into hell.[c]

Adultery As Fostered By Divorce.

31 "It was also said, *(Dt.24:1,3)*
'Whoever divorces his wife,
let him give her a certificate of divorce.'
32 But I say to you *(§ 152,p.167-8,Lk.16:18,p.158)*
that every one who divorces his wife,
except on the ground of unchastity,
makes her an adulteress;
and whoever marries a divorced woman commits adultery.

(c) Swearing

The Futility Of All Oaths Profanity, Perjury, or Any Other Oath

33 "Again you have heard that it was said to the men of old,
'You shall not swear falsely, *(Dt.24:12; Num.30:2)*
but shall perform to the Lord what you have sworn.'
34 "But I say to you, *(Mt.23:16-22,p.192)*
Do not swear at all,
either by heaven, for it is the throne of God,
35 or by the earth, for it is his footstool,
or by Jerusalem, for it is the city of the great king.
36 And do not swear by your head,
for you cannot make one hair white or black.

The Adequacy Of Simple Truth

37 "Let what you say be simply
'Yes' or 'No';
Anything more than this
comes from evil.[d]

---

[a] *Many ancient authorities insert* without cause. [b] *Greek*, says Raca to *(an obscure term of abuse)*.
[c] *Greek* Gehenna. [d] *Or* the evil one.

	Matthew	Luke
(d) How to Meet Evil *Overcoming Evil*		
The Old Way *"Getting Even"*	38" You have heard that it was said, *(Ex.21:24;Lev.24:20;Dt.19:2)* 'An eye for an eye, and a tooth for a tooth.'	
Christ's Way *By "Loving Helpfulness"* *By Doing Good* *By Blessing* *By Prayer*	39But I say to you, *(Cf. v. 44)*	*Lk.* 27" But I say to you that hear, " Love your enemies, *(v.35;Lk.23:34,p.240)* do good to those who hate you, 28bless those who curse you, pray for those who abuse you.
By non-Violence *By Meekness* *By Patient Suffering* *By Going The Second Mile*	" Do not resist one who is evil. But if any one strikes you on the right cheek, turn to him the other also; 40" and if any one would sue you and take your coat, let him have your cloak as well; 41" and if any one forces you to go one mile, go with him two miles.	29" To him who strikes you on the cheek, offer the other also; and from him who takes away your cloak do not withhold your coat as well.
By Suffering Oneself to Be Defrauded" *(1 Cor. 6:1-8; Hebr. 10:32-36)*	42" Give to him who begs from you, and do not refuse him who would borrow from you.	30" Give to every one who begs from you; " and of him who takes away your goods, do not ask them again.
By The Golden Rule	*(Cf. 7:12)*	31And as you wish that men would do to you, do so to them.
(e) How to Meet Enemies *The Old Way*	43" You have heard that it was said, 'You shall love your neighbor *(Lev.19:18)* and hate your enemy.'	
Christ's Way *Winning Enemies Through Love and Prayer*	44But I say to you, 'Love your enemies and pray for those who persecute you,'	*(Cf. v. 27-28)*
Our Father's Example	45" so that you may be sons of your Father who is in heaven; for he makes his sun rise *(v.9;Lk.6:35)* on the evil and on the good, and sends rain on the just and on the unjust.	
The Christian Must Do More Than Others,- *More than Publicans,* *More than Heathen,*	46" For if you love those who love you what reward have you? Do not even the tax collectors do the same? 47" And if you salute only your brethren, what more are you doing than others? Do not even the Gentiles do the same?	32" If you love those who love you, what credit is that to you? for even sinners love those who love them.
More than Sinners.		33" And if you do good to those who do good to you, what credit is that to you? For even sinners do the same. 34 And if you lend to those from whom you hope to receive, what credit is that to you? Even sinners lend to sinners, to receive as much again.
Christian Love and Unselfish Helpfulness		35" But love your enemies, *(v.27)* and do good, and lend, expecting nothing in return;[a]
The Great Reward	*(Mt.5:9,45)*	and your reward will be great, and you will be sons of the Most High; for he is kind to the ungrateful and the selfish.
God's Example		36" Be merciful even as your Father is merciful.

(3) The Final Summary of Christian Righteousness

Summary of (vs. 17-47 *The Perfect Ideal of Righteousness*	48You, therefore, must be perfect,* *(Lev.19:2)* as your heavenly Father is perfect.	

[a] *Some ancient authorities read* despairing of no man.

* *Of course, this is possible only through the grace of Christ, by faith. But God can be satisfied only by perfect righteousness, as revealed in Christ; and according to Him will we be judged (Ac.17:31a). His righteousness is our perfect ideal, and if we believe in it, and are utterly committed to it and seek it with all our heart, it will be reckoned as our own; we will be "justified" in the sight of God.*

B. CHRISTIAN RIGHTEOUSNESS IN THE FOUR ESSENTIAL RELATIONSHIPS OF LIFE***
Mt. 6:1-34

Christian Righteousness
1. General Statement

1 "Beware of practicing your piety* before men
in order to be seen by them; (Mt.23:5ff.)
for then you will have no reward from your father who is in heaven.

2. Typical Illustrations

(1) Alms Doing, *or Our Attitude towards Others - Sacrificial Service.*

2 "Thus, when you give alms, **
sound no trumpet before you,
as the hypocrites do
in the synagogues and in the streets,
that they may be praised by men.

One's Attitude Toward Men

(a) Negatively

Truly, I say to you,
they have their reward.

(b) Positively

3 "But when you give alms,
do not let your left hand know what your right hand is doing,
4 so that your alms may be in secret;
and your Father who sees in secret
will reward you.

(2) Praying, *or Our Attitude towards God - Absolute Devotion*

Ones Attitude Toward God

5 "And when you pray,
you must not be like the hypocrites;
for they love to stand and pray in the synagogues and at the street corners,
that they may be seen by men. (Lk.18:12f.,p.167)
Truly, I say to you,
they have their reward.

(a) Negatively, Don't Pray Like a Hypocrite

(b) Positively, But in Absolute sincerity

6 "But when you pray
go into your room
and shut the door
and pray to your Father who is in secret;
and your Father who sees in secret will reward you.

(c) Negatively, Don't Pray Like a Heathen

7 "And in praying do not heap up empty phrases
as the Gentiles do;
for they think they will be heard for their many words.

(d) Positively, But Pray As a Child

8 "Do not be like them,
for your Father knows what you need (v.32,p.64)
before you ask him.

THE MODEL PRAYER
I. Invocation
II. Petitions
1. For God's Cause
a. His Name
b. His Kingdom
c. His Will
2. For Human Need
a. Sustenance
b. Forgiveness
c. Guidance
d. Deliverance
III. Doxology (See footnote)

9 "Pray then like this:
'Our Father who art in heaven, (Lk.11:2-4 and margin,p.138)
Hallowed be thy name.
10 Thy kingdom come,
Thy will be done, (Mt.26:42,p.222)
On earth as it is in heaven.
11 Give us this day our daily bread;[a]
12 And forgive us our debts, as we also have forgiven our debtors;
13 And lead us not into temptation,
but deliver us from evil.'[b]

One Point Emphasized (Forgiveness)

14 "For if you forgive men their trespasses,
your heavenly Father also will forgive you; ((Mt.18:21-35,p.116-117; Mk.11:25-26,p.182 Note)
15 But if you do not forgive men their trespasses,
neither will your Father forgive your trespasses.

---

*Greek righteousness.
**Greek do alms.
[a]Or our bread for the morrow.
[b]Or the evil one. *Many authorities, some ancient add, in some form,* For thine is the kingdom, and the power, and the glory, forever. Amen.
****T.Z.Koo quotes Confucius as saying that there are* three *"Essential Relationships" in life, and therefore* th[ree] *"Fundamental Attitudes in Ethical Conduct."*
Jesus, however, here sets forth four, *and He also shows what the truly ethical attitude is toward each. Here, then,* is the essential foundation for all moral conduct.

(3) Fasting, *or Our Attitude towards Ourselves - Self-Denial and Self-Sacrifice.*

One's Attitude Toward Self:- (a) Negatively

16 " And when you fast
do not look dismal,
like the hypocrites,
for they disfigure their faces
that their fasting may be seen by men.
Truly, I say to you,
they have their reward.

(b) Positively

17 " But when you fast, (§ 55, p.48)
anoint your head and wash your face,
18 that your fasting may not be seen by men
but by your Father who is in secret;
and your Father who sees in secret
will reward you.

(4) Wealth, *or Our Attitude towards Things - Mastery over Them, and Using Them As Means to Kingdom Ends. (Cf.Gen.1:28)*

One's Attitude Toward Things:-

(a) AVARICE (The Sin of the Rich) Rebuked

19 " Do not lay up for yourselves treasures on earth,
where moth and rust[a] consume
and where thieves break in and steal,

Avarice Robs you of Treasure

20 " but lay up for yourselves treasures in heaven, (Mt.19:21; p.143; Lk.12:33)
where neither moth nor rust[a] consumes,
and where thieves do not break in and steal;

21 " for where your treasure is,
there will your heart be also.

Avarice Blinds Insight

22 " The eye is the lamp of the body. (Lk.11:33-34, p.140)
So, if your eye is sound, your whole body will be full of light;
23 but if your eye is not sound, your whole body will be full of darkness.
If then the light in you is darkness,
how great is the darkness!

Avarice cripples service

24 " No one can serve two masters; (Lk.16:13, p.158)
for either he will hate the one and love the other,
or he will be devoted to the one and despise the other.
You cannot serve God and mammon.

(b) ANXIETY (The Sin of the poor) Rebuked

Trust God Instead,

25 " Therefore I tell you,
do not be anxious about your life,
what you shall eat or what you shall drink,
nor about your body,
what you shall put on.
Is not life more than food,
and the body more than clothing?

As the Birds Do For Food,

26 " Look at the birds of the air:
they neither sow nor reap
nor gather into barns,
and yet your heavenly Father feeds them.
Are you not of more value than they?

27 " And which of you by being anxious
can add one cubit to his span of life?[b]

As the Flowers Do For Dress:

28 " And why be anxious about clothing?
Consider the lilies of the field, how they grow;
they neither toil nor spin;
29 yet I tell you, even Solomon in all his glory
was not arrayed like one of these.

God Will Provide

30 " But if God so clothes the grass of the field,
which today is alive and tomorrow is thrown into the oven,
will he not much more clothe you, O men of little faith?

....

[a] *Or* worm. [b] *Or* to his stature.

Worry About Food and Clothing Is Unworthy of a Christian

31 “Therefore do not be anxious, saying,
‘What shall we eat?’
or ‘What shall we drink?’
or, ‘What shall we wear?’
32 For the Gentiles seek all these things;
and your heavenly Father knows that you need them all.

Seek The Consummation of the Kingdom; This Is The Supreme Good; Seek Other Things As Means To This End.

33 “But seek first his kingdom and his righteousness,
and all these things shall be yours as well.

The Folly of Anxiety About the Future.

34 “Therefore do not be anxious about tomorrow,
for tomorrow will be anxious for itself.
Let the day's own trouble be sufficient for the day.”

C. THE ESSENTIAL DIFFICULTIES AND DANGERS OF CHRISTIAN RIGHTEOUSNESS
(Mt. 7; Lk. 6:37-49)

a. “Censorious judgments of Others, vs. Practical Estimates (7:1-6)

	Matthew 7	Luke 6
Censorious Judging To Be Avoided	1 “Judge not, that you be not judged. 2 For with the judgment you pronounce you will be judged,	37 “Judge not, and you will not be judged;
The Resulting Reward		“Condemn not, and you will not be condemned; forgive, and you will be forgiven; 38 give, and it will be given to you; good measure, pressed down, shaken together, running over, will be put into your lap.
	and the measure you give will be the measure you get.	For the measure you give will be the measure you get back.”
Illustrative Comparisons		39 He also told them a parable: *(Mt.15:14,p.103)* “Can a blind man lead a blind man? Will they not both fall into a pit? 40 A disciple is not above his teacher, but every one when he is fully taught will be like his teacher.
Censorious Condemnation of Others Indicates Hidden Sin in ourselves;	3 “Why do you see the speck that is in your brother's eye, but do not notice the log that is in your own eye? 4 “Or how can you say to your brother, ‘Let me take the speck out of your eye,’ when there is the log in your own eye?	41 “Why do you see the speck that is in your brother's eye, but do not notice the log that is in your own eye? 42 Or how can you say to your brother, ‘Brother, let me take out the speck that is in your eye,’ when you yourself do not see the log that is in your own eye?
Hence It Is Hypocrisy.	5 “You hypocrite, first take the log out of your own eye, and then you will see clearly to take the speck out of your brother's eye.	“You hypocrite, first take the log out of your own eye, and then you will see clearly to take out the speck that is in your brother's eye.
Practical Estimates However Are Necessary.	6 “Do not give dogs what is holy; and do not throw your pearls before swine, lest they trample them underfoot and turn to attack you.	

b. All True Prayer Will Be Answered (7:7-11) or Varying Method In Prayer

The Command (Personal Appropriation)

7 “Ask, and it will be given you;
seek, and you will find;
knock, and it will be opened to you.

“Asking” means, choosing, willing
“Seeking” means, hunting, Research
“Knocking” means, Perseverance, in spite of barriers.

The Reason, or (Universal Law)

8 “For every one who asks receives,
and he who seeks finds,
and to him who knocks it will be opened.

An Illustration Human Fathers,

9 "Or what man of you
if his son asks him for a loaf,
will give him a stone?
10 Or if he asks for a fish,
will give him a serpent?

Our Divine Father,

11 "If you then, who are evil,
know how to give good gifts to your children,
how much more will your Father who is in heaven
give good things to those who ask him?

c. A Practical Universal Rule of Conduct Towards Others (7:12)

The Golden Rule of Conduct

12 "So whatever you wish that men would do to you,
do so to them; *(Cf. 6:31)*
for this is the law and the prophets.

d. The Essential Dangers of the Christian Life (7:13-27)

(a) The Inherent Danger (13-14)

Heedless drifting is Easy, But Ruinous

13 "Enter by the narrow gate;
for the gate is wide and the way is easy,[a]
that leads to destruction,
and those who enter by it are many.

Creative Effort Is Difficult, But Rewarding

14 For the gate is narrow and the way is hard
that leads to life,
and those who find it are few.

(b) The Danger from False Teachers (15-20)

How False Teachers Come

15 "Beware of false prophets, *(Mt.21:11, p.198)*
who come to you in sheep's clothing
but inwardly are ravenous wolves.

How To Detect Them,

16 "You will know them by their fruits.

The General Law,

Are grapes gathered from thorns, or figs from thistles?

Lk.6:43-45

It is Universally True,

17 So, every sound tree bears good fruit,
but the bad tree bears evil fruit.

43 "For no good tree bears bad fruit,
nor again does a bad tree bear good fruit;

It is Necessarily True

18 "A sound tree cannot bear evil fruit, *(Mt.12:33, p.72)*
nor can a bad tree bear good fruit.

It is Fatally True

19 "Every tree that does not bear good fruit
is cut down and thrown into the fire.

So It Is A Dependable Rule.

20 "Thus you will know them
by their fruits.
(v.16)

44 "for each tree is known by its own fruit.
For figs are not gathered from thorns,
nor are grapes picked from a bramble bush.

Good Deeds and Good Words Come From Right Inner Attitudes *(Cf.Mt.12:34, p.72)*

45 "The good man out of the good treasure of his heart
produces good,
and the evil man out of his evil treasure
produces evil;
for out of the abundance of the heart his mouth speaks.

(c) The Danger of Self-Deception (Mt.7:21-27; Lk.6:46-49)

46 "Why do you call me 'Lord, Lord,'
and not do what I tell you?

Loud Profession vs. Obeying The Will of God

21 "Not every one who says to me,
'Lord, Lord,'
shall enter the kingdom of heaven,
but he who does the will of my Father who is in heaven.

---

[a] *Some ancient authorities read* for the way is wide and easy.

Mt.

22 "On that day many will say to me,
'Lord, Lord, did we not prophesy in your name,
and cast out demons in your name,
and do many mighty works in your name?' *(Lk.13:25-27, p.152)*

Doing Iniquity Is Fatal to Eternal Destiny

23 "And then will I declare to them,
'I never knew you;
depart from me, you evil doers.

(d) The Danger of Hearing and Not Doing

An Illustration

A Wise Builder

24 "Every one then who
hears these words of mine
and does them
will be like
a wise man
who built his house
upon the rock;

25 "and the rain fell,
and the floods came,
and the winds blew
and beat upon that house,
but it did not fall,
because it had been founded on the rock.

47 "Every one who comes to me
and hears my words
and does them,
I will show you what he is like:
48 he is like a man
building a house,
who dug deep,
and laid the foundation
upon rock;

" and when a flood arose,
the stream broke against that house,
and could not shake it,
because it had been well built.[a]

A Foolish Builder

26 "And every one who
hears these words of mine
and does not do them
will be like
a foolish man who built
his house upon the sand.

27 "And the rain fell,
and the floods came,
and the winds blew
and beat against that house,
and it fell;
and great was the fall of it."

49 "But he who
hears
and does not do them
is like
a man who built
a house on the ground
without a foundation;
against which the stream broke,
and immediately it fell,
and the ruin of that house was great."

The Immediate Effect of the Sermon On the Mount

The People Are Startled At Christ's Authoritative Teaching

28 And when Jesus finished these sayings,
the crowds were astonished at his teaching,
29 for he taught them as one who had authority,
and not as their scribes.

(4) Jesus Returns to Capernaum and Heals the Centurion's Servant. § 62

Mt. 8: 1, 5-13

Jesus Returns To Capernaum

1 When he came down from the mountain
great crowds followed him;
5 As he entered Ca-per´na-um,

Lk. 7:1-10

1 After he had ended all his sayings
in the hearing of the people
he entered Ca-per´na-um.

A Roman Captain Appeals for Help

2 Now a centurion had a slave
who was dear[b] to him,
who was sick and at the point of death.

3 When he heard of Jesus,

---

[a] *Some ancient authorities read* founded upon the rock.
[b] Or valuable.

YOU CAN REMEMBER "The Sermon on the Mount" if you will note carefully the outline that is followed on pp.56-66, and here recapitulated on page 66. "THE SERMON ON THE MOUNT - A. The Righteousness of the Sons of the Kingdom of God; B. Christian Righteousness In The Four Essential Relationships of Life; and C. The Essential Difficulties and Dangers of Christian Righteousness.

	Mt.	Lk.
His Servant Is Sick He Sends to Jesus for Help	a centurion came forward to him, beseeching him	he sent to him elders of the Jews, asking him to come and heal his slave.
	6 and saying, "Lord, my servant is lying paralyzed at home in terrible distress."	4 And when they came to Jesus, they besought him earnestly, saying, "He is worthy to have you do this for him, 5 for he loves our nation, and he built us our synagogue."
Jesus Is Going to Heal Him	7 And he said to him, "I will come and heal him."	
He Sends a Message To Jesus:		6 And Jesus went with them. When he was not far from the house, the centurion sent friends to him,
	8 But the centurion answered him,	saying to him,
His Humility	"Lord, I am not worthy to have you come under my roof;	"Lord, do not trouble yourself, for I am not worthy to have you come under my roof; 7 therefore I did not presume to come to you.
His Faith	but only say the word, and my servant will be healed.	But say the word, and let my servant be healed.
His Illustration from Experience	9 "For I am a man under authority, with soldiers under me; and I say to one, 'Go,' and he goes, and to another, 'Come,' and he comes, and to my slave, 'Do this,' and he does it."	8 "For I am a man set under authority, with soldiers under me; and I say to one, 'Go,' and he goes; and to another, 'Come,' and he comes; and to my slave, 'Do this,' and he does it."
Jesus Marvels	10 When Jesus heard him, he marveled, *(Contrast Mt.13:58)*	9 When Jesus heard this he marveled at him,
At His Faith *And Comments About It*	and he said to those who followed him, "Truly, I say to you, not even[a] in Israel have I found such faith.	and turned and said to the multitude that followed him, "I tell you not even in Israel have I found such faith."
He Predicts Gentile Acceptance	11 I tell you, many will come from east and west *(Mal.1:11)* and will sit at table with Abraham, and Isaac, and Jacob *(Lk.13:28-29,p.152)* in the kingdom of heaven,	
And Jewish Apostacy	12 while the sons of the kingdom will be thrown into the outer darkness; there men will weep *(Mt.13:42;22:13;24:51;25:30; Lk.13:28)* and gnash their teeth."	
He Speaks A Healing Word	13 And to the centurion Jesus said, "Go; be it done for you as you have believed." *(Mt.9:22,29; Mk.10:52,p.174; Lk.7:50)*	
The Servant Is Cured,	And the servant was healed at that very moment.	
They Find, On Return.		10 And when those who had been sent returned to the house, they found the slave well.

---

[a] *Some ancient authorities read* With no one.

(1) A Widow's Son Is Restored to Life. § 63

Lk. 7:11-17

*Jesus With a Multitude Journeys to Nain***	11 Soon afterward[a] he went to a city called Na'in, and his disciples and a great crowd went with him.
He Meets A Funeral At The City Gate	12 As he drew near to the gate of the city, behold, a man who had died was being carried out, the only son of his mother, and she was a widow; and a large crowd from the city was with her.
He Comforts the Widow	13 And when the Lord saw her, he had compassion on her and said to her, "Do not weep."
He Stops The Procession *He Raises the Dead*	14 And he came and touched the bier, and the bearers stood still. And he said, "Young man, I say to you, arise."
	15 And the dead man sat up, and began to speak.
He Gives the Son To His Mother	And he gave him to his mother.
The People Are Awed	16 Fear seized them all; and they glorified God, saying, "A great prophet has arisen among us!" and "God has visited his people!"
The News Spreads Far and Wide	17 And this report concerning him spread through the whole of Judea, and all the surrounding country.

(2) John the Baptist Sends Messengers to Jesus. § 64

	Mt. 11:2-6	*Lk. 7:18-23*
		18 The disciples of John told him of all these things.
John Hears of Jesus' Doings	2 Now when John heard in prison about the deeds of the Christ,	
He Sends Men to Jesus	he sent word by his disciples 3 and said to him,	19 And John, calling to him two of his disciples, sent them to the Lord, saying, "Are you he who is to come, or shall we look for another?"
They Come to Jesus		20 And when the men had come to him, they said, "John the Baptist has sent us to you, saying, 'Are you he who is to come, or shall we look for another?'"
They State Their Errand	"Are you he who is to come, or shall we look for another?"	
They Hear Him Teach *They See Him Heal*		21 In that hour he cured many of diseases and plagues and evil spirits, and on many that were blind he bestowed sight.
Jesus Answers John's Question By Many Miracles	4 And Jesus answered them, "Go and tell John what you hear and see: 5 the blind receive their sight and the lame walk, lepers are cleansed and the deaf hear,	22 And he answered them, "Go and tell John what you have seen and heard: the blind receive their sight, the lame walk, lepers are cleansed, and the deaf hear,
By The Message He Preaches,	and the dead are raised up, and the poor have good news preached to them.	the dead are raised up, the poor have good news preached to them.
And by A Mild Rebuke	6 And blessed is he who takes no offense at me."	23 And blessed is he who takes no offense at me!"

....

[a] *Some ancient authorities read* next day.

**For the journey Through Southern Galilee we follow the order of Luke because Mark omits these events altogether (see Mk. 3:19) and Matthew gives them only in part (see Mt. 11:2-29).*

***See Map, p.50.*

(3) Jesus Evaluates John and Laments His Rejection. § 65

	Mt. 11:7-19	*Lk. 7:24-35*
(a) What Jesus Thinks of John. *Jesus Speaks to the Crowds Concerning John;*	7As they went away, Jesus began to speak to the crowds concerning John:	24When the messengers of John had gone, he began to speak to the crowds concerning John:
What John Was Not;	" What did you go out into the wilderness to behold? a reed shaken by the wind?	" What did you go out into the wilderness to behold? A reed shaken by the wind?
Not A Fickle Man, *Not an Ostentatious One,*	8" Why then did you go out? To see a man[a] clothed in soft raiment? Behold, those who wear soft raiment are in kings' houses.	25" What then did you go out to see? A man clothed in soft raiment? Behold, those who are gorgeously apparelled and live in luxury are in kings' courts.
Not Merely a Prophet, But Much More.	9" Why then did you go out? To see a prophet[b]? Yes, I tell you, and more than a prophet.	26" What then did you go out to see? A prophet? Yes, I tell you, and more than a prophet.
He Is to Introduce the Messiah,	10" This is he, of whom it is written, 'Behold, I send my messenger before thy face, who shall prepare thy way before thee.'	27" This is he of whom it is written, *(Mal.3:1)* 'Behold, I send my messenger before thy face, who shall prepare thy way before thee.'
The Unparalleled Greatness Of His Mission As a Prophet.	11" Truly, I say to you, among those born of women there has risen no one greater than John the Baptist; yet he who is least* in the kingdom of heaven is greater than he.	28" I tell you, among those born of women none is greater than John; yet he who is least* in the kingdom of God is greater than he."
(b) How John was Received,	12" From the days of John the Baptist until now the kingdom of heaven has suffered violence,[c]	*(Cf.Lk.16:16,p.158)*
By the populace, *(Mt.21:31-32,p.184)*		29(When they heard this all the people and the tax collectors justified God, having been baptized with the baptism of John;
	and men of violence take it by force.	
By the Religious Aristocracy, Even Though His Coming Had Often Been Prophesied	13For all the prophets and the law prophesied until John;	30but the Pharisees and the lawyers rejected the purpose of God for themselves, not having been baptized by him.) *(Cf.Lk.16:16,p.158)*
Culminating in Malachi 4:5-6	14and if you are willing to accept it, he is Elijah who is to come. *(Lk.1:17,p.11;Mt.11:10-13,p.110)* 15He who has ears to hear,[d] let him hear.	
(c) Their Arbitrary Rejection of Both John and Jesus	16But to what shall I compare this generation?	31" To what then shall I compare the men of this generation, and what are they like?
Like Pouting Children,	It is like children sitting in the marketplaces and calling to their playmates,	32" They are like children sitting in the marketplace and calling to one another,
Playing Wedding and Funeral	17'We piped to you, and you did not dance; we wailed, and you did not mourn.'	'We piped to you, and you did not dance; we wailed, and you did not weep.'
Thus John was Rejected and So Also was Jesus	18For John came neither eating nor drinking, and they say, 'He has a demon;' 19the Son of man came eating and drinking, and they say,	33" For John the Baptist has come eating no bread and drinking no wine; and you say, 'He has a demon.' 34" The Son of man has come eating and drinking; and you say,
Such Conduct is not Justifiable	'Behold, a glutton and a drunkard, a friend of tax-collectors and sinners!' Yet wisdom is justified by her deeds."[e]	'Behold, a glutton and a drunkard, a friend of tax-collectors and sinners!' 35Yet wisdom is justified by all her children.

[a]*Or* What then did you go out to see? A man. [b]*Many ancient authorities read* " What then did you go out to see? A prophet? [c]*Or* has been coming violently. [d]*Some ancient authorities omit* to hear. [e]*Many ancient authorities read* children *but little, *Greek* lesser.

[*For Mt. 11:20-30 see* § 134, *p.147*]

(4) Jesus is Anointed By a Sinful Woman. § 66 [*Contrast?* § 161]

Lk. 7:36-50

Jesus Is Dining With a Pharisee

36 One of the Pharisees asked him to eat with him, *(Compare* §§ 130,139 *)*
and he went into the Pharisee's house, and sat at table.

A Reclaimed Sinner Shows Her Unbounded Love By Anointing Jesus.

37 And behold, a woman of the city, who was a sinner,
when she learned that he was sitting at table in the Pharisee's house,
brought an alabaster flask of ointment,

38 and standing behind him at his feet, weeping,
she began to wet his feet with her tears,
and wiped them with the hair of her head,
and kissed his feet,
and anointed them with the ointment.

Prejudice Misconstrues Her Act

39 Now when the Pharisee who had invited him saw it,
he said to himself,
"If this man were a prophet,
he would have known who and what sort of woman this is who is touching him,
for she is a sinner."

Jesus Explains Her Conduct

40 And Jesus answering said to him,
"Simon, I have something to say to you."
And he answered,
"What is it, Teacher?"

(a) By a Parable,

41 "A certain creditor had two debtors;
one owed five hundred denarii, and the other fifty.

42 "When they could not pay, he forgave them both.
Now which of them will love him more?"

43 Simon answered,
"The one, I suppose, to whom he forgave more."
And he said to him,
"You have judged rightly."

(b) And Its Application,

44 Then turning toward the woman he said to Simon,
"Do you see this woman?

"I entered into your house, you gave me no water for my feet,
but she has wet my feet with her tears and wiped them with her hair.
45 You gave me no kiss,
but from the time I came in she has not ceased to kiss my feet.
46 You did not anoint my head with oil,
but she has anointed my feet with ointment.

(c) The Conclusion,

47 "Therefore I tell you, her sins, which are many, are forgiven,
for she loved much;
but he who is forgiven little, loves little."

Jesus Comforts The Woman

48 And he said to her,
"Your sins are forgiven."

The Guests Are Astonished

49 Then those who were at table with him
began to say among themselves,
"Who is this who even forgives sins?"

Jesus Speaks A Final Word To The Woman

50 And he said to the woman,
"Your faith has saved you;
Go in peace."

(5) Jesus Has Women Helpers in His Work. § 67

Lk. 8:1-3

The Work of Jesus is Supported By Women Who Attend Him

1 Soon afterward he went on through cities and villages,
preaching and bringing the good news of the kingdom of God.

And the twelve were with him,
2 and also some women who had been healed of evil spirits and infirmities:
Mary, called Mag´da-lene, from whom seven demons had gone out,
3 and Jo-an´na, the wife of Chu´za, Herod's steward, and Susanna, and many others,
who provided for them[a] out of their means.

[a] *Many ancient authorities read* him.

(Mk. 3:19b-5:20; Mt. 8:28-34; 12:22-13:53; Lk.8:4-39)

(1) Jesus' Friends Say He Is Beside Himself. § 68

Mk. 3:19b-21

	Mk. 3:19b-21
Jesus Comes Home	19b Then he went home,*
He is Teaching in the Synagogue at Home.	20 And the crowd came together again, so that they could not even eat.
His Friends Think He is Crazy	21 And when his friends heard it, they went out to seize him, for they said, "He is beside himself."

(2) Scribes and Pharisees Say His Power is From the Devil.** § 69

	Mt. 12:22-45	*Mk. 3:22-30 (Cf. Lk. 11:14-26 and footnote; p.139)*
A Pitifully Helpless Man Is Brought.	22 Then a blind and dumb demoniac was brought to him,	
He is Marvelously Healed	and he healed him, so that the dumb man spoke and saw.	
The Crowds Are Amazed	23 And all the people were amazed, and said, "Can this be the Son of David?"	
The Jealous Scribes Attribute His Miraculous Power to the Devil.	24 But when the Pharisees heard it they said, "It is only by Be-el'ze-bub,[a] the prince of demons, that this man casts out demons."	22 And the scribes who came down from Jerusalem*** said, "He is possessed by Be-el'ze-bub,[a] and by the prince of demons he casts out the demons."

The Reply of Jesus to This Charge

Jesus Refutes Their Charge	25 Knowing their thoughts he said to them,	23 And he called them to him, and said to them in parables, "How can Satan cast out Satan?
a. His First Argument,	"Every kingdom divided against itself is laid waste, And no city or house divided against itself will stand,	24 If a kingdom is divided against itself, that kingdom cannot stand. 25 "And if a house is divided against itself, that house will not be able to stand.
	26 "And if Satan casts out Satan he is divided against himself; how then will his kingdom stand?	26 "And if Satan has risen up against himself and is divided, he cannot stand, but is coming to an end.
b. His Second Argument	27 "And if I cast out demons by Be-el'ze-bub,[a] by whom do your sons cast them out? Therefore they shall be your judges.	

i.e., to Capernaum.* *****This explanation of His miraculous power was several times repeated. They could not deny His superhuman power; so they attempted to discredit it. (Cf. Mt. 9:34; Lk. 11:14-36; Jn. 8:48; 10:20-21)*

******These officials were seeking a chance to kill Him (as John 5:18 says), and had followed him like blood hounds, from place to place (Mk.2:2;3:2-6).***

[a]*Greek* Beelzebul.

A Practical Corollary,

Mt.

28 "But if it is by the Spirit of God *(Lk.11:20,p.140)*
that I cast out demons,
then the kingdom of God has come upon you.

c. A Third Argument–

Mt.

29 "Or how can one enter
a strong man's house
and plunder his goods,
unless he first binds the strong man?
Then indeed he may plunder his house.

Mk.

27 "But no one can enter
a strong man's house
and plunder his goods,
unless he first binds the strong man;
then indeed he may plunder his house.

Satan, Instead of Helping me, Fights me.

Mt.

30 "He who is not with me *(Cf.Mk.9:40,p.115)*
is against me,
and he who does not gather with me
scatters.

Then Jesus Warns Them About Blasphemy Against The Holy Spirit

Mt.

31 "Therefore I tell you,
every sin and blasphemy
will be forgiven men,

but the blasphemy against the Spirit
will not be forgiven.

32 "And whoever
says a word against the Son of man
will be forgiven;
but whoever speaks
against the Holy Spirit
will not be forgiven,
either in this age
or in the age to come.

Mk.

28 "Truly, I say to you,
all sins
will be forgiven the sons of men,
and whatever blasphemies they utter;

29 "but whoever blasphemes
against the Holy Spirit
never has forgiveness,

but is guilty of* "eternal sin"

30 for they had said,
"He has an unclean spirit."

For That Would Be "Eternal Sin"

Why They Say Such Things

Mt.

33 "Either make the tree good, and its fruit good;
or make the tree bad, and its fruit bad; *(Mt.7:18,p.65)*
for the tree is known by its fruit.

Evil Words Come Out of Evil Hearts,

34 "You brood of vipers! *(Mt.9:7,p.23)*
how can you speak good, when you are evil?
For out of the abundance of the heart the mouth speaks. *(Cf.Lk.7:45,p.65)*

and so

35 "The good man out of his good treasure
brings forth good,
and the evil man out of his evil treasure
brings forth evil.

We Shall Be Judged For Evil Words Also.

36 "I tell you on the day of judgment
men will render account for every careless word they utter;
37 for by your words you will be justified,
and by your words you will be condemned."

Demanding a Sign From Heaven *(Cf.§ 99,p.106;Lk.11:29-30,p.140; Jn.2:18-22,p.31)*

Then The Scribes Demand A Sign from Heaven.

38 Then some of the scribes and Pharisees said to him,
"Teacher, we wish to see a sign from you."

Jesus Replies that Their Demand Shows Moral Perversity He Points

39 But he answered them,
"An evil and adulterous generation seeks a sign;
but no sign shall be given to it
except the sign of the prophet Jonah.

**RSV inserts an. Jesus does not here speak of any one specific sin, but of persistence in sin to the point of moral reprobacy, or moral suicide, when it is no longer possible to repent. As Heb.6:6 says, "It is impossible to get them to repent" · And no sin is forgivable without repentance.*

	Mt.
To The Resurrection As The All-sufficient Sign.	40 "For as Jonah was three days and three nights in the belly of the whale, so will the Son of man be three days and three nights in the heart of the earth.
Then Jesus Shows The Enormity of The Guilt of That Generation In Rejecting Him.	41 "The men of Nin'e-veh will arise at the judgment with this generation and condemn it; for they repented at the preaching of Jonah, and behold, something greater than Jonah is here. 42 The queen of the south will arise at the judgment with this generation and condemn it; for she came from the ends of the earth to hear the wisdom of Solomon; and behold, something greater than Solomon is here.
He Illustrates by A Parable	43 "When the unclean spirit has gone out of a man, he passes through waterless places seeking rest, but he finds none. 44 "Then he says, 'I will return to my house from which I came.' And when he comes he finds it empty, swept, and put in order.
He Says It Applies To That Generation,	45 Then he goes and brings with him seven other spirits more evil than himself, and they enter and dwell there; and the last state of that man becomes worse than the first.
They Are Worse Than Before.	"So shall it be also with this evil generation."

(3) Jesus' Relatives Interfere. § 70

	Mt. 12:46-50	*Mk. 3:31-35*	*Lk. 8:19-21*
Jesus' Mother and His Brothers Come to Interfere	46 While he was still speaking to the people, behold, his mother and his brothers	31 And his mother and his brothers came;	19 Then * his mother and his brothers came to him, but they could not reach him for the crowd.
They Call For Him	stood outside, asking to speak to him.[a]	and standing outside they sent to him and called him.	
		32 And a crowd was sitting about him;	
The Crowd Tell Him About It	*(See footnote)*	and they said to him, "Your mother and your brothers[b] are outside, asking for you."	20 And he was told, "Your mother and your brothers are standing outside, desiring to see you."
He Replies Raising the Question About the Deepest Kinship	48 But he replied to the man who told him, "Who is my mother, and who are my brothers?"	33 And he answered, "Who are my mother and my brothers?"	21 But he said to them,
		34 And looking around on those who sat about him,	
The Object Lesson	49 And stretching out his hand towards his disciples, he said, "Here are my mother and my brothers!	he said, "Here are my mother and my brothers!	"My mother and my brothers are those who hear
The Deepest Basis of Kinship Is Pointed Out.	50 "For whoever does the will of my Father in heaven is my brother, and sister, and mother."	35 "Whosoever does the will of God is my brother, and sister, and mother."	the word of God and do it.

....

[a] *Some ancient authorities insert verse 47.* Some one told him, "Your mother and your brothers are standing outside asking to speak to you." [b] *Some early authorities add* and your sisters. **Or* Now.

	Mt. 13:1-53	Mk. 4:1-34	Lk. 8:4-18
		The Occasion	
The Setting	1 That same day Jesus went out of the house		
(See also Mt.13:36 Mk.4:33-34)	and sat beside the sea. 2 And great crowds gathered about him,	1 Again he began to teach beside the sea. And a very large crowd gathered about him,	4 And when a great crowd came together people from town after town came to him,
	so that he got into a boat and sat there; and the whole crowd stood on the beach.	so that he got into a boat and sat in it on the sea; and the whole crowd was beside the sea on the land.	
		The Teaching	
He Speaks Many Parables	3 And he told them many things in parables, saying:	2 And he taught them many things in parables,	he said in a parable:
		The Parable of the Sower	
The Parable of the Sower:		and in his teaching he said to them: 3 "Listen!	
	"A sower went out to sow.	A sower went out to sow.	5 "A sower went out to sow his seed;
1. Seeds Upon the Wayside Are Tramped On And Eaten Up	4 And as he sowed, some seeds fell along the path, and the birds came and devoured them.	4 And as he sowed, some seed fell along the path and the birds came and devoured it.	and as he sowed, some fell along the path, and was trodden underfoot, and the birds of the air devoured it.
2. Seeds Upon Rocky Ground Make A Quick Growth	5 "Other seeds fell on rocky ground, where they had not much soil, and immediately they sprang up, since they had no depth of soil,	5 "Other seed fell on rocky ground, where it had not much soil, and immediately it sprang up, since it had no depth of soil;	6 "And some fell on the rock;
But Soon Are Withered	6 "but when the sun rose they were scorched; and since they had no root they withered away.	6 "and when the sun rose it was scorched, and since it had no root it withered away.	and as it grew up, it withered away, because it had no moisture.
3. Seeds Among Thorns Are Choked Out	7 "Other seeds fell upon thorns, and the thorns grew up and choked them.	7 "Other seed fell among thorns and the thorns grew up and choked it, and it yielded no grain.	7 "And some fell among thorns; and the thorns grew with it and choked it.
4. Seeds In Good soil Grow According to The Strength of the Soil	8 "Other seeds fell on good soil and brought forth grain, some a hundredfold, some sixty, some thirty.	8 "And other seeds fell into good soil and brought forth grain, growing up and increasing and yielding thirtyfold and sixtyfold and a hundredfold."	8 "And some fell into good soil and grew, and yielded a hundredfold."
The Appeal for Understanding	9 "He who has ears,[a] let him hear." *(Cf.v.16-17)*	9 And he said, "He who has ears to hear, let him hear."	As he said this, he called out, "He who has ears to hear, let him hear."

[a] *Some ancient authorities add here and in verse 43* to hear.

Why Jesus Teaches By Parables

	Mt.	Mk.	Lk.
They Ask Why He Speaks in Parables	10 Then the disciples came, and said to him, "Why do you speak to them in parables?"	10 And when he was alone, those who were about him with the twelve asked him concerning the parables.	9 And when his disciples asked him what this parable meant,
His Answer: (a) To Reveal to Those Who Are Ready to Hear	11 And he answered them "To you it has been given to know the secrets of the kingdom of heaven, but to them it has not been given.	11 And he said to them, "To you has been given the secret of the kingdom of God, but for those outside everything is in parables;	10 he said, "To you it has been given to know the secrets of the kingdom of God; but for others they are in parables,
According to A Psychological Principle)	12 "For to him who has will more be given, and he will have abundance; but from him who has not, even what he has will be taken away. 13 This is why I speak to them in parables,	*(Cf.Mk.4:24-25)*	
(b) And to Conceal From Those Who Are Not Ready	because seeing they do not see, and hearing they do not hear, nor do they understand.	12 "so that they may indeed see but not perceive, and may indeed hear but not understand;	"so that seeing they may not see, and hearing they may not understand.
Isaiah Had Understood This, (Is.6:9-10) Why Some Cannot Understand (See Mk.4:24 24-25)	14 "With them indeed is fulfilled the prophecy of Isaiah which says: 'You shall indeed hear but never understand, and you shall indeed see but never perceive. 15 For this people's heart has grown dull, and their ears are heavy of hearing, and their eyes they have closed, lest they should perceive with their eyes, and hear with their ears, and understand with their heart, and turn for me to heal them.'	*(Atrophy through disuse. Cf. another example in Jn.5:44,47)* *Mk.* lest they should, turn again and be forgiven."	
Understanding Brings Blessing As Prophets and Saints Of Old Discerned	16 "But blessed are your eyes, for they see, *(Cf.v.9)* and your ears, for they hear. 17 "Truly, I say to you, many prophets and righteous men longed to see what you see, and did not see it, and to hear what you hear, and did not hear it.	*(cf. Mk.4:21-22)*	*(Cf.Lk. 8:16-18)* *(Cf.Lk.10:23-24,p.174)*

Jesus Explains The Parable of The Sower.

	Mt.	Mk.	Lk.
Christ's Own Interpretation of the Parable of the Sower!	18 "Hear then the parable of the sower.	13 And he said to them, "Do you not understand this parable? How then will you understand all the parables? 14 "The sower sows the word. 15 And these are the ones along the path where the word is sown;	11 "Now the parable is this: The seed is the word of God. 12 "The ones along the path
The Way Side	19 "When any one hears the word of the kingdom and does not understand it, the evil one comes and snatches away	"When they hear, Satan immediately comes and takes away	are those who have heard; then the devil comes and takes away

	Mt.	Mk.	Lk.
	what is sown in his heart;	the word which is sown in them.	the word from their hearts, that they may not believe and be saved.
	this is what was sown along the path.		
The Rocky Places	20 " As for what was sown on rocky ground, this is he who hears the word and immediately receives it with joy;	16 " And these in like manner are the ones sown upon the rocky ground, who, when they hear the word, immediately receive it with joy;	13 " And the ones on the rock are those who, when they hear the word, receive it with joy;
	21 " yet he has no root in himself, but endures for a while, and when tribulation or persecution arises on account of the word, immediately he falls away.[a]	17 " and they have no root in themselves, but endure for a while; then, when tribulation or persecution arises on account of the word, immediately they fall away.[a]	" but these have no root, they believe for a while and in time of temptation fall away.
The Thorny Places	22 " As for what was sown among thorns, this is he who hears the word,	18 " And others are the ones sown among thorns; they are those who hear the word,	14 " And as for what fell among the thorns, they are those who hear, but as they go on their way they are choked
	but the cares of the world and the delight in riches choke the word, and it proves unfruitful.	19 but the cares of the world, and the delight in riches, and the desire for other things, enter in and choke the word, and it proves unfruitful.	by the cares and riches and pleasures of life, and their fruit does not mature.
The Good Soil	23 " As for what was sown on good soil, this is he who hears the word * and understands it;*	20 " But those that were sown upon the good soil are the ones who hear the word and accept it*	15 " And as for that in the good soil, they are those who,* hearing the word, hold it fast* in an honest and good heart,*
(1) An Honest And a Good Heart (2) Hear (3) Understand (4) Accept (5) Hold Fast (6) Until They Bear Fruit (7) In Patience*	he indeed bears fruit, and yields, in one case a hundredfold, in another sixty, and in another thirty."	and bear fruit, thirtyfold and sixtyfold and a hundredfold."	and bring forth fruit with patience.*

The Use of Parables

	Mk.	Lk.
Further Comments	21 And he said to them, " Is a lamp brought in[b]	(Cf. Mt. 5:15; 11:33, p. 140)
What Lamps Are For	to be put under a bushel, or under a bed, and not on a stand?	16 " No one after lighting a lamp covers it with a vessel, or puts it under a bed, but puts it on a stand, that those who enter may see the light.
The Reason For Secrecy	22 " For there is nothing hid, except to be made manifest; nor is anything secret,	17 " For nothing is hid that shall not be made manifest, nor anything secret
Is More Effectual: Publicity	except to come to light.	that shall not be known and come to light.
Personal Responsibility for What and How We Hear	23 " If any man has ears to hear, let him hear." 24 And he said to them, " Take heed what you hear;	 18 " Take heed then how you hear;

[a]Or stumbles. Or stumble. [b]Or lighted.

**These seven conditions summarize all four gospels and give a complete program, analyzing and explaining why some are fruitful and others are not. Test it out and see.*

And The Result

(Compare Mt.v.15, "Why He Teaches by Parables" p. 75)

Mk.

the measure you give
will be the measure you get,
and still more will be given you.

25 "For to him who has
will more be given;
and from him who has not,
even what he has
will be taken away."

Lk.

"for to him who has
will more be given,
and from him who has not,
even what he thinks that he has
will be taken away."

The Parable of the Growing Seed

The Parable of Seed Growing Mysteriously

26 And he said,
"The kingdom of God is
as if a man should scatter seed upon the ground,
27 and should sleep and rise night and day,
and the seed should sprout and grow, he knows not how.
28 The earth produces of itself,
first the blade, then the ear,
then the full grain in the ear.
29 But when the grain is ripe,
at once he puts in the sickle, because the harvest has come."

The Parable of the 'Tares', or Weeds

Mt.

A Man Sows Good Seed

24 Another parable he put before them, saying,
"The kingdom of heaven may be compared to *(Cf.v.36f.)*
a man who sowed good seed in his field;

His Enemy Sows Bad Seed

25 "but while men were sleeping,
his enemy came
and sowed weeds among the wheat,
and went away.

The Discovery

26 "So when the plants came up and bore grain,
then the weeds appeared also.

The Explanation

27 "And the servants[a] of the householder came and said to him,
'Sir, did you not sow good seed in your field?
How then has it weeds?'

28 "He said to them,
'An enemy has done this.'

The Servants Ask What to Do

"The servants[a] said to him,
'Then do you want us to go and gather them?'

29 "But he said,
'No;
lest in gathering the weeds you root up the wheat along with them.

The Remedy

30 'Let both grow together until the harvest; *(Mt.24:30-31,p.200)*
and at harvest time I will tell the reapers, *(Rev.14:14-19)*
Gather the weeds first
and bind them in bundles to be burned, *(vs.36-43)*
but gather the wheat into my barn.'"

The Parable of the Mustard Seed

The Tiniest of Seeds Grows into The Greatest shrub

Mt.

31 Another parable he put before them,
saying,

"The kingdom of heaven
is like a grain of mustard seed
which a man took
and sowed in his field;
32 it is the smallest of all seeds,
but when it has grown,
it is the greatest of shrubs
and becomes a tree,

Mk. *(Cf.Lk.13:18,19,p.146)*

30 And he said,
"With what can we compare the kingdom of God,
or what parable shall we use for it?

31 "It is like a grain of mustard seed,
which,
when sown upon the ground,
is the smallest of all the seeds on earth;
32 yet when it is sown it grows up
and becomes the greatest of all shrubs,

and puts forth large branches,

[a] Or slaves.

	Mt.	*Mk.*
An Extensive Growth	so that the birds of the air come and make nests in its branches."	so that the birds of the air can make nests in its shade."

The Parable of the leaven

[33]He told them another parable. *(Cf.Lk.13:20-21,p.146)*
" The kingdom of heaven is like leaven
which a woman took and hid in three measures of meal,
till it was all leavened."

Intensive Transforming Growth

Many Other Parables

	Mt.	*Mk.*
Many Other Parables	[34]All this Jesus said to the crowds in parables;	[33]With many such parables he spoke the word to them,
		[34]as they were able to hear it;
	indeed he said nothing to them without a parable.	he did not speak to them without a parable,

[35]This was to fulfill
what was spoken by the prophet: [a]
" I will open my mouth in parables, *(Jn.10:6;16:25,pp.132,219)*
I will utter what has been hidden
since the foundation of the world."

Explanations Privately

	Mt.	*Mk.*
Retiring to the House	[36]Then he left the crowds and went into the house.	
		but privately to his own disciples he explained everything.

Explaining The Parable of "The Tares," or Weeds

And his disciples came to him,
saying,
" Explain to us the parable *(v.24ff. Mt.15:15,p.103)*
of the weeds of the field."

[37]He answered,
" He who sows the good seed is the Son of man; *The Sower*
[38]the field is the world, *The Field*
and the good seed means the sons of the kingdom; *The Good Seed*
the weeds are the sons of the evil one, *The Tares*
[39]and the enemy who sowed them is the devil; *The Enemy*
the harvest is the close of the age, *The Harvest*
and the reapers are angels. *The Reapers*

The Harvest (a) Of Weeds

[40]" Just as the weeds are gathered
and burned with fire,
so will it be at the close of the age.
[41]The Son of man will send his angels,
and they will gather out of his kingdom
all causes of sin and all evil-doers,
[42]and throw them into the furnace of fire;
there men will weep and gnash their teeth. *(v.50;Mt.8:12,p.67)*

(b) Of the Good Seed

[43]" Then the righteous will shine like the sun
in the kingdom of their Father.

" He who has ears, let him hear."

The Parable of the Hidden Treasure

Our total Surrender To Obtain Salvation

[44]" The kingdom of heaven is like treasure hidden in a field,
which a man found and covered up;
then in his joy he goes and sells all that he has
and buys that field.

[a]*Some ancient authorities read* the prophet Isaiah.

The Parable of the Merchant Seeking Goodly Pearls

Mt.

Christ's Total Surrender To Provide Our Salvation

45 "Again,
the kingdom of heaven is like a merchant in search of fine pearls,
46 who, on finding one pearl of great value,
went and sold all that he had
and bought it.

The Parable of the Drag-Net

The Drag-Net Full of Bad and Good

47 "Again,
the kingdom of heaven is like a net which was thrown into the sea
and gathered fish of every kind;
48 when it was full, men drew it ashore
and sat down and sorted the good into vessels
but threw away the bad.

Partial Interpretation

49 "So it will be at the close of the age.
The angels will come out
and separate the evil from the righteous,
50 and throw them into the furnace of fire;
there men will weep and gnash their teeth.

What Parables are For

The Use of Parables

51 "Have you understood all this?"

They said to him,
"Yes."

52 And he said to them,
"Therefore every scribe
who has been trained for the kingdom of heaven
is like a householder
who brings out of his treasure what is new and what is old."

Jesus Leaves

53 And when Jesus had finished these parables,
he went away from there.

(5) Jesus Withdraws Across the Lake He Stills a Tempest. § 72

	Mt. 8:18,23-27	*Mk. 4:35-41*	*Lk. 8:22-25*
At Sunset They Get Away by Boat	18 Now when Jesus saw great crowds around him,	35 On that day, when evening had come,	22 One day he got into a boat with his disciples,
Across the Lake	he gave orders to go over to the other side.	he said to them, "Let us go across to the other side."	and he said to them, "Let us go across to the other side of the lake."
		36 And leaving the crowd,	
	23 And when he got into the boat his disciples followed him.		
		they took him with them, just as he was, in the boat.	
As They Sail Jesus Falls Asleep		And other boats were with him.	So they set out, 23 and as they sailed he fell asleep.
A Storm Comes	24 And behold, there arose a great storm on the sea,	37 And a great storm of wind arose,	And a storm of wind came down on the lake,
		and the waves beat into the boat,	
	so that the boat was being swamped by the waves;	so that the boat was already filling.	and they were filling with water, and were in danger.
	....		

**Note that in this case " the kingdom of heaven", is like, not " the pearl of great price," but like " A merchant seeking goodly pearls," which he purchases in order to sell them again.*

	Mt.	*Mk.*	*Lk.*
		38 But he was in the stern,	
	but he was asleep.	asleep on the cushion;	
The Disciples waken Jesus	25 And they went and woke him, saying, "Save, Lord; we are perishing."	and they woke him and said to him, "Teacher, do you not care if we perish?"	24 And they went and woke him, saying, "Master, Master, we are perishing!"
		39 And he awoke *(v. 40)*	And he awoke *(v. 25)*
	26 And he said to them, "Why are you afraid, O men of little faith?"		
He Stills The Storm	Then he rose and rebuked the winds and the sea;	and rebuked the wind, and said to the sea, "Peace! Be still!"	and rebuked the wind and the raging waves;
	and there was a great calm.	And the wind ceased, and there was a great calm.	and they ceased and there was a calm.
He Rebukes Their Fears.	*(cf. v.26)*	40 He said to them, "Why are you afraid? Have you no faith?"	25 He said to them, "Where is your faith?"
They Stand in Awe of Him		41 And they were filled with awe,	And they were afraid,
	27 And the men marveled, saying, "What sort of man is this, that even winds and sea obey him?"	and said to one another, "Who then is this, tht even wind and sea obey him?" *(Cf. Mk. 1:27)*	and they marveled, saying to one another, "Who then is this, that he commands even wind and water, and they obey him?"

(6) Jesus Cures the Gadarene Demoniacs. § 73

	Mt. 8:28-34	*Mk. 5:1-16*	*Lk. 8:26-36*
They Arrive in Gerasa	28 And when he came to the other side, to the country of the Gad-a-renes´[a],	1 They came to the other side of the sea, to the country of the Ger´a-senes.[a]	26 Then they arrived at the country of the Ger´a-senes,[a] which is opposite Galilee.
		2 And when he had come out of the boat,	27 And as he stepped out on land,
They Are Met By Two Demoniacs	two demoniacs met him,	there met him	there met him a man from the city
The Men Are Characterized	coming out of the tombs,	out of the tombs a man with an unclean spirit,	who had demons;
			for a long time he had worn no clothes,
		3 who lived among the tombs;	and he lived not in a house but in the tombs.
	so fierce that no one could pass that way.		
		and no one could bind him any more, even with a chain; 4 for he had often been bound with fetters and chains, but the chains he wrenched apart and the fetters he broke in pieces; and no one had the strength to subdue him.	*(Cf. vs. 29b)*

[a] *Some ancient authorities read* Gergesenes; *some* Gerasenes; *some Gadarenes.*

	Mt.	Mk.	Lk.
		[5]Night and day among the tombs and on the mountains he was always crying out, and bruising himself with stones.	
The Demoniacs See Jesus, They Run to Him, Kneel To Him.	[29]And behold, they cried out,	[6]And when he saw Jesus from afar, he ran and worshipped him; [7]and crying out with a loud voice, he said,	[28]When he saw Jesus, he cried out and fell down before him, and said with a loud voice,
They Beg Him To Let Them Alone. He Commands Them To Come Out They Protest	"What have you to do with us, O Son of God? Have you come here to torment us before the time?"	"What have you to do with me, Jesus, Son of the Most High God? I adjure you by God, do not torment me."	"What have you to do with me, Jesus, Son of the Most High God? I beseech you, do not torment me."
Jesus Commands the Demons to Come out		[8]For he had said to him, "Come out of the man, you unclean spirit!"	[29]For he had commanded the unclean spirit to come out of the man.
		(Cf. vs. 4-5)	(For many a time it had seized him; he was kept under guard, and bound with chains and fetters, but he broke the bonds and was driven by the demon into the desert.)
Jesus Asks The Man His Name He Says, "Legion"		[9]And Jesus[a] asked him, "What is your name?" He replied, "My name is Legion; for we are many."	[30]Jesus then asked him, "What is your name?" And he said, "Legion;" for many demons had entered him.
Then They Beg Not to Be Sent Away		[10]And he begged him eagerly not to send them out of the country.	[31]And they begged him not to command them to depart into the abyss.
A Large Herd of Swine Is Near	[30]Now a herd of many swine was feeding at some distance from them.	[11]Now a great herd of swine was feeding there on the hillside;	[32]Now a large herd of swine was feeding there on the hillside;
The Demons Beg To Enter Them	[31]And the demons begged him, "If you cast us out, send us away into the herd of swine."	[12]and they begged him, "Send us to the swine, let us enter them."	and they begged him to let them enter these.
Jesus Says, "Go"	[32]And he said to them, "Go."	[13]So he gave them leave.	And he allowed them.
The Demons Come Out, Enter The Swine; and They stampede Down The Hill Into The Lake	So they came out and went into the swine; and behold, the whole herd rushed down the steep bank into the sea, and perished in the waters.	And the unclean spirits came out, and entered the swine; and the herd, numbering about two thousand, rushed down the steep bank into the sea, and were drowned in the sea.	[33]Then the demons came out of the man and entered the swine, and the herd rushed down the steep bank into the lake and were drowned.

[a]Greek he.

	Mt.	*Mk.*	*Lk.*
The Swineherds Flee And Report	33 The herdsmen fled, and going into the city they told everything, and what had happened to the demoniacs.	14 The herdsmen fled, and told it in the city and in the country.	34 When the herdsmen saw what had happened, they fled, and told it in the city and in the country.
Many Come to See The Demoniacs Who Were cured	34 And behold, all the city came out to meet Jesus; and when they saw him,	And people came to see what it was that had happened. 15 And they came to Jesus, and saw the demoniac sitting there, clothed and in his right mind, the man who had had the legion; and they were afraid.	35 Then people went out to see what had happened, and they came to Jesus, and found the man from whom the demons had gone, sitting at the feet of Jesus, clothed and in his right mind; and they were afraid.
Those Who Had Seen Tell What Had Happened		16 And those who had seen it told what had happened to the demoniac and to the swine.	36 And those who had seen it told them how he who had been possessed with demons was healed.

(7) Jesus Leaves Their Country. § 74

	Mt. 8:34b	*Mk. 5:17-20*	*Lk. 8:37-39*
The People Beg Jesus to Leave	they begged him to leave their neighborhood.	17 And they began to beg Jesus[b] to depart from their neighborhood.	37 Then all the people of the surrounding country of the Ger′a-senes[a] asked him to depart from them;
Because They Are Afraid			for they were seized with great fear; so he got into the boat and returned.

	Mk.	*Lk.*
The Cured Man Asks to Go Along	18 And as he was getting into the boat, the man who had been possessed with demons begged him that he might be with him.	38 The man from whom the demons had gone begged that he might be with him;
Jesus Tells Him to Go Home and Testify	19 But he refused, and said to him, "Go home to your friends, and tell them how much the Lord has done for you, and how he has had mercy on you."	 but he sent him away, saying, 39 "Return to your home, and declare how much God has done for you."
He Testifies in His Own Country	20 And he went away and began to proclaim in the De-cap′o-lis	And he went away, proclaiming throughout the whole city
What Jesus Had Done For Him	how much Jesus had done for him; And all men marveled.	how much Jesus had done for him.

....

[a] *Some ancient authorities read* Gadarenes, *some* Gergesenes.
[b] *Greek* him.

(V) IN CAPERNAUM AGAIN

(1) Jesus Returns to Capernaum And Is Welcomed by the Multitudes. § 75

	Mt. 9:1	Mk. 5:21	Lk. 8:40
They Return to Capernaum	1 And getting into a boat he crossed over	21 And when Jesus had crossed again in the boat to the other side,	40 Now when Jesus returned,
The Multitude Welcomes Jesus	and came to his own city.	a great crowd gathered about him;	the crowd welcomed him, for they were all waiting for him.
On The Beach		and he was beside the sea.	

[*Mt.9:14-17. Note: for the analysis of these verses and the parallel in Mk. and Lk. see* § 55,*p.48*]

(2) Jairus Pleads with Jesus to Heal His Daughter. § 76

	Mt. 9:18-19	Mk. 5:22-24	Lk. 8:41-42
Just Then Jairus Comes To Jesus and Kneels Before Him	18 While he was thus speaking* to them, behold, a ruler came in* and he knelt before him,	22 Then came one of the rulers of the synagogue, Ja'i-rus by name; and seeing him, he fell at his feet,	41 And there came a man named Ja'i-rus, who was a ruler of the synagogue; and falling at Jesus' feet
He Tells of His Sick Daughter	saying, "My daughter has just died;	23 and besought him, saying, "My little daughter is at the point of death.	he besought him to come to his house, 42 for he had an only daughter, about twelve years of age, and she was dying.
And Pleads for Help.	but come and lay your hand on her, and she will live."	Come and lay your hands on her, so that she may be made well, and live."	
Jesus Goes with Jairus.	19 And Jesus rose and followed him, with his disciples.	24 And he went with him.	

(3) A Woman Touches the Hem of Jesus' Garment. § 77

	Mt. 9:20-22	Mk. 5:25-34	Lk. 8:43-48
		And a great crowd followed him and pressed round him.	As he went, the people pressed round him.
A Suffering Woman Comes	20 And behold, a woman who had suffered from a hemorrhage for twelve years	25 And there was a woman who had had a flow of blood for twelve years,	43 And a woman who had a flow of blood for twelve years[a] **

*Or up, *Mk. 5:21 says,* He was beside the sea.

** [a]*Some ancient authorities add* and had spent all her living upon physicians. *(See v.26 of Mk.)*

	Matthew	Mark	Luke
She Had Suffered Much Was No Better But Grew Worse		26and who had suffered much under many physicians, and had spent all that she had, and was no better but rather grew worse.	*(See footnote on p. 83)* - and could not be healed by anyone,
She Presses Through The Crowd Behind Jesus		27She had heard the reports about Jesus,	
She	came up behind him	and came up behind him in the crowd	44came up behind him,
Touches Jesus' Robe	and touched the fringe of his garment.	and touched his garment.	and touched the fringe of his garment;
She Has Great Faith	21For she said to herself, "If I only touch his garment, I shall be made well."	28For she said, "If I touch even his garments, I shall be made well."	*(Cf.Mk.6:56,p.97)*
She Is Cured And She Feels It In Her Body	*(Cf. v. 22c)*	29And immediately the hemorrhage ceased; and she felt in her body that she was healed of her disease.	and immediately her flow of blood ceased. *(Mt.v.33;Mk.v.47)* *(Cf. vs. 46 below)*
Jesus Also Felt That Healing Power Had Gone Out From Him He Turns	22Jesus turned,	30And Jesus, perceiving in himself that power had gone forth from him, immediately turned about in the crowd,	
He Asks Who Touched Him (a) He Questions the Crowd		and said, "Who touched my garments?"	45And Jesus said, "Who was it that touched me?"
(b) They All Deny (c) The Disciples' Explain It Away		31And his disciples said to him, "You see the crowd pressing around you, and yet you say, 'Who touched me?'"	When all denied it, Peter and those who were with him[a] said, "Master, the multitudes surround you and press upon you!"
(d) Jesus, However, Presses His Question And Tells What He Felt		32And he looked around to see who had done it.	46But Jesus said, "Some one touched me; for I perceive that power has gone forth from me
(e) The Woman Comes Up Trembling Kneels Before Him And Confesses Before The Crowd What She Had Done And How Well She Felt	*(Cf.v.29)* *(Cf.v.29)*	33But the woman, knowing what had been done to her, came in fear and trembling and fell down before him, and told him the whole truth.	47And when the woman *(v.46)* saw that she was not hidden, she came trembling, and falling down before him declared in the presence of all the people why she had touched him, and how she had been immediately healed.
(f) Jesus Encourages Her	and seeing her, he said, "Take heart, daughter; your faith has made you well." *(Mk.10:52;Lk.17:19;18:42; Mt.9:29)*	34And he said to her, "Daughter, your faith has made you well; go in peace, and be healed of your disease."	48And he said to her, "Daughter, your faith has made you well; go in peace." *(Cf. v. 44b)*
She Is completely cured	And instantly the woman was made well.	*(Cf. v. 29)*	

[a]*Some ancient authorities omit* and those who were with him.

	Mt. 9:23-26	Mk. 5:35-43	Lk. 8:49-56
Special Messengers Bring Bad News to Jairus		35 While he was still speaking, there came from the ruler's house some who said, "Your daughter is dead. Why trouble the Teacher any further?"	49 While he was still speaking, a man from the ruler's house came and said, "Your daughter is dead; do not trouble the Teacher anymore."
Jesus Urges Him to Believe and not to Fear		36 But ignoring[a] what they said, Jesus said to the ruler of the synagogue, "Do not fear, only believe."	50 But Jesus on hearing this answered him, "Do not fear; only believe, and she shall be well."
Jesus lets Only Three Follow		37 And he allowed no one to follow him except Peter and James and John the brother of James.	
They Reach the House and Enter	23 And when Jesus came to the ruler s house	38 When they came to the house of the ruler of the synagogue,	51 And when he came to the house he permitted no one to enter with him except Peter and John and James, and the father and mother of the maiden.
Great Wailing Is Going On	and saw the flute players and the crowd making tumult,	he saw a tumult and people weeping and wailing loudly,	52 And all were weeping and bewailing her;
Jesus Quiets the Tumult	24 he said, "Depart; for the girl is not dead but sleeping."	39 And when he had entered, he said to them, "Why do you make a tumult and weep? The child is not dead but sleeping."	but he said, "Do not weep; for she is not dead but sleeping."
They Laugh at Him	And they laughed at him.	40 And they laughed at him.	53 And they laughed at him, knowing that she was dead.
He Clears the Room and takes Two Witnesses	25 But when the crowd had been put outside, he went in	But he put them all outside, and took the child's father and mother and those who were with him, and went in where the child was.	*(Cf. v.51 above)*
The Girl Is Restored to Life Jesus, taking Her Hand, Calls to Her. Her Spirit Returns. She Gets Up And Walks.	and took her by the hand,	41 Taking her by her hand he said to her, "Tal´i-tha cu´mi;" which means, "Little girl, I say to you, arise."	54 But taking her by the hand he called, saying, "Child, arise."
	and the girl arose.	42 And immediately the girl got up and walked; for she was twelve years old.	55 And her spirit returned, and she got up at once. *(Cf. v. 42 above)*
Jesus Tells Them To Feed Her		*(Cf. v. 43 below)*	And he directed that something should be given her to eat.
They Are Amazed		And immediately they were overcome with amazement.	56 And her parents were amazed;
Jesus Charges Secrecy		43 And he strictly charged them that no one should know this.	but he charged them to tell no one what had happened.
		And told them to give her something to eat.	*(Cf. v. 55)*
But His Fame Spreads	26 And the report of this went through all that district.		

[a] Or overhearing. *Many ancient authorities read* hearing.

(5) Jesus Cures Two Blind Men. § 79

Mt. 9:27-31

Two Blind men Appeal to Jesus in the Street

27And as Jesus passed on from there,
two blind men followed him,
crying aloud,
"Have mercy on us, Son of David."

They Follow Him Into the House

28When he entered the house,
the blind men came to him.

He Arouses Their Faith

And Jesus said to them,
"Do you believe that I am able to do this?"

They Confess Their Faith

They said to him,
"Yes, Lord."

He Touches Their Eyes

29Then he touched their eyes, saying,
"According to your faith be it done to you." *(v.21)*

They Are Cured

30And their eyes were opened.

Jesus Charges Secrecy

And Jesus sternly charged them,
"See that no one knows it."

They Publicize Him Instead

31But they went away,
and spread his fame through all that district.

(6) Jesus Cures A Dumb Demoniac. § 80

Mt. 9:32-34

Jesus Comes Out of the House

32As they were going away,

A Demoniac Is Brought

behold, a dumb demoniac was brought to him.

He is Cured

33And when the demon had been cast out,
the dumb man spoke.

The Crowds Marvel

And the crowds marveled, saying,
"Never was anything like this seen in Israel."

The Pharisees Blaspheme

34But the Pharisees said,
"He casts out demons by the prince of the demons." *

****Note how determined these men are to discredit Jesus.*** *This is the same set Jesus so completely answered and so sternly rebuked in John 5:30-47 (p.53), Mt.12:14 (p.55), and again in Mt.12:22-45 (pp.71-73). Here they are still hounding Jesus about, and pressing the same old charges against Him. They are still doing it much later, in John 8:48-59 (p.128), at the Feast of Tabernacles; and then they break out in mob-violence against Him (p.128 , v.59).*

(VI) THE TWELVE SENT THROUGHOUT GALILEE

(1) Jesus' Last Visit to Nazareth. § 81 *(Cf. § 41, p.38)*

	Mt. 13:54-58	Mk. 6:1-6a
Jesus Goes out from Capernaum.		1 He went away from there *
He Arrives in His Home Town, Nazareth.	54 And coming to his own country	and he came to his own country; and his disciples followed him.
		2 And on the sabbath
He is Teaching in the Synagogue,	he taught them in their synagogue,	he began to teach in the synagogue;
The People Are Astonished	so that they were astonished, and said, "Where did this man get this wisdom	and many who heard him were astonished, saying, "Where did this man get all this? What is the wisdom given to him?
	and these mighty works?	What mighty works are wrought by his hands!
Because They Know Him,	55 "Is not this the carpenter's Son? Is not his mother called Mary? and are not his brothers ** James and Joseph and Simon and Judas?	3 "Is not this the carpenter, the son of Mary and brother of ** James and Joseph and Judas and Simon?
So They Reject Him.	56 "And are not all his sisters with us? Where then did this man get all this?"	"And are not his sisters here with us?"
	57 And they took offense[a] at him.	And they took offense[a] at him.
Jesus Replies to Them	But Jesus said to them, "A prophet is not without honor except in his own country *(Mt.13:57;Mk.6:4) Lk.4:24;Jn.4:44)* and in his own house."	4 And Jesus said to them, "A prophet is not without honor, except in his own country, and among his own kin, and in his own house."
His Work Is Prevented by Their Unbelief	58 And he did not do many mighty works there, because of their unbelief.	5 And he could do no mighty work there, except that he laid his hands upon a few sick people and healed them.
Jesus Marvels At Their Unbelief		6 And he marveled because of their unbelief.

(2) Jesus' Last Tour Through Galilee. § 82

	Mt. 9:35-38	Mk. 6:6b
Jesus Goes on Tour, Preaching and Healing	35 And Jesus went about all the cities and villages, teaching in their synagogues and preaching the gospel of the kingdom, and healing every disease and every infirmity.	And he went about among the villages teaching.
He Has Compassion for the Shepherdless Multitude	36 When he saw the crowds, he had compassion for them, because they were harassed and helpless, like sheep without a shepherd.	
He Appeals for Helpers To Reap The Ripened Harvest	37 Then he said to his disciples, "The harvest is plentiful, but the laborers are few; 38 Pray therefore the Lord of the harvest that he send out laborers into his harvest."	

....

[a]Or stumbled.

*Because there was too much excitement in Capernaum. (See previous section)

**Mt.1:18;2:11;12:46;13:55;Mk.3:31;6:3; Lk.1:43;2:33,48,51;Jn.2:1,5,12;7:3,5,10;19:25.

(3) Jesus Sends Out the Twelve. § 83 *(Cf. Sending the 70, § 125, p. 135)*

	Mt. 10:1, 5-42	*Mk. 6:7-13*	*Lk. 9:1-6*
(1) He Calls Them			
He Sends Them By Twos	1 And he called to him his twelve disciples. [*In vs. 2-4 their names are given. See p. 57, § 60.* *Both Mk. and Lk. give their names in that context.*]	7 And he called to him the twelve, and began to send them out two by two. *He Empowers Them*	1 And he called the twelve together,
He Gives Them Both The Right And The Power	And gave them authority over unclean spirits, to cast them out, and to heal every disease and every infirmity.	And gave them authority over the unclean spirits.	And gave them power and authority over all demons and to cure diseases.
(2) He Charges Them			
He Gives Them Instructions *(a) Where to Go*	5 These twelve Jesus sent out, charging them, "Go nowhere among the Gentiles, and enter no town of the Samaritans, 6 but go rather to the lost sheep of the house of Israel.	8 He charged them	2 And he sent them out
(b) What to Do	7 "And preach as you go, saying, 'The kingdom of heaven is at hand.' 8 "Heal the sick, raise the dead, cleanse lepers, cast out demons. You received without pay, give without pay.		to preach the kingdom of God and to heal.
(c) How to Equip Themselves	9 "Take *(Cf. v. 10 below)* no gold, nor silver, nor copper in your belts; [a] 10 no bag for your journey, nor two tunics, nor sandals, nor a staff; for the laborer deserves his food.	to take nothing for their journey except a staff; no bread, no bag, no money in their belts, 9 but to wear sandals and not put on two tunics. 10 And he said to them,	3 And he said to them, "Take nothing for your journey, no staff, nor bag, nor bread, nor money; and do not have two tunics.
(d) How to Proceed	11 "And whatever town or village you enter, find out who is worthy in it, and stay with him until you depart. 12 "As you enter the house, salute it. 13 And if the house is worthy, let your peace come upon it; but if it is not worthy, let your peace return to you.	"Where you enter a house, stay there until you leave the place."	4 "And whatever house you enter, stay there, and from there depart.

Matthew	Mark	Luke
14 " And if any one will not receive you or listen to your words,	11 " And if any place will not receive you and they refuse to hear you,	5 " And wherever they do not receive you,
	when you leave,	when you leave that town
shake off the dust from your feet	shake off the dust that is on your feet for a testimony against them."	shake off the dust from your feet as a testimony against them."
as you leave that house or town.		

The Responsibility of the Hearers

15 " Truly, I say to you,
it shall be more tolerable on the day of judgment
for the land of Sodom and Go-mor´rah
than for that town.

(3) He Warns and Instructs Them

(a) Be Expert in Meeting Danger

16 " Behold, I send you out
as sheep in the midst of wolves;
so be wise as serpents
and innocent as doves.

17 " Beware of men;

(b) Expect Persecution by Jewish and by Gentile Courts

for they will deliver you up to councils,*
and flog you in their synagogues,
18 and you will be dragged before governors and kings (Lk.21:12-13,p.197)
for my sake,
to bear testimony before them and the Gentiles.

(c) Don't Worry; The Spirit of God Will Help You

19 " When they deliver you up,
do not be anxious how you are to speak (Mk.13:11; Lk.21:14-15,p.198)
or what you are to say;
for what you are to say will be given to you in that hour.
20 For it is not you who speak,
but the Spirit of your Father speaking through you. (Cf.Lk.12:11-12,p.142)

(d) You Will Be Persecuted by All Classes

21 " Brother will deliver up brother to death, (Mk.13:12,p.198)
and the father his child,
and children will rise against parents
and have them put to death;
22 and you will be hated by all for my name's sake.
But he who endures to the end
will be saved.

(e) Flee When Necessary

23 " When they persecute you in one town,
flee to the next;
for truly, I say to you,
you will not have gone through all the towns of Israel,
before the Son of man comes.

(f) Be Like The Master

24 " A disciple is not above his teacher,
nor a servant[a] above his master;
25 it is enough for the disciple to be like his teacher,
and the servant[a] like his master.
If they have called the master of the house Be-el´ze-bub,[b]
how much more will they malign those of his household.

(g) Do Not Fear. Risk All For the Gospel God will Reward

26 " So have no fear of them;
for nothing is covered that will not be revealed,
or hidden that will not be known.
27 What I tell you in the dark,
utter in the light;
and what you hear whispered,
proclaim upon the housetops.

28 " And do not fear those who kill the body
but cannot kill the soul;
rather fear him who can destroy both soul and body in hell.[c]

---

[a] *Or* slave. [b] *Greek* Beelzebul. [c] *Greek* Gehenna.

*Sanhedrins, Gk.

Mt.

And Protect You

29 "Are not two sparrows sold for a penny? *(Lk.12:6-7,p.142)*
And not one of them will fall to the ground without your Father's will.
30 But even the hairs of your head are all numbered.
31 Fear not, therefore;
you are of more value than many sparrows.

(4) He Warns Converts

(a) Confessing and Denying

32 "So every one who acknowledges me before men,
I also will acknowledge before my Father who is in Heaven;
33 but whoever denies me before men,
I also will deny before my Father who is in heaven.

(b) Dissensions and Enmity Inevitable

34 "Do not think that I have come to bring peace on earth;
I have not come to bring peace, but a sword. *(Lk.12:51-53,p.144)*
35 For I have come to set a man against his father,
and a daughter against her mother,
and a daughter-in-law against her mother-in-law;
36 and a man's foes will be those of his own household.

(c) The Supreme Cost of Discipleship and It's Reward

37 "He who loves father or mother more than me *(Lk.14:26-27,p.154)*
is not worthy of me;
and he who loves son or daughter more than me
is not worthy of me;
38 and he who does not take his cross and follow me
is not worthy of me.
39 He who finds his life
will lose it,
and he who loses his life for my sake
will find it.

(5) He Promises Rewards for All Helpers

(a) For Helping Christ

40 "He who receives you receives me, *(Jn.12:44-45,p.195;14:9-10,p.215)*
and he who receives me
receives him who sent me.

(b) For Helping Prophets

41 "He who receives a prophet because he is a prophet
shall receive a prophet's reward,

(c) For Helping Saints

and he who receives a righteous man because he is a righteous man
shall receive a righteous man's reward.

(d) For Helping the Little Ones

42 "And whoever gives to one of these little ones
even a cup of cold water
because he is a disciple,
truly, I say to you, he shall not lose his reward." *(Cf.Mt.25:40,45,p.204)*

(6) They Go Out

They Go

(7) The Work They Accomplished

Mk.	*Lk.*
12 So they went out	6 And they departed
	and went through the villages,
and preached that men should repent.	preaching the gospel
13 And they cast out many demons,	
and anointed with oil many that were sick	
and healed them.	and healing everywhere.

(Cf.James 5:14f.)

(4) Jesus Also Goes Out. § 84

Mt. 11:1

Jesus Goes Out Also To Preach

1 And when Jesus had finished
instructing his twelve disciples,
he went on from there
to teach and preach in their cities.

	Mt. 14:1-12	*Mk. 6:14-29*	*Lk. 9:7-9*
		The Excitement and Rumors Stirred up by Jesus' campaign.	
Herod Hears About Jesus	1At that time Herod the tetrarch heard about the fame of Jesus;	14King Herod heard of it; for Jesus'[a] name had become known.	7Now Herod the tetrarch heard of all that was done, and he was perplexed, because that it was said by some
His Interpretation			that John had been raised from the dead,
	2and he said to his servants, "This is John the Baptist, he has been raised from the dead; that is why these powers are at work in him."	Some[a] said, "'John the Baptizer has been raised from the dead; that is why these powers are at work in him."	
The Opinion of Others		15But others said, "It is Elijah." And others said, "It is a prophet, like one of the prophets of old."	8by some that Elijah had appeared, and by others that one of the old prophets had risen.
Herod Wants to See Jesus		16But when Herod heard of it he said, "John, whom I beheaded, has been raised."	9Herod said, "John I beheaded; but who is this about whom I hear such things?" And he sought to see him.*
		The Story of how Herod Had Killed John The Baptist.	
John is Arrested Bound Imprisoned To Appease Herodias	3For Herod had seized John and bound him and put him in prison, for the sake of He-ro´di-as, his brother Philip's wife;[b]	17For Herod had sent and seized John, and bound him in prison for the sake of He-ro´di-as, his brother Philip's wife; because he had married her.	*(Cf. Lk.3:19-20,p.33)*
The Reason	4Because John said to him, "It is not lawful for you to have her."	18For John had said to Herod, "It is not lawful for you to have your brother's wife."	
Herod's Wife Seeks Revenge		19And Herodias had a grudge against him, and wanted to kill him. But she could not,	
But Herod Is Afraid		20for Herod feared John, knowing that he was a righteous and holy man, and kept him safe. When he heard him, he was much perplexed; and yet he heard him gladly.	
	5And though he wanted to put him to death, he feared the people, because they held him to be a prophet.		
Then Comes The Fatal Occasion	6But when Herod's birthday came,	21But an opportunity came when Herod on his birthday gave a banquet for his courtiers and officers and the leading men of Galilee.	
	the daughter of He-ro´di-as danced before the company, and pleased Herod,	22For when He-ro´di-as' daughter came in and danced, she pleased Herod and his guests;	

---

[a] *Some ancient authorities read* he.
[b] *A few ancient authorities read* his brother's wife.
*Or And he kept seeking to see Him ***(Cf.Lk.13:31;23:8,p.234). This is a very significant statement. Josephus tells us of Herod's sinister attitude at this time: he had killed John the Baptist, Josephus says, because he feared John's great popularity with the people. And now Herod turns his suspicions on Jesus, for just now Jesus has been carrying on a campaign which is touching every city and village of Galilee. Jesus is aware of Herod's treachery and from now on carefully avoids him, as we shall see.***

The Rash Vow Is Made		And the king said to the girl, "Ask me for whatever you wish, and I will grant it."
The Wicked Oath Is Sworn	7 so that he promised with an oath to give her whatever she might ask.	23 And he vowed to her, "Whatever you ask me I will give you, even half of my kingdom."
The Treachery of Malice Has Its Way		24 And she went out, and said to her mother, "What shall I ask?" And she said, "The head of John the baptizer."
	8 Prompted by her mother,	
The Weak and Dissolute King Is Overcome	she said, "Give me the head of John the Baptist here on a platter."	25 And she came in immediately with haste to the king, and asked, saying, "I want you to give me at once The head of John the Baptist on a platter."
He Gives The Command	9 And the king was sorry; but because of his oaths and his guests	26 And the king was exceedingly sorry; but because of his oaths and his guests he did not want to break his word to her.
	he commanded it to be given;	27 And immediately the king
The Revolting Crime Is Committed	10 he sent	sent a soldier of the guard and gave orders to bring his head. He went
	and had John beheaded in the prison,	and beheaded him in the prison,
	11 and his head was brought on a platter and given to the girl, and she brought it to her mother.	28 and brought his head on a platter, and gave it to the girl; and the girl gave it to her mother.
The Last Reverent Tribute of Love Is Paid.	12 And his disciples came and took the body and buried it.	29 When the disciples heard of it, they came and took his body, and laid it in a tomb.
The News Is Brought to Jesus.	And they went and told Jesus.	

(6) The Twelve Apostles Return* and Report to Jesus. § 86

	Mk. 6:30	*Lk. 9:10*
*The Apostles Report Their Adventures**	30 The apostles returned to Jesus and told him all that they had done and taught.	10 On their return * the apostles told him what they had done.

....

****1.** It is some weeks since Jesus sent out The Twelve, in teams of two, unaccompanied by Himself, (Mk.6:7, § 83, pp. 88ff). Now they are returning to Capernaum, (See preceding § 86), as it had been prearranged, for it is just Passover time (Jn. 6:4). They are all excited over their new experiences of miraculous power (Mk. 6:30) and eager to tell him "all about it." He wants to talk it all over with them, encouraging them, correcting their mistakes as he used to do (See Mk. 9:38 ff.; Lk. 9:53-56).*

2. But amidst the vast Passover crowds they haven't a chance (Mk. 6:31): so Jesus proposes a "retreat" across the lake into the hills, so as to get a bit of leisure, for they needed some rest.

3. Furthermore their intensive campaigning through "all the cities and villages of Galilee" (a couple hundred of them, as Josephus tells us) had so stirred up the masses of Galilee that Herod Antipas got anxious about it, fearing a mass uprising against Rome. Josephus also tells us this about Herod. (Cf.Lk.23:5)

4. So he had foully murdered John the Baptist. And now he was looking for Jesus (Mt. 14:1; Lk. 9:9).

5. Also there was a move afoot to take Jesus by force and make Him king (Jn. 6:15), and the Apostles doubtless fell for it.

6. Jesus had also just learned of John's death and was sick at heart over it. So there were several reasons why Jesus wanted to get the Apostles out of that jam, to some quiet retreat across the lake.

(I) The Five Thousand Fed. § 87 [Cp. § 97, p.105]

	Mt. 14:13-21	Mk. 6:31-44	Lk. 9:11-17	Jn. 6:1-14
		Jesus and The Apostles Seek Privacy		
*Jesus Proposes Retirement** *(a) When He Hears of John's Death (Mt. v. 13)* *(b) To Get Away from Herod (Lk. 9:9b)* *(c) For Rest (Mk. 6:31)* *(d) And Reports (Mk.6:30)* *(e) To Head Off A Political Move (Jn.6:15)*	[13]Now when Jesus heard this,	[31]And he said to them, "Come away by yourselves to a lonely place, and rest a while." For many were coming and going, and they had no leisure even to eat.		[1]After this
Then They Go To the Other Side By Boat	he withdrew from there in a boat	[32]And they went away in a boat	And he took them and withdrew apart	Jesus went to the other side of the Sea of Galilee, which is the sea of Ti-be'ri-as.
	to a lonely place apart.	to a lonely place by themselves.*	to a city called Beth-sa'i-da.	
The Persistent Crowd Pursues Jesus	But when the crowds heard it,	[33]Now many saw them going, and knew them,	[11]When the crowds learned it,	[2]And a multitude
	they followed him		they followed him;	followed him,
	on foot from the towns.	And they ran there on foot from all the towns, and got there ahead of them.		
The Reason For Their Curiosity			*Jn.* because they saw the signs which he did on those who were diseased.	
Jesus and the Apostles Arrive They Go To The Hills	[14]As he went ashore	[34]As he landed	[3]Jesus went up into the hills, and there sat down with his disciples.	
		The Passover Crowds Arrive And Jesus Teaches and Heals Them		
The Crowds Arrive			[4]Now the Passover, the feast of the Jews, was at hand.	
	he saw a great throng;	he saw a great throng	[5]Lifting up his eyes, then, and seeing that a multitude was coming to him,	
He Has Compassion and Welcomes Them	and he had compassion on them,	and he had compassion on them, because they were like sheep without a shepherd;	*Lk.* and he welcomed them	
He Teaches and Heals All Day	and healed their sick.	and he began to teach them many things.	and spoke to them of the kingdom of God, and cured those who had need of healing.	
		In the Evening A Problem Arises		
The Apostles Are Worried	[15]When it was evening, the disciples came to him	[35]And when it grew late, his disciples came to him	[12]Now the day began to wear away; and the twelve came	
	and said,	and said,	and said to him,	
	"This is a lonely place, and the day is now over;	"This is a lonely place, and the hour is now late;		

....

**For all the reasons see the historical footnote on p. 92.*

	Mt.	*Mk.*	*Lk.*	*Jn.*
The Problem of Feeding the Crowd	send the crowds away to go into the villages and buy food for themselves."	36send them away to go into the country and villages round about and buy themselves something to eat."	"Send the crowd away, to go into the villages and country round about, to lodge and get provisions; for we are here in a lonely place."	
The Disciples Suggest Sending Them Away				
Jesus Proposes A Better Way				Jesus said to Philip, "How are we to buy bread, so that these people may eat?" 6This he said to test him, for he himself knew what he would do.
Philip Answers				7Philip answered him, "Two hundred denarii[a*] would not buy enough bread for each of them to get a little."
Jesus Suggests That They Feed Them	16Jesus said, "They need not go away; you give them something to eat."	37But he answered them, "You give them something to eat."	13But he said to them, "You give them something to eat."	
They Ask How That Can Be		And they said to him,	They said, "We have no more than five loaves and two fish-- unless we are to go and buy food for all these people."	
They Canvass The Alternatives	*(Cf. v. 21)*	*(Cf. v. 44)* "Shall we go and buy two hundred denarii[a*] worth of bread, and give it to them to eat?"	14 For there were about five thousand men.	
Jesus Asks How Much Food They Have		38And he said to them, "How many loaves have you? Go and see."		
They Take Stock		And when they had found out,		8One of his disciples, Andrew, Simon Peter's brother, said to him,
And Report	They said to him, "We have only five loaves [here and two fish."	they said, "Five, and two fish."		9"There is a lad here who has five barley loaves and two fish; but what are they among so many?"
He Says, Bring What You Have	18And he said, "Bring them here to me."			
		The Miracle		
Jesus Deals With the Multitude	19Then he ordered the crowds to sit down	39Then he commanded them all to sit down	14bAnd he said to his disciples, "Make them sit down	10Jesus said, "Make the people sit down."
(a) Organizing The Crowd		by companies	in companies, about fifty each."	
	on the grass;	upon the green grass.		Now there was much grass in the place;
		40So they sat down in groups, by hundreds and by fifties.	15And they did so, and made them all sit down.	so the men sat down,
	(Cf. 21)	*(Cf. 44)*	*(Cf. 14a)*	in number about five thousand.

[a] *The denarius was worth about twenty cents.* * *It was a day's wage for a laboring man.*

	Mt.	Mk.	Lk.	Jn.
(b) Taking and Blessing The Food	and taking the five loaves and the two fish he looked up to heaven, and blessed,	41 And taking the five loaves and the two fish he looked up to heaven, and blessed,	16 And taking the five loaves and the two fish he looked up to heaven, and blessed	11 Jesus then took the loaves, and when he had given thanks,
(c) Breaking and Distributing It	and broke and gave the loaves to the disciples, and the disciples gave them to the crowds.	and broke the loaves, and gave them to the disciples to set before the people; and he divided the two fish among them all.	and broke them, and gave them to the disciples to set before the crowd.	he distributed them to those who were seated; so also the fish, as much as they wanted.
(d) Eating To The Full	20 And they all ate and were satisfied.	42 And they all ate, and were satisfied.	17 And all ate and were satisfied.	12 And when they had eaten their fill, he told his disciples, "Gather up the fragments left over, that nothing may be lost."
(e) Gathering The Fragments	And they took up twelve baskets full of the broken pieces left over.	43 And they took up twelve baskets full of broken pieces and of the fish.	And they took up what was left over, twelve baskets of broken pieces.	13 So they gathered them up and filled twelve baskets with fragments from the five barley loaves, left by those who had eaten.
		Talking Over What Had Happened		
(f) The Number Fed	21 And those who ate were about five thousand men, besides women and children.	44 And those who ate the loaves were five thousand men.	*(cf. 14a)*	*(cf. 10b above)*
(g) The Effect of The Miracle				*Jn.* 14 When the people saw the sign which he had done, they said, "This is indeed the prophet who is to come into the world!"

(2) Jesus Spends The Night In Prayer.* § 88

	Mt. 14:22-23a	*Mk. 6:45-46*	*Jn. 6:15*
Jesus Sends The Disciples Away	22 Then he made the disciples get into the boat and go before him to the other side, while he dismissed the crowds.	45 Immediately he made his disciples get into the boat and go before him to the other side, to Beth-sa′i-da, while he dismissed the crowd.	
The Boundless Enthusiasm of The Crowds			15 Perceiving then that they were about to come and take him by force to make him king,
He Sends The Multitudes Away	23 And after he had dismissed the crowds,	46 And after he had taken leave of them,	
He Seeks Solitude For Prayer	he went up into the hills by himself to pray.	he went into the hills to pray.	Jesus withdrew again to the hills by himself.

....

To realize how serious the situation is, read again the Footnotes on pp. 92 and 98 and visualize realistically what it would mean, if He didn't nip that movement in the bud. Then see what He does about it next day (just after this night of prayer) in the synagogue at Capernaum (Jn.6). And note especially what the **people did when He disappointed their expectations (Jn.6:66, also 70 and 71).*

(3) Jesus Walking On The Water. § 89

	Mt. 14:23b-33	Mk. 6:47-52	Jn. 6:16-21
The Disciples Are Caught In A Storm	When evening came, he was there alone,	47 And when evening came,	16 When evening came, his disciples went down to the sea, 17 got into a boat, and started across the sea to Ca-per′na-um.
Night Comes On,			It was now dark, and Jesus had not yet come to them. 18 The sea rose because a strong wind was blowing.
The Disciples Are In Peril.	24 but the boat by this time was out on the sea,[a] beaten by the waves; for the wind was against them.	the boat was out on the sea, and he was alone on the land.	
Jesus Sees Their Plight;		48 And he saw that they were distressed in rowing, for the wind was against them.	
He Comes to Their Rescue Walking On The Water.	25 And in the fourth watch of the night he came to them, walking on the sea.	And about the fourth watch of the night he came to them, walking on the sea.	*Jn.* 19 When they had rowed about three or four miles,[b]
They See Him Coming		He meant to pass by them,	they saw Jesus walking on the sea and drawing near the boat.
(a) They Are Suspicious And Afraid	26 But when the disciples saw him walking on the sea, they were terrified, saying, "It is a ghost!" And they cried out for fear.	*Mk.* 49 but when they saw him walking on the sea, they thought it was a ghost, and cried out; 50 for they all saw him, and were terrified.	*Jn.* They were frightened,
(b) He Reassures Them	27 But immediately he spoke to them, saying, "Take heart, It is I; have no fear."	But immediately he spoke to them and said, "Take heart, It is I; have no fear."	20 but he said to them, "It is I; do not be afraid."
(c) Peter Impulsively Challenges Jesus	28 And Peter answered him, "Lord, if it is you, bid me come to you on the water."		
(d) Jesus Bids Him Come	29 He said, "Come." So Peter got out of the boat and walked on the water and came to Jesus;		
(e) Fearing, He Sinks	30 but when he saw the wind,[c] he was afraid, and beginning to sink he cried out, "Lord, save me."		
(f) He Is Rescued By Jesus	31 Jesus immediately reached out his hand and caught him, saying to him, "O man of little faith, why did you doubt?"		

[a] *Some ancient authorities read* was many furlongs distant from the land. [b] *Greek* twenty-five or thirty stadia. [c] *Many ancient authorities read* strong wind.

	Mt.	Mk.	Jn.
			21 Then they were glad to take him into the boat,
Jesus Enters The Boat *The Wind Stops Blowing*	32 And when they got into the boat, the wind ceased.	51 And he got into the boat with them and the wind ceased.	
They Are Filled With Awe	33 And those in the boat worshiped him, saying, "Truly you are the Son of God."	And they were utterly astounded,	
		52 for they did not understand about the loaves, but their hearts were hardened.	
			and immediately the boat was at the land to which they were going.

(4) Jesus Heals Many In Gennesaret. § 90

	Mt. 14:34-36	Mk. 6:53-56
They Arrive At Gennesaret	34 And when they had crossed over they came to land at Gen-nes´a-ret. *(See Map, p.50)*	53 And when they had crossed over, they came to land at Gen-nes´a-ret, and moored to the shore.
The Crowds Recognize Him	35 And when the men of that place recognized him,	54 And when they got out of the boat, immediately the people recognized him,
Again They Throng Him *They Bring All Their Sick To Jesus*	they sent round to all that region and brought to him all that were sick,	55 and ran about the whole neighborhood and began to bring sick people on their pallets to any place where they heard he was.
Wherever He Goes *This Is Repeated*	36 and besought him that they might only touch the fringe of his garment;	56 And wherever he came, in villages, cities, or country, they laid the sick in the market places, and besought him that they might touch even the fringe of his garment;
He Heals Them All	and as many as touched it were made well.	and as many as touched it *(Cp. § 77, p.83)* were made well.

(5) The Sermon on the Bread of Life. § 91

Jn. 6:22-59

(The Spiritual Character and Mission of the Messianic King)

The Occasion

*The Multitudes Return To Capernaum, Seeking Jesus**

22 On the next day
the people who remained on the other side of the sea
saw that there had been only one boat there,
and that Jesus had not entered the boat with his disciples,
but that his disciples had gone away alone.*
23 However, boats from Tiberias came near
the place where they ate the bread after the Lord had given thanks.
24 So when the people saw that Jesus was not there,*
nor his disciples,
they themselves got into the boats
and went to Ca-per´na-um, seeking Jesus.

They Find Him

25 When they found him on the other side of the sea,** they said to him,
"Rabbi, when did you come here?"**

. . . .

**What had become of Jesus? (See Mt.14:22-24).*

***For answer as to how and when He Got there, see §§89 and 90 just preceding.*

***The Discourse** (See v.59 to locate this event)*

He Urges Them To Labor For Spiritual Food

26 Jesus answered them,
"Truly, truly, I say to you, you seek me*, not because you saw signs,*
but because you ate your fill of the loaves.

27 "Do not labor for the food which perishes,
but for the food which endures to eternal life, *(Jn.5:20;10:28-30,p.149)*
which the Son of man will give to you;
for on him has God the Father set his seal."

How Can They Work for Such Food?

28 Then they said to him,
"What must we do, to be doing the work of God?"

By Believing in Jesus.

29 Jesus answered them,
"This is the work of God, that you believe in him whom he has sent."

They Demand a Sign From Heaven,

30 So they said to him,
"Then what sign** do you do, that we may see, and believe you?

Like The Manna- If They Are to Believe.

"What work do you perform?
31 Our fathers ate the manna in the wilderness; as it is written,
'He gave them bread from heaven to eat.'" *(Ex.16;Neh.9:15;Ps.78:24;105:40)*

Jesus Answers God Is Now Giving You the Real Bread from Heaven. Of This The Manna Was Only a Symbol

32 Jesus then said to them,
"Truly, truly, I say to you,
it was not Moses who gave you the bread from heaven;
my Father gives you the true bread from heaven. *(Jn.3:31,p.33;6:32-42*
33 For the bread of God is that which comes down from heaven,
and gives life to the world."

They Say Give Us This Bread.

34 They said to him,
"Lord, give us this bread always." *(Cf.Jn.4:15,p.34)*

He Replies I Am the Bread of Life That Satisfies.

35 Jesus said to them,
"I am the bread of life;
he who comes to me shall not hunger, *(Jn.4:13,p.34;7:37-38,p.124)*
and he who believes in me shall never thirst.

It Is Available Only Thru Faith, But You Do Not Believe in Me.

36 "But I said to you that you have seen me, and yet do not believe.
37 All that the Father gives me will come to me;
and him who comes to me I will not cast out.

As The Messiah And Savior

38 "For I have come down from heaven,
not to do my own will, but the will of him who sent me;

If You Do Thus Believe in Me, I Will Give You This Bread Which Brings Life Eternal

39 "and this is the will of him who sent me,
that I should lose nothing of all that he has given me,
but raise it up at the last day.
40 For this is the will of my Father,
that every one who sees the Son and believes in him
should have eternal life;
and I will raise him up at the last day."

The Jewish Rulers Murmur Against Jesus

They Murmur and are Bewildered

41 The Jews then murmured at him, because he said,
"I am the bread which came down from heaven."

And Go Off On a Tangent

42 They said,
"Is not this Jesus, the son of Joseph, *(Cf.Mk.6:3;p.87;Jn.7:27,p.123)*
whose father and mother we know?
How does he now say,
'I have come down from heaven'?" *(Jn.7:28,p.124)*

**They want to make Jesus their Jewish King on earth and reign from Jerusalem (See verse 15). This would have meant war with Rome. So He must quell the conspiracy, and teach them the true mission of the Messiah,-- which is not to set up a political Jewish Kingdom, but to save the world (Jn. 4:42). He is the Spiritual Messiah-King, and His kingdom is not of this world. (Jn.18:36)*

***Many Jews, Pharisees especially, had been taught to expect the Messiah to proclaim himself by stupendous "signs from heaven". This is what they are now asking for.*

If They Are Drawn of God and Taught of God They Will Come To Him and Believe in Him (See Jn.14:26,p.215 16:7-13, p.218)

43 Jesus answered them,
"Do not murmur among yourselves.
44 No one can come to me unless the Father who sent me draws him; *(v.45. Cf. Jn. 15:7-11, p.218)*
and I will raise him up at the last day.

45 "It is written in the prophets,
'And they shall all be taught by God.'
Every one who has heard and learned from the Father *(v.44)*
comes to me.

Physical Eyes Cannot See Spiritual Realities But Only the "Eye of Faith"

46 "Not that any one has seen the Father except him who is from God;
he has seen the Father.

He Who Believes Has the Life Which is Eternal

47 "Truly, truly, I say to you,
he who believes has eternal life.

Jesus Is The Heavenly Manna Which Gives Life Eternal

48 "I am the bread of life.
49 Your fathers ate the manna in the wilderness, and they died.
50 This is the bread which comes down from heaven,
that a man may eat of it and not die.

51 "I am the living bread which came down from heaven;
if any one eats of this bread, he will live for ever.*

*(Here Jesus Introduces a New Thought)**

Christ Will Give His Flesh

And* the bread which I shall give for the life of the world
is my flesh." *((v.52-57f.)*

How Can He? (By His Death)

52 The Jews then disputed among themselves, saying,
"How can this man give us his flesh to eat?"

If They Do Not Eat and Drink Him They do not Have Eternal Life

53 So Jesus said to them,
"Truly, truly, I say to you,
unless you eat the flesh of the Son of man and drink his blood, *(v.51b)*
you have no life in you;

If They Do Eat and Drink Him They Will Have Life

54 "he who eats my flesh and drinks my blood has eternal life,
and I will raise him up at the last day.
55 For my flesh is food indeed,
and my blood is drink indeed.

They Must Eat Him As He Eats The Father (By Utter Obedience Jn.4:32-34)

56 "He who eats my flesh and drinks my blood
abides in me, and I in him.
57 As the living Father sent me, and I live because of the Father,
so he who eats me will live because of me.

Jesus Summarizes His Message (Cf. vs. 31-32)

58 "This is the bread which came down from heaven,
not such as the fathers ate and died;
he who eats this bread will live for ever."

A Footnote by the Author

Where This Discussion Took Place

59 This he said in the synagogue, as he taught at Ca-per´na-um.

....

*Or moreover; *a new sentence and a new paragraph begin here, for Jesus changes the subject. They must accept, not only His* life, *but also His* death. *This is what finally stumbles them. A crucified Messiah was unthinkable to a Jew. His "blood" equals His "life" or the Spirit (v. 63); His flesh equals His "Word" (1:14). Jesus is both "The Truth and The Life."*

(6) Many Disciples Forsake Jesus. § 92

*(" The Great Galilean Crisis")**

Jn. 6:60-71

Many Disciples Murmur At Jesus For Insisting Upon Faith in His Death**

60 Many of his disciples, when they heard it*, said,
" This is a hard saying; *(vs.51b-58)*
who can listen to it?"

He Further Sifts Them

He Will Not Only Die But Also Ascend To Heaven

61 But Jesus knowing in himself that his disciples murmured at it,
said to them,
" Do you take offense at this?
62 Then what if you were to see the Son of man
ascending where he was before? *(See Jn.3:31 and ref. p.33)*

And His Kingdom Will Be A Kingdom of the Spirit (See Jn.18:36-38,p.234)

63 " It is the spirit that gives life, the flesh is of no avail;
the words that I have spoken to you are spirit and life.
64 But there are some of you that do not believe."

Many Do Not Believe This

For Jesus knew from the first
who those were that did not believe,
and who it was that should betray him.

Such Faith Must Be Wrought In the Heart By God, and So,

65 And he said,
" This is why I told you *(vs.43-45)*
that no one can come to me unless it is granted him by the Father."

*Many Forsake Him****

66 After this many of his disciples drew back ***
and no longer went about with him.

Jesus Tests the Twelve

67 Jesus said to the twelve,
" Will you also go away?"

Peter Is True Blue

He had Caught The Very Essence Of Living By Faith In Christ

68 Simon Peter answered him,
" Lord, to whom shall we go?
You have the words of eternal life;
69 and we have believed, and have come to know
that you are the Holy One of God."

70 Jesus answered them,
" Did I not choose you, the twelve, and one of you is a devil?"

*Judas (in His Heart) Turns Against Jesus***

71 He spoke of Judas the son of Simon Iscariot, **
for he, one of the twelve, was to betray him.

Jn.7:1

When the Crowds Go On to Jerusalem Jesus Remains In Galilee

1 After this
Jesus went about in Galilee;
he would not go about in Judea,
because the Jews sought to kill him.***

....

This great crisis just about closes Jesus' public work at Capernaum, and also in Galilee. The Jewish rulers were against Him; Herod Antipas, the Jewish King of Galilee, was watching Him suspiciously, and had just before this killed John the Baptist. And now the crowds, and even many of His disciples, forsake Him. Henceforth the " Settled" Ministry is broken up, and Jesus becomes a fugitive and a wanderer; but He still evangelizes, but in widely scattered sections in the north, very carefully keeping out of Herod Antipas's territory all the while.

***When Judas here discerns that Jesus is not going to set up an earthly kingdom, he turns against Jesus. In Jn. 18:36-37, note how Jesus disclaims an earthly kingship; the* spiritual *nature of his kingdom is here (in Jn. 6) brought out emphatically.*

****" They were about to come and take him by force to make him king"(6:15); so after a night of prayer (6:15), Jesus next day in the synagogue of Capernaum, very plainly indicates just what kind of a king he had come down from heaven to be (cf. Jn. 6:38-40; with Jn. 18:36-37). He disclaimed in the most emphatic terms that he aspired to be a political king, but king of a kingdom " not of this world," --a Kingdom of the Spirit.*

The Jewish rulers understood this only too well. That is why they rejected him. The people too understood him; that is why they left him. That is why Judas turned against him (vs. 70-71). Only those clung to him who perceived, however imperfectly, that " He" had the words of eternal life (vs. 67-69).

Jesus evidently abandons this plan of going on with the crowds to the Passover. The Crowds leave him and go on to the feast. But it is too dangerous for Jesus and His apostles to do so; so He stays away from Jerusalem (Jn.7:1).

As soon as the Passover is ended, the Jewish Rulers come back to Capernaum hunting for Jesus, as pages 102 and 3 reveal.

Then on page 104 Jesus gets out of Galilee entirely. (See special footnotes page 104) and keeps out for six months from Passover, in April, to Feast of Tabernacles, in October (p.121).

III. THE SPECIALIZED MINISTRY (TRAINING THE TWELVE)

Mostly Outside Galilee

(From the Great Galilean Crisis, April A.D. 29;
To the Final Departure from Galilee, October, A.D. 29)

(I) IN CAPERNAUM AND PHOENICIA [1] *(p. 102ff.)*
1. Disputing about the "Traditions of the Elders" (Mt. 15:1-20; Mk. 7:1-23; Jn. 7:1) p. 102-103.
2. Withdrawing to Tyre and Sidon (Mt. 15:21; Mk. 7:24) p. 104.
3. Healing the Phoenician Woman's Daughter (Mt. 15:22-28; Mk. 7:25-30) p. 104.

(II) THROUGH DECAPOLIS [2] *(p. 105)*
1. Withdrawing through Decapolis (Mt. 15:29; Mk. 7:31) p. 105.
2. Teaching and Healing Multitudes There (Mt. 15:30-31; Mk. 7:32-37) p. 105.
3. Feeding Four Thousand (Mt. 15:32-39a; Mk. 8:1-9) p. 105-106.

(III) TO DALMANUTHA (MAGADAN) [3] *(p. 106)*
1. Withdrawing by Boat to Dalmanutha (Mt. 15:39b; Mk. 8:10) p. 106.
2. Pharisees and Sadducees Demand a sign from Heaven (Mt. 16:1-4a; Mk. 8:11-12) p. 106.

(IV) TO BETHSAIDA [4] *(p. 107)*
1. Withdrawing by Boat Across the Lake (Mt. 16:4b; Mk. 8:13) p. 107.
2. Warning Against the Leaven of the Pharisees (Mt. 16:5-12; Mk. 8:14-21) p. 107.
3. Healing a Blind Man of Bethsaida (Mk. 8:22-26) p. 107.

(V) NEAR CAESARAEA-PHILIPPI [5] *(p. 108ff.)*
1. Peter's Great Confession (Mt. 16:13-20; Mk. 8:27-30; Lk. 9:18-21) p. 108.
2. Jesus Foretells His Death (Mt. 16:21-28; Mk. 8:31-9:1; Lk. 9:22-27) p. 109.
3. Jesus is Transfigured (Mt. 17:1-13; Mk. 9:2-13; Lk. 9:28-36) p. 110-111.
4. A Demoniac Boy is Healed (Mt. 17:14-21; Mk. 9:14-29; Lk. 9:37-43a) p. 111-113.

(VI) THROUGH GALILEE [6] *(p. 113)*
Returning Secretly Through Galilee (Mt. 17:22-23; Mk. 9:30-32; Lk. 9:43b-45) p. 113.

(VII) IN CAPERNAUM [7] *(p. 114)*
1. Jesus and the Temple Tax (Mt. 17:24-27; Mk. 9:33a) p. 114.
2. "The Greater" and "The Little" in the Kingdom of Heaven (Mt. 18:1-35; Mk. 9:33b-50; Lk. 9:46-50) p. 114-117.

(VIII) THE FINAL DEPARTURE FROM GALILEE [7] *(p. 117)*
(Mt. 19:1a; Mk. 10:1a; cf. Lk. 9:51)

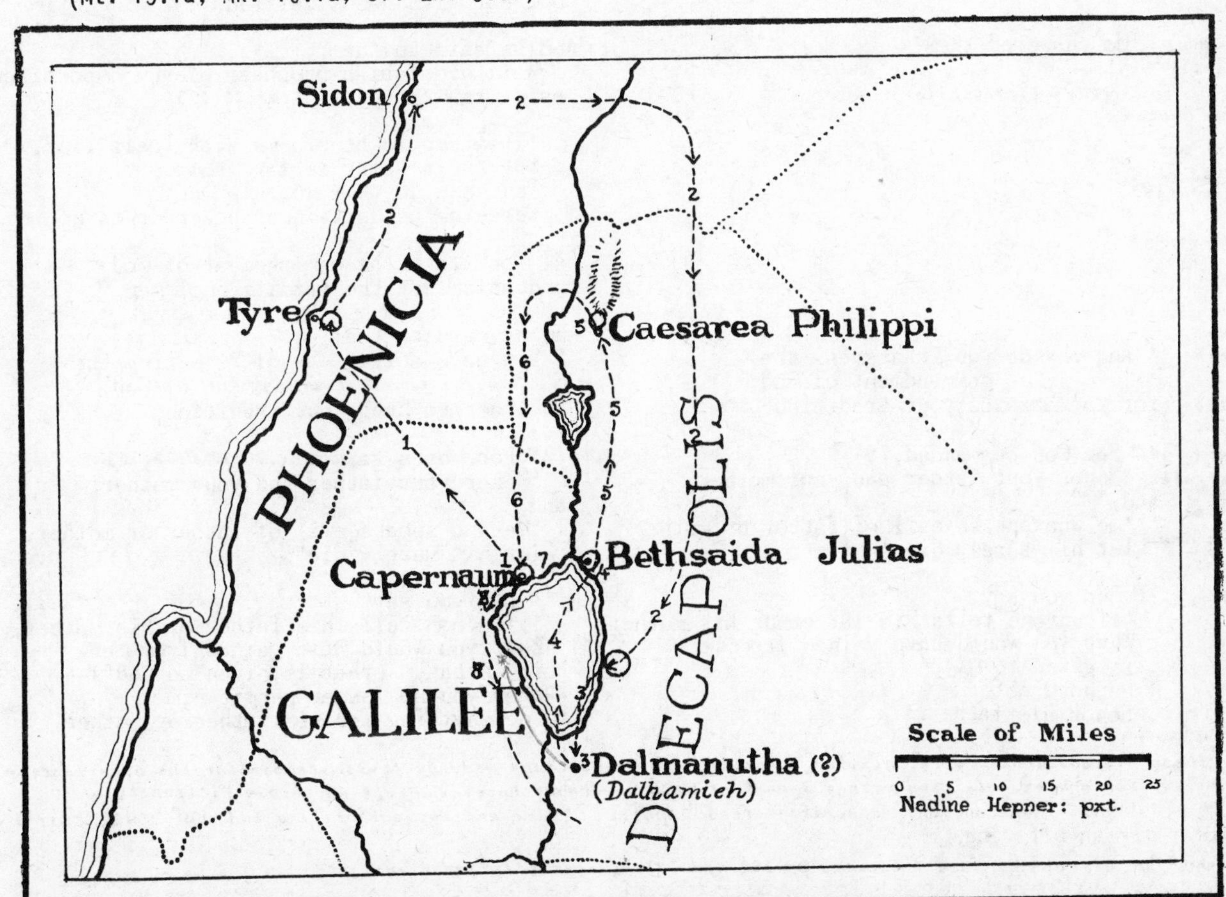

Mostly Outside Galilee (See Map p. 101)

(I) IN CAPERNAUM AND PHOENICIA

1. The Conflict About the "Traditions of the Elders".* § 93

Mt. 15:1-20	*Mk. 7:1-23*	*Jn. 7:1*

(1) Jesus Stays Away From Jerusalem Even at Passover Time Because Jewish Rulers Are Seeking To Kill Him**

Jn. 7:1

[[1]After this
Jesus went about in Galilee;
He would not go about in Judea,
because the Jews[a] sought to kill him].

(This verse covers all that Jesus did throughout the whole of the six months of "The Specialized Ministry," which follows. It is much more fully recorded by the other Gospels. See pp. 102-118)

(2) Jewish Rulers Come to Capernaum Looking for Jesus

So the Jewish Rulers Send Spies from Jerusalem to "Shadow" Him

Mt.

[1]Then Pharisees and scribes
came to Jesus
from Jerusalem

Mk.

[1]Now when the Pharisees
gathered together to him,
with some of the scribes,
who had come from Jerusalem,

They Soon Find Occasion Against Him

[2]they saw that some of his disciples
ate with hands defiled,
that is, unwashed.

The Background of Their Contention

[3](For the Pharisees, and all the Jews,
do not eat unless they wash their hands,
observing the tradition of the elders;
[4]and when they come from the market place,
they do not eat unless they purify[b] themselves.

And there are many other traditions which they observe,
the washing of cups and pots and vessels of bronze.[c])

(3) Jewish Rulers Criticise Jesus In The Presence of the Multitude

a. They Accuse Jesus of Violating Their Traditions

Mt.

and said,
[2]"Why do your disciples transgress
the tradition of the elders?
For they do not wash their hands
when they eat."

Mk.

[5]And the Pharisees and the scribes asked him,
"Why do your disciples not live[d]
according to the tradition of the elders,
but eat with hands defiled?"

b. Jesus Answers Them

(a) He Quotes Isaiah and Accuses Them Of Violating God's Commandments

Mt.

[3]He answered them,
(Cf. vs. 7-9 below)

Mk.

[6]And he said to them,
"Well did Isaiah prophesy of you hypocrites,
as it is written, *(Isa.29:13)*

'This people honors me with their lips,
but their heart is far from me;
[7]in vain do they worship me,
teaching as doctrines the precepts of men.'

[8]"You leave the commandment of God,
and hold fast the tradition of men."

(b) He Answers Their Question

Mt.

"And why do you transgress the
commandment of God
for the sake of your tradition?

Mk.

[9]And he said to them,
"You have a fine way of rejecting the
commandment of God,
in order to keep your tradition!

(c) He Illustrates With One Of The Ten Commandments

Mt.

[4]"For God commanded,
'Honor your father and your mother,'
and,
'He who speaks evil of father or mother,
let him surely die.'
[5]"But you say,
'If anyone tells his father or his mother,
What you would have gained from me
is given to God.[e]
he need not
honor his father.'

Mk.

[10]"For Moses said, *(Ex.20:12, Dt.5:16)*
'Honor your father and your mother;'
and,
'He who speaks evil of father or mother,
let him surely die';
[11]"but you say,
'If a man tells his father or his mother,
What you would have gained from me
is Corban,' (that is, Given to God[e])--
[12]then you no longer permit him
to do anything for his father or mother,

---

* *These "Traditions" were detailed teachings and regulations made by Jewish rabbis for the observance of the law. For one example read verses 3 to 5 of Mark's account here. Consult any Bible Dictionary.*

[a]*Or* Judeans. [b]*Some ancient authorities read* baptize. [c]*Some ancient authorities add* and beds. [d]*Greek* walk. [e]*Or* an offering.

***Or*, kept seeking. *See footnotes pp.104 and 121. (Especially important.)*

	Mt. 15	Mk. 7
(d) He Re-states His Answer	6 So, for the sake of your tradition, you have made void the law[a] of God.	13 " thus making void the word of God through your tradition which you hand on. And many such things you do."
(e) He Renews His Charge of Hypocrisy	7 " You hypocrites! Well did Isaiah prophesy of you, when he said: 8 'This people honors me with their lips, but their heart is far from me; 9 in vain do they worship me, teaching as doctrines the precepts of men.' "	*(Cf. vs. 6-8 above)*

(4) Jesus Calls The People and Explains to Them

	Mt. 15	Mk. 7
Jesus Explains to the Multitude	10 And he called the people to him and said to them, " Hear and understand: 11 not what goes into the mouth defiles a man, but what comes out of the mouth, this defiles a man."	14 And he called the people to him again and said to them, " Hear me, all of you, and understand: 15 there is nothing outside a man which by going into him can defile him; but the things which come out of a man are what defile him."[b]

(5) Later, Jesus Explains To The Twelve Alone.

	Mt. 15	Mk. 7
They Enter A House		17 And when he had entered the house, and left the people,
The Disciples Warn Jesus	12 Then the disciples came and said to him, " Do you know that the Pharisees were offended when they heard this saying?"	
He Explains His Own Attitude To the Rulers	13 He answered, " Every plant which my heavenly Father has not planted will be rooted up. 14 " Let them alone; they are blind guides. And if a blind man leads a blind man, both will fall into a pit."	*(Lk.6:39,p.64;Jn.9:39-41;Mt.23:17,p.192)*
He Gives a Fuller Explanation of His Teaching	15 But Peter said to him, " Explain the parable to us." 16 And he said, " Are you also still without understanding? 17 Do you not see,	his disciples asked him about the parable. 18 And he said to them, " Then are you also without understanding? Do you not see
(a) Negatively	that whatever goes into the mouth passes into the stomach and so passes on?[c]	that whatever goes into a man from outside cannot defile him, 19 since it enters, not his heart but his stomach, and so passes on?"[c] (Thus he declared all foods clean.)
(b) Positively	18 " But what comes out of the mouth proceeds from the heart, and this defiles a man. 19 For out of the heart come evil thoughts, murder, adultery, fornication, theft, false witness, slander.	20 And he said, " What comes out of a man is what defiles a man. 21 " For from within, out of the heart of man, come evil thoughts, fornication, theft, murder, adultery, 22 coveting, wickednesses, deceit, licentiousness, an evil eye, slander, pride, foolishness. *(Cf. Paul's "Work of the Flesh," Gal.5:19-21 and his other lists.)*
(c) In Conclusion	20 These are what defile a man; but to eat with unwashed hands does not defile a man."	23 " All these evil things come from within, and they defile a man."

[a] *Many ancient authorities read* word. [b] *Many ancient authorities add verse 16,* " If any man has ears to hear, let him hear." [c] *Or* is evacuated.

2. The Withdrawal* to Tyre and Sidon. § 94

	Mt. 15:21	Mk. 7:24a
They Journey To Tyre and Sidon (Map, p.101)	21 And Jesus went away from there* and withdrew to the district of Tyre and Sidon.	24 And from there he arose and went away* to the region of Tyre and Sidon.[a]

3. The Syrophoenician Woman's Daughter Healed. § 95

	Mt. 15:22-28	Mk. 7:24b-30
Jesus Desires Privacy		And he entered a house, and would not have anyone know it. Yet he could not be hid;
A Woman's Plea Is Unheeded	22 And behold, a Canaanite woman from that region	25 but immediately a woman,
		whose little daughter was possessed by an unclean spirit, heard of him,
	came out	and came and fell down at his feet.
		26 Now the woman was a Greek, a Sy-ro-phoe-ni´cian by race.
	and cried, "Have mercy on me, O Lord, Son of David; my daughter is severely possessed by a demon."	And she begged him to cast the demon out of her daughter.
	23 But he did not answer her a word.	
The Disciples' Plea Is Answered Mysteriously	And his disciples came and begged him, saying, "Send her away, for she is crying after us."	
	24 He answered, "I was sent only to the lost sheep of the house of Israel."	
The Woman, Pleading More Earnestly, Is Answered Enigmatically	25 But she came and knelt before him, saying, "Lord, help me."	
	26 And he answered, "It is not fair to take the children's bread and throw it to the dogs."	27 And he said to her, "Let the children first be fed, for it is not right to take the children's bread and throw it to the dogs."
Persisting in her Faith	27 She said, "Yes, Lord, yet even the dogs eat the crumbs that fall from their master's table."	28 But she answered him, "Yes, Lord; yet even the dogs under the table eat the children's crumbs."
Her Request Is Granted.	28 Then Jesus answered her, "O woman, great is your faith! Be it done for you as you desire."	29 And he said to her, "For this saying you may go your way; the demon has left your daughter."
She Goes Home	And her daughter was healed instantly.	30 And she went home,
She Finds Her Child Well		And found the child lying in bed, and the demon gone.

....

*"There was too much excitement among the people, too much bitterness [and malicious envy] among the Pharisees, too much suspicion on the part of Herod Antipas, too much dullness on the part of the disciples, for Jesus to remain in Galilee."

**Jesus wanted to be alone after all the strain in Galilee. He craved a little privacy and rest." -A.T. Robertson, in "Word Pictures in N.T.", Vol.I, p.325.- Used by permission. (Cf.footnote,p.121)

[a] Some ancient authorities omit and Sidon.

(II) IN DECAPOLIS

1. The Journey Through Decapolis. § 96

	Mt. 15:29a	*Mk. 7:31*
They Go From Tyre Thru Sidon, and Decapolis, To Lake Galilee (See Map p.101)	29 And Jesus went on from there, and passed along the sea of Galilee.	31 Soon after this he returned from the region of Tyre, and went through Sidon to the sea of Galilee, through the region of the Decapolis.

2. The Many Miracles of Healing There. § 97

	Mt. 15:29b-31	*Mk. 7:32-37*
Jesus Goes to a Hillside	And he went up into the hills,* and sat down there.	
Many Come and are Healed	30 And great crowds came to him, bringing with them the lame, the maimed, the blind, the dumb, and many others, and they put them at his feet, and he healed them,	
		A Deaf and Dumb Man Healed
A Deaf and Dumb Man Is Brought		32 And they brought to him a man who was deaf and had an impediment in his speech; and they besought him to lay his hand upon him.
Jesus By Sign Language Arouses His Faith	*(Mk.8:23,p.107)*	33 And taking him aside from the multitude privately, he put his fingers into his ears, and he spat and he touched his tongue; 34 and looking up to heaven, he sighed, and said to him, "Eph´pha-tha," that is, "Be opened."
The Man Is Cured		35 And his ears were opened, his tongue was released, and he spoke plainly.
Secrecy is Enjoined, but not Heeded		36 And he charged them to tell no one; but the more he charged them, the more zealously they proclaimed it.
They are Greatly Astonished At His Great Miracles and Glorify God	31 so that the crowd wondered, when they saw the dumb speaking, the maimed whole, the lame walking, and the blind seeing; and they glorified the God of Israel.	37 And they were astonished beyond measure, saying, "He has done all things well; he even makes the deaf hear and the dumb speak.

3. The Four Thousand Fed. § 98 [*See* § 87, *p.93*]

	Mt. 15:32-39a	*Mk. 8:1-10a*
The Compassionate Plea of Jesus To The Disciples	32 Then Jesus called his disciples to him and said, "I have compassion on the crowd, because they have been with me now three days, and have nothing to eat; and I am unwilling to send them away hungry, lest they faint on the way."	1 In those days, when again a great crowd had gathered, and they had nothing to eat, he called his disciples to him, and said to them, 2 "I have compassion on the crowd, *(Mt.9:36;Mk.1:41;10:33;13:20)* because they have been with me now three days, and have nothing to eat; 3 and if I send them away hungry to their homes, they will faint on the way; and some of them have come a long way."

....

**This was the region in which Jesus had told the healed demoniac to publish what He had done for him (See p.82, especially vv.17-20 of Mk.).*

	Mt. 15:32-39a	Mk. 8:1-10a
The Disciples' Embarrassment	33And the disciples said to him, "Where are we to get bread enough in the desert to feed so great a crowd?"	4And his disciples answered him, "How can one feed these men with bread here in the desert?"
Our Lord's Question	34And Jesus said to them, "How many loaves have you?" They said, "Seven, and a few small fish."	5And he asked them, "How many loaves have you?" They said, "Seven." *(Cf. v.7)*
The Crowd Is Seated	35And commanding the crowd to sit down on the ground,	6And he commanded the crowd to sit down on the ground;
Blessing and Distributing the Bread and the Fish	36he took the seven loaves and the fish, and having given thanks he broke them and gave them to the disciples, And the disciples gave them to the crowds.	and he took the seven loaves, *(Cf. v.7)* and having given thanks he broke them and gave them to his disciples to set before the people. And they set them before the crowd. 7And they had a few small fish. And having blessed them, he commanded that these also should be set before them.
Gathering up the Remainder	37And they all ate and were satisfied. And they took up seven baskets full of the broken pieces left over.	8And they ate, and were satisfied And they took up the broken pieces left over, seven baskets full.
The Number Fed	38Those who ate were four thousand men, besides women and children.	9And there were about four thousand people.
Sending Away the Crowds	39And sending away the crowds,	10And he sent them away.

(III) IN DALMANUTHA (MAGADAN)

The Pharisees and Sadducees Demand a Sign. § 99

(Cf.Mt.12:38-39,p.72; Lk.11:29-30,p.140; Jn.2:18-22)

	Mt. 15:39b-16:4a	*Mk. 8:10-12*
Going to Dalmanutha	He got into the boat, and went to the region of Magadan.*	10bAnd immediately he got into the boat with his disciples, and went into the district of Dal-ma-nu´-tha. [a]*
Pharisees and Sadducees Demand a Sign	1And the Pharisees and Sad´du-cees came, and to test him they asked him to show them a sign from heaven.**	11The Pharisees came and began to argue with him, ** seeking from him a sign from heaven, to test him.
Jesus Answers Them	2He answered them, [b]	12And he sighed deeply in his spirit, and said, "Why does this generation seek a sign?
(a) Why Men Seek for Signs *(b) Read the Signs You Have*	"When it is evening, you say, 'It will be fair weather; for the sky is red.' 3"And in the morning, 'It will be stormy today, for the sky is red and threatening.' You know how to interpret the appearance of the sky, but you cannot interpret the signs of the times. 4An evil and adulterous generation seeks for a sign,	*(Lk.12:54-56,p.145)*
(c) No Others Will Be Given *(d) Except One* ***	but no sign shall be given to it except the sign of Jonah.***"	"Truly, I say unto you, no sign shall be given to this generation."

[a]*Some ancient authorities read* Magadan *or* Magdala. **Dalmanutha may be the ruin today called Dalhamieh (See map p. 101).*

[b]*Many ancient authorities omit the following words to the end of verse 3.*

***The Pharisees taught that the true Messiah would prove himself by some stupendous miracles like those of Joshua and Moses.*

****That is, His resurrection from the dead. This is the only sign Jesus ever gave them, when they demanded a sign. See further examples in Mt.12:38,p.72,Lk.11:29-30,p.140;Jn.2:18-22,p.31.*

1. Warning Against the Leaven of the Pharisees. § 100

	Mt. 16:4b-12	Mk. 8:13-21
In crossing the Lake	So he left them and departed.	13And he left them, and getting into the boat again he departed to* the other side.
	5When the disciples reached the other side,**	
Provisions Are Forgotten.	they had forgotten to bring any bread.	14Now they had forgotten to bring bread; and they had only one loaf with them in the boat.
En Route Jesus Warns of Bad Leaven	6Jesus said to them, "Take heed and beware of the leaven of the Pharisees and Sad´du-cees."	15And he cautioned them, saying, "Take heed, beware of the leaven of the Pharisees (Lk.12:1-3,p.142) and of the leaven of Herod."[a]
They Misunderstand Him	7And they discussed it among themselves, saying, "We brought no bread."	16And they discussed it with one another, saying, "We have no bread."
Jesus Rebukes Them With an Unmatched Battery of Questions	8But Jesus, aware of this, said, "O men of little faith, Why do you discuss among yourselves the fact that you have no bread?	17And being aware of it, Jesus said to them, "Why do you discuss the fact that you have no bread?
	9"Do you not yet perceive?	"Do you not yet perceive or understand? Are your hearts hardened? 18Having eyes do you not see, and having ears do you not hear?
	"Do you not remember (§ 87,p.93)	And do you not remember?
	the five loaves of the five thousand, and how many baskets you gathered?	19"When I broke the five loaves for the five thousand, how many baskets full of broken pieces did you take up?"
		They said to him, "Twelve."
	10"Nor the seven loaves of the four thousand, and how many baskets (§ 98, p.105) you gathered?	20"And the seven for the four thousand, how many baskets full of broken pieces did you take up?" And they said to him, "Seven."
Then He Gives A Fuller Explanation		21And he said to them, "Do you not yet understand?"
	11"How is it that you fail to perceive that I did not speak about bread? Beware of the leaven of the Pharisees and Sad´du-cees."	
And They Understand	12Then they understood that he did not tell them to beware of the leaven of bread, but of the teaching of the Pharisees and Sad´du-cees.	

2. A Blind Man of Bethsaida Healed. § 101

Mk. 8:22-26

Passing Through Bethsaida	22And they came to Beth-sa i-da.
A Blind Man Is Brought	And some people brought to him a blind man, and begged him to touch him.
Jesus Takes Him Aside	23And he took the blind man by the hand, and led him out of the village. (Mk.7:33,p.105)
He Heals by Arousing His Faith	And when he had spit on his eyes and laid his hands upon him, he asked him, "Do you see anything?"
	24And he looked up and said, "I see men; but they look like trees, walking."
Step by Step	25Then again he laid his hands upon his eyes; and he looked intently and was restored, and saw everything clearly.
He Sends Him Home	26And he sent him away to his home, saying, "Do not even enter the village."

---

*left for. **Literally, And the disciples, going to the other side, forgot to take bread. (See vs.13,14 and 22 of Mk.)

[a]Some ancient authorities read the Herodians.

1. Peter's Great Confession § 102
(That Jesus Is the Messiah).

	Mt. 16:13-20 (Cf. Jn.6:68-69)	Mk. 8:27-30	Lk. 9:18-21
Jesus Goes to Caesarea-Philippi	13 Now when Jesus came into the district of Caes-a-re´a Philippi,	27 And Jesus went on with his disciples, to the villages of Caes-a-re´a Philippi;	
He Retires for Prayer			18 Now it happened *(Lk.9:29;11:1)* that as he was praying alone the disciples were with him;
He Asks The Disciples Who People Say He Is	He asked his disciples, "Who do men say that the Son of man is?"	and on the way he asked his disciples, "Who do men say that I am?"	and he asked them, "Who do the people say that I am?"
They Answer, John, Elijah, Jeremiah, A Prophet Resurrected.	14 And they said, "Some say John the Baptist, others say, Elijah, and others, Jeremiah, or one of the prophets."	28 And they told him, "John the Baptist"; and others, "Elijah"; and others, "One of the prophets."	19 And they answered, "John the Baptist; but others say, Elijah; and others, that one of the old prophets has risen."
Jesus Asks Who Do You Say?	15 He said to them, "But who do you say that I am?"	29 And he asked them, "But who do you say that I am?"	20 And he said to them, "But who do you say that I am?"
Peter Answers.	16 Simon Peter replied, "You are the Christ, the Son of the living God."	Peter answered him, "You are the Christ."	And Peter answered, "The Christ of God."
Our Lord Replies (a) Such Faith Comes Only By The Spirit's Teaching	17 And Jesus answered him, "Blessed are you, Simon Bar-Jona! For flesh and blood has not revealed this to you, but my Father who is in heaven.		
(b) Such Faith Is the Sure Foundation of all True Discipleship	18 "And I tell you, You are Peter,[a] and on this rock[b]* I will build my church; and the powers of death[c] shall not prevail against it.		
(c) Such Faith Alone Confers Great Privileges and Powers On All Who So Believe	19 "I will give you the keys of the kingdom of heaven,* *(Mt.18:18,p.116)* and whatever you bind on earth shall be bound in heaven, and whatever you loose on earth shall be loosed in heaven."		
He Forbids Them to Tell That He Is The Messiah	20 Then he strictly charged the disciples to tell no one that he was the Christ.	30 And he charged them to tell no one about him.	21 But he charged and commanded them to tell this to no one,

....

[a] *Greek* Petros. [b] *Greek* Petra. [c] *Greek* the gates of Hades.

**Ponder deeply the marginal notes on vv. 17,18,19. Also compare John 6:43,44,45,46,47, p.99)*

***All these opinions quoted in verse of Mt. accept Jesus as a* prophet. *But Jesus was never satisfied with that, or any faith in Him, less than that He was "The Messiah," or as they would say 'The Son of Man' or 'The Son of God.' The Samaritans said "We know that this is truly 'The Savior of the World.'" (Jn.4:19-25,29,42). The woman already in v.19 believes Him to be "a Prophet," but is still wondering whether or not He could be "The Messiah." (vs.25 and 29). Cf. also Nicodemus (Jn.3); The man in Jn.4:50 and 53; the man in Jn.9. First, he believed in Jesus as healer; then v.17 as prophet; then in v.35-38 as Savior.*

2. Jesus Foretells His Death and Resurrection. § 103

	Mt. 16:21-28	*Mk. 8:31-9:1*	*Lk. 9:22-27*
Jesus Begins to Teach About His Death and Resurrection ***(Cf.§ 106, p.113)*** ***[He Had Long Ago Forseen it For Himself]***	21 From that time Jesus began to show his disciples that he must go to Jerusalem and suffer many things from the elders and chief priests and scribes, and be killed, and on the third day be raised.	31 And he began to teach them (§ 106,§ 155) that the Son of man must suffer many things, and be rejected by the elders and the chief priests and the scribes, and be killed, and after three days rise again. 32 And he said this plainly.	22 saying, "The Son of man must suffer many things, and be rejected by the elders and chief priests and scribes, and be killed, and on the third day be raised."
Peter Privately Rebukes Jesus.	22 And Peter took him and began to rebuke him saying; "God forbid, Lord! This shall never happen to you."	And Peter took him, and began to rebuke him.	
Our Lord Rebukes Peter.	23 But he turned and said to Peter, "Get behind me, Satan! You are a hindrance[a] to me; for you are not on the side of God but of men."	33 But turning and seeing his disciples, he rebuked Peter, and said, "Get behind me, Satan! For you are not on the side of God, but of men."	
Then Jesus Speaks to All:	24 Then Jesus told his disciples,	34 And he called to him the multitude with his disciples, and said to them,	23 And he said to all,
The Death of Self Applies to all Who Follow Christ.	"If any man would come after me, let him deny himself and take up his cross and follow me.	"If any man would come after me let him deny himself and take up his cross and follow me.	"If any man would come after me, let him deny himself and take up his cross daily and follow me. *(Lk.14:27,p.154)*
Obtaining Life Eternal or else The Death of the Soul, Depend On It,	25 "For whoever would save his life will lose it, and whoever loses his life for my sake will find it.	35 "For whoever would save his life will lose it; and whoever loses his life for my sake and the gospel's will save it.	24 "For whoever would save his life will lose it; but whoever loses his life for my sake, he will save it.
And He Who Loses Himself Loses All,	26 For what will it profit a man if he gains the whole world and forfeits his life?	for what does it profit a man to gain the whole world and forfeit his life?	25 For what does it profit a man if he gains the whole world and loses or forfeits himself?
In The Final Round-up All Will Be Apparent.	"Or what shall a man give in return for his life?	37 "For what can a man give in return for his life? 38 "For whoever is ashamed of me and of my words in this adulterous and sinful generation, of him will the Son of man also be ashamed,	26 "For whoever is ashamed of me and of my words, of him will the Son of man be ashamed
Jesus Is Coming "in Glory" to Judge All Men-- At The End Of The Age	27 For the Son of man is to come with his angels in the glory of his Father and then he will repay every man for what he has done.	when he comes in the glory of his Father with the holy angels.	when he comes *(Cf.Mt.25:31,p.204)* in his glory and the glory of the Father and of the holy angels.
But Soon* He Is Coming "in Power" into His Kingdom	28 "Truly, I say to you, there are some standing here who will not taste death before they see the Son of man coming in his kingdom."	*Mk. 9* 1 And he said to them, "Truly, I say to you, there are some standing here who will not taste death before they see the kingdom of God come with power." *(Lk.21:31-32,p.201)*	27 "But I tell you truly, there are some standing here who will not taste of death before they see the kingdom of God."

[a] *Greek* stumbling-block. **i.e. on Pentecost, through His death, resurrection, glorification and the outpouring of the Spirit, of which the "Transfiguration which follows, is a "vision" (Cf.Mt.17:9; Lk.24:26) When the Jewish kingdom is hastening to an end, the Messiah's kingdom will "come in power," even while some of those standing there are yet alive (v.28).*

Jesus Has a Vision of Resurrection Glory

	Mt. 17:1-13	*Mk. 9:2-13*	*Lk. 9:28-36*
Jesus Chooses Peter, James and John.	1 And after six days	2 And after six days	28 Now about eight days after these sayings
	Jesus took with him Peter and James and John his brother,	Jesus took with him Peter and James and John,	he took with him Peter and John and James,
They Retire into the Mountain To Pray.	and led them up a high mountain apart.	and led them up a high mountain apart by themselves;	and went upon the mountain to pray.
As Jesus Prays He is Transfigured	2 And he was transfigured before them, and his face shone like the sun, and his garments became white as the light.	And he was transfigured before them, 3 and his garments became glistening, intensely white,[d] as no fuller on earth could bleach them.	29 And as he was praying, *(Lk.9:18;11* [was alte the appearance of his countenance and his raiment became dazzling white.
Then Moses and Elijah Come "in Glory" And Speak With Jesus of His "Exodus" (Gk.)	3 And behold, there appeared to them Moses and Elijah, talking with him.	4 And there appeared to them Elijah with Moses; and they were talking to Jesus.	30 And behold, two men talked with him, Moses and Elijah, 31 who appeared in glory and spoke of his departure, which he was to accomplish at Jerusalem.
The Apostles At First Fight Sleep Then They Awake And See His Glory			32 Now Peter and those who were with him were heavy with sleep but kept awake, and they saw his glory *(II Pet.1:16-18)* and the two men who stood with him.
Peter Feels He Must Say Something	4 And Peter said to Jesus, "Lord, it is well that we are here; if you wish, I will make three booths here. one for you one for Moses and one for Elijah." *(Cf. v. 6b below)*	5 And Peter said to Jesus, "Master,[a] it is well that we are here: let us make three booths, one for you and one for Moses and one for Elijah." 6 For he did not know what to say, for they were exceedingly afraid.	33 And as the men were parting from him, Peter said to Jesus, "Master, it is well that we are here; let us make three booths, one for you and one for Moses and one for Elijah"-- not knowing what he said. *(Cf. v. 34b below)*
A Radiant Cloud Envelops Them	5 He was still speaking, when lo, a bright cloud overshadowed them. *(Cf. v. 6b below)*	7 And a cloud overshadowed them. *(Cf. v. 6b above)*	34 As he said this, a cloud came and overshadowed them; and they were afraid as they entered the cloud.
And a Divine Voice Speaks To Them	And a voice from the cloud said, "This is my beloved Son,[b] with whom I am well pleased; listen to him." *(Ps.2:7b;Is.42:1)*	And a voice came out of the cloud, "This is my beloved Son;[b] *(Cf.§ 20:v.11,p.25)* listen to him."	35 And a voice *(Cf.Jn.12:28,p.194)* came out of the cloud, saying, "This is my Son, my Chosen;[b] listen to him!"
The Disciples Are Prostrated by Fear.	6 When the disciples heard this, they fell on their faces, and were filled with awe.	*(Cf. v. 6b above)*	*(Cf. v. 34b above)*
Jesus Comes and Reassures Them	7 But Jesus came and touched them, saying, "Rise, and have no fear."		
They Look Up And See Jesus Only with Them	8 And when they lifted up their eyes, they saw no one but Jesus only	8 And suddenly looking around they no longer saw any one with them but Jesus only.	36 And when the voice had spoken, Jesus was found alone.

[a] Or Rabbi. [b] Or My Son, my (or the) Beloved. [c] Many ancient authorities read my beloved.
[d] white as snow.

	Mt.	*Mk.*	*Lk.*
They Go down the mountain	9 And as they were coming down the mountain, Jesus commanded them,	9 And as they were coming down the mountain, he charged them	
They are Bound to Secrecy Until After the Resurrection	"Tell no one the vision, until the Son of man is raised from the dead."	to tell no one what they had seen, until the Son of man should have risen from the dead.	
		10 So they kept the matter to themselves,	And they kept silence and told no one in those days anything of what they had seen.
They Question About The Resurrection, and		questioning what the rising from the dead meant.	
About the Coming of Elijah;	10 And the disciples asked him, "Then why do the scribes say that first Elijah must come?"	11 And they asked him, "Why do the scribes say that first Elijah must come?"	
He Replies That Elijah Has Come, Meaning John the Baptist	11 He replied, "Elijah does come, and he is to restore all things, *(Cf. v.12 below)*	12 And he said to them, "Elijah does come first to restore all things; and how is it written of the Son of man, that he should suffer many things and be treated with contempt?	*(Mal.4:5-6;Lk.1:17;Mt.11:14,p.69)*
He Alludes To John The Baptist and His Fate, and His Own	12 "But I tell you that Elijah has already come, and they did not know him, but did to him whatever they pleased. "So also the Son of man will suffer at their hands."	13 "But I tell you that Elijah has come, and they did to him whatever they pleased, as it is written of him."	
They Understand About John	13 Then the disciples understood that he was speaking to them of John the Baptist.		

4. A Demoniac Boy Healed. § 105

	Mt. 17:14-21	*Mk. 9:14-29* *The Miracle*	*Lk. 9:37-43a*
The Next Day			37 On the next day,
They Come to the Crowds at the Foot of the mountain	14 And when they came to the crowd,	14 And when they came to the disciples, they saw a great crowd about them, and scribes arguing with them.	when they had come down from the mountain,
*Who Are Amazed * at Jesus.*		15 And immediately all the crowd, when they saw him, were greatly amazed, and ran up to him and greeted him.	a great crowd met him.
He Questions Them		16 And he asked them, "What are you discussing with them?"	

....

**Why? Perhaps, as in the case of Moses coming down from Mt. Sinai, (Ex.34:29-35) because of some lingering radiance in His face (See also II Cor.3:7-4:6).*

112 A Demoniac Boy Healed (Continued) *Mt. 17:14-21; Mk. 9:14-29; Lk. 9:37-43a*

	Matthew	Mark	Luke
A Father Brings His Son and Explains	a man came up to him and kneeling before him, said, 15 "Lord,	17 And one of the crowd answered him, "Teacher, I brought my son to you,	38 And behold, a man from the crowd cried, "Teacher,
The Boy's Affliction Is Graphically Described	have mercy on my son, for he is an epileptic and suffers terribly; for often he falls into the fire, and often into the water.	for he has a dumb spirit; 18 "and wherever it seizes him, it dashes him down; *(Cf. v.22)* and he foams and grinds his teeth and becomes rigid.	I beg you to look upon my son, for he is my only child; 39 "and behold, a spirit seizes him, and he suddenly cries out; it convulses him till he foams, and shatters him, and will hardly leave him.
The Disciples Had Tried and Had Failed	16 "And I brought him to your disciples, and they could not heal him."	"And I asked your disciples to cast it out, and they were not able."	40 "And I begged your disciples to cast it out, but they could not."
Our Lord Expresses His Chagrin And Asks Them To Bring The Boy To Him	17 And Jesus answered, "O faithless and perverse generation, how long am I to be with you? How long am I to bear with you? Bring him here to me."	19 And he answered them, "O faithless generation, how long am I to be with you? How long am I to bear with you? Bring him to me."	41 Jesus answered, "O faithless and perverse generation, how long am I to be with you and bear with you? Bring your son here."
They Bring The Boy To Him		20 And they brought the boy to him; and when the spirit saw him, immediately	
Just Then The boy Has A Convulsion		it convulsed the boy, and he fell on the ground and rolled about, foaming at the mouth.	42 While he was coming, the demon tore him and convulsed him.
The Trouble Has Been Since Childhood		21 And Jesus[a] asked his father, "How long has he had this?" And he said, "From childhood.	
The Father Makes a Desperate Plea	*(Cf. v. 15b)*	22 And it has often cast him into the fire and into the water, to destroy him; but if you can do anything, have pity on us and help us."	
	(Cf. Mt.v.20)	23 And Jesus said to him, "If you can! All things are possible to him who believes." *(Mk.11:22-24, p.182)*	
The Father's Halting Faith Is Helped		24 Immediately the father of the child cried out,[b] and said, "I believe; help my unbelief!"	
Jesus Cures The Boy He Gives A Stern Command	18 And Jesus rebuked him,	25 And when Jesus saw that a crowd came running together, he rebuked the unclean spirit, saying to it, "You dumb and deaf spirit, I command you, Come out of him, and never enter him again."	But Jesus rebuked the unclean spirit,

[a] *Greek* he. [b] *Many ancient authorities add* with tears.

	Matthew	Mark	Luke
The Boy Gives A Loud Shriek And Has A Convulsion	and the demon came out of him,	26 And after crying out, and convulsing him terribly, it came out,	
The Limp Body Seems Dead		and the boy was like a corpse; so that most of them said, "He is dead."	
Jesus Takes The Boy By The Hand		27 But Jesus took him by the hand and lifted him up, and he arose.	
He Is Cured	and the boy was cured instantly.		and healed the boy,
He Is Given To The Father			and gave him back to his father.
Everybody Is Astonished			43 And all were astonished at the majesty of God.

An Explanation Privately

	Matthew	Mark
In the House		28 And when he had gone home,
The Disciples Ask Jesus Why They Had Failed	19 Then the disciples came to Jesus privately and said, "Why could we not cast it out?"	his disciples asked him privately, "Why could we not cast it out?"
Jesus Answers, It Is Their Lack of Faith	20 He said to them, "Because of your little faith. For truly, I say to you, if you have faith as a grain of mustard seed, *(Lk.17:6,p.159)*	29 And he said to them,
Faith Can Do What is Impossible Otherwise	you will say to this mountain, *(Mt. Hermon)* 'Move hence to yonder place,' and it will move; and nothing will be impossible to you.[a] *(Cf.Mk.9:23)*	
Such Faith Comes Through Prayer and Fasting		"This kind cannot be driven out by anything but prayer."[b]

(VI) THE SECRET RETURN THROUGH GALILEE TO CAPERNAUM. § 106 [§ 103, § 155]

Jesus Again Foretells His Death and Resurrection

	Mt. 17:22-23	*Mk. 9:30-32*	*Lk. 9:43b-45*
Jesus Seeks Privacy for Further Teaching	22 As they were gathering[c] in Galilee,	30 They went on from there and passed through Galilee. And he would not have any one know it;	43b But while they were all marveling at everything he did,
		31 for he was teaching his disciples,	
The Lesson About His Death Is Repeated	Jesus said to them,	saying to them,	he said to his disciples, 44 "Let these words sink into your ears;
	"The Son of man is to be delivered into the hands of men,	"The Son of man will be delivered into the hands of men,	for the Son of man is to be delivered into the hands of men."
	23 and they will kill him, and he will be raised on the third day."	and they will kill him; and when he is killed, after three days he will rise."	
They Do Not Understand What He Means		32 But they did not understand the saying, *(Cf.Lk.18:34,p.172)*	45 But they did not understand this saying, and it was concealed from them, that they should not perceive it;
But It Worries Them	And they were greatly distressed.	and they were afraid to ask him.	and they were afraid to ask him about this saying.

[a] *Some ancient authorities insert verse 21,* "But this kind never comes out except by prayer and fasting." *See Mk. 9:29.* [b] *Many ancient authorities add* and fasting. [c] *Some ancient authorities read* abode.

1. Peter and the Temple Tax. § 107

Mt. 17:24-27 | **Mk. 9:33a**

They Return Home

24When they came to Ca-per′na-um,

33And they came to Ca-per′na-um;

The Temple Tax Collectors Question Peter

the collectors of the half-shekel tax went up to Peter
and said,
"Does not your teacher pay the tax?"*

25He said,
"Yes."

Christ Questions Peter In a Parable About Liability To Taxes

And when he came home,**
Jesus spoke to him first, saying,
"What do you think, Simon?
From whom do kings of the earth take toll or tribute?
From their sons, or from others?"

26And when he said,
"From others,"

What It Meant

Jesus said to him,
"Then the sons are free."

Another Parable About How the Money Was To Be Provided

27"However, not to give offense to them,
go to the sea and cast a hook,
and take the first fish that comes up,
and when you open its mouth
you will find a shekel;
take that and give it to them for me and for yourself."

2. "The Greater" and "The Little" in the Kingdom of Heaven And Their Relations to Each Other. § 108

(1) How To Be Great in The Kingdom

Mt. 18:1-35 | **Mk. 9:33b-50** | **Lk. 9:46-50**

On The Way

The Disciples Argue About Rank in the Kingdom

46An argument arose among them
as to which of them was the greatest.

In The House

And when he was in the house

They Ask Jesus Who Is Greatest

1At that time
the disciples came to Jesus, saying, *(Cf. § 156, p.172; Lk.22:24-30, p.209)*
"Who is the greatest
in the kingdom of heaven?"

He Asks About Their Dispute

47But when Jesus perceived
the thought of their hearts,

he asked them,
"What were you discussing on the way?"

They Do Not Answer Because They Are Ashamed

34But they were silent;
for on the way they had discussed with one another
who was the greatest.

Jesus Rebukes Their selfish Ambitions and Reveals the greatest secret of True Greatness.

35And he sat down and called the twelve;
and he said to them,
"If any one would be first, *(Cf. vs.48c below)*
he must be last of all
and servant of all."

Jesus Gives Them An Object Lesson; The Discourse:

2And calling to him a child,
He put him in the midst of them,

36And he took a child,
and put him in the midst of them;

He took a child
and put him
by his side,

and said,

a. Entering the Kingdom

3"Truly, I say to you,
Unless you turn and become like children, *(Cf. § 153)*
you will never enter the kingdom of heaven.

b. Rank in the Kingdom

4"Whoever humbles himself like this child,
he is the greatest in the kingdom of heaven. *(Mt.5:19b, p.59; § 156, p.172; Mt.23:11, p.191)*

*This was a poll tax, levied on every adult Israelite. It was for the support of the temple worship.

**Greek into the house.

(2) How to Treat the Lesser Ones

c. Attitude to the Little Ones In The Kingdom

(a) Receiving Them

Mt.

5 " Whoever receives
one such child
in my name,
receives me,

Mk.

And taking him in his arms,
he said to them,
37 " Whoever receives
one such child
in my name,
receives me;
and whoever receives me,
receives not me
but him who sent me."

Lk.

48 And said to them,
" Whoever receives
this child
in my name
receives me,
and whoever receives me
receives
him who sent me;
for he who is least among you all
is the one who is great."

John's Interruption

Mk.

38 John said to him,
" Teacher, we saw a man
casting out demons in your name;[a]
and we forbade him,
because he was not following us."

Lk.

49 John answered,
" Master, we saw a man
casting out demons in your name,
and we forbade him,
because he does not follow with us."

Christ's Answer

Mk.

39 But Jesus said,
" Do not forbid him;
for no one
who does a mighty work in my name
will be able soon after to speak evil of me.
40 For he that is not against us
is for us. *(Cf.Mt.12:30,p.72)*

41 " For truly, I say to you,
whoever gives you
a cup of water to drink
because you bear the name of Christ,
will by no means lose his reward.

Lk.

50 But Jesus said to him,
" Do not forbid him;
for he that is not against you
is for you."

(b) Causing The Weak to Stumble

Mt.

6 " But whoever causes
one of these little ones
who believe in me to sin,[b]
it would be better for him
to have a great millstone *(Lk.17:2,p.159)*
fastened round his neck
and to be drowned in the depths of the sea.

Mk.

42 " Whoever causes
one of these little ones
who believe in me to sin,[b]
it would be better for him
if a great millstone were
hung round his neck
and he were thrown into the sea.

Causes of Stumbling are Bad

Mt.

7 " Woe to the world for temptations to sin![c]
For it is necessary that temptations come, *(Lk.17:1,p.159)*
but woe to the man by whom the temptation comes!

Do Not Allow Yourself to Stumble at Any Cost

Mt.

8 " And if your hand
or your foot
causes you to sin,[b]
cut it off
and throw it from you;
it is better for you to enter life maimed or lame
than with two hands or two feet to be thrown
into the eternal fire.

Mk.

43 " And if your hand
(Cf. vs. 45 below)
causes you to sin,[b]
cut it off;
it is better for you to enter life maimed
than with two hands to go to hell,[d]
to the unquenchable fire.[e]

Better Forfeit A Hand, Or Foot

Mk.

45 " And if your foot causes you to sin,[b]
cut it off;
it is better for you to enter life lame
than with two feet to be thrown into hell.[c]

Or An Eye.

Mt.

9 " And if your eye causes you to sin,[b]
pluck it out
and throw it from you;

" It is better for you
to enter life
with one eye
than with two eyes to be thrown into the hell[d]
of fire.

Mk.

47 " And if your eye causes you to sin,[b]
pluck it out;

it is better for you
to enter into the kingdom of God
with one eye
than with two eyes to be thrown into hell,[d]

---

[a] *Some ancient authorities add* who does not follow us. [b] *Or* stumble. [c] *Greek* stumbling-blocks. [d] *Greek* Gehenna. [e] *Verses 44 and 46 (which are identical with verse 48) are omitted by the best ancient authorities.*

Mt. | *Mk.*

[48]where their worm does not die,
and the fire is not quenched.

(Cf.Mt.5:13,p.59; Lk.14:34-36; p.155)

[49] "For every one will be salted with fire.[a]

The Necessity of Severe Self-Discipline

[50]Salt is good;
but if the salt has lost its saltness,
how will you season it?
Have salt in yourselves,
and be at peace with one another."

(c) About Not Despising the Little Ones

The Angels' Concern For Them

[10]"See that you do not despise one of these little ones;
for I tell you
that in heaven their angels
always behold the face of my Father who is in heaven.[b]

(3) How to Save the Sinning

A Shepherd's Concern for the Weak

[12]"What do you think?
If a man has a hundred sheep,
and one of them has gone astray, *(Cf.Lk.15:4-7,p.155)*
does he not leave the ninety-nine on the hills
and go in search of the one that went astray?

And His Rejoicing Over Them When Rescued

[13]"And if he finds it,
truly, I say to you,
he rejoices over it more
than over the ninety-nine that never went astray.

The Heavenly Father's Concern For The Little Ones

[14]"So it is not the will of my[c] Father who is in heaven
that one of these little ones should perish.

d. How to Win Back an Erring Brother

(a) Make Personal Effort

[15]"If your brother sins against you,
go and tell him his fault,
between you and him alone.
If he listens to you,
you have gained your brother.

(b) Get One or Two Helpers

[16]"But if he does not listen,
take one or two others along with you,
that every word may be confirmed
by the evidence of two or three witnesses.

(c) Enlist the Strength of the Whole Congregation

[17]"If he refuses to listen to them,
tell it to the church;
and if he refuses to listen even to the church,
let him be to you as a Gentile and a tax collector.

(d) Assurance of Divine Cooperation

[18]"Truly, I say to you,
whatever you bind on earth *(Mt.16:19,p.108)*
will be bound in heaven,
and whatever you loose on earth
will be loosed in heaven.

(e) The Power of Agreement in Prayer for Christ's Work

[19]"Again I say to you,
if two of you agree on earth
about anything they ask,
it will be done for them by my Father in heaven.
[20]For where two or three are gathered
in my name,
there am I in the midst of them."

(4) How To Forgive Those Who Offend Us

Forgiveness Whenever There is Penitence

[21]Then Peter came up and said to him,
"Lord, how often shall my brother sin against me and I forgive him?
As many as seven times?"

[22]Jesus said to him,
"I do not say to you seven times,
but seventy times seven.[d]

---

[a]*Many ancient authorities add* and every sacrifice will be salted with salt. [b]*Some ancient authorities add verse 11,* For the Son of Man came to save that which was lost. [c]*Some ancient authorities read* your. [d]*Or* seventy seven times.

a) Illustrating the Importance of Forgiveness

23 "Therefore the kingdom of heaven may be compared to a king
who wished to settle accounts with his servants.

A King Makes A Reckoning With His Servants

24 "When he began the reckoning,
one was brought to him
who owed him ten thousand talents;[a]
25 and as he could not pay,
his lord ordered him to be sold,
with his wife
and children
and all that he had,
and payment to be made.

One Is Found Wanting And Is Condemned

The Servant Pleads for Mercy

26 "So the servant fell on his knees, imploring him,
'Lord, have patience with me, and I will pay you everything.'
27 And out of pity for him
the lord of that servant released him
and forgave him the debt.

The Servant Makes Demands On a Fellow-Servant And Refuses Mercy

28 "But that same servant, as he went out,
came upon one of his fellow servants
who owed him a hundred denarii;[b]
and seizing him by the throat he said,
'Pay what you owe.'

29 "So his fellow servant fell down and besought him,
'Have patience with me, and I will pay you.'

30 "He refused
and went and put him in prison
till he should pay the debt.

His Fellow-Servants Reported Him

31 "When his fellow servants saw what had taken place,
they were greatly distressed.

And they went and reported to their lord all that had taken place.

He Is Tried

32 "Then his lord summoned him and said to him,
'You wicked servant!
I forgave you all that debt because you besought me;
33 and should not you have had mercy on your fellow servant,
as I had mercy on you?'

He Is Punished

34 "And in anger his lord
delivered him to the jailors,[c]
till he should pay all his debt.

b) We Endanger Our Own Salvation, If We Do Not Forgive

35 "So also my heavenly Father will do to every one of you,
if you do not forgive your brother from your heart." *(Mt.6:12,14-15,p.62)*

(VIII) THE FINAL DEPARTURE FROM GALILEE.* § 109

	Mt.19:1a	*Mk.10:1a*	*Lk.9:51*	*Jn.7:2,3,10*
Jesus Determines to Carry His Campaign to Judea			[*51 When the days drew near for him to be received up, he set his face to go up to Jerusalem.*]	
	1 Now when Jesus had finished these sayings,			
And Leaves Galilee				[*2 Now the Jews' feast of Tabernacles was at hand. 3 So his brothers said to him, "Leave here and go to Judea." 10 But after his brothers had gone up to the feast, Then he also went up.*]
(Mt. and Mk. continued in § 151, p.167 ff.)	he went away from Galilee and entered into the region of Judea.	1 And he left there and went to the region of Judea.		

After this section, Mt.and Mk. leap forward in their accounts. They omit entirely the "Later Judean Ministry" and the accounts given by John of the feasts of Tabernacles in Jn.7-10:21; "The Feast of Dedication," (Jn.10:22-39); The first half of the "Perean Ministry" (Jn.10:40-42); and the "Return of Jesus to Judea to raise Lazarus from the dead" (Jn.11:1-53); "Jesus' Retirement to Ephraim" (Jn.11:54). Mt.and Mk. also omit the many details of these events given by Luke in Chapters 10:1-17:10. For the argument see Outline and Notes on next two pages, and the maps on pp.118 and 150.

[a] *This talent was probably worth about a thousand dollars.* [b] *The Denarius was worth about twenty cents.*
[c] *Greek* tortures.

THE CONCLUDING MINISTRY

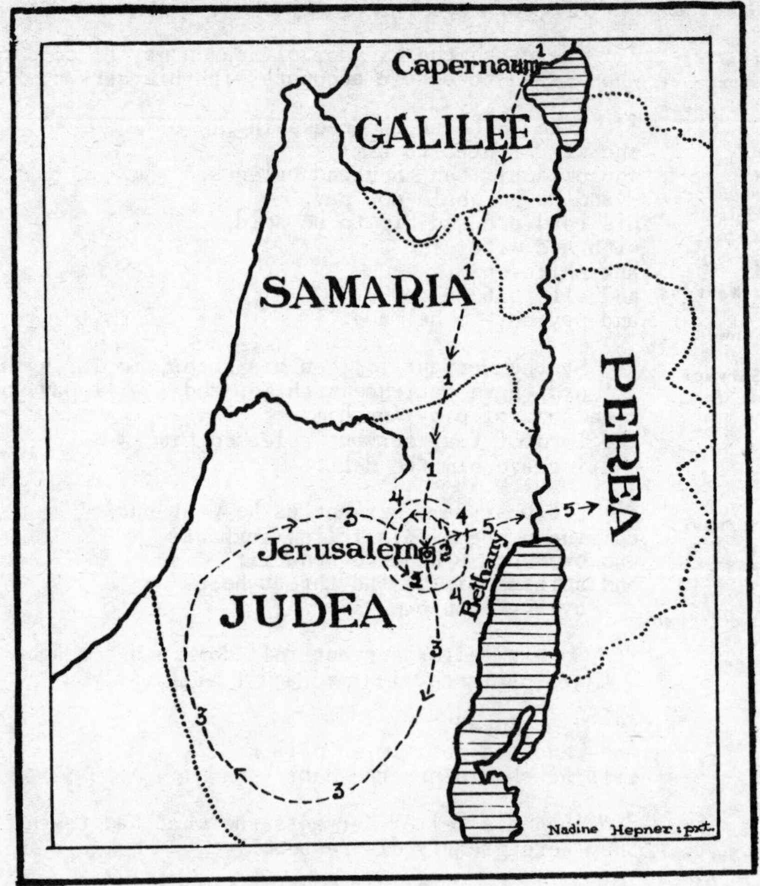

MAP OF THE JUDEAN MINISTRY

(For map of the Perean Ministry see p.150)

INTRODUCTION TO THE CONCLUDING MINISTRY

At the "Feast of the Jews" mentioned in Jn. 5, the persecution of Jesus by the Jewish rulers had reached such a pitch that they were seeking to kill Him. (Jn.5:16-18; and Jn.7:19). So Jesus stayed away from Jerusalem (Jn. 7:1) from that time on until the Feast of Tabernacles; it may have been for a year and a half. He did not even go up for the intervening passover (see Jn. 6:1 and 4), tho urged to become king (Jn.6:15) With the end of His life drawing near (Lk.9:51), He still has Judea and Perea to thoroughly evangelize; only six months remain. So Jesus "steadfastly set his face" to accomplish this part of his task, by an intensive campaign in each of these two provinces, before the tragic end comes which He so vividly foresees. §§ 103,106).

THE EVANGELIZATION OF JUDEA requires all the time from The Feast of Tabernacles (Jn. 7) in October to The Feast of Dedication (Jn. 10:22) in the end of December, i.e., 3 months. This constitutes the "Later Judean Ministry." (Jn. 7:3-10:21 and Lk. 9:51-13:21). It began with a feast in Jerusalem and ended there at another feast.

THE EVANGELIZATION OF PEREA required from The Feast of Dedication (see Jn. 10:40), to the Raising of Lazarus (see Jn. 11:7), some time in February or March. It is recorded briefly in Jn.10:22-42; and more fully by Luke in 13:22-17:10, and also the tour through Perea to the last Passover (Lk.17:11-19:28; Mt.19:1b-20:34; Mk.10:1b-52).

In both these campaigns Jesus worked intensively, using both the twelve and the seventy in teams of two each, as Lk. 10:1 suggests, for the time was exceedingly short. But with six plus thirty-five teams of two He could visit "every city and village", healing and teaching and heralding the kingdom's coming.

There is no hint that Jesus left Judea until Jn. 10:40-42. But that was after the Feast of Dedication (Jn.10:22-39). Where then was Jesus between the "Tabernacles" in October and the "Dedication" in December? The only account we have is that of Lk. 10:1-13:21. In Lk. 10:38-42, Luke tells of Jesus at Bethany - which is in Judea; in 10:30 the allusion is also to Judea. Luke also refers to his moving about. So He must be outside Jerusalem, but still in Judea. It seems conclusive then that this is a "Judean Ministry,", between the two visits to Jerusalem, at the two feast times mentioned by John. (Sometimes these events are made part of "The Perean Ministry." This is evidently a mistake)

Note how completely Luke and John supplement each other, and how they dovetail into each other. In the arrangement outlined on page 119 and tabulation of the Gospel materials in detail on the pages that follow Jn.7:2ff. explains Lk.9:51; Jn.7:2-10:21 explains "after this" of Lk.10:1; Jn.10:22-42 explains the fresh start in Luke's narrative at Lk.13:22; and Jn.11:1-54 explains the vague general expression at Lk.17:11.

So John's specifications of time and places and circumstances, like an eye-witness account, furnish the frame of reference, while Luke's detailed history of events supplements John and fills in the concrete picture.

The case for the present arrangement is argued at length by A.T.Robertson and the authors he quotes, in the Appendix of His Harmony of the Gospels (Harper and Brothers).

While Matthew and Mark give no account of these intensive campaigns in Judea and Perea, what they do say, of the events preceding and following, fits in perfectly with these accounts of Luke and John.

The "Concluding Ministry" is shown in general outline (p.119) and the movements mentioned by the writers of Luke and John are indicated in two outline maps, one of the Evangelization of Judea (p. 118) and the other The Evangelization of Perea (p.150).

IV. THE CONCLUDING MINISTRY [*In General Outline*]

Intensive Campaigning in the Remaining Provinces

"When the days were well-nigh come that he should be received up" (Lk.9:51a)
(From the Feast of Tabernacles, Oct.,A.D.29; To the Feast of the Passover, Apr.A.D.30;6 months)

(I) FROM GALILEE TO JUDEA

("The Later Judean Ministry") *"Leave this place and go to Judea." (Jn.7:3)*

INTRODUCTION

(a) The Time.- *"Now the Feast of the Jews, The Feast of Tabernacles was at hand" (Jn.7:2;cf.Lk.9:51)*

(b) The Purpose.- *"He steadfastly set His face to go to Jerusalem." (Lk.9:51b)*

(c) The Event.- *Mark says, "He arose from thence" - i.e. Capernaum. (Mk.10:1). MATTHEW SAYS, "He departed from Galilee" (Mt.19:1a)*

(d) The Manner.- *"He went up to the Feast, not publically, but as it were in secret" (Jn.7:10b) i.e., through Samaria (Lk.9:51-62), and not with the thousands of Passover pilgrims.*

MAIN DIVISIONS

(A) CONFLICTS WITH THE JEWISH RULERS AT THE FEAST OF TABERNACLES §§ 110-124, *pp.121-133.* [1,2]
(Oct.A.D.29) (Jn.7:2-10:21-39) Outlines and Map pp. 118-20.

1. BEFORE THE FEAST (Jn.7:2-13) [2]
2. IN THE MIDST OF THE FEAST (Jn.7:14-36) [2]
3. ON THE LAST DAY OF THE FEAST (Jn.7:37-8:59) [2]
   (1) Two Great Ceremonies Interpreted by Jesus.
   (2) Two Great Appeals Made by Jesus.
4. AFTER THE FEAST (Jn.9:1-10:21) [2]
   (1) Healing the Man Born Blind, and The Ensuing Controversies (Jn.9:1-34)
   (2) Winning the Healed Man to Discipleship, and The Ensuing Controversy (Jn.9:35-10:18)
   (3) The Resulting Division (Jn.10:19-21)

(B) EVANGELIZING IN JUDEA. § 125, pp.134-147. *Outline, p.134; Map p.118.*
(From the Feast of Tabernacles, Oct.,A.D.29; To the Feast of Dedication, Dec.,A.D.29) (Lk.10:1-13:21)

1. Opening Events
2. Controversies
3. The Seventy Return (Lk.10:17-24; Mt.11:25-28)

(C) CONFLICT WITH THE JEWISH RULERS AT THE FEAST OF DEDICATION. § 135, pp.148-149.
(Late Dec.A.D.29) (Jn.10:22-39)

1. Jesus Is Teaching In Solomon's Porch (22-23)
2. The Jews Ask Him to Tell Whether He IS The Messiah (24-30)
3. They Attempt to Stone Him (31-38)
4. They Try to Seize Him
5. But He Escapes (39)

(II) FROM JUDEA TO PEREA *(FIRST PART OF THE PEREAN MINISTRY)* § 136, pp.150-159. *Outline and Map p.150.*

(Evangelizing in Perea)
"He went beyond the Jordan." (Jn.10:40)
(From the Feast of Dedication Dec.A.D.29; To the Resurrection of Lazarus, Feb. or March,A.D.30)

1. *JOHN'S GENERAL SUMMARY (Jn.10:40-42)*
2. *LUKE'S SPECIFIC INCIDENTS (Lk.13:22-17:10)*

(III) FROM PEREA TO BETHANY AND EPHRAIM *(INTERRUPTION OF THE PEREAN MINISTRY)* §§ 145,146, pp.160-162.

(Conflict with Jewish Rulers At Bethany)
"Let us go to Bethany." (Jn.11:15)
(A fleeting visit shortly before Passover, A.D.30) (Jn.11:1-44)

(1) The Resurrection of Lazarus and the Result.
(2) Retirement in Ephraim.

(IV) FROM EPHRAIM TO BETHANY *(SECOND PART OF THE PEREAN MINISTRY)* § 147, pp.164-177. *See Map p.164.*

(Evangelizing in Perea on His Final Return to Jerusalem)
"Jesus came to Bethany." (Jn.12:1)
(A Week or Two Before The Last Passover - April A.D. 30)
(Journeying with the Passover crowds through Samaria, Perea, and Judea)
(Jn.11:55-12:11; Lk. 17:11-19:28; Mt.19:1b-20:34; Mk.10:1b-52)

1. Approaching Perea Along the Boundary of Samaria and Galilee. (Lk.17:11)
2. Journeying Through Perea. 3. Passing Through Jericho.
4. Nearing Jerusalem. 5. Arriving at Bethany.

(A) CONFLICTS WITH JEWISH RULERS AT THE FEAST OF TABERNACLES (Jn.7:1-10:21)

Various Opinions About Who Jesus Is, and Conflicting Attitudes to Him

1. BEFORE THE FEAST (Jn. 7:1-13) pp.121-123.

   (1) The Murderous Attitude of the Rulers--Ever since His Last Visit § 110
   (Jn.7:1; cf. Jn. 5:18 and Mt. 12:14; Mk. 3:6)
   (2) This Attitude Well-Known to Jesus (Jn.7:2-7) § 111
   (3) What Jesus Does About it (Jn. 7:8-10; cf. Lk. 9:51-62) § 112
   (4) How it was Revealed at Jerusalem before Jesus arrived (Jn. 7:11-13) § 114

2. IN THE MIDST OF THE FEAST (Jn. 7:14-36) § 115 pp. 123-124.

   (1) The Divine Source of Jesus Teachings (14-24)
   (2) The Divine Origin of Jesus Himself(25-31)
   (3) The Divine Destiny of Jesus (32-36)

3. ON THE LAST DAY OF THE FEAST (Jn. 7:37-8:59) pp. 124-128.

   (1) Two Great Ceremonies Interpreted by Jesus

   a. The Water-Pouring Ceremony--In the Morning (Jn. 7:37-52) § 116
   (Jesus Gives the Water of Life)
   (a) The Ceremony and Its Meaning
   (b) The Fulfilment in Jesus
   a1 His Claim
   b1 The Resulting Division of Sentiment (40-52) § 117

   b. The Lamp-Lighting Ceremony--In the Evening (Jn. 8:12-20)* § 119
   (Jesus is the Light of Life)
   (a) The Ceremony and Its Meaning
   (b) Its Fulfilment in Jesus
   a1 His Claim (12)
   b1 The Resulting Contention (13-20)

   (2) Two Great Appeals Made by Jesus (21-59)

   a. The First -- To Believe on Him as the Messianic Savior From Sin (21-30)
   (Jesus is the only Savior from Sin) § 120

   (a) The Occasion (20)
   (b) His Appeal - " Except ye believe, ye shall die in your sins"
   (c) Their Replies

   b. The Second -- To Continue in His Word (31-59)
   (Jesus is the Truth that makes Men Free) § 121

   (a) The Occasion
   (b) His Appeal - " The Truth shall Make you free"
   (c) Their Replies
   a1 Their Claims about Themselves (33-47)
   b1 Their Accusations and Violence Against Him (48-59)

4. AFTER THE FEAST (Jn. 9:1-10:21) pp. 129-133.

   (1) Healing of the Man Born Blind and the Ensuing Controversies (9:1-34)
   (Jesus is the Light of the World) § 122
   a. The Cure of the Man (1-7)
   b. His Controversies with The Pharisees (8-34a)
   c. Their Excommunication of Him (34b)

   (2) Winning the Healed Man to Discipleship and the Ensuing Controversy (9:35-10:21)
   (Jesus is the Judge of the World, and The True Shepherd of His Sheep) § 123

   a. Jesus Wins the Healed Man to Discipleship (35-38)
   b. The Pharisees are Embittered (39-41)
   c. Jesus Replies to Them by Parable (10:1-21) § 124
   (a) The Parable of the Good Shepherd (1-6)
   (b) Its Interpretation (7-18)
   (c) The Resulting Division (19-21)

**Most ancient Manuscripts omit Jn. 7:53-8:11;* § 118. *While it is probably a true incident, it does not belong here. Some manuscripts place it near the end of Lk. 21; where it fits very well.*

Jn. 7:1-10:21

1. BEFORE THE FEAST (Who Jesus Is)

(Jn. 7:1-13; Cp. Lk. 9:51-62)

Prefatory Note By John

(1) The Jewish Rulers Have Been Plotting to Kill* Jesus Ever Since His Last Visit to Jerusalem. § 110

Jn. 7:1; Cp. Jn. 5:18; Mt. 12:14; Mk.3:6

Prefatory Note Jesus Stays Away from Jerusalem for 18 months

[1After this Jesus went about in Galilee;*
he would not go about in Judea,
because the Jews[a] sought to kill him.] *(Jn.5:18; Mt.12:14,p.55;Jn.7:19,p.123)*

(2) In Spite of This, Jesus Resolutely Determines to Face the Issue. § 111

Lk. 9:51

Then He Plans to Evangelize Jerusalem and Judea (See Notes, p.118)

51When the days drew near *(See Jn.7:6,8,30 below)*
for him to be received up,
he set his face
to go to Jerusalem.

(3) His Brothers Urge Him to Go To the Feast With the Crowds. § 112

(Even His brothers do not believe in Him as Messiah. V.5)

Jn. 7:2-9

If you are the Messiah Declare Yourself

The Feast of Tabernacles Is Approaching

2Now the Jews' feast of tabernacles was at hand.

His Brothers Urge Jesus to Go And There Declare Himself.

3So his brothers said to him,
"Leave here and go to Judea,
that your disciples may see the works you are doing.

Their Reasoning: a. Its Background is the Whole Period of Withdrawals (see 7:1b)

4"For no man works in secret
if he seeks to be known openly.

b. What They Say

"If you do these things,
show yourself to the world."

c. Why They Say it

5For even his brothers did not believe in him.

Jesus Replies: He Well Knows the Bitterness of the Rulers

6Jesus said to them,
"My time has not yet come, *(v.8,30;Jn.2:4;8:20)*
but your time is always here.
7The world cannot hate you,

Why They Hate Him

but it hates me *(Jn.15:18-25,p.217;Mt.5:10-12,p.59)*
because I testify of it that its works are evil.

8"Go to the feast yourselves;
I am not going up to the feast,[b]
for my time has not yet fully come." *(v.6)*

Jesus Does Not Go With the Crowds of Pilgrims But Lets Them Go On

9So saying, he remained in Galilee.

---

[a]Or Judeans. [b]*Many ancient authorities add* yet.

**He had stayed away from Jerusalem (and from all the feasts), for a full year and a half (Cf. Jn.5:1 and 6:4), because he knew the hostility and malignity of the Jewish rulers. When last he had been attending the Passover they were plotting to kill Him (see Jn.5:18). Ever since, they had hounded Him about opposing Him at every turn, and plotting against Him, (for their motives, see Jn.7:7). [See almost the entire "Later Galilean Ministry."] Then it became not even safe for Him to stay in Herod Antipas' territory, for Herod had now killed John the Baptist, and was becoming suspicious of Jesus (See Lk.9:7-9). [See the whole of "The Specialized Ministry", just preceding--and note how carefully Jesus keeps out of Herod's territory (i.e., out of Galilee and Perea)]. (Cf.footnote,p.104)*

(4) Jesus Goes to the Feast Privately. § 113

(Remember Jn.7:1,25)

Mt. 19:1a, 8:19-22 | *Mk. 10:1a* | *Lk. 9:51b-62* | *Jn. 7:10*

Later, When Others Are Gone

Mt.: [[1]He went away from Galilee.]*

Mk.: [[1a]And he left there.]*

Jn.: [10]But after his brothers
had gone up to the feast,
then he also went up,
not publicly but in private.

[See § 109, p.100]

Jesus Also Goes to Jerusalem But "Secretly", i.e. Thru Samaria

Lk. 9:51-56

[51b]And he sent messengers ahead of him,

He Sends Messengers Ahead to Prepare Lodgings

[52]who went
and entered a village of the Samaritans,
to make ready for him;

They Were Refused Hospitality

[53]but the people would not receive him,
because his face was set toward Jerusalem.

James and John Threaten Vengeance

[54]And when his disciples James and John saw it,
they said,
"Lord, do you want us to bid fire come down from heaven
and consume them?"[a]

Jesus Rebukes Them

[55]But he turned *(Note and ponder His reason, in footnote)*
and rebuked them.[b]

He Suggests a Better Way

[56]And they went on to another village.

A Scribe Asks to Go Along

Mt. 8:19-22

[19]And a scribe came up
and said to him,
"Teacher, I will follow you
wherever you go."

Lk.: [57]As they were going along the road,
a man
said to him,
"I will follow you
wherever you go."

Jesus Warns of Hardships

[20]And Jesus said to him,
"Foxes have holes,
and birds of the air have nests;
but the Son of man
has nowhere to lay his head."

Lk.: [58]And Jesus said to him,
"Foxes have holes,
and birds of the air have nests;
but the Son of man
has nowhere to lay his head."

[59]To another he said,
"Follow me."

Two Others Plead For Delay

[21]Another of the disciples
said to him,
"Lord, let me first
go and bury my father."

Lk.: But he said,
"Lord, let me first
go and bury my father."

Jesus Insists on Immediate Decisions

[22]But Jesus said to him,
"Follow me,
and leave the dead to bury their own dead."

Lk.: [60]But he said to him,
"Leave the dead to bury their own dead;
but as for you, go and proclaim
the kingdom of God."

[61]Another said,
"I will follow you, Lord;
but let me first say farewell
to those at my home."

He Warns Against Looking Back

[62]Jesus said to him,
"No one who puts his hand to the plow
and looks back
is fit for the kingdom of God."

---

[a]*Some ancient authorities add* as Elijah did. *(Cp. 2 K. 1:10-12).* [b]*Some ancient authorities add* and he said, "You do not know what manner of spirit you are of. For the Son of man came not to destroy men's lives but to save them."

*For continuance of the record of Mt. and Mk. see § 151, p.167.

Jn. 7:11-13

Is Jesus a Good man or An Impostor?

The Tension at the Feast Before He Arrives
a. The Officials Hunt Him
b. The Crowds Discuss Him

11The Jews were looking for him at the feast, and saying,
"Where is He?"

12And there was much muttering about him among the people,
while some said,
"He is a good man,"
others said,
"No, he is leading the people astray."

But Everyone Speaks Secretly

13Yet for fear of the Jews no one spoke openly of him.

2. IN THE MIDST OF THE FEAST. § 115

Jn. 7:14-36

Jesus Is The Revealer of God's Message

(1) The Divine Source of Jesus' Teaching

Jesus Arrives. Is Teaching in the Temple

14About the middle of the feast
Jesus went up into the temple
and taught.

a. The Jews Marvel

15The Jews marveled at it, saying,
"How is it that this man has learning,[a] when he has never studied?"

b. Jesus Explains That His Teaching Is God's Message And Not His Own

16So Jesus answered them,
"My teaching is not mine, *(Jn.12:47-50,p.195; See also Jn.8:31,p.127)*
but his who sent me;
17if any man's will is to do his will,
he shall know whether the teaching is from God
or whether I am speaking on my own authority.
18He who speaks on his own authority seeks his own glory;
but he who seeks the glory of him who sent him is true,
and in him there is no falsehood.

c. They Plot to Kill Him (Ever since Jn.5,p.51-52)

19Did not Moses give you the law?
Yet none of you keeps the law.
Why do you seek to kill me?" *[Jn.5:18; Mt.12:14;Mk.3:6 (p.55); Jn.7:1 (p.121), v.20,25;8:40,44,59; footnote p.121]*

d. The Crowds sneer at Jesus

20The people answered,
"You have a demon!
Who is seeking to kill you?"

e. He Tells Why They Hate Him. Healing A Man On the Sabbath Is No More Sabbath breaking Than Circumcision On the Sabbath

21Jesus answered them,
"I did one deed, and you all marvel at it. *(Jn.5,p.51-52)*
22Moses gave you circumcision
(not that it is from Moses, but from the fathers),
and you circumcise a man upon the sabbath.
23If on the sabbath a man receives circumcision,
so that the law of Moses may not be broken,
are you angry with me
because on the sabbath I made a man's whole body well?
24Do not judge by appearances,
but judge with right judgment."

(2) The Divine Origin of Jesus Himself

a. Some of the People Try to Figure Out Why The Rulers Allow Him To Go On

25Some of the people of Jerusalem therefore said,
"Is not this the man whom they seek to kill? *[v.19]*
26And here he is, speaking openly,
and they say nothing to him!
Can it be that the authorities really know that this is the Christ?

27"Yet we know where this man comes from;
and when the Christ appears, no one will know where he comes from."

[a]*Or* this man knows his letters.

b. Jesus Claims To Know God And To Have Come From Him

28 So Jesus proclaimed, as he taught* in the temple,
"You know me, and you know where I come from?
But I have not come of my own accord;
He who sent me is true,
and him you do not know.
29 I know him, for I come from him,
and he sent me."

c. Some Wanted To Arrest Him

30 So they sought to arrest him; *(v.32,44,45,10:39)*
but no one laid hands on him,
because his hour had not yet come. *(Jn.2:4;7:6,8,30)*

They Accepted His Claim To Be Messiah

31 Yet many of the people believed in him;
they said,
"When the Christ appears,
will he do more signs than this man has done?"

(3) The Divine Destiny of Jesus

a. They Do Attempt to Arrest Him

32 The Pharisees heard the crowd thus muttering about him,
and the chief priests and Pharisees sent officers to arrest him.

b. He Says He Will Continue For A Time And Then Go Where They Can't Come

33 Jesus then said,
"I shall be with you a little longer,
and then I will go to him who sent me;
34 you will seek me and you will not find me;
where I am you cannot come."

c. They are Mystified and Baffled

35 The Jews said to one another,
"Where does this man intend to go that we shall not find him?
Does he intend to go to the Dispersion among the Greeks and teach the Greeks?
36 What does he mean by saying,
'You will seek me and you will not find me,'
and,
'Where I am you cannot come?'"

3. ON THE LAST DAY OF THE FEAST

Jn.7:37-8:59

(1) Two Great Ceremonies Interpreted by Jesus

a. The Water Pouring Ceremony** § 116

In the Morning
Jn.7:37-44

Jesus Is The Water of Life

a. The Meaning of the Ceremony

37 On the last day of the feast, the great day,
Jesus stood up and proclaimed,
"If any one thirst, let him come to me and drink. *(Jn.4:13-14,p.34;6:35,p.98)*
38 He who believes in me,
as[a] the scripture has said,
'Out of his heart shall flow rivers of living water.'"

b. Its Fulfillment in Jesus

39 Now this he said about the Spirit,
which those who believed in him were to receive;
for as yet the Spirit had not been given,
because Jesus was not yet glorified.

c. Conflicting Opinions Cause a Division

40 When they heard these words, some of the people said,
"This is really the prophet."
41 Others said,
"This is the Christ."
But some said,
"Is the Christ to come from Galilee?
42 Has not the scripture said that the Christ is descended from David
and comes from Bethlehem, the village where David was?"

Some Believe Him A Prophet Some Believe That He Is The Messiah; Some Wish To Arrest Him, But No One Acts

43 So there was a division among the people over him.
44 Some of them wanted to arrest him,
but no one laid hands on him.

---

[a] Or let him come to me, and let him who believes in me drink. As.

*was teaching. ***This took place each morning of the feast (except perhaps the last). It was in commemoration of the water from the rock of Sinai (Ex.17:1-7;1 Cor.10:4). It was also supposed to point forward to the time of the Messiah, as Ezekiel had prophesied (Ezek.47:1-5). On this last day the crowds awaited in great expectancy for its fulfilment; then Jesus spoke, claiming to be the Messianic fulfilment of the prophecy.*

Confusion in the Sanhedrin. § 117

Jn. 7:45-52
During The Day

Jesus is The Despair of The Jewish Rulers

a. Their Police Return to Report, but Empty Handed

45The officers then went back to the chief priests and Pharisees,
who said to them,
"Why did you not bring him?" *(v.30,32,44)*

They Excuse Themselves

46The officers answered,
"No man ever spoke like this man!"

b. The Pharisees Reprimand Them

47The Pharisees answered them,
"Are you led astray, you also?
48Have any of the authorities or of the Pharisees believed in him?
49But this crowd, who do not know the law, are accursed."

c. Nicodemus Defends Jesus Timidly

50Nic-o-de´mus, *(Jn.3:1,p.31;19:39,p.246)*
who had gone to him before, and who was one of them,
said to them,
51"Does our law judge a man without first giving him a hearing
and learning what he does?"

But He Is Squelched

52They replied,
Are you from Galilee too?
Search and you will see that no prophet is to rise from Galilee." [a]

[a] *Most of the ancient authorities either omit 7:53-8:11, or insert it, with variations of the text, here or at the end of this gospel or after Luke 21:38.*

Judging An Adulterous Woman. § 118

Jn.7:53-8:1-11

53They went each to his own house,
1but Jesus went to the Mount of Olives.

Jesus Is Teaching In The Temple

2Early in the morning
he came again to the temple;

The Crowds Flock to Him

all the people came to him,
and he sat down, and taught them.

The Jews Bring An Adulterous Woman to Him to Trap Him

3The scribes and the Pharisees
brought a woman who had been caught in adultery,

and placing her in the midst,
4they said to him,

They Accuse The Woman

"Teacher, this woman
has been caught in the act of adultery.

They Quote The Law

5"Now in the law
Moses commanded us to stone such.

Then Ask His Advice

"What do you say about her?"

Their Motive, Jesus Sees Thru Their scheme

6This they said to test him,
that they might have some charge to bring against him.

He Writes On the Ground

Jesus bent down
and wrote with his finger on the ground.

They Insist

7And as they continued to ask him,
he stood up and said to them,

He Answers Them;

"Let him who is without sin among you
be the first to throw a stone at her."

Again He Writes

8And once more he bent down
and wrote with his finger on the ground.

CONTINUED ON NEXT PAGE

b. The Lamp-Lighting Ceremony.* § 119

In the Evening

Jn. 8:12-20

Jesus is The Light of The World

The Ceremony and Its Meaning: He Claims to be The Light of Life

12Again Jesus spoke to them, saying,
"I am the light of the world; *(Cp.Jn.1;5,8,9;9:5;12:35,36,46)*
he who follows me will not walk in darkness,
but will have the light of life."

They Sneer at His Claims

13The Pharisees then said to him,
"You are bearing witness to yourself;
your testimony is not true." *(v.17-18)*

Jesus Appeals to the Father's Testimony

14Jesus answered,
"Even if I do bear witness to myself,
my testimony is true,
for I know whence I have come and whither I am going,
but you do not know whence I come or whither I am going.

Which Corrobarates His Own

15"You judge according to the flesh, I judge no one.
16Yet even if I do judge, my judgment is true,
for it is not I alone that judge, but I and he[a] who sent me.
17In your law it is written
that the testimony of two men is true;
18I bear witness to myself,
and the Father who sent me bears witness to me." *(v.13)*

They Ask Where His Father Is,

19They said to him therefore,
"Where is your Father?"

Jesus Answers.

Jesus answered,
"You know neither me nor my Father;
if you knew me, you would know my Father also." *(Jn.12:44)*

Why They Didn't Arrest Him

20These words he spoke in the treasury
as he taught in the temple;
but no one arrested him, *(7:30,32,44,45;10:39)*
because his hour had not yet come. *(Jn.2:4;7:6,8,30)*

(2) Two Great Appeals Made By Jesus

a. The First Appeal - To Accept Jesus as Savior from Sin. § 120

Jn.8:21-30

Jesus is our only Savior from sin

Jesus Warns They Will Die in Sin And Cannot Come Where He Is Going, They Don't Understand

21Again he said to them,
"I go away, and you will seek me
and die in your sin;
Where I am going, you cannot come."

22Then said the Jews,
"Will he kill himself, since he says,
'Where I am going, you cannot come'?"

[a]*Many ancient authorities read* the Father. **This took place each evening of the feast, in remembrance of the pillar of fiery cloud that led Israel through the desert. It became an apt symbol of the Messiah. Jesus claims to be its fulfilment. (Ex.13:20-22;40:34;Num.7:89;9:15ff).*

Jn. 7:53-8:1-11 CONTINUED FROM BOTTOM OF PRECEDING PAGE

They All Slink Out

9But when they heard it
they went away, one by one,
beginning with the eldest,

Only the Woman is Left

And Jesus was left alone
with the woman standing before him.

Jesus Asks Where They Are

10Jesus looked up and said to her,
"Woman, where are they?
Has no one condemned you?"

He Deals With The Woman,

11She said, "No one, Lord."

He Seeks Not Condemnation But Repentance,

And Jesus said,
"Neither do I condemn you;
go, and do not sin again." *(Jn.5:14,p.52)*

Jesus Says
Unless They Believe
They Will Die

23He said to them,
"You are from below, I am from above;
you are of this world, I am not of this world.
24I told you that you would die in your sins,
for you will die in your sins unless you believe that I am he."

They Ask Who He Is

25They said to him,
"Who are you?"

He Answers,
The Messenger
Of God

Jesus said to them,
"Even what I have told you from the beginning.[a]
26I have much to say about you and much to judge;
but he who sent me is true,
and I declare to the world what I have heard from him."

They Fail
to Understand

27They did not understand that he spoke to them of the Father.

Jesus Replies
That After
They Crucify Him
They Will Understand
That He Always
Does God's Will

28So Jesus said,
"When you have lifted up the Son of man, *(Jn.12:32-34,p.194;Jn.3:14,p.32)*
then you will know that I am he,
and that I do nothing on my own authority
but speak thus as the Father taught me.

29"And he who sent me is with me;
he has not left me alone, *(Jn.16:31,p.219)*
for I always do what is pleasing to him."

Many Do Believe
But Superficially

30As he spoke thus, many believed in him.

b. The Second Appeal - To Continue In His Word. § 121

Jn. 8:31-59

Jesus Reveals the Truth That Makes Men Free, As They Obey It

True Freedom.
So Jesus
Urges Them
To Continue
Until They Are Free

31Jesus then said to the Jews who had believed in him, *(See Jn.7:16-18,p.123;12:47-50, p.195)*
"If you continue in my word, you are my disciples,
32and you will know the truth, and the truth will make you free."

They Retort
That They
Are No Slaves

33They answered him,
"We are descendants of Abraham,
and have never been in bondage to anyone.
How is it that you say,
'You will be made free'?"

He Says
Sin Enslaves

34Jesus answered them,
"Truly, truly, I say to you,
every one who commits sin is a slave to sin.

But That
He
Makes Free

35The slave does not continue in the house forever;
the son continues forever.
36So if the Son makes you free,
you will be free indeed.

Then Jesus Answers
Their Other Claim

Real Parentage, Too,
is Spiritual

37"I know that you are descendants of Abraham;
yet you seek to kill me,
because my word finds no place in you.
38I speak of what I have seen with my Father,
and you do what you have heard from your father."

(a) Jesus says
They Are Not
True Children of
Abraham

39They answered him,
"Abraham is our father." *(Cf.Mt.3:9,p.23)*

If They Were
They Would
Act Like It

Jesus said to them,
"If you were Abraham's children,
you would do what Abraham did,
40but now you seek to kill me,
a man who has told you the truth
which I heard from God;
this is not what Abraham did.
41You do what your father did."

Then They
Claim To Be
Children of God

They said to him,
"We were not born of fornication;
we have one Father, even God."

[a]Or Why do I talk to you at all?

(b) Jesus Says Neither Are They True Sons of God

42Jesus said to them,
"If God were your Father, you would love me,
for I proceeded and came forth from God;
I came not of my own accord, but he sent me.

(c) But in Reality, Sons of The Devil Because They Do The Devil's Will

43"Why do you not understand what I say?
It is because you cannot bear to hear my word.
44You are of your father the devil,
and your will is to do your father's desires.

Because They Do The Works of The Devil

"He was a murderer from the beginning, [*Gen.1:1*]
and has nothing to do with the truth,
because there is no truth in him. [*Gen.3*]
When he lies, he speaks according to his own nature,
for he is a liar and the father of lies.

and Because They Refuse To Believe Him.

45"But, because I tell the truth, you do not believe me.
46Which of you convicts me of sin?
If I tell the truth, why do you not believe me?
47He who is of God hears the words of God;
the reason why you do not hear them is that you are not of God."

Then They Make A Double Accusation: You Are a Samaritan And Have A Demon

48The Jews answered him,
"Are we not right in saying that you are a Samaritan
and have a demon?" *(Cf.§ 69 and footnote,p.71)*

No: But Because I Honor God, You Dishonor Me

49Jesus answered,
"I have not a demon;
I honor my Father,
and you dishonor me.

But God Will Judge. If They Believe, They Will Not Die in Sin

50Yet I do not seek my own glory; *(5:41,p.53)*
there is One who seeks it and he will be the judge.
51Truly, truly, I say to you,
if any one keeps my word, he will never see death."

Then They Accuse Him of Vaunting Himself, Claiming To Be Greater Than Abraham Or The Prophets

52The Jews said to him,
"Now we know that you have a demon.
Abraham died, as did the prophets;
and you say,
'If any one keeps my word, he will never taste death.'
53Are you greater than our father Abraham, who died?
And the prophets died!
Whom do you make yourself to be?"

He Is Not Guilty, But Is True to God

54Jesus answered,
"If I glorify myself, my glory is nothing;
it is my Father who glorifies me,
of whom you say that he is your God.

They Do Not Know God But He Knows God He Dare Not Deny It And He Keeps God's Word

55"But you have not known him;
I know him.
If I said, I do not know him,
I should be a liar like you;
but I do know him
and I keep his word.

Abraham Rejoiced As He Foresaw The Messianic Glory

56"Your father Abraham rejoiced that he was to see my day;
he saw it and was glad."

They Misunderstand And Are Horrified

57The Jews then said to him,
"You are not yet fifty years old,
and have you seen Abraham?"[a]

Christ Asserts His Preexistence

58Jesus said to them,
"Truly, truly, I say to you,
before Abraham was, I am."

They Attempt to Mob Jesus

59So they took up stones to throw at him;*
but Jesus hid himself, *(Jn.12:36,p.194;cf.Lk.4:30, p.38)*
and went out of the temple.

....

[a] *Some ancient authorities read* has Abraham seen you? **Although there have been bitter controversies, and they even "sought to kill" Jesus, yet this is the first time that physical violence is actually attempted. The attempt is repeated when next He comes to Jerusalem, three months later (Jn.10: 39-40)*

Jn.9:1-10:21

(1) Healing A Man Born Blind, And the Ensuing Controversy. § 122

Jn. 9:1-34

Jesus is the Light of the World

a. THE CURE

(a) Jesus Heals The Man

As They Flee They See A Blind Man

1As he passed by, he saw a man blind from his birth.

*The Disciples Ask Who's To Blame**

2And his disciples asked him,
"Rabbi, who sinned,* this man or his parents,
that he was born blind?"

Jesus Answers Our Part Is Not to Fix Blame, But to Rescue From Evil

3Jesus answered,
"It was not that this man sinned, or his parents,
but that the works of God might be made manifest in him.
4We must work the works of him who sent me, while it is day;
night comes, when no one can work.
5As long as I am in the world, I am the light of the world." *(Jn.1:5,8,9; 8:12; 12:35-36,46)*

Jesus Anoints The Man's Eyes With Clay

6As he said this, he spat on the ground
and made clay of the spittle
and anointed the man's eyes with the clay,

And Instructs Him To Go, Wash.

7saying to him,
"Go, wash in the pool of Si-lo′am"(which means Sent).

He Obeys

So he went and washed

And Is Healed.

and came back seeing.

(b) The Neighbors Verify the Cure

The Neighbors Are Bewildered And Doubt His Identity,

8The neighbors
and those who had seen him before as a beggar, said,
"Is not this the man who used to sit and beg?"

9Some said,
"It is he";
others said,
"No, but he is like him."

The Man Asserts His Identity

He said,
"I am the man."

They Ask How He Was Cured

10They said to him,
"Then how were your eyes opened?"

He Explains

11He answered,
"The man called Jesus made clay
and anointed my eyes
and said to me, 'Go to Si-lo′am and wash';

so I went and washed
and received my sight."

12They said to him,
"Where is he?"

He said,
"I do not know."

....

*The Disciples were interested in fixing blame; and since sickness was believed to be the result of sin; some believed he had sinned before he was born, either in the prenatal state, or in a previous existence; some believed the sins of the parents are "visited upon the children."

b. THE CONTROVERSY

(a) The Pharisees Discuss the Case

The Man Is Brought to The Pharisees

13 They brought to the Pharisees the man who had formerly been blind.
14 Now it was a sabbath day
when Jesus made the clay
and opened his eyes.

They Ask Him How He Has Been Healed

15 The Pharisees again asked him how he had received his sight.

And he said to them,

"He put clay on my eyes, and I washed, and I see."

They Dispute Among Themselves

16 Some of the Pharisees said,
"This man is not from God,
for he does not keep the sabbath."

But others said,
"How can a man who is a sinner do such signs?"

There was a division among them.

They Ask The Man

17 So they again said to the blind man,
"What do you say about him,
since he has opened your eyes?"

He said,
"He is a prophet."

(b) The Pharisees Interview His Parents

The Jews Call His Parents and Question Them

18 The Jews did not believe
that he had been blind and had received his sight,
until they called the parents of the man who had received his sight,
19 and asked them,
"Is this your son,
who you say was born blind?
How then does he now see?"

His Parents Dodge the Issue

20 His parents answered,

"We know that this is our son,
and that he was born blind;
21 but how he now sees we do not know,
nor do we know who opened his eyes.
Ask him; he is of age,
he will speak for himself."

*Because They Fear Persecution and Excommunication**

22 His parents said this because they feared the Jews,
for the Jews had already agreed
that if any one should confess him to be Christ,
he was to be put out of the synagogue. *(v.34-35;Lk.11:52,p.141;Jn.12:42; Mt.23;13,p.19*

23 Therefore his parents said,
"He is of age,
ask him."

....

**Such excommunication from the synagogue was a serious affair inasmuch as it involved both social ostracism and economic boycott. Noone would sell to him or buy from him.*

(c) The Pharisees Again Summon The Man and Put Him On Trial

The Pharisees Give Pious Advice

24 So for the second time
they called the man who had been blind,
and said to him,
"Give God the praise;
we know that this man is a sinner."

The Man Defends Himself

25 He answered,
"Whether he is a sinner, I do not know;
one thing I know, that though I was blind, now I see."

They Probe Further

26 They said to him,
"What did he do to you?
How did he open your eyes?"

He Thrusts Home

27 He answered them,
"I have told you already,
and you would not listen.
Why do you want to hear it again?
Do you too want to become his disciples?"

They Are Exasperated and Revile Him

28 And they reviled him, saying,
"You are his disciple,
but we are disciples of Moses.
29 We know that God has spoken to Moses,
but as for this man,
we do not know where he comes from."

The Courageous Eloquence of Conviction

30 The man answered,
"Why, this is a marvel!
You do not know where he comes from,
and yet he opened my eyes.

The Petty Contempt Of Dishonest Officials

31 "We know that God does not listen to sinners,
but if any one is a worshiper of God and does his will,
God listens to him.

32 "Never since the world began
has it been heard that any one opened the eyes of a man born blind.

33 "If this man were not from God,
he could do nothing."

They Revile Him

34 They answered him,
"You were born in utter sin,
and would you teach us?"

(d) They Excommunicate Him

And they cast him out. *(v.22,35;15:18-26; p.217)*

(2) Winning the Healed Man to Discipleship

And the Ensuing Controversy. § 123

Jn. 9:35-10:21

Jesus Seeks Out the Man and Wins Him to Discipleship

(Jesus is the Judge of the World, and the True Shepherd of His Sheep)

Jesus Hunts Him Up

35 Jesus heard that they had cast him out,
and having found him he said,
"Do you believe in the Son of man?[a]*

He Wins the Man to Discipleship

36 He answered,
"And who is he, sir,
that I may believe in him?"

37 Jesus said to him,
"You have seen him,
and it is he who speaks to you." (*Or who is speaking with you*)

38 He said,
"Lord, I believe";

and he worshiped him.

Jesus Comments On The Situation

39 Jesus said,
"For judgment I came into this world, (*cf. Jn. 3:17-19, p. 32; 5:22ff. p. 52; Jn. 12:47-48, p. 195*)
that those who do not see may see,
and that those who see may become blind."

The Pharisees Are Embittered

40 Some of the Pharisees near him heard this,
and they said to him,
"Are we also blind?"

Jesus Sternly Rebukes Them And Enforces His Rebuke With a Priceless Parable

41 Jesus said to them,
"If you were blind, you would have no guilt;
but now that you say,
'We see,'
your guilt remains."

The Parable of the Good Shepherd.** § 124

Jn. 10:1-21

(a) The Parable

Jesus Replies to Them by Parable

1 "Truly, truly, I say to you,
he who does not enter the sheepfold by the door
but climbs in by another way,
that man is a thief and a robber;

God's Sheep and False Shepherds

2 but he who enters by the door
is the shepherd of the sheep.

The True Shepherd and His Sheep

3 "To him the gatekeeper opens;
the sheep hear his voice,
and he calls his own sheep by name
and leads them out.

4 "When he has brought out all his own,
he goes before them,
and the sheep follow him,
for they know his voice.

5 "A stranger they will not follow,
but they will flee from him,
for they do not know the voice of strangers."

They Do Not Understand His Parable

6 This figure Jesus used with them,
but they did not understand what he was saying to them.

....

[a] *Many ancient authorities read* the Son of God. *(In either case it meant "The Messiah").

***This Parable was Christ's further discussion of the excommunication of the man who defended Jesus and "believed in Him as Messiah." (See 9:34 and 35). It is a stern rebuke of the Jewish Rulers for that wicked decision.*

(b) The Interpretation of the Parable

Jn. 10:7-18

He Explains Jesus is the Door of the Sheep

7So Jesus again said to them,
" Truly, truly, I say to you,
I am the door of the sheep.
8All who came before me are thieves and robbers;
but the sheep did not heed them.

9" I am the door;
if any one enters by me,
he will be saved,
and will go in and out and find pasture.

10" The thief comes only to steal and kill and destroy;
I came that they may have life,
and have it abundantly.

Jesus is the Good Shepherd of the Sheep

11" I am the good shepherd.
The good shepherd lays down his life for the sheep.

12" He who is a hireling, and not a shepherd,
whose own the sheep are not,
sees the wolf coming
and leaves the sheep and flees;

13" and the wolf snatches them and scatters them.
He flees because he is a hireling
and cares nothing for the sheep.

He is Faithful to Death

Jesus Knows His Sheep

14" I am the good shepherd;
I know my own and my own know me,
15as the Father knows me and I know the Father;
and I lay down my life for the sheep.

There is One Flock and One Shepherd

16" And I have other sheep,
that are not of this fold; *(cf. Jn. 11:52, p. 163)*
I must bring them also,
and they will heed my voice.
So there shall be one flock, one shepherd.

The Commandment to Lay Down His Life

God Has Commanded Jesus to Lay Down His Life, In Order That He May Take It Again

17" For this reason the Father loves me,
because I lay down my life
that I may take it again.
18No one takes it from me,
but I lay it down of my own accord.

So He Has Been Authorized By The Father To Do It

" I have power* to lay it down,
and I have power* to take it again;
this charge I have received from my Father."

(c) The Outcome of the Controversy

Jn. 10:19-21

Again

19There was again a division among the Jews because of these words.

The Result Is Division

20Many of them said,
" He has a demon, and he is mad; why listen to him?" *(Jn. 8:48, 52, p. 128)*

21Others said,
" These are not the sayings of one who has a demon.
Can a demon open the eyes of the blind?"

....

**Gk. authority, or the right.*

(B) EVANGELIZING IN JUDEA OUTSIDE JERUSALEM (Luke 10:1-13:21*)*
(From the Feast of Tabernacles, Oct. A.D. 29;
To the Feast of Dedication, Dec. A.D. 29)

**Footnote to Lk. 10:1 - next page.*

"After this" evidently refers to the section just preceding. This section speaks specifically of time and places (Lk.9:51,52,56,57,p.122).

These statements make it plain that the time *is somewhere near the end. It is also clear that Jesus and his disciples are on the way to Jerusalem.*

The situation of Lk. 9:51 corresponds rather exactly with Mt. 19:1a, and Mk. 10:1a. Then Jn.7:2-10 comes to our aid and makes these general statements concrete and specific. Jesus went "privately" to the feast (i.e. not when the pilgrim crowds went, and clamored for Him to go along, see Jn.7:2-9, but 3 or 4 days after they were gone). Also he went, not by the usual round about pilgrim route, through Perea, but by the direct route, through Samaria.

Then "in the midst of the feast," Jesus arrives (Jn. 7:14) and is teaching. So also "on the last day of the feast" he is teaching (7:37). Things work up to a climax in Jn. 10:19-20.

All of these considerations would seem to explain the phrase, "after this" in Lk. 10:1. And it would make this phrase equal to, "After the Feast of Tabernacles" *Jesus sent out the Seventy.*

If then we ask where *Jesus was just then? and where (to what places) He sent the Seventy, all we can say is that there is no hint anywhere that Jesus had, in the meantime, left Judea. In Jn. 10:22, two and a half months later, at the Feast of Dedication, Jesus is still in Judea and shows up again at Jerusalem. Now if He was in Jerusalem at Jn. 7:14 and again at 10:22 the best guess is that He remained in Judea during those months; and there is nothing to contradict this idea.*

Then when Jesus does *leave Judea, after the Feast of Dedication, John expressly says so (Jn.10:40), and proceeds to characterize and sum up His work there and its results, Luke again supplying the details (see next division* § 136-144*)*
So then John 7:14-10:21 fits exactly into the gap between Lk. 9 and 10.

Between Jn. 10:21 and 10:22 there is a gap of three months, from the Feast of Tabernacles to The Feast of Dedication. John tells us nothing of what went on during that time. Neither do Matthew or Mark. Only to Luke are we indebted for the detailed, concrete incidents of these three months from the last half of October to the last week of December. These events follow next, and they all, so far as any evidence to the contrary is concerned, took place in Judea. See also footnotes on next two pages.

***Just when The Seventy* returned *we do not know. Certainly it was not immediately. It may have been at the close of this period of "Evangelizing in Judea" (i.e.* after *Lk. 13:21). Compare the return of "The Twelve", just before Passover, at the* close *of "The Last Tour Throughout Galilee." (See Mk. 6:7; and Mk. 6:30; p. 92,* § 86 *).*

(B) EVANGELIZING IN JUDEA
Lk. 10:1-13:21

1. OPENING EVENTS

(1) Sending Out the Seventy. § 125

Mt. 11:20-24 *Lk. 10:1-16*

(Probably Just After the Feast of Tabernacles)

Lk.

a. Jesus Sends Messengers Ahead

1After this* the Lord appointed seventy[a] others,
and sent them on ahead of him, two by two,
into every town and place where he himself was about to come.

b. He Commands Them To Pray For Other Workers

2And he said to them,
"The harvest is plentiful,**
but the laborers are few;
pray therefore the Lord of the harvest
to send out laborers into his harvest.

c. He Gives The Charge

(a) Their Danger

3"Go your way;
behold, I send you out as lambs in the midst of wolves.

(b) No Impediments

4"Carry no purse, no bag, no sandals;
and salute no man on the road.

(c) Their Method of Procedure

5"Whatever house you enter, first say,
'Peace be to this house!'
6And if a son of peace is there, your peace shall rest upon him;
but if not, it shall return to you.
7And remain in the same house,
eating and drinking what they provide,
for the laborer deserves his wages;
do not go from house to house.

(d) If Received

8"Whenever you enter a town and they receive you,
eat what is set before you;
9heal the sick in it
and say to them,
'The kingdom of God has come near to you.'

(e) If Rejected

10"But whenever you enter a town and they do not receive you,
go into its streets and say,
11'Even the dust of your town that clings to our feet,
we wipe off against you;
nevertheless know this, that the kingdom of God has come near.'

(f) The Penalty for Rejecting

12"I tell you,
It shall be more tolerable on that day for Sodom
than for that town."

---

[a]*Many ancient authorities read* seventy-two.

**See footnote on previous page.*

***We can get an idea of just how "plenteous the harvest" was, if we recall that up to now, Jesus had thoroughly evangelized only Galilee and Jerusalem. But all of Judea, outside the capital was almost untouched. Neither had He more than touched Perea. Now that He has been practically excluded from Galilee, He will concentrate on the up-to-now neglected provinces, Judea and Perea. And that is where nearly all the recorded events that follow take place,--Lk. 10:1-13:21 in Judea; and Lk. 13:22-19:28, in Perea. After that there remains only the consummation of His whole life and work at Jerusalem.*

And since only six months remain till "His hour will have come," and since "the harvest is so great," He appoints seventy more helpers, making 35 plus 6 teams of two each.

The Peril of Rejecting God's Messengers

	Mt.	*Lk.*
	20Then he began to upbraid the cities where most of his mighty works had been done, because they did not repent.	
Woe to Chorazin and Bethsaida	21"Woe to you, Cho-ra'zin! woe to you, Beth-sa'i-da! For if the mighty works done in you had been done in Tyre and Sidon, they would have repented long ago in sackcloth and ashes.	13"Woe to you, Cho-ra'zin! woe to you, Beth-sa'i-da! For if the mighty works done in you had been done in Tyre and Sidon, they would have repented long ago, sitting in sackcloth and ashes.
A Worse Judgment Than That Of Tyre and Sidon Awaits Them	22"But I tell you, it shall be more tolerable on the day of judgment for Tyre and Sidon than for you.	14"But it shall be more tolerable in the judgment for Tyre wnd Sidon than for you.
Woe to Capernaum	23"And you, Ca-per'na-um, will you be exalted to heaven? You shall be brought down to Hades. For if the mighty works done in you had been done in Sodom, it would have remained until this day.	15"And you, Ca-per'na-um, will you be exalted to heaven?. You shall be brought down to Hades.
A Worse Judgment Than That of Sodom	24"But I tell you that it shall be more tolerable on the day of judgment for the land of Sodom. than for you."	*Cf. v. 12*
Rejecting Christ's Messengers Means Rejecting Christ		16"He who hears you hears me, *(Jn.12:44-50)* and he who rejects you rejects me, and he who rejects me rejects him who sent me."

[2. The Return of the Seventy*, See § 134]
Lk. 10:17-24

[17The seventy returned with joy, saying,
"Lord, even the demons are subject
to us in your name."

18And he said to them,
"I saw Satan fall like lightning from heaven.
19Behold, I have given you authority
to tread upon serpents and scorpions,
and over all the power of the enemy;
and nothing shall hurt you.
20Nevertheless do not rejoice in this,
that the spirits are subject to you;
but rejoice that your names are written in heaven."

21In that same hour
he rejoiced in the Holy Spirit and said,
"I thank thee, Father,
Lord of heaven and earth,
that thou hast hidden these things
from the wise and understanding,
and hast revealed them to babes;
yea, Father,
for such was thy gracious will.[a]

22"All things have been delivered
to me by my Father;
and no one knows who the Son is except the Father,
or who the Father is except the Son
and anyone to whom
the Son chooses to reveal him."

23Then turning to the disciples he said privately,
"Blessed are the eyes which see what you see!
24For I tell you that many prophets and kings
desired to see what you see,
and did not see it,
and to hear what you hear,
and did not hear it."]

....

**How long after they were sent out, they returned is nowhere indicated. So it seems best not to disturb the order of Luke's record. The best guess is that they returned at the close of this period when Jesus came back to Jerusalem--after about 3 months-to the Feast of Dedication. (See pp.134 for the fuller explanation, and also § 134] for the probable chronological sequence of events.)*

[a]Or it was well-pleasing before Thee.

(3) The Good Samaritan. § 126
Lk. 10:25-37

The Occasion.

A Lawyer's Question

25And behold, a lawyer stood up to put him to the test, saying,
"Teacher, what shall I do to inherit eternal life?"

Our Lord's Question

26He said to him,
"What is written in the law? How do you read?"

The Lawyer's Reply

27And he answered,
"You shall love the Lord your God with all your heart,
and with all your soul,
and with all your strength,
and with all your mind;
and your neighbor as yourself."

Jesus says "You Are Right"

28And he said to him,
"You have answered right;
do this, and you will live."

The Lawyer Quibbles

29But he, desiring to justify himself, said to Jesus,
"And who is my neighbor?"

The Story

Jesus Tells a Story, A Desperately Needy Situation

30Jesus replied,
"A man was going down from Jerusalem to Jericho,
and he fell among robbers,
who stripped him and beat him,
and departed, leaving him half dead.

A Priest Shuns His Duty

31"Now by chance a priest was going down that road;
and when he saw him he passed by on the other side.

A Levite also

32So likewise a Levite,
when he came to the place and saw him,
passed by on the other side.

A Samaritan Shows Compassion

33"But a Samaritan, as he journeyed, came to where he was;
and when he saw him, he had compassion,

Gives Him First Aid

34and went to him,
and bound up his wounds, pouring on oil and wine;

Takes Him To a Shelter

"Then he set him on his own beast,
and brought him to an inn,
and took care of him.

Provides Expenses, Promises Further Care

35"And the next day he took out two denarii,[a]
and gave them to the innkeeper, saying,
'Take care of him;
and whatever more you spend,
I will repay you when I come back.'

Its Interpretation

The Moral Is Revealed By a Question

36"Which of these three, do you think,
proved neighbor to the man who fell among the robbers?"

The Truth Is Brought Home

37He said,
"The one who showed mercy on him."

It Remains To Be Done

And Jesus said to him,
"Go and do likewise."

....

[a]*See note on Mt. 18:28.*

(4) Visiting Martha and Mary. § 127

Lk. 10:38-42

Jesus is Received by Martha

38 Now as they went on their way,
he entered a village;
and a woman named Martha received him into her house.

Mary Shows Deeper Interest

39 And she had a sister called Mary,
who also sat at the Lord's feet
and listened to his teaching.

Martha Is Distracted and Complains Fretfully

40 But Martha was distracted with much serving;
and she went to him and said,
"Lord, do you not care that my sister has left me to serve alone?
Tell her then to help me."

The Master Rebukes Her and Commends Mary

41 But the Lord answered her,
"Martha, Martha, you are anxious and troubled about many things;
42 one thing is needful.[a]
Mary has chosen the good portion,
which shall not be taken away from her."

(5) Teaching How To Pray. § 128

Lk. 11:1-13

The Occasion

Jesus Prays

1 He was praying in a certain place,
and when he ceased, one of his disciples said to him,

The Disciples Request To Be Taught To Pray

"Lord, teach us to pray,
as John taught his disciples."

The Lesson

A Former Lesson Is Reviewed (See Mt. 6:9ff.)*

2 And he said to them,
"When you pray, say: *
'Father,
hallowed be thy name.
Thy kingdom come.

3 "Give us each day our daily bread;[b]
4 And forgive us our sins,
for we ourselves
forgive every one who is indebted to us;
and lead us not into temptation."

Whole-hearted Perseverance in Praying Is Urged By a Striking Illustration

5 And he said to them,
"Which of you who has a friend
will go to him at midnight and say to him,
'Friend, lend me three loaves;
6 for a friend of mine has arrived on a journey,
and I have nothing to set before him;'

7 "And he will answer from within,
'Do not bother me; the door is now shut,
and my children are with me in bed;
I cannot get up and give you anything'?

8 "I tell you,
though he will not get up and give him anything because he is his friend,
yet because of his importunity
he will rise and give him whatever he needs.

---

[a] *Many ancient authorities read* few things are needful, or only one.
[b] *Or,* our bread for the morrow.
**In Chapters 10-17 of Luke many sayings and teachings are also given by Mt. and Mk. but in other life situations; we must either suppose that Jesus taught numerous truths on various occasions like every other great teacher, or else tear Luke's story into fragments and thus disregard his fine sense of both historical and literary sequences. (See footnote, p.146)*

Another Lesson Reviewed

The Method of Persevering in Prayer Is Suggested

9 "And I tell you,
Ask, and it will be given you;
seek, and you will find;
knock, and it will be opened to you.

The Reason: is The Certainity of God's Answer To Prayer

10 "For every one who asks receives,
and he who seeks finds,
and to him who knocks it will be opened.

An Illustration

A Loving Father's Good Gifts Are Certain

11 "What father among you,
if his son asks for[a] a fish, will instead of a fish give him a serpent;
12 or if he asks for an egg, will give him a scorpion?

A New Turn of Thought

His All-Inclusive Gift Is Promised

13 "If you then, who are evil,
know how to give good gifts to your children,
how much more will the heavenly Father
give the Holy Spirit to those who ask him?"

2. CONTROVERSIES AND WARNINGS

(I) Casting Out Demons by the "Finger of God". § 129

*Lk. 11:14 -36**

[*Cf. Mt. 12:22-45.* § 69 *,p.71ff.*]

The Occasion

A Stupendous Miracle Is Witnessed

14 Now he was casting out a demon that was dumb;

when the demon had gone out,
the dumb man spoke,

The People Are Amazed

and the people marveled.

Some Criticise Blasphemously
Others Ask For A Catastrophic Sign

15 But some of them said,
"He casts out demons by Be-el´ze-bub,[b] the prince of demons";
16 while others, to try him,
sought from him a sign from heaven.

The Teaching of Jesus

He Rebukes Their Cavils

Jesus Refutes Their False Explanation
a. He Shows Its Absurdity

17 But he, knowing their thoughts,
said to them,
"Every kingdom divided against itself is laid waste,
and house falls upon house.

b. He Disproves by their Own Practices.

18 "And if Satan also is divided against himself,
how will his kingdom stand?
For you say that I cast out demons by Be-el´ze-bub.

c. He Gives The True Explanation:

19 "And if I cast out demons by Be-el´ze-bub,
by whom do your sons cast them out?
Therefore they shall be your judges.

(a) His Power to Cast Out Demons Comes from God

20 "But if it is by the finger of God that I cast out demons,
then the kingdom of God has come upon you.

[a] *Some ancient authorities insert* a loaf, will give him a stone? or if he asks for. [b] *Greek* Beelzebul.
**Compare Mt. 12:22-45. This is either the same event (in part) as that in Mt., or a similar one on a much later occasion, and not in Galilee, but in Judea. (See footnote p.146)*

(b) Satan Jealously Guards His Possessions and Must be Overpowered

21 "When a strong man, fully armed, guards his own palace,
his goods are in peace;
22 but when one stronger than he assails him and overcomes him,
he takes away his armor in which he trusted,
and divides his spoil.

(c) Satan Does Not Help Jesus But Hinders

23 "He who is not with me is against me;
and he who does not gather with me scatters.

(d) The Evil Spirit Is Persistent

24 "When the unclean spirit has gone out of a man,
he passes through waterless places seeking rest;
and finding none he says,
'I will return to my house from which I came.'

25 "And when he comes, he finds it swept and put in order.

(e) And Will Return Whenever He Can

26 "Then he goes
and brings seven other spirits more evil than himself,
and they enter and dwell there;
and the last state of that man becomes worse than the first."

A Woman Is Answered

d. An Interruption Is Turned to Account A Woman's Enthusiasm for Jesus

27 As he said this,
a woman in the crowd raised her voice and said to him,
"Blessed is the womb that bore you, and the breasts that you sucked!"

Jesus' Reply

28 But he said,
"Blessed rather are those who hear the word of God and keep it!"

Jesus Rebukes The Demand for "A Sign"
The True Sign from Heaven

e. An Unreasonable Demand Is Rejected

29 When the crowds were increasing,

he began to say,

(a) Evil Men Demand Signs

"This generation is an evil generation;
it seeks a sign,

(b) No Sign Is Given Except That of The Resurrection

but no sign shall be given to it except the sign of Jonah.
30 For as Jonah became a sign to the men of Nin´e-veh,
so will the Son of man be to this generation.

(c) Christ's Wisdom Is Greater Than That of Solomon

31 "The queen of the south will arise at the judgment
with the men of this generation and condemn them;
for she came from the ends of the earth to hear the wisdom of Solomon,
and behold, something greater than Solomon is here.

(d) His Preaching Is Better Attested Than Jonah's

32 "The men of Nin´e-veh will arise at the judgment
with this generation and condemn it;
for they repented at the preaching of Jonah,
and behold, something greater than Jonah is here.

(e) Christ Is God's Light Exhibited to Men

33 "No one after lighting a lamp
puts it in a cellar or under a bushel,
but on a stand,
that those who enter may see the light.

(f) Hence Darkness Is Due to Bad Eyes

34 "Your eye is the lamp of your body;
when your eye is sound, your whole body is full of light;
but when it is not sound, your body is full of darkness.

(g) Examine Your Own Eyes, So That

35 "Therefore be careful lest the light in you be darkness.

(h) You May Have Fulness of Light

36 "If then your whole body is full of light, having no part dark,
it will be wholly bright, as when a lamp with its rays gives you light."

(2) Dining With a Pharisee. § 130 *(Cf.* §§ 66 *and* 139

Lk. 11:37-54

A Pharisee's Selfrighteous Formalism Rebuked

Jesus Is Invited to Dine With A Pharisee

37While he was speaking, a Pharisee asked him to dine with him;
so he went in and sat at table.

He Is Criticized For Not Washing Ceremonially

38The Pharisee was astonished to see
that he did not first wash before dinner.

He Teaches About Inward Cleansing vs. Outward

39And the Lord said to him,
"Now you Pharisees cleanse the outside of the cup and of the dish,
but inside you are full of extortion and wickedness. *(Mt.23:26,p.192)*
40You fools! Did not he who made the outside make the inside also?
41But give for alms those things which are within;
and behold, everything is clean for you.

And of Moral Defilement vs. Ceremonial Pollution

42"But woe to you Pharisees!
For you tithe the mint and rue and every herb, *(Mt.23:23,p.192)*
and neglect justice and the love of God;
these you ought to have done
without neglecting the others.

He Warns Against Ostentation and Hypocrisy

43"Woe to you Pharisees!
For you love the best seats in synagogues *(Cp. § 175)*
and salutations in the market places.
44Woe to you!
For you are like the graves which are not seen,
and men walk over them without knowing it."

A Lawyer's Objection Overruled

A Lawyer Challenges Him

45One of the lawyers answered him,
"Teacher, in saying this you reproach us also."

He Gives A Three-Fold Warning In Reply
(a) Because of Harsh Demands

46And he said,
"Woe to you lawyers also!
For you load men with burdens hard to bear, *(Mt.23:4,p.191)*
and you yourselves do not touch the burdens with one of your fingers.

(b) Because of Persecuting Prophets and Apostles

47"Woe to you! *(Mt.23:29-36,p.192)*
For you build the tombs of the prophets whom your fathers killed.
48So you are witnesses and consent to the deeds of your fathers;
for they killed them, and you build their tombs.
49Therefore also the wisdom of God said,
'I will send them prophets and apostles, *(Mt.23:34)*
some of whom they will kill and persecute,'

Blood-Guilt Results

50"that the blood of all the prophets, *(Mt.23:30-36,p.193)*
shed from the foundation of the world
may be required of this generation,
51from the blood of Abel to the blood of Zech-a-ri´ah,
who perished between the altar and the sanctuary.
Yes, I tell you,
It shall be required of this generation.

(c) Because of Perverting God's Message

52"Woe to you lawyers!
For you have taken away the key of knowledge;
you did not enter yourselves, *(Jn.9:22,p.130)*
and you hindered those who were entering."

They Vehemently Attack Jesus As He Comes Out

53As he went away from there,
the scribes and the Pharisees began to press him hard,
and to provoke him to speak of many things,
54lying in wait for him, to catch at something he might say.

(3) Warning His Disciples Against the Spirit of Pharisaism. § 131

Lk. 12:1-59

a. Beware of Hypocrisy (1-12)

(To His Disciples In the Crowd)

The Immense And Eager Crowds

1 In the meantime,
when so many thousands of the multitude had gathered together
that they trod upon one another,

Jesus Warns Against Hypocrisy It is Useless

he began to say to his disciples first,
"Beware of the leaven of the Pharisees, which is hypocrisy. *(§ 100, p.107)*
2 Nothing is covered up that will not be revealed,
or hidden that will not be known.
3 Whatever you have said in the dark *(Mt.10:27, p.89)*
shall be heard in the light,
and what you have whispered in private rooms
shall be proclaimed upon the housetops.

Fear Only To Do Wrong

4 "I tell you, my friends,
do not fear those who kill the body, *(Mt.10:26-28, p.89)*
and after that have no more that they can do.
5 But I will warn you whom to fear:
fear him, who after he has killed, has power to cast into hell;[a]
yes, I tell you, fear him!

God Will Protect

6 "Are not five sparrows sold for two pennies? *(Mt.10:29-31, p.90)*
And not one of them is forgotten before God.
7 Why, even the hairs of your head are all numbered.
Fear not; you are of more value than many sparrows.

Confessing and Denying Christ

8 "And I tell you,
every one who acknowledges me before men,
the Son of man also will acknowledge before the angels of God;
9 but he who denies me before men
will be denied before the angels of God. *(Mt.10:32-33, p.90)*
10 And every one who speaks a word against the Son of man
will be forgiven;
but he who blasphemes against the Holy Spirit
will not be forgiven.

The Spirit of God Will Defend You When Accused (e.g. Ac. 4:8f.)

11 "And when they bring you before the synagogues *(Mt.10:19-20, p.89)*
and the rulers and the authorities,
do not be anxious how or what you are to answer or what you are to say;
12 for the Holy Spirit will teach you in that very hour *(Mk.13:11, p.198)*
what you ought to say."

b. Beware of Covetousness (13-21)

(The Sin of the Rich) *(Lk.16:19-31, p.158)*

(To a Man In The Crowd/ Who Interrupts)

The Occasion
A Man Makes a Request;
Jesus Answers Him.

13 One of the multitude said to him,
"Teacher, bid my brother divide the inheritance with me."

14 But he said to him,
"Man, who made me a judge or divider over you?"

Then He Speaks to All: About The Fundamental Fallacy of Covetousness

15 And he said to them,
"Take heed, and beware of all covetousness;
for a man's life does not consist
in the abundance of his possessions."

He Illustrates What He Means By the Parable of The Rich Farmer

16 And he told them a parable, saying,
"The land of a rich man brought forth plentifully;

Who has a Bumper Crop, His Barns won't Hold It;

17 "and he thought to himself,
'What shall I do, for I have nowhere to store my crops?'
18 And he said,
'I will do this:
I will pull down my barns, and build larger ones;
and there I will store all my grain and my goods.
19 And I will say to my soul,
Soul, you have ample goods laid up for many years;
take your ease, eat, drink, be merry.'

So He Plans To Build Bigger, And Then To Take Things Easy-- Self Indulgence Not self-discipline And self-sacrifice

[a] *Greek* Gehenna.

But God Calls Him a Fool Because He Is "Rich For Self," (Thru Self-Indulgence) And Not "Rich Towards God." (Thru Self-Discipline And Service of Others.)

20"But God said to him,
'Fool! This night your soul is required of you;
and the things you have prepared, whose will they be?'

21"So is he who lays up treasure for himself,
and is not rich toward God."

c. Beware of Anxiety (22-34) *(Cf.Mt.6:25-33,p.63)*
(The Sin of the Poor)

To His Disciples Again

Don't Worry About the Necessities of Food and Clothing

22And he said to his disciples,
"Therefore I tell you,
Do not be anxious about your life, what you shall eat,
nor about your body, what you shall put on.
23For life is more than food,
and the body more than clothing.

For God Will Provide All Necessities As Surely As He Does For The Birds

24"Consider the ravens: they neither sow nor reap,
they have neither storehouse nor barn,
and yet God feeds them.
Of how much more value are you than the birds!
25And which of you by being anxious
can add a cubit to his span of life?[a]
26If then you are not able to do as small a thing as that,
why are you anxious about the rest?

Or The Flowers

27"Consider the lilies, how they grow;
they neither toil nor spin;[b]
yet I tell you,
even Solomon in all his glory
was not arrayed like one of these.
28But if God so clothes the grass which is alive in the field today
and tomorrow is thrown into the oven,
how much more will he clothe you,
O men of little faith?

If You Do Not Do As Non-Christians

29"And do not seek what you are to eat and what you are to drink,
nor be of anxious mind.
30For all the nations of the world seek these things;
and your Father knows that you need them.

But Seek First The Kingdom of God.

31"Instead, seek his[c] kingdom,
and these things shall be yours as well.

The Kingdom of God Is the Supreme End: All Else is Means to That End.

32"Fear not, little flock,
for it is your Father's good pleasure to give you the kingdom.

For Nothing Can Rob You of Treasure in Heaven and Your Life Will be Rightly Centered

33"Sell your possessions, and give alms;
provide yourselves with purses that do not grow old,
with a treasure in the heavens that does not fail, *(v.21;Mt.6:20,21,p.63)*
where no thief approaches
and no moth destroys.
34For where your treasure is, there will your heart be also.

....

[a]*Or* to his stature.
[b]*A few ancient authorities read* Consider the lilies; they neither spin nor weave.
[c]*Some ancient authorities read* God's.

d. But Be Always Watchful (35-48)

A Parable of Servants Watching For Their Master's Return

35" Let your loins be girded and your lamps burning,

36and be like men who are waiting (§ 190,p.202)
for their master to come home from the marriage feast,
so that they may open to him at once when he comes and knocks.
37Blessed are those servants
whom the master finds awake when he comes;
truly, I say to you, he will gird himself
and have them sit at table and come and serve them.
38If he comes in the second watch, or in the third,
and finds them so,
blessed are those servants!

A Parable about Guarding Against a Thief

39" But know this, that
if the householder had known at what hour the thief was coming,
he would have been awake and[a]
would not have left his house to be broken into.

The Application

40" You also must be ready;
for the Son of man is coming at an hour you do not expect."

(To Peter, Who Speaks Up)

Special Watchfulness in Stewards, or (Business Managers)

41Peter said,
" Lord, are you telling this parable for us or for all?"

42And the Lord said,
" Who then is the faithful and wise steward,
whom his master will set over his household,
to give them their portion of food at the proper time?

Illustrated by A Parable of A Faithful Manager

43" Blessed is that servant
whom his master when he comes will find so doing.
44Truly I tell you,
he will set him over all his possessions.

A Parable Contrasting Good and Evil Servants

45" But if that servant says in his heart, (Mt.24:48-51,p.202)
'My master is delayed in coming,'
and begins to beat the menservants and the maidservants,
and to eat and drink and to get drunk,
46the master of that servant will come on a day when he does not expect him
and at an hour he does not know,
and will punish[b] him,
and put him with the unfaithful.

Varying Rewards, According to Faithfulness

47" And that servant who knew his master's will,
but did not make ready or act according to his will,
shall receive a severe beating.
48But he who did not know, and did what deserved a beating,
shall receive a light beating.

Responsibility Varying, According to Opportunity

" Everyone to whom much is given, of him will much be required;
and of him to whom men commit much they will demand the more.

e. Endure Persecution (49-53)

You Will Be Tested by Baptisms of Fire

49" I came to cast fire upon the earth;
and would that it were already kindled! (Mk.10:38-39,p.172)
50I have a baptism to be baptized with;
and how I am constrained until it is accomplished!

Even Divisions In Families Will Occur

51" Do you think that I have come to give peace on earth?
No, I tell you, but rather division; (Mt.10:34-36,p.90)
52for henceforth in one house there will be five
divided, three against two, and two against three;
53they will be divided, father against son and son against father,
mother against daughter and daughter against her mother,
mother-in-law against her daughter-in-law,
and daughter-in-law against her mother-in-law."

---

[a] *Some ancient authorities omit* would have been awake and.
[b] *Or* cut him in pieces.

(4) Heeding The Signs of the Times. § 131a

Lk. 12:54-59

(To The Multitudes)

Signs of The Weather and

54He also said to the multitudes,
"When you see a cloud rising in the west,
you say at once
'A shower is coming;'
and so it happens.
55And when you see the south wind blowing you say,
'There will be scorching heat;'
and it happens.

Signs of The Times

56You hypocrites!
You know how to interpret the appearance of earth and sky; (§ 99, p.106)
but why do you not know how to interpret the present time?

Righteousness and Wisdom

57And why do you not judge for yourselves what is right?
58As you go with your accuser before the magistrate,
make an effort to settle with him on the way,
lest he drag you to the judge, *(Mt.5:25-26, p.60)*
and the judge hand you over to the officer,
and the officer put you in prison.
59I tell you
you will never get out
till you have paid the very last copper!"

(5) Averting Judgment Through Repentance. § 132

Lk. 13:1-9

(To New Arrivals)

Fresh News of A Tragedy

1There were some present at that very time*
who told him of the Galileans
whose blood Pilate had mingled with their sacrifices.

The Lesson:
(a) From Galilean Victims

2And he answered them,
"Do you think that these Galileans were worse sinners than
all the other Galileans,
because they suffered thus?

3"I tell you,
No;
but unless you repent you will all likewise perish.

(b) From a Jerusalem Tragedy

4"Or those eighteen upon whom the tower in Siloam fell and killed them,
do you think that they were worse offenders than all the others
who dwelt in Jerusalem?
5I tell you,
No; but unless you repent you will all likewise perish."

Judgment of the Jewish Nation Prefigured

6And he told this parable:
"A man had a fig tree planted in his vineyard;
and he came seeking fruit on it and found none.

Her Fruitlessness

7"And he said to the vinedresser,
'Lo, these three years I have come seeking fruit on this fig tree,
and I find none.
Cut it down;
Why should it use up the ground?'

Why Her Fate Is Deferred

8"And he answered him,
'Let it alone, sir, this year also,
till I dig about it and put on manure.
9And if it bears fruit next year, well and good;
but if not, you can cut it down.'"

*[*or just then some arrived*]

(6) In The Synagogue On The Sabbath. § 133

Lk. 13:10-21

a. Healing a Crippled Woman (10-17)

Jesus Is Teaching in a Synagogue

10Now he was teaching in one of the synagogues on the sabbath.

A Deformed Woman Is There

11And there was a woman who had had a spirit of infirmity for eighteen years;
she was bent over and could not fully straighten herself.

Jesus Heals Her

12And when Jesus saw her, he called her and said to her,
"Woman, you are freed from your infirmity."
13And he laid his hands upon her,
and immediately she was made straight.
And she praised God.

The Ruler of The Synagogue Objects

14But the ruler of the synagogue,
indignant because Jesus had healed on the sabbath,
said to the people,
"There are six days on which work ought to be done;
come on those days and be healed,
and not on the sabbath day."

Our Lord Rebukes Him

15Then the Lord answered him,
"You hypocrites!
Does not each of you on the sabbath
untie his ox or his ass from the manger,
and lead it away to water it?

16"And ought not this woman,
a daughter of Abraham
whom Satan bound for eighteen years,
be loosed from this bond on the sabbath day?" *(See § 58 and Note p.54-55)*

The Two-fold Effect of The miracle

17As he said this,
all his adversaries were put to shame;
and all the people rejoiced at all the glorious things that were done by him.

The Power of the Kingdom of God

The Expanding Power-- of the Kingdom is like a Mustard Seed

18He said therefore,
"What is the kingdom of God like? And to what shall I compare it?
19It is like a grain of mustard seed
which a man took and sowed in his garden; *(Mt.13:31-32,p.77)*
and it grew and became a tree,
and the birds of the air made nests in its branches."

Its Transforming Power-- is Like Leaven

20And again he said,
"To what shall I compare the kingdom of God? *(Mt.13:33,p.78)*
21It is like leaven
which a woman took and hid in three measures of meal,
till it was all leavened."

In this whole section (Evangelizing in Judea, pp. 135-149) there are some incidents and many teachings of Christ that are repetions of passages in Matthew and Mark. There they are often assigned to other occasions (time and place being different). On the logical principle of "economy" the simplest explanation would be the best. And that would be not to disturb the literary sequence of Luke too much. At least that would be the best pedagogically.

It is not strange that in evangelizing in Judea the same life-situations would arise as had risen previously in Galilee; and so the same questions would be asked and the same answers given.

We know for example that Paul often repeated himself in this way, e.g. in Galatians and Romans, also in Ephesians and Colossians.

In fact all great teachers frequently repeat their most striking sayings, illustrations and teachings.

Besides Each one of the Gospels reports Jesus as repeating on different occasions, the same sayings, enunciating the same principles, or using the same illustrations.

(7) The Return of the Seventy. § 134 (See §134, p.136, and Note, p.134)

	Mt. 11:25-30	*Lk. 10:17-24*
The Disciples Rejoice in Their Experience of Power		17 The seventy[a] returned with joy, saying, "Lord, even the demons are subject to us in your name!"
They Should Rejoice More In Their Salvation		18 And he said to them, "I saw Satan fall like lightning from heaven. 19 Behold, I have given you authority to tread upon serpents and scorpions, and over all the power of the enemy; and nothing shall hurt you. 20 Nevertheless do not rejoice in this, that the spirits are subject to you; but rejoice that your names are written in heaven."
Christ Exults, in the Holy Spirit, over Their Success	25 At that time* Jesus declared, "I thank thee, Father, Lord of heaven and earth, that thou hast hidden these things from the wise and understanding and revealed them to babes; 26 yea, Father, for such was thy gracious will.[b]	21 In that same hour * he rejoiced in the Holy Spirit and said, "I thank thee, Father, Lord of heaven and earth, that thou hast hidden these things from the wise and understanding and revealed them to babes; yea, Father, for such was thy gracious will.[b]
Christ Has Absolute Authority as Savior	27 "All things have been delivered to me by my Father; *(Jn.3:25;Mt.28:18)* and no one knows the Son except the Father, and no one knows the Father except the Son and anyone to whom the Son chooses to reveal him.	22 "All things have been delivered to me by my Father; *(Jn.17:2)* and no one knows who the Son is except the Father, or who the Father is except the Son and anyone to whom the Son chooses to reveal him."
Christ Alone Can Give Rest From Life's Excessive Toil and Burdens	28 "Come to me, all who labor and are heavy laden, and I will give you rest. 29 Take my yoke upon you, and learn from me;** for I am gentle*** and lowly**** in heart, and you will find rest for your souls. 30 For my yoke is easy, and my burden is light."	
	A Private Word To The Disciples	
The Exalted Privilege of His Followers Was Eagerly Desired By Prophets and Kings	*(Cf.Mt.13:16-17,p.75)*	23 Then turning to the disciples he said privately, "Blessed are the eyes which see what you see! 24 For I tell you that many prophets and kings desired to see what you see, and did not see it, and to hear what you hear, and did not hear it."

Just when The Seventy returned we do not know. It may have been at the close of this period of "Evangelizing in Judea" (i.e. after Lk. 13:21).

Compare the return of "The Twelve", at the close of "The Last Tour Throughout Galilee." (See Mk.6: 7-30; and Lk.9:1-10, pp.88-92)

[a] *Many ancient authorities read* seventy-two.
[b] *Or* so it was well-pleasing before thee.
* Greek season. *Mt.'s word is general; Lk.'s is very specific. Lk. also gives more graphic details.*
** *"Take my yoke upon you" was a technical expression used by the Jewish Rabbis, which meant, "become my pupil," or, "enroll in my school."*
*** *Greek* meek.
**** *Or* humble.

(See General Outline, p.118,119)

Conflict With the Jewish Rulers at The Feast of Dedication.* § 135

(Late December A.D. 29) (John 10:22-39) [4] [Map.p.119]

1. *Jesus is Teaching in Solomon's Porch (22-23)*

2. *The Jews ask Him to Tell Whether He is The Messiah (24-30)*

   a. *Their Explicit Demand (24)*

   b. *His Profound Reply (25-30)*

      (a) *He has told them,*
      (b) *His works declare Him*
      (c) *His sheep recognize His Voice*
      (d) *And He knows them*
      (e) *They Follow (obey) Him*
      (f) *He gives them life eternal*
      (g) *If they abide in Him, (Ro. 11:20-23) They are eternally secure.*
      (h) *Because He and the Father will safe-guard them.*
      (i) *And The Father is greater than all.*
      (j) *And He and The Father work together as one.*

3. *They Attempt to Stone Him (31-38)*

   a. *They Threaten Him (31)*

   b. *He Dissuades Them (32-38)*

4. *They Try to Seize Him,*

5. *But He Escapes. (39)* [5]

....

(C) Conflict With the Jewish Rulers at The Feast of Dedication.* § 135

Jn. 10:22-39

1. *Jesus is Teaching in Solomon's Porch*

Jn. 10:22, 23

Their Determined Attack: The Time, Place, and Circumstances

22 It was the feast of the Dedication* at Jerusalem;
23 it was winter,
and Jesus was walking in the temple, in the portico of Solomon.

2. *The Jews Ask Him to Tell Them Whether He is the Messiah*

Jn. 10:24-30

Their Tactics and Their Question

24 So the Jews gathered round him
and said to him,
"How long will you keep us in suspense?
If you are the Christ, tell us plainly."

Christ's Defense: He Has Told Them,

25 Jesus answered them,
"I told you, and you do not believe.

But They Disbelieved. The Reason for Their Unbelief is Not Lack of Evidence, But Moral Perversity

"The works that I do in my Father's name,
they bear witness to me;
26 but you do not believe,
because you do not belong to my sheep.

....

*The Feast of Dedication *was the anniversary of the rededication of the temple by the Maccabees (165 B.C.), after it had been defiled by Antiochus Epiphanes (Macc. 4:56-59). This all took place between Old Testament and New Testament times. Hence this feast is not mentioned in the Old Testament.*

Those Who Believe And Obey, Receive Life Eternal;

[27]" My sheep hear my voice, (*Jn.18:37,p.234*)
and I know them, and they follow me;

[28]" and I give them eternal life, (*Jn.5:20f.;6:27ff.,p.98*)

Those Who Trust Him *Are Eternally Secure*

and they shall never perish,
and no one shall snatch them out of my hand. (*Cf.Ro.11:20-23*)

Because of:
(a) The Supreme Greatness of The Father and

[29]" My Father, who has given them to me,[a]
is greater than all,
and no one is able to snatch them out of the Father's hand.

(b) The United Action of Christ and The Father.

[30]" I and the Father are one." (*Cf.Jn.5:19-29,p.52;Mt.11:27;Lk.10:22,p.147*)

3. They Attempt to Stone Him *Jn. 10:31-38*

The Rulers Threaten Violence

[31]The Jews took up stones again to stone him. (*Jn.8:59,p.128*)

Jesus Remonstrates

[32]Jesus answered them,
" I have shown you many good works from the Father;
for which of these do you stone me?"

They Charge Him With Blasphemy

[33]The Jews answered him,
" We stone you for no good work
but for blasphemy;
because you, being a man, make yourself God."

In Defense,
(a) He Appeals to Scripture as Justifying His Statement

[34]Jesus answered them,
" Is it not written in your law,
'I said, You are gods?'
[35]If he called them gods to whom the word of God came
(and scripture cannot be broken),

[36]do you say of him whom the Father consecrated and sent into the world,
'You are blaspheming,'
because I said, 'I am the Son of God'?

(b) He Appeals to His Works as Demonstrating His Unity With God

[37]" If I am not doing the works of my Father,
then do not believe me;
[38]but if I do them, (*Jn.5:17,36,p.53*)
even though you do not believe me, believe the works, (*Jn.14:11,p.215*)
that you may know and understand that the Father is in me
and I am in the Father." (*Jn.14:10,p.120-23,*

4. They Try to Arrest Jesus

Jn. 10:39

They Try To Seize Jesus But He Eludes Them

[39]Again they tried to arrest him, (*Jn.7:30,45ff.,p.124*)
but he escaped from their hands.

....

[a]*Many ancient authorities read* what my Father has given to me.

IV. THE CONCLUDING MINISTRY *(Continued)* [*For General Outline see p.118*]

[(I) FROM GALILEE TO JUDEA *(THE LATER JUDEAN MINISTRY) pp.118-149*]]

(II) FROM JUDEA TO PEREA, *(FIRST PART OF THE PEREAN MINISTRY*)* [1,2] *See map*
(Jn. 10:40-42; Lk. 13:22-17:10)
(From the Feast of Dedication, Dec. A.D. 29;
To The Raising of Lazarus, Spring, A.D. 30)

(A) JOHN'S GENERAL SUMMARY (Jn.10:40-42) § 136 p. 152.
*(Jesus Leaves Judea to Minister in Perea, Jn.10:40)**

(1) Great Crowds Come to Him (41a)
(2) Many Miracles are Wrought (41b)
(3) Many Believers Are Won (42)

(B) LUKE'S SPECIFIC INCIDENTS (Lk. 13:22-17:10) pp. 152-177.
(Jesus Is Teaching as He Journeys on to Jerusalem, Lk.13:22-17:10)

1. JESUS AND THE PHARISEES (Lk.13:23-14:24)
(Correcting False Views of Salvation and The Kingdom) § 137 pp. 152-154.

(1) One Asks Whether Few Are Saved (22-30) p. 152.
(2) Some Warn Jesus Against Herod (31-35) § 138 p. 153.
(3) A Pharisee Invites Jesus to Dine With Him (14:1-24) § 139 pp. 153-154.
a. He Heals A Dropsical Man Who Is Present (2-6)
b. He Reproves the Guests (7-11)
c. He Instructs the Host (12-14)
d. He Warns Against Excuses (15-24)

2. JESUS AND THE MULTITUDES (14:25-16:31) pp. 154-159.
(Great Crowds Are Eagerly Following Jesus, 14:25 and 15:1)

(1) Jesus Warns Them of the Cost of Discipleship (14:25-35) § 140 pp. 154-155.
(2) He Eats with the Publicans § 141 pp. 155-159.
(The Pharisees Murmur at This and He Explains by Parables (15:1-2)
a. Three Parables About Repentant Sinners
(a) The Lost Sheep (3-7)
(b) The Lost Coin (8-10)
(c) The Lost Son (11-32)
b. Two Parables About the Use of Temporal Things (16) §§ 142-143
(a) The Right Use of Wealth (16:1-18)
(b) The Wrong Use of Wealth (16:19-31)

....

Jesus had not yet evangelized in* **Perea. *During the great Galilean Ministry, He made repeated tours "throughout all* **Galilee**". *He had also preached a bit in* **Decapolis** *and even as far north as* **Caesarea-Philippi.** *More recently He had, with the help of the seventy and The Twelve, campaigned intensively in* **Judea.** *Now there remains* **only Perea.** *And here is where He concentrates His repeated efforts henceforth.*

3. JESUS AND HIS DISCIPLES (17:1-10) § 144
(He Is Teaching Them, 17:1)

(1) About Offenses and Forgiveness (1-4)
(2) About Faith and Humility (5-10) p. 159.

[(III) FROM PEREA TO BETHANY AND EPHRAIM pp.160-163
(INTERRUPTION OF THE PEREAN MINISTRY)]

[(IV) FROM EPHRAIM BACK TO BETHANY pp.164-177
(SECOND PART OF THE PEREAN MINISTRY)]

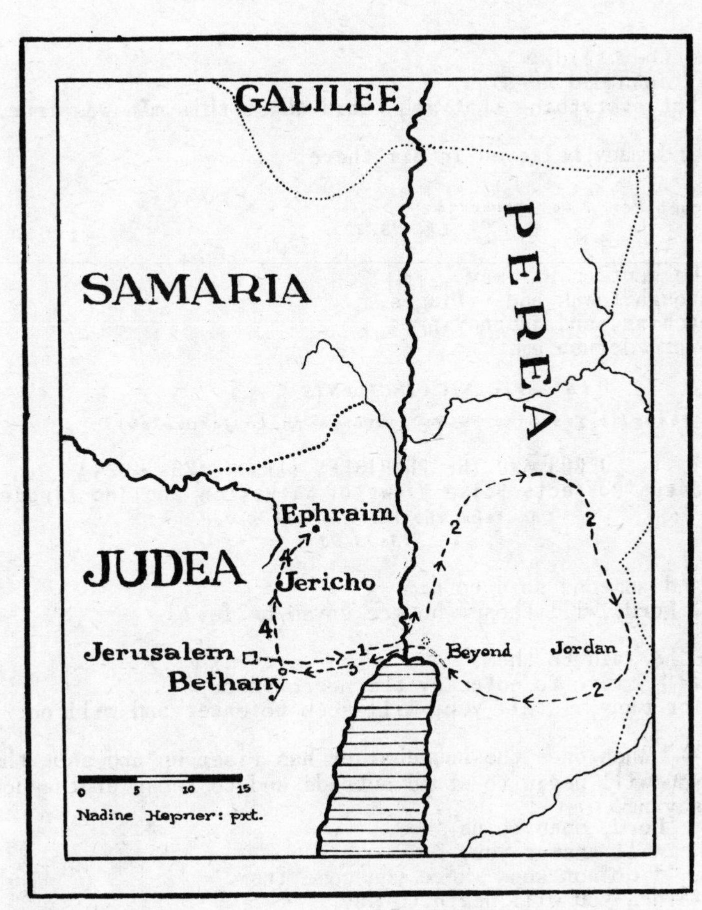

(II) FROM JUDEA TO PEREA, or EVANGELIZING IN PEREA

(FIRST PART OF THE PEREAN MINISTRY)
Lk. 13:22-17:10; Jn. 10:40-42

(A) GENERAL STATEMENTS § 136
Jn. 10:40-42; Lk. 13:22

(1) Jesus Withdraws from Judea to Perea. [1] *(See map page 150)*
Jn. 10:40

Jesus Withdraws to Perea	40He went away again, across the Jordan, to the place where John at first baptized,

(2) Jesus Is Evangelizing in Perea [2]
Jn. 10:40-42

He Stays in Perea	and there he remained.
Great Crowds Come to Him	41And many came to him;
They Are Convinced By His Signs	and they said, " John did no sign, but everything that John said about this man was true."
Many Believe	42And many believed in him there.

(3) Jesus Is Returning Through Perea to Jerusalem.
Lk. 13:22

Jesus Continues Teaching As He Journeys on to Jerusalem	22He went on his way [2] through towns and villages, teaching, and journeying toward Jerusalem.

(B) SPECIFIC INCIDENTS

(Jesus is Teaching as He journeys on to Jerusalem)

1. JESUS AND THE PHARISEES (Lk. 13:23-14:24)
(1) Jesus Corrects False Views of Salvation and The Kingdom. § 137
One Asks Whether Few Are Saved
Lk. 13:23-30

*They Ask Will Few Be Saved**	23And someone said to him, " Lord, will those who are saved be few?"
Jesus Answers:	And he said to them,
(a) Some Seek and Fail	24" Strive to enter by the narrow door; for many, I tell you, will seek to enter and will not be able.
(b) Others Are Self-deceived *By Formal Profession Instead of Faithful Obedience*	25" When once the householder has risen up and shut the door, you will begin to stand outside and to knock at the door, saying, 'Lord, open to us.' He will answer you, 'I do not know where you come from.' 26Then you will begin to say, 'We ate and drank in your presence, and you taught in our streets.' 27But he will say, 'I tell you, I do not know where you come from; depart from me, all you workers of iniquity!'
(c) Many Will Weep and Rave When Too Late	28" There you will weep and gnash your teeth, when you see Abraham and Isaac and Jacob and all the prophets in the kingdom of God, and you yourselves thrust out.
(d) Many Gentiles Will Be Saved	29" And men will come from east and west, and from north and south, and sit at table in the kingdom of God.
(e) Many Earthly Estimates Will Be Reversed	30" And behold, some are last who will be first, and some are first who will be last."

**This question probably arose because they had been taught that no Gentiles except those who became proselytes will be saved--and only those Jews who kept the law strictly. (Consider Peter's astonishment when this belief of his was uprooted in Ac.10; and what a time he had convincing the rest, upon his return and report at Jerusalem (Ac.11:1-18).*

(2) Some Warn Jesus Against Herod. § 138

Lk. 13:31-35

The Hypocritical Warning

31At that very hour some Pharisees came, and said to him,
"Get away from here* for Herod wants to kill you."

Jesus' Profound Reply

32And he said to them,
"Go and tell that fox,
'Behold, I cast out demons and perform cures today and tomorrow,
and the third day I finish my course.
33Nevertheless I must go on my way
today and tomorrow and the day following;
for it cannot be that a prophet should perish away from Jerusalem.'

(a) His Clear Vision of His Own Fate

(Cf.Lk.19:41-44 p.180; and Mt.23:37-39, p.193)

(b) And The Fate Of His Nation

34"O Jerusalem, Jerusalem,
killing the prophets and stoning those who are sent to you!
How often would I have gathered your children together
as a hen gathers her brood under her wings,
and you would not!

(c) He Had Done His Utmost To Prevent It

(d) Now It Is Too Late

35"Behold, your house is forsaken!
And I tell you, you will not see me until you say,
'Blessed be he who comes in the name of the Lord!'"

(3) A Pharisee Invites Jesus to Dine With Him. § 139 *(See §§ 66 and 130)*

Lk. 14:1-24

a. Jesus Heals a Dropsical Man Who Is Present (2-6)
A Lesson About Sabbath Observance

(As They Enter) Jesus is Being Watched, And a Trap Is Set for Him But He Sees It.

1One sabbath
when he went to dine at the house of a ruler who belonged to the Pharisees,
they were watching him. *(§ 58, p.55)*

A Sick Man Is There.

2And behold, there was a man before him who had dropsy.

Jesus Asks A Question

3And Jesus spoke to the lawyers and Pharisees, saying,
"Is it lawful to heal on the sabbath, or not?"

They Do Not Answer

4But they were silent.

He Heals the Sick Man

Then he took him and healed him,
and let him go.

Jesus' Comment Goes Unanswered Because They Could Not

5And he said to them,
"Which of you, having an ass[a] or an ox that has fallen into a well,
will not immediately pull him out on a sabbath day?"
6And they could not reply to this. *(For other Sabbath controversies see pp.52-55 and footnotes)*

b. He Reproves the Guests (7-11)
A Lesson in Honor vs. Courtesy

(When Being Seated) Seeking Honor Discourteously Is Self-Defeating

7Now he told a parable to those who were invited,
when he marked how they chose the places of honor,
saying to them,
8"When you are invited by anyone to a marriage feast,
do not sit down in a place of honor,
lest a more eminent man than you be invited by him;
9and he who invited you both will come and say to you,
'Give place to this man,'
and then you will begin with shame to take the lowest place.

The Right Way (Be Truly Humble)

10"But when you are invited,
go and sit in the lowest place,
so that when your host comes
he may say to you,
'Friend, go up higher;'
Then you will be honored in the presence of all who sit at table with you.

The Reason Why

11"For every one who exalts himself will be humbled,
and he who humbles himself will be exalted."

....

[a] Many ancient authorities read a son.

**He is in Perea (Herod's Territory).*

c. He Instructs The Host (12-14)
A Lesson In Hospitality

(Table Talk)

The Wrong Practice	12He said also to the man who had invited him, "When you give a dinner or a banquet, do not invite your friends or your brothers or your kinsmen or rich neighbors lest they also invite you in return, and you be repaid.
The Right Way	13"But when you give a feast, invite the poor, the maimed, the lame, the blind, *(v.21)* 14and you will be blessed, because they cannot repay you. You will be repaid at the resurrection of the just."

d. He Warns Against Excuses (15-24)
A Lesson About Pre-Occupation With Earthly Things

(Table Talk Cont.)

A Fellow-Guest Makes A Pious Remark	15When one of those who sat at table with him heard this, he said to him, "Blessed is he who shall eat bread in the kingdom of God!"
Jesus Replies With a Story	16But he said to him, "A man once gave a great banquet, and invited many; *(Cf.Mt.22:2-14,p.186)*
Invitations To a Banquet Are Sent Out	17"and at the time for the banquet he sent his servant to say to those who had been invited, 'Come; for all is now ready.' *(Mt.22:4f.)*
Excuses Attempt To Hide Indifference	18"But they all alike began to make excuses. "The first said to him, 'I have bought a field, and I must go out and see it; I pray you, have me excused.' 19And another said, 'I have bought five yoke of oxen, and I go to examine them; I pray you have me excused.' 20And another said, 'I have married a wife, and therefore I cannot come.'
Others Are Invited From The City	21"So the servant came and reported this to his master. Then the householder in anger said to his servant, 'Go out quickly to the streets and lanes of the city, and bring in the poor and maimed and blind and lame.' *(v.13)*
Still Others Are Brought in From the Country	22"And the servant said, 'Sir, what you commanded has been done, and still there is room.' 23And the master said to the servant, 'Go out to the highways and hedges, and compel people to come in, that my house may be filled.
The Fate of Those Who Refused	24'For I tell to you, none of those men who were invited shall taste my banquet.'"

2. JESUS AND THE MULTITUDES

(Great Crowds Are Eagerly Following Jesus)
Lk. 14:25-16:31

(1) Jesus Warns of The Cost of Discipleship. § 140

Lk. 14:25-35

Great Crowds Mill About Jesus	25Now great multitudes accompanied him; *(Cf.Lk.12:1)*
He Warns Of What True Discipleship May Cost (Renouncing All, cf.v.33)	and he turned and said to them, 26"If any one comes to me and does not hate his own father and mother *(Cf.Mt.10:35-38,p.90)* and wife and children and brothers and sisters, yes, and even his own life, he cannot be my disciple.
Doggedly Bearing One's Own Cross To The End	27"Whoever does not bear his own cross *(Lk.9:23, p.109)* and come after me, cannot be my disciple.

Counting the Cost Before Building A Vinyard Watch Tower

28" For which of you, desiring to build a tower,
does not first sit down and count the cost,
whether he has enough to complete it?
29Otherwise, when he has laid a foundation, and is not able to finish,
all who see it begin to mock him,
30saying,
'This man began to build, and was not able to finish.'

A Second Illustration

31" Or what king, going to encounter another king in war,
will not sit down first and take counsel
whether he is able with ten thousand
to meet him who comes against him with twenty thousand?

Counting the Cost Before Rushing Into War

32And if not, while the other is yet a great way off,
he sends an embassy and asks terms of peace.

The Master Key: True Discipleship Is Renouncing All For Christ

33" So therefore, whoever of you
does not renounce all that he has *(Cf.v.26)*
cannot be my disciple.

Saltless Religion Is Worthless

34" Salt is good;
but if salt has lost its taste, *(Mt.5:13,p.59;Mk.9:50,p.116)*
how shall its saltness be restored?
35It is fit neither for the land nor for the dunghill;
men throw it away.

Each One Must Make The Application To Himself

" He who has ears to hear, let him hear."

(2) Jesus Eats With the Publicans and Sinners. § 141

(The Pharisees Murmur at This (15:1-2) and Jesus Explains)

Lk. 15

(1) The Occasion *Publicans and Outcasts Respond, Pharisees Criticize*

1Now the tax collectors and sinners were all drawing near to him to hear him.
(§ 54, p.47)
2And the Pharisees and the scribes murmured, saying,
" This man receives sinners and eats with them."

a. *Three Parables About Repentant Sinners*

Lk. 15:3-32

(2) The Teaching

(a) The Parable about a Lost Sheep Which Was Found (3-7)

The Shepherd Goes After His Lost Sheep

3So he told them this parable: *(Cf.Mt.18:12-14,p.116)*
4" What man of you, having a hundred sheep, if he has lost one of them,
does not leave the ninety-nine in the wilderness,
and go after the one which is lost, until he finds it?

He Rejoices When He Finds It

5" And when he has found it, he lays it on his shoulders, rejoicing.

6" And when he comes home, he calls together his friends and his neighbors,
saying to them,
'Rejoice with me, for I have found my sheep which was lost.'

So God Rejoices Over Repentant Sinners

7" Even so, I tell you,
there will be more joy in heaven *(v.10)*
over one sinner who repents than over
ninety-nine righteous persons who need no repentance.

(b) The Parable of A Lost Coin Which Was Found (8-10)

A Woman Searches for Her Lost Coin

8" Or
what woman, having ten silver coins[a],
if she loses one coin,
does not light a lamp and sweep the house
and seek diligently until she finds it?

She Rejoices When She Finds It

9" And when she has found it,
she calls together her friends and neighbors,
saying,
'Rejoice with me,
for I have found the coin which I had lost.'

So God Rejoices Over Repentant Sinners

10" Even so, I tell you
there is joy before the angels of God *(v.7)*
over one sinner who repents."

[a]*The* drachma, *rendered here by* silver coin, *was about sixteen cents.*

(c) The Parable About A Lost Son Who Was Found

A Good Father Has Two Bad Boys
The Younger Son Breaks With His Father

11 And he said,
" There was a man who had two sons;
12 and the younger of them said to his father,
'Father, give me the share of property that falls to me.' *(Dt.21:17)*
And he divided his living between them.

13 " Not many days later,
He Leaves Home
the younger son gathered all he had
He Goes Far Away
and took his journey into a far country,
He Lives Recklessly
" and there he squandered his property in loose living.

He Comes to Want

14 " And when he had spent everything,
a great famine arose in that country,
and he began to be in want.

He Comes To Disgrace

15 " So he went and joined himself to one of the citizens of that country,
who sent him into his fields to feed swine.

He Comes to Desperation

16 " And he would gladly have fed on[a]
the pods that the swine ate;
and no one gave him anything.

He Comes to Himself

17 " But when he came to himself he said,
'How many of my father's hired servants have bread enough and to spare,
but I perish* here with hunger!

He Comes To Repentance

18[b] I will arise and go to my father,
and I will say to him,
Father, I have sinned against heaven and before you;
19 I am no longer worthy to be called your son;
treat me as one of your hired servants.'

He Comes Home

20 " And he arose and came to his father.
But while he was yet at a distance, his father saw him
and had compassion,
and ran and embraced him and kissed him.

He Confesses His Sin

21 " And the son said to him,
'Father, I have sinned against heaven and before you;
I am no longer worthy to be called your son.'

He Is Welcomed
He Is Forgiven

22 " But the father said to his servants,
'Bring quickly the best robe, and put it on him;
and put a ring on his hand, and shoes on his feet;
23 and bring the fatted calf and kill it,
and let us eat and make merry;
24 for this my son was dead, and is alive again;
he was lost, and is found.'

He Is Honored

" And they began to make merry.

His Older Brother Comes In
Hears The Celebration

25 " Now his elder son was in the field;
and as he came and drew near the house,
he heard music and dancing.

He Calls A Servant

26 " And he called one of the servants
and asked what this meant.

He Gets The News

27 " And he said to him,
'Your brother has come,
and your father has killed the fatted calf,
because he has received him safe and sound.'

He Is Angry and Resentful

28 " But he was angry and refused to go in.

The Father Entreats Him

" His father came out
and entreated him.

....

[a] *Many ancient authorities read* filled his belly with.
[b] *Some ancient authorities add* treat me as one of your hired servants.
*am perishing.

He Remains Stubbornly Scornful

29 But he answered his father,
'Lo, these many years I have served you,
and I never disobeyed your command;
yet you never gave me a kid,
that I might make merry with my friends.
30 But when this son of yours came,
who has devoured your living with harlots,
you killed for him the fatted calf!'

The Father Pleads Again

31 "And he said to him,
'Son, you are always with me,
and all that is mine is yours.

The Cause For Rejoicing

32 'It was fitting to make merry and be glad,
for this your brother was dead, and is alive;
he was lost, and is found.'"

(The Occasion is the same as 15:1-2)

b. *Two Parables Concerning the Right and Wrong Use of Temporal Things*
A Lesson to His Disciples

(a) The Parable about An Unrighteous Steward. § 142

(The Right *Use of Wealth)*
Lk. 16:1-18

A Lesson to His Disciples

1 He said also to the disciples,
"There was a rich man who had a steward,
and charges were brought to him
that this man was wasting his goods.

(1) The story of A Rich Man And His Manager

2 And he called him and said to him,
"What is this that I hear about you?
Turn in the account of your stewardship,
for you can no longer be steward.'

The Manager's Dilemma

3 "And the steward said to himself,
'What shall I do,
since my master is taking the stewardship away from me?
I am not strong enough to dig, and I am ashamed to beg.

His Resolve

4 'I have decided what to do,
so that people may receive me into their houses
when I am put out of the stewardship.'

His Provision for the Future By Making Friends For the Future

5 "So summoning his master's debtors one by one,
he said to the first,
'How much do you owe my master?'
6 He said,
'A hundred measures of oil.'
And he said to him,
'Take your bill, and sit down quickly and write fifty.'

7 Then he said to another,
'And how much do you owe?'
He said,
'A hundred measures of wheat.'
He said to him,
'Take your bill, and write eighty.'

He is Selfish but Shrewd

8 "The master commended the dishonest steward
for his prudence;
for the sons of this world[a] are wiser in their own generation
than the sons of light.

(2) The Application *To Gain Eternal Values Use Temporal Things*

9 "And I tell you,
make friends for yourselves by means of unrighteous mammon,
so that when it fails
they may receive you into the eternal habitations.

(a) Faithfully

10 "He who is faithful in a very little is faithful also in much;
and he who is dishonest in a very little is dishonest also in much.

---

[a] *Greek* age.

(One's Use of Material Wealth Prepares for The Use of True Riches)

11 "If then you have not been faithful in the unrighteous mammon,
who will entrust to you the true riches?
12 And if you have not been faithful in that which is another's
who will give you that which is your own?

(b) Whole-Heartedly

13 "No servant can serve two masters; *(Mt.6:24,p.63)*
for either he will hate the one and love the other,
or he will be devoted to the one and despise the other.
You cannot serve God and mammon."

(3) The Effect
(a) The Scoffing of avarice

14 The Pharisees, who were lovers of money, heard all this,
and they scoffed at him.

15 But he said to them,

(b) The Judgment of God

"You are those who justify yourselves before men,
but God knows your hearts;
for what is exalted among men
is an abomination in the sight of God.

(c) As Expressed in the New Law and the Old

16 "The law and the prophets were until John; *(Cf.Mt.11:13,p.69)*
since then the good news of the kingdom of God is preached,
and every man enters it violently. *(Mt.11:12)*

(d) God's Law Cannot Fail

17 "But it is easier for heaven and earth to pass away,
than for one dot of the law to become void.

(e) For Example-Divorce is Adultery

18 "Every one who divorces his wife
and marries another *(Cf.Mt.5:27-32,p.60;* § 152*,p.167-8)*
commits adultery,
and he who marries a woman divorced from her husband
commits adultery.

(b) The Parable of the Rich Man and Lazarus. § 143

(The Wrong Use of Wealth)
Lk. 16:19-31)

(1) Rich and Poor Contrasted:
(a) Here

19 "There was a rich man, *(Cf.Lk.12:13-21,p.142)*
who was clothed in purple and fine linen
and who feasted sumptuously every day.
20 And at his gate lay a poor man named Lazarus,
full of sores,
21 who desired to be fed
with what fell from the rich man's table;
moreover the dogs came and licked his sores.

(b) Hereafter

22 "The poor man died
and was carried by the angels to Abraham's bosom.
The rich man also died and was buried;
23 and in Hades, being in torment, he lifted up his eyes,
and saw Abraham afar off and Lazarus in his bosom.

(2) A Rich Man's Despairing Plea
(a) For Himself

24 "And he called out,
'Father Abraham, have mercy upon me,
and send Lazarus
to dip the end of his finger in water and cool my tongue;
for I am in anguish in this flame.'

25 "But Abraham said,
'Son, remember that you in your lifetime received your good things,
and Lazarus in like manner evil things;
but now he is comforted here, and you are in anguish.

26 'And besides all this,
between us and you a great chasm has been fixed,
in order that those who would pass from here to you may not be able,
and none may cross from there to us.'

(b) For His Brothers

27 "And he said,
'Then I beg you, father,
to send him to my father's house,

28'for I have five brothers,
so that he may warn them,
lest they also come into this place of torment.'

Abraham's Stern Reply

29"But Abraham said,
'They have Moses and the prophets; let them hear them.'

He Pleads Further

30"And he said,
'No, father Abraham;
but if some one goes to them from the dead, they will repent.'

But to No Avail

31"He said to him,
'If they do not hear Moses and the prophets,
neither will they be convinced if some one should rise from the dead.'"

3. JESUS AND HIS DISCIPLES. § 144

(He is Teaching Them)
Lk. 17:1-10

a. About Causes of Stumbling

Do Not Tempt Anyone To Sin

1And he said to his disciples,
"Temptations to sin[a] are sure to come; *(Mt.18:7,p.115)*
but woe to him by whom they come!

Better Die Than Do That (Cf.Mt.18:6;Mk.9:42, p.115)

2"It would be better for him if a millstone were hung round his neck
and he were cast into the sea,
than that he should cause one of these little ones to sin.[b]

b. About The Duty To Forgive

If Another Sins Against You Forgive Him and be Reconciled as Often as He Repents

3"Take heed to yourselves;
if your brother sins, rebuke him,
and if he repents, forgive him;

4"and if he sins against you seven times in the day,
and turns to you seven times, and says,
'I repent',
you must forgive him."

c. Aboutthe Power of Faith

True Faith Will Win

5And the apostles said to the Lord,
"Increase our faith!"

Against All Odds

6And the Lord said,
"If you had faith as a grain of mustard seed, *(Mt.17:20,p.113)*
you could say to this sycamine tree,
'Be rooted up, and be planted in the sea,'
and it would obey you.

d. About Humility

We Must Be Humble

7"Will any one of you, who has a servant plowing or keeping sheep,
say to him when he has come in from the field,
'Come at once and sit down at table'?

Not Demanding

8"Will he not rather say to him,
'Prepare supper for me,
and gird yourself and serve me, till I eat and drink;
and afterward you shall eat and drink'?

9"Does he thank the servant
because he did what was commanded?

For We Are Unworthy

10"So you also,
when you have done all that is commanded you, say,
'We are unworthy servants;
we have only done what was our duty.'"

---

[a]Or stumbling blocks. [b]Or stumble.

1. *FATAL CONFLICT WITH JEWISH RULERS, THROUGH THE RAISING OF LAZARUS (Jn.11:1-46)*
   (1) Jesus Raises Lazarus From the Dead (Jn.11:1-44)
   (2) The Double Result (45-46)
      a. Many Believe (45)
      b. Some Report to The Pharisees (46)

2. *RETIREMENT IN EPHRAIM (Jn.11:47-54) (See* § 146, *page 163)*
   (1) The Sanhedrin Votes to Seek The Death of Jesus
   (2) So Jesus Retires to Ephraim

---

1. Jesus Raises Lazarus from the Dead. § 145

Jn. 11:1-46

A Message Is Sent to Jesus

Lazarus Is Sick

1Now a certain man was ill,
Lazarus of Bethany,
the village of Mary and her sister Martha.
2It was Mary who anointed the Lord with ointment *(Jn.* § 161*; p.176)*
and wiped his feet with her hair,
whose brother Lazarus was ill.

His Sisters Send for Jesus

3So the sisters sent to him, saying,
"Lord, he whom you love is ill."

Jesus Delays

Jesus Delays Two Days

4But when Jesus heard it he said,
"This illness is not unto death; it is for the glory of God.
so that the Son of God may be glorified by means of it."

For Love's Sake.

5Now Jesus loved Martha and her sister and Lazarus.
6So when he heard that he was ill,
he stayed two days longer in the place where he was.

He Discusses the Situation with His Disciples

7Then after this he said to the disciples,
"Let us go into Judea again." *(Jn.10:31,p.149)*

They Fear Foul Play Against Jesus

8The disciples said to him,
"Rabbi, the Jews were but now seeking to stone you,
and are you going there again?"

Jesus Walks by Faith Securely "As Long As It Is Day"

9Jesus answered,
"Are there not twelve hours in the day?
If anyone walks in the day, he does not stumble, *(Jn.12:35-36,46,p.194)*
because he sees the light of this world.
10But if anyone walks in the night, he stumbles,
because the light is not in him."

Jesus is Aware That Lazarus Has Died

11Thus he spoke, and then he said to them,
"Our friend Lazarus has fallen asleep,
but I go to awake him out of sleep."

And Discusses The Matter With His Disciples

12The disciples said to him,
"Lord, if he has fallen asleep, he will recover."

13Now Jesus had spoken of his death,
but they thought that he meant taking rest in sleep.

He Rejoices By Faith In The Greater Good

14Then Jesus told them plainly
"Lazarus is dead;
15and for your sake I am glad that I was not there,
so that you may believe.
But let us go to him."

The Disciples Agree to Return

16Thomas, called the twin, said to his fellow disciples,
"Let us also go, that we may die with him."

Jesus Arrives at Bethany

When They Arrive At Bethany

17Now when Jesus[a] came,
he found that Lazarus had already been in the tomb four days.

A Funeral Crowd Is There

18Bethany was near to Jerusalem, about two miles[b] off,
19and many of the Jews had come to Martha and Mary
to console them concerning their brother.

Martha Goes Secretly to Meet Jesus

20When Martha heard that Jesus was coming,
she went and met him,
while Mary sat in the house.

She Talks With Him

21Martha said to Jesus,
"Lord, if you had been here, my brother would not have died.
22And even now I know that whatever you ask from God,
God will give you."

Jesus Nurtures Her Faltering Faith

23Jesus said to her,
"Your brother will rise again."

24Martha said to him,
"I know that he will rise again in the resurrection at the last day."

True Believers Never Die

25Jesus said to her,
"I am the resurrection and the life[c];
he who believes in me, though he die, yet shall he live;
26and whoever lives and believes in me shall never die.
Do you believe this?"

Martha does not quite understand

27She said to him,
"Yes, Lord; I believe that you are the Christ, the Son of God,
he who is coming into the world."

Martha goes to Call Mary

28When she had said this, she went
and called her sister Mary, saying quietly,
"The Teacher is here and is calling for you."

Mary Comes to Meet Jesus

29And when she heard it, she rose quickly, and went to him.

30Now Jesus had not yet come to the village,
but was still in the place where Martha had met him.

The Crowd Follows

31When the Jews who were with her in the house, consoling her,
saw Mary rise quickly and go out,
they followed her, supposing that she was going to the tomb to weep there.

Mary Meets Jesus

32Then Mary, when she came where Jesus was and saw him,
fell at his feet, saying to him,
"Lord, if you had been here, my brother would not have died."

All Proceed to the Tomb

33When Jesus saw her weeping,
and the Jews who came with her also weeping,
he was deeply moved in spirit and troubled;
34and he said,
"Where have you laid him?"

They said to him,
"Lord, come and see."

Jesus Weeps

35Jesus wept.

The Jews Draw a Hasty Inference

36So the Jews said,
"See how he loved him!"
37But some of them said,
"Could not he who opened the eyes of the blind man
have kept this man from dying?"

---

[a] *Greek* he. [b] *Greek* fifteen stadia. [c] *A few ancient authorities omit* and the life.

Jesus Raises Lazarus From the Tomb

Jesus Comes to the Tomb

38 Then Jesus, deeply moved again, came to the tomb;

It was a cave, and a stone lay upon it.

They Take Away the Stone

39 Jesus said,
"Take away the stone."

Martha Interferes

Martha, the sister of the dead man, said to him,
"Lord, by this time there will be an odor,
for he has been dead four days."

Jesus Reproves Her

40 Jesus said to her,
"Did I not tell you that if you would believe,
you would see the glory of God?"

They remove The Stone

41 So they took away the stone.

*Jesus Gives Thanks for Answered Prayer**

And Jesus lifted up his eyes and said,
"Father, I thank thee that thou hast* heard me.
42 I knew* that thou hearest me always,
but I have said this on account of the people standing by,
that they may believe that thou didst send me."

He Calls to Lazarus

43 When he had said this, he cried with a loud voice,
"Lazarus, come out!"

Lazarus Comes Out Of the Tomb, Bound

44 The dead man came out,
his hands and feet bound with bandages,
and his face wrapped with a cloth.

Jesus Frees Him

Jesus said to them,
"Unbind him, and let him go."

2. The Double Result

Many Believe

45 Many of the Jews therefore,
who came with Mary and had seen what he did,
believed in him;

Some Report to The Pharisees

46 but some of them went to the Pharisees
and told them what Jesus had done.

....

****He already, before leaving Perea, had prayed and accepted the answer to His prayer. (Study verses 4,11,13).***

2. "RETIREMENT IN EPHRAIM"* (Jn. 11:47-54)

(1) The Sanhedrin Decides on Jesus' Death (47-53)
(2) So Jesus and His Apostles Flee to Ephraim (54a)
(3) They Remain There Until Passover Time (54b-55)
(4) The People Seek for Jesus at The Passover (56) p.175.
(5) The Jewish Rulers Make Official Search for Him (57) p. 175.

"Ephraim" was such an out of the way and obscure place, that we cannot be sure just where it was. But it was a fine place to remain hidden, until "His hour had come"

The Retirement in Ephraim.* § 146

Jn. 11:47-54

The Sanhedrin Decides to Seek The Death of Jesus

The Sanhedrin Assembles

47So the chief priests and the Pharisees
gathered the council, and said,
"What are we to do?

They Are In Consternation

For this man performs many signs.
48If we let him go on thus,

They Fear Roman Vengeance

everyone will believe in him,
and the Romans will come
and destroy both our holy place[a] and our nation."

The High Priest Speaks Ominously Proposing Drastic Action

49But one of them, Ca´ia-phas,
who was high priest that year, said to them,
"You know nothing at all;
50you do not understand that it is expedient for you
that one man should die for the people,
and not that the whole nation should perish."

The Author Interprets It Prophetically And Extends It

51He did not say this of his own accord,
but being high priest that year
he prophesied that Jesus should die for the nation,
52and not for the nation only,
but to gather into one *(Cf.Jn.10:16,p.133)*
the children of God who are scattered abroad.

The Sanhedrin Takes Official Legal Action And From Then On They Seek Jesus' Death

53So from that day on
they took counsel how to put him to death.

So Jesus Flees Secretly to Retirement in Ephraim

54Jesus therefore no longer went about openly among the Jews,
but went from there to the country near the wilderness,
to a town called Ephraim;
and there he stayed with the disciples.

(Meanwhile The Passover Crowds Await Jesus' Coming § 160,p.175

[a]*Greek* our place.

(55Now the Passover of the Jews was at hand,
and many went up from the country to Jerusalem
before the Passover,
to purify themselves.
56They were looking for Jesus
and saying to one another, as they stood in the temple,
"What do you think?
That he will not come to the feast?"
57Now the chief priests and the Pharisees had given orders that
if any one knew where he was,
he should let them know, so that they might arrest him.)

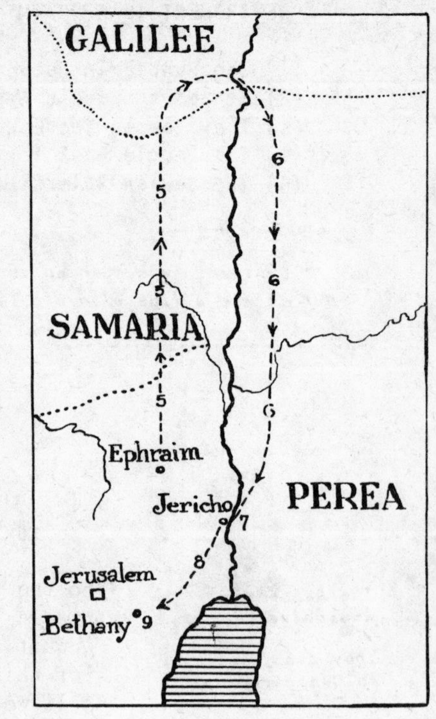

(IV) FROM EPHRAIM TO BETHANY, or

SECOND PART OF "THE PEREAN MINISTRY"

EVANGELIZING ON HIS FINAL RETURN TO JERUSALEM pp. 164-177

(Journeying through Samaria, Galilee, Perea, and Judea, to Bethany)

(A week or two before Passover, A.D. 30)

1. *APPROACHING PEREA (Lk. 17:11)*

(1) Jesus Cleanses Ten Lepers (Lk. 17:11-19) § 147 p. 165.

(2) Jesus Explains The Coming of the Messianic Kingdom (Lk. 17:20-37) § 148 pp.165-166.

a. *The Essential Nature of the Messiah's Kingdom (20-21)*

b. *The Coming of the Messianic King (22-24)*

c. *The Rejection of the Messiah, And The Judgmants that follow (25-37)*

(3) Overcoming Both Despair and Self-Righteousness Through Prayer (Lk.18:1-14) pp.166-167.

a. *The Widow and the Judge.* § 149

b. *The Pharisee and the Publican.* § 150

2. *JOURNEYING THROUGH PEREA (Mt 19:1'-20;28; Mk.10:1-45)* pp.167-173.

(1) Jesus Teaches and Heals Great Multitudes (Mt. 19:2, Mk. 10:1c) § § 151 p.167.

(2) Jesus Teaches About Marriage, Divorce, and Celibacy (Mt. 19:3-12; Mk. 10:2-12) § 152 pp.167-168.

(3) Jesus Blesses Little Children (Mt. 19:13-15; Mk. 10:13-16; Lk. 18:15-17) § 153 p.168.

(4) Jesus Instructs a Rich Young Ruler (Mt. 19:16-20:16; Mk. 10:17-31; Lk. 18:18-30) § 154 pp.169-171.

(5) Jesus Teaches the Twelve about His Death (Mt. 20:17-18; Mk. 10:32-34; Lk. 18:31-34) § 155 p.172.

(6) Jesus Rebukes the Selfish Ambition of the Twelve (Mt. 20:20-28; Mk. 10:35-45) § 156 pp.172-173.

3. *PASSING THROUGH JERICHO (Mt. 20:29-34; Mk.10:46-52; Lk.18:35-19:10)* pp.173-175.

(1) Jesus Heals Two Blind Men at Jericho (Mt. 20:29-34; Mk. 10:46-52; Lk.18:35-43) § 157 pp.173-174

(2) Jesus Lodges with a Publican and Saves Him (Lk. 19:1-10) § 158 p.174.

4. *NEARING JERUSALEM (Lk. 19:11a and 28)* pp.174-175.

(1) Jesus Teaches by Parable, on Approaching Jerusalem (Lk. 19:11-28) § 159 pp.174-175.

(2) The Passover Crowds Await Jesus' Coming, in Jerusalem (Jn. 11:55-57) § 160 p.175

5. *ARRIVING AT BETHANY (Mk. 11:1a; Lk. 19:29a; Jn. 12:1a)* p.176-177.

(1) Mary Anoints Jesus at Bethany (Mt. 26:6-13; Mk. 14:3-9; Jn. 12:1-8) § 161 p.176.

(2) The Crowds Hear the News of Jesus' Arrival at Bethany (Jn. 12:9-11) § 162 p.177.

(IV) FROM EPHRIAM TO BETHANY,* or
SECOND PART OF "THE PEREAN MINISTRY"
JESUS EVANGELIZING ON HIS FINAL RETURN TO JERUSALEM
1. APPROACHING PEREA (Lk. 17:11)

(1) Jesus Cleanses Ten Lepers. § 147
Lk. 17:11-19

Setting Out on the Last Journey to Jerusalem

11On the way to Jerusalem
he was passing along between Sa-ma΄ri-a and Galilee.*

Ten Lepers Meet Jesus and Ask For His Mercy

12And as he entered a village,
he was met by ten lepers,
who stood at a distance
13and lifted up their voices and said,
"Jesus, Master, have mercy on us."

He Instructs Them

14When he saw them he said to them,
"Go and show yourselves to the priests." *(Lev.13:2ff,Mt.8:4, § 49)*

They Obey and Are Cleansed

And as they went they were cleansed.

One Returns To Give Thanks

15Then one of them, when he saw that he was healed,
turned back, praising God with a loud voice;
16and he fell on his face at Jesus' feet, giving him thanks.

He Is A Foreigner

Now he was a Samaritan.

Jesus Commends Him

17Then said Jesus,
"Were not ten cleansed?
Where are the nine?
18Was no one found to return and give praise to God
except this foreigner?"

And Encourages Him

19And he said to him,
"Rise and go your way;
your faith has made you well." *(Lk.8:48,p.84)*

(2) Jesus Explains the Coming of the Messianic Kingdom.*** § 148
Lk. 17:20-18:14

a. The Essential Nature of the Messianic Kingdom

(a) Wrong Ideas About The Kingdom: It Is Not Outward Show but Inner Experience of Transformation and Control

20Being asked by the Pharisees when the kingdom of God was coming,***
he answered them,
"The kingdom of God is not coming with signs to be observed;
21nor will they say,
'Lo, here it is!' or 'There!'
for behold, the kingdom of God is in the midst[a] of you."

b. The Coming of the Messianic King

(b) Mistaken Desires About the Kingdom

22And he said to the disciples,
"The days are coming
when you will desire to see one of the days of the Son of man,**
and you will not see it.

(c) False Rumors About Its Coming

23"And they will say to you,
'Lo, there!' or 'Lo, here!' *(Mt.24:26-27,p.200)*
Do not go, do not follow them.

(d) The True Sign of Its Consummation

24"For as the lightning flashes *(Mt.24:27)*
and lights up the sky from one side to the other,
so will the Son of man be in his day.[b]

---

[a]Or within you. [b]Some ancient authorities omit in his day.

*Ephraim is north of Jerusalem, not far from Bethel. So it is clear that Jesus did not take the direct road south to Jerusalem, only a few miles away. For security reasons (because a reward was offered for news of His whereabouts). He travelled north through Samaria to Southern Galilee. From There He sought safe conduct to Jerusalem by journeying with the great crowds of pilgrims en route to the Passover. In the crowds He would be safe, and could continue His evangelizing work, all the way through Perea to Judea, and from there on through Jericho to Jerusalem.

**"The Son of Man," meaning, The Messiah. They had extravagant notions about what He would do and how He would come. Jews would live in a fairy land, and their Gentile oppressors would be destroyed. And they were eagerly expectant then. Many expected Him, by some stupendous miracle, to usher in The Messianic Kingdom, when they got to Jerusalem. This feeling was especially rampant during this last journey to Jerusalem.(Compare this incident, and §155,§156,§159,§163. Note how tense the situation is, all through the journey.

***By which they meant Jewish Independence, (as in Acts 1:6) "restore the kingdom to Israel."

c. But First,--The Rejection of the Messiah And the Judgments that Follow

But For The Present The Messiah Will be Rejected

25" But first he* must suffer many things
and be rejected by this generation.

And Judgments Will Come Unexpectedly

26" As it was in the days of Noah, (Cf.Mt.24:37-41,p.202)
so will it be in the days of the Son of man. *

(a) As They Did in the Days of Noah

27" They ate, they drank, they married, they were given in marriage,**
until the day when Noah entered the ark,
and the flood came and destroyed them all.

And in the Days of Lot

28" Likewise as it was in the days of Lot--
they ate, they drank, they bought, they sold, they planted, they built,**
29but on the day when Lot went out from Sodom
fire and brimstone rained from heaven and destroyed them all--
30so will it be on the day when the Son of man is revealed.

(b) Many Will Not Escape

31" On that day,***
let him who is on the housetop, with his goods in the house,
not come down to take them away;
and likewise let him who is in the field not turn back.

Whoever Is Faithful At All Cost Will Be Saved

32Remember Lot's wife.
33Whoever seeks to gain his life will lose it,
but whoever loses his life will preserve it.

But Some Will Not Pay The Price

34I tell you,
in that night there will be two men in one bed;
one will be taken and the other left.
35There will be two women grinding together;
one will be taken and the other left." [a]

(c) Judgments Will Strike Where Corruption Abounds

37And they said to him,
"Where, Lord?"
He said to them,
"Where the body is, (Cf.Mt.24:28,p.200)
there the eagles[b] will be gathered together.

(3) Overcoming Both Despair and Self-Righteousness Through Prayer

a. The Widow and the Judge. § 149

Lk. 18:1-8

(1) The Purpose of the Parable

1And he told them a parable,
to the effect that they ought always to pray and not lose heart.

(2) The Story

A Conscienceless Judge and a Helpless Widow

2He said,
"In a certain city there was a judge
who neither feared God nor regarded man;
3and there was a widow in that city
who kept coming to him and saying,
'Vindicate me against my adversary.'

Her Plea For Justice Is Ignored Her Persistence Wins Out

4" For a while he refused;
but afterward he said to himself,
'Though I neither fear God nor regard man,
5yet because this widow bothers me, I will vindicate her,
or she will wear me out by her continual coming.'"

(3) Its Meaning

6And the Lord said,
"Hear what the unrighteous judge says.

Never Despair But Persist In Prayer

7" And will not God vindicate his elect,
who cry to him day and night?
Will he delay long over them? (2 Pet.3:3-10)

God's Answer Is Sure;

8I tell you, he will vindicate them speedily.

But Will People Have Enough Faith

"Nevertheless, when the Son of man* comes,
will he find faith on earth?"

---

[a]*Some ancient authorities add verse 36,* Two men will be in the field; one will be taken and the other will be left. [b]*Or* vultures.

**The Messiah (See v. 26). **Life going on as usual. ***When Jerusalem will be destroyed (See Lk. 21:20-24; compare Mk. 13:14-19).*

b. The Pharisee and the Publican. § 150

Lk. 18:9-14

The Purpose of Jesus	9He also told this parable to some who trusted in themselves that they were righteous and despised others:
The Story	10"Two men went up into the temple to pray, one a Pharisee and the other a tax collector.
A Self-Righteous Pharisee Prays "With Himself"	11"The Pharisee stood and prayed thus with himself, 'God, I thank thee that I am not like other men, extortioners, unjust, adulterers, or even like this tax collector. 12I fast twice a week, I give tithes of all that I get.'
A Conscience-smitten Publican Prays	13"But the tax collector, standing far off, would not even lift up his eyes to heaven, but beat his breast, saying, 'God, be merciful to me a sinner!'
Which Prayer was Effectual	14"I tell you, this man went down to his house justified rather than the other;
and Why	"for every one who exalts himself will be humbled, *(Lk.14:11,p.153;Mt.23:12,p.191)* but he who humbles himself will be exalted."

2. JOURNEYING THROUGH PEREA

(1) Jesus Teaches and Heals Great Multitudes. § 151

	*Mt. 19:1b-2 **	*Mk. 10:1b**
Jesus Comes into Perea Bordering on Judea	1band entered the region of Judea beyond the Jordan;	1band went to the region of Judea and beyond the Jordan:
Multitudes of Pilgrims En Route to the Passover Join Him.	2and large crowds followed him,	and crowds gathered to him again;
He Teaches and Heals All	and he healed them there.	and again, as his custom was, he taught them.

(2) Jesus Teaches About Marriage, Divorce, and Celibacy. § 152

(Cf.Mt.5:27-32,p.60; Lk.16:18,p.158)

	Mt. 19:3-12	*Mk. 10:2-12*
The Pharisees Question Jesus	3And Pharisees came up to him and tested him by asking, "Is it lawful to divorce one's wife for any cause?"	2And Pharisees came up and in order to test him asked, "Is it lawful for a man to divorce his wife?"
Jesus Questions Them	*(Cf. 7 and 8 below)*	3He answered them, "What did Moses command you?"
They Answer		4They said, "Moses allowed a man to write a certificate of divorce, and to put her away."
Jesus Replies (a) Moses' Sufferance and Why	4He answered,	5But Jesus said to them, "For your hardness of heart he wrote you this commandment.
(b) The Nature of Marriage as God Intended It	"Have you not read that he who made them from the beginning made them male and female,	6"But from the beginning of creation, 'God made them male and female.'
An Ideal Union	5"and said, 'For this reason a man shall leave his father and mother and be joined to his wife, and the two shall become one'?[b] 6So that they are no longer two but one.[b]	7'For this reason a man shall leave his father and mother and be joined to his wife,[a] 8and the two shall become one.'[b] So they are no longer two but one.[b]

[a]*Some ancient authorities omit* and be joined to his wife. [b]*Greek* one flesh.

**The records of Mt. and Mk. are continued here from* § 113 *p.122.*

(c) Therefore It Is a Permanent Union

Mt. "What therefore God has joined together, let not man put asunder."

Mk. 9 "What therefore God has joined together, let not man put asunder."

(d) Why Then Did Moses Permit Divorce?

Mt. 7 They said to him,
"Why then did Moses command one
to give a certificate of divorce,
and to put her away?"

His Answer: Divorce Comes From Sinfulness, and Violates Nature

Mt. 8 He said to them,
"For your hardness of heart
Moses allowed you to divorce your wives,
but from the beginning it was not so.

Mk. 10 And in the house
the disciples asked him again about this matter.
(Cf. vs. 3-5 above)

Divorce Encourages Adultery

Mt. 9 "And I say to you:
whoever divorces his wife,
except for unchastity,[a]
and marries another
commits adultery."[b]

Mk. 11 And he said to them,
"Whoever divorces his wife *(Cf. Mt. 5:27-32, p. 60, Lk. 16:18, p. 158)*
and marries another,
commits adultery against her;

It Works Both Ways

Mk. 12 "and if she divorces her husband
and marries another,
she commits adultery."

Celibacy

Mt.

The Disciples Question Jesus Further

10 The disciples said to him,
"If such is the case of a man with his wife,
it is not expedient to marry."

He Answers
(a) In General Marriage Is Best

11 But he said to them,
"Not all men can receive this precept,
but only those to whom it is given.

(b) In Special Cases Celibacy May Be Better,— Because of One's Makeup, Because of Necessity,

12 "For there are eunuchs
who have been so from birth,
and there are eunuchs
who have been made eunuchs by men,

Because of The Kingdom

"and there are eunuchs
who have made themselves eunuchs
for the sake of the kingdom of Heaven.

Each Must Decide For Himself

"He who is able to receive this,
let him receive it."

(3) Jesus Blesses Little Children. § 153

	Mt. 19:13-15	*Mk. 10:13-16*	*Lk. 18:15-17*
Children Are Brought to Jesus	13 Then children were brought to him that he might lay his hands on them and pray.	13 And they were bringing children to him, that he might touch them;	15 Now they were bringing even infants to him that he might touch them;
The Disciples Interfere	The disciples rebuked the people;	and the disciples rebuked them.	and when the disciples saw it, they rebuked them.
Jesus Rebukes Them and Lauds the Childlike Spirit	14 but Jesus said, "Let the children come to me,	14 But when Jesus saw it he was indignant, and said to them, "Let the children come to me,	16 But Jesus called them to him, saying, "Let the children come to me,
The Kingdom Belongs To Those Who Have It	and do not hinder them; for to such belongs the kingdom of heaven." *(Cf. Mt. 18:3, p. 114)*	do not hinder them; for to such belongs the kingdom of God.	and do not hinder them; for to such belongs the kingdom of God.
		15 "Truly, I say to you, whoever does not receive the kingdom of God	17 "Truly, I say to you, whoever does not receive the kingdom of God

[a] *Some ancient authorities, after* unchastity *read* makes her commit adultery. [b] *Some ancient authorities insert* and he who marries a divorced woman commits adultery.

		like a child shall not enter it."	like a child shall not enter it."
He Takes The Children In His Arms and Blesses Them	15 And he laid his hands on them and went away.	16 And he took them in his arms and blessed them, laying his hands upon them.	

(4) Jesus Instructs a Rich Young Ruler. § 154

	Mt. 19:16-20:16	*Mk. 10:17-31*	*Lk. 18:18-30*
		The Story	
A Ruler Comes and Kneels Before Jesus	16 And behold, one came up to him, saying,	17 And as he was setting out on his journey a man ran up and knelt before him, and asked him,	18 And a ruler asked him,
(a) His first Question How to Enter Into Life.	"Teacher, what good deed must I do, to have eternal life?"	"Good Teacher, what must I do to inherit eternal life?"	"Good Teacher, *(Cf.10:25ff.,p.137)* what shall I do to inherit eternal life?"
Christ's Answer	17 And he said to him, "Why do you ask me about what is good? One there is who is good.	18 And Jesus said to him, "Why do you call me good? No one is good but God alone.	19 And Jesus said to him, "Why do you call me good? No one is good but God alone.
Entering into Life by Keeping the commandments	If you would enter life, keep the commandments." 18 He said to him, "Which?"	19 "You know the commandments:	20 You know the commandments:
Jesus Enumerates Sample Commands	And Jesus said, "You shall not kill, You shall not commit adultery, You shall not steal, You shall not bear false witness, 19 Honor your father and your mother, and, You shall love your neighbor as yourself."	'Do not kill, Do not commit adultery, Do not steal, Do not bear false witness, Do not defraud, Honor your father and mother!'	Do not commit adultery, Do not kill, Do not steal, Do not bear false witness, Honor your father and mother."
And The Young Man Claims Full Obedience			
(b) His Second Question How to Be Perfect	20 The young man said to him, "All these I have observed; what do I still lack?"	20 And he said to him, "Teacher, all these I have observed from my youth."	21 And he said, "All these I have kept from my youth."
Christ's Answer: Becoming "Perfect" Through Absolute Consecration	21 Jesus said to him, "If you would be perfect, go, sell what you possess and give it to the poor, and you will have treasure in heaven; and come, follow me."	21 And Jesus looking upon him loved him, and said to him, "You lack one thing; go, sell all that you have, and give it to the poor, and you will have treasure in heaven; and come, follow me."	22 And when Jesus heard it, he said to him, "One thing you still lack. Sell all that you have and distribute to the poor, and you will have treasure in heaven; and come, follow me."

	Mt.	Mk.	Lk.
The man's Refusal and the Result	22 When the young man heard this he went away sorrowful; for he had great possessions.	22 At that saying his countenance fell and he went away sorrowful; for he had great possessions.	23 But when he heard this he became sad, for he was very rich.

The Comment of Jesus on the Incident

	Mt.	Mk.	Lk.
Jesus says Riches Make Salvation Difficult	23 And Jesus said to his disciples, "Truly, I say to you, it will be hard for a rich man to enter the kingdom of heaven."	23 And Jesus looked around and said to his disciples, "How hard it will be for those who have riches to enter the kingdom of God!"	24 Jesus looking at him said, "How hard it is for those who have riches to enter the kingdom of God!
*The Disciples Are Amazed**		24 And the disciples were amazed at his words.	
Jesus Explains With Further Emphasis	24 "Again I tell you, It is easier for a camel to go through the eye of a needle than for a rich man to enter the kingdom of God."	But Jesus said to them again, "Children, how hard it is[a] to enter the kingdom of God! 25 "It is easier for a camel to go through the eye of a needle than for a rich man to enter the kingdom of God."	25 "For it is easier for a camel to go through the eye of a needle than for a rich man to enter the kingdom of God."
*They Are Still More Dumbfounded**	25 When the disciples heard this, they were greatly astonished, saying, "Who then* can be saved?"	26 And they were exceedingly [astonished, and said to him,[b] "Then who can be saved?"	26 Those who heard it said, "Then who can be saved?"
A Final Word	26 But Jesus looked at them and said to them, "With men this is impossible, but with God all things are possible."	27 Jesus looked at them and said, "With men it is impossible, but not with God; for all things are possible with God."	27 But he said, "What is impossible with men is possible with God."

Peter's Question

	Mt.	Mk.	Lk.
Peter's Assumption of Merit	27 Then Peter said in reply, "Lo, we have left everything and followed you. What then shall we have?"	28 Peter began to say to him, "Lo, we have left everything, and followed you." *(Cf.Mk.1:20,p.41)*	28 And Peter said, "Lo, we have left our homes and followed you."
In Eternal Life Great Power and Glory will be enjoyed By Those Who Had Followed Christ and To Those Who Sacrifice Here	28 Jesus said to them, "Truly, I say to you, in the new world, when the Son of man shall sit on his glorious throne, you who have followed me will also sit on twelve thrones, judging the twelve tribes of Israel." 29 "And every one who has left houses or brothers or sisters or father or mother or children or lands, for my name's sake,	29 Jesus said, "Truly I say to you, "There is no one who has left house, or brothers, or sisters, or mother, or father, or children, or lands, for my sake, and for the gospel,	29 And he said to them, "Truly, I say to you, *(Cf.Lk.22:24-30,p.209)* "There is no man who has left house or wife or brothers or parents or children, for the sake of the kingdom of God,

[a] *Some ancient authorities add* for those who trust in riches. [b] *Many ancient authorities read* to one another.

**That is, if a rich man cannot? They had been taught that riches were evidence of God's approval and blessing. A poor man found it impossible to keep all the "traditions of the elders."*

	Mt.	Mk.	Lk.
	" will receive a hundredfold,[a]	30" who will not receive a hundredfold	30who will not receive manifold more
A Hundred-Fold Here In This Life Would Be Given		now in this time, houses, and brothers, and sisters, and mothers, and children, and lands, with persecutions,	in this time,
However God Doesn't Count As We Do	and inherit eternal life.	and in the age to come eternal life.	and in the age to come eternal life."
The Last First: (1) The General Statement	30" But many that are first will be last, and the last first." *(20:16)*	*Mk.* 31" But many that are first will be last, and the last first."	

(Lk. 13:30, p. 152)

Mt. 20

(2) The Parable: a. The Householder Hiring Workmen

1" For the kingdom of heaven
is like a householder
who went out early in the morning
to hire laborers for his vineyard.

(a) In the Morning

2" After agreeing with the laborers for a denarius[b] a day,
he sent them into his vineyard.

(b) At Nine

3" And going out about the third hour
he saw others standing idle in the market-place;

4" and to them he said,
'You go into the vineyard too, and whatever is right I will give you.'

" So they went.

(c) At Twelve and at Three

5" Going out again about the sixth hour and the ninth hour,
he did the same.

(d) In the Evening

6" And about the eleventh hour he went out and found others standing;
and he said to them,
'Why do you stand here idle all day?'

7" They said to him,
'Because no one has hired us.'

" He said to them,
'You go into the vineyard too.'

b. Paying The Men At Night

8" And when evening came,
the owner of the vineyard said to his steward,
'Call the laborers and pay them their wages,
beginning with the last, up to the first.'

9" And when those hired about the eleventh hour came,
each of them received a denarius.[b]

10" Now when the first came, they thought that they would receive more;
but each of them also received a denarius.

Some Grumble

11" And on receiving it, they grumbled at the householder,
12saying,
'These last worked only one hour,
and you have made them equal to us
who have borne the burden of the day and the scorching heat."

The Grumblers Are Answered

13" But he replied to one of them,
'Friend, I am doing you no wrong;
did you not agree with me for a denarius?

14'Take what belongs to you, and go;
I choose to give to this last as I give to you.
15Am I not allowed to do what I choose with what belongs to me?
Or do you begrudge my generosity?'[c]

(3) The General Principle Reiterated (cf. 19:30)

16" So the last will be first,
and the first last." *(19:30)*

[a]*Some ancient authorities read* manifold. [b]*About twenty cents. Note on Mt. 18:28.,* [c]*Or* is your eye evil because I am good?

(5) Jesus Again Teaches the Twelve About His Death. § 155 [§103, §106]

	Mt. 20:17-19	Mk. 10:32-34	Lk. 18:31-34
Jesus and the Disciples Are On The Way to Jerusalem	17And as Jesus was going up to Jerusalem	32And they were on the road, going up to Jerusalem, and Jesus was walking ahead of them; and they were amazed. and those who followed were afraid.	*(Cf.Lk.19:11)*
Jesus Foretells His Sufferings, Death, and Resurrection in Great Detail.	he took the twelve disciples aside, and on the way he said to them, 18"Behold we are going up to Jerusalem;	And taking the twelve again, he began to tell them what was to happen to him, 33saying, "Behold, we are going up to Jerusalem;	31And taking the twelve aside, he said to them, "Behold, we are going up to Jerusalem, and everything that is written of the Son of man by the prophets will be accomplished.
As Prophesied.	*Mt.*	*Mk.*	
He Will Be Betrayed Arrested Condemned	and the Son of man will be delivered to the chief priests and scribes, and they will condemn him to death,	and the Son of man will be delivered to the chief priests and the scribes, and they will condemn him to death,	
Handed Over To the Romans	19and deliver him to the Gentiles	*Mk.* and deliver him to the Gentiles.	*Lk.* 32"For he will be delivered to the Gentiles,
Who will Mock	to be mocked	34And they will mock him, and spit upon him,	and will be mocked and shamefully treated and spit upon;
and Scourge	and scourged	and scourge him,	33they will scourge him
and Crucify, He Will Rise Again,	and crucified, and he will be raised on the third day."	and kill him; and after three days he will rise."	and kill him, and on the third day he will rise."
The Disciples Fail to Understand		*(Cf.Lk.9:45,p.113)*	34But they understood none of these things; this saying was hid from them, and they did not grasp what was said.

(6) Jesus Rebukes the Selfish Ambition of the Twelve. § 156

a. The Ambition of the Two

	Mt. 20:20-28	Mk. 10:35-45
An Ambitious Mother's Homage	20Then the mother of the sons of Zeb´e-dee came up to him, with her sons, and kneeling before him she asked him for something.	35And James and John, the sons of Zeb´e-dee, came forward to him, and said to him, "Teacher, we want you to do for us whatever we ask of you."
	21And he said to her, "What do you want?"	36And he said to them, "What do you want me to do for you?"
Her Request	She said to him, "Command that these two sons of mine may sit, one at your right hand and one at your left, in your kingdom."	37And they said to him, "Grant us to sit, one at your right hand and one at your left, in your glory."
Christ's Rebuke and Question	22But Jesus answered, "You do not know what you are asking. Are you able to drink the cup* that I am to drink?	38But Jesus said to them, "You do not know what you are asking. Are you able to drink the cup* that I drink, or to be baptized with the baptism with which I am baptized?"*
Their Ready Reply	They said to him, "We are able."	39And they said to him, "We are able."
Christ's Profound Reply	23He said to them, "You will drink my cup, *(Mt.26:39,p.222)*	And Jesus said to them, "The cup that I drink you will drink; and with the baptism with which I am baptized, you will be baptized;
	but to sit at my right hand and at my left is not mine to grant; ** but it is for those for whom it has been prepared** by my Father."	40but to sit at my right hand or at my left, is not mine to grant; ** but it is for those for whom it has been prepared."

....

**Here (as in Lk.12:49-50) Jesus refers to His death as a "baptism", or a "cup" to drink.*

***Literally, "Is not mine to grant except to those for whom it has been prepared." Rank In Christ's Kingdom is bestowed not arbitrarily, by favoritism, but is bestowed on a basis of intrinsic merit.*

b. The Jealousy of the Ten

	Mt. 20:20-28	Mk. 10:35-45
The other Apostles Are Jealous	24 And when the ten heard it, they were indignant at the two brothers.	41 And when the ten heard it, they began to be indignant at James and John,
Jesus Explains: (a)Apparent Greatness Consists in Exercising Authority	25 But Jesus called them to him and said, "You know that the rulers of the Gentiles lord it over them, and their great men exercise authority over them.	42 And Jesus called them to him and said to them, "You know that those who are supposed to rule over the Gentiles lord it over them, and their great men exercise authority over them.
(b)True Greatness consists in Greatly Serving	26 Not so shall it be among you; *(Mt.5:4;18:4,p.58)* but whoever would be great among you must be your servant, *(Mt.23:11,p.191)* 27 and whoever would be first among you must be your slave;	43 But it shall not be so among you; but whoever would be great among you must be your servant, 44 and whoever would be first among you must be slave of all.
(c) Christ's Greatness Is Thus Judged	28 even as the Son of man came not to be served but to serve, and to give his life as a ransom for many."	45 For the Son of man also came not to be served but to serve, and to give his life as a ransom for many."

3. PASSING THROUGH JERICHO (Mt. 20:29a; Mk. 10:46a; Lk.18:35a)

(1) Jesus Heals Two Blind Men at Jericho. § 157

	Mt. 20:29-34	*Mk. 10:46-52*	*Lk. 18:35-43*
		46 And they came to Jericho;	35 As he drew near to Jericho,
Jesus and a Multitude Are Passing by	29 And as they went out of Jericho, a great crowd followed him.	and as he was leaving Jericho, with his disciples and a great multitude,	
Two Blind Beggars Hear Them	30 And behold, two blind men sitting by the roadside, when he heard	Bar-ti-mae´us, a blind beggar, the son of Ti-mae´us, was sitting by the roadside. 47 And when he heard	a blind man was sitting by the roadside begging;
They Learn that It Is Jesus	that Jesus was passing by,	that it was Jesus of Nazareth,	36 and hearing a multitude going by, he inquired what this meant. 37 They told him, "Jesus of Nazareth is passing by."
They Plead for Help	cried out,[a] "Have mercy on us, Son of David!"	he began to cry out, and say, "Jesus, Son of David, have mercy on me!"	38 And he cried, "Jesus, Son of David, have mercy on me!"
The Crowds Rebuke Them	31 The crowd rebuked them, telling them to be silent;	48 And many rebuked him, telling him to be silent;	39 And those who were in front rebuked him, telling him to be silent;
The Beggars Insist the More,	but they cried out the more, "Lord, have mercy on us, Son of David!"	but he cried out all the more, "Son of David, have mercy on me!"	but he cried out all the more, "Son of David, have mercy on me!"
Jesus Calls Them.	32 And Jesus stopped and called them,	49 And Jesus stopped and said, "Call him." And they called the blind man, saying to him, "Take heart; rise, he is calling you."	40 And Jesus stopped, and commanded him to be brought to him;
They Jump Up And Go To Him		50 And throwing off his mantle he sprang up and came to Jesus.	
Jesus Asks What they want	saying, "What do you want me to do for you?"	51 And Jesus said to him, "What do you want me to do for you?"	and when he came near, he asked him, 41 "What do you want me to do for you?"
They Ask To Be Cured	33 They said to him, "Lord, let our eyes be opened."	And the blind man said to him, "Master,[b] let me receive my sight."	He said, "Lord, let me receive my sight."

[a] *Many ancient authorities insert* Lord. [b] *Or* Rabbi.

	Matthew	Mark	Luke
Jesus Touches Their Eyes	34 And Jesus, in pity, touched their eyes.	52 And Jesus said to him,	42 And Jesus said to him,
They Are Healed		"Go your way; Your faith has made you well."	"Receive your sight; your faith has made you well."
	And immediately they received their sight,	And immediately he received his sight	43 And immediately he received his sight
They follow Jesus Praising God;	and followed him.	and followed him on the way.	and followed him, glorifying God;
The Crowds Praise God			and all the people, when they saw it, gave praise to God.

(2) Jesus Lodges with a Publican and Saves Him. § 158

Lk. 19:1-10

Jesus is Passing Through Jericho

1 He entered Jericho and was passing through.

2 And there was a man named Zac-chae´us;
he was a chief tax collector,
and rich.

Zacchaeus Wants to See Him

3 And he sought to see who Jesus was,
but could not, on account of the crowd,
because he was small of stature.

So He Climbs Up So He Can See

4 So he ran on ahead
and climbed up into a sycamore tree to see him,
for he was to pass that way.

Jesus Says He Must Go Home With Him

5 And when Jesus came to the place,
he looked up and said to him,
"Zac-chae´us, make haste and come down;
for I must stay at your house today."

He Comes Down And Takes Jesus Home With Him

6 So he made haste and came down
and received him joyfully.

The People Sneer

7 And when they saw it they all murmured,
"He has gone in to be the guest of a man who is a sinner." (§ 54)

A Sinner Repents

8 And Zac-chae´us stood and said to the Lord,
"Behold, Lord, the half of my goods I give to the poor;
and if I have defrauded any one of anything, I restore it fourfold."

Salvation Comes to His Household

9 And Jesus said to him,
"Today salvation has come to this house,
since he also is a son of Abraham.*
10 For the Son of man came to seek and to save that which was lost."

4. NEARING JERUSALEM (Lk. 19:11a and 28)

(1) Jesus Teaches by Parable, on Approaching Jerusalem. § 159 [*Contrast* § 192]

Lk. 19:11-28

On Nearing Jerusalem They Grow Tensely Expectant

11 As they heard these things,
he proceeded to tell a parable,
because he was near to Jerusalem,
and because they supposed that the kingdom of God was to appear immediately.** *(Mk.10:32)*

Jesus Teaches By Parable

A King Goes To get a Kingdom

12 He said therefore,
"A nobleman went into a far country
to receive kingly power[a] and then return.

He Assigns Responsibilities To His Servants

13 "Calling ten of his servants,
he gave them ten pounds,[b] and said to them,
'Trade with these till I come. *(Cf.Mt.25:16 and footnote)*

....

[a] *Greek* a kingdom.
[b] *The mina, rendered here by* pound, *was equal to about twenty dollars.*

**And not a hopeless outcast as they thought. It is said that publicans were even forbidden to attend synagogue.*
***See footnote p.165.*

His Citizens Send Men To Oppose Him

14 "But his citizens hated him
and sent an embassy after him, saying,
'We do not want this man to reign over us.'

The King, Returning, Reckons with His Servants

15 "When he returned,
having received the kingly power,[a]
he commanded these servants, to whom he had given the money, to be called to him,
that he might know what they had gained by trading.

and Rewards Each

16 "The first came before him, saying,
'Lord, your pound has made ten pounds more.'

17 "And he said to him,
'Well done, good servant!
Because you have been faithful in a very little,
you shall have authority over ten cities.'

Faithfulness In Duty Earns Greater Responsibility

18 "And the second came, saying,
'Lord, your pound has made five pounds.'
19 And he said to him,
'And you are to be over five cities.'

Failure and Neglect, Due to Fear and Mistrust,

20 "Then another came, saying,
'Lord, here is your pound, which I kept laid away in a napkin; *(Cf. Mt. 25:25, p. 204)*
21 for I was afraid of you, because you are a severe man;
you take up what you did not lay down,
and reap what you did not sow.'

Are Condemned

22 "He said to him,
'I will condemn you out of your own mouth, you wicked servant!
You knew that I was a severe man,
taking up what I did not lay down
and reaping what I did not sow?
23 Why then did you not put my money into the bank,
and at my coming I should have collected it with interest?'

They Are Inexcusable

They Are Punished

24 "And he said to those who stood by,
'Take the pound from him,
and give it to him who has the ten pounds.'

25 (And they said to him,
'Lord, he has ten pounds!')

This Law Is Universal

26 "I tell you, that to every one who has will more be given;
but from him who has not, even what he has will be taken away.'

The King also Punishes His Enemies

27 "But as for these enemies of mine, who did not want me to reign over them,
bring them here and slay them before me.'"

Jesus Continues His Journey

Jesus Then Leads on to Jerusalem

28 And when he had said this,
he went on ahead,
going up to Jerusalem.

(2) The Passover Crowds Await Jesus' Coming, in Jerusalem. § 160

Jn. 11:55-57

Meanwhile At Jerusalem The Passover Is At Hand

55 Now the Passover of the Jews was at hand,

The Crowds Come Early

and many went up from the country to Jerusalem
before the Passover,
to purify themselves.

They Seek Eagerly for Jesus. Everybody Is Talking About Him.

56 They were looking for Jesus

and saying to one another, as they stood in the temple,
"What do you think?
That he will not come to the feast?"

The Officials Serve Notice and Plan to Arrest Him

57 Now the chief priests and the Pharisees had given orders that
*if any one knew where he was, *(See Jn. 11:54, and § 146, p. 163)*
he should let them know, so that they might arrest him.

[a] *Greek* a kingdom.

**Here was Judas' chance:* In the light of this verse and Jn. 12:6, p. 176, study §§ 194, 195.*

(1) Mary Anoints Jesus at Bethany. § 161 [Contrast § 66]

	Mt. 26:6-13	Mk. 14:3-9 *	Jn. 12:1-8
Jesus Arrives at Bethany		(*i.e., Friday Afternoon, reckoning from Mk.15:42. See p.245, footnote)	1 Six days before the Passover*, Jesus came to Bethany, where Laz´a-rus was, whom Jesus had raised from the dead.
He Is A Guest of Simon	6 Now when Jesus was at Bethany in the house of Simon the leper,	3 And while he was at Bethany in the house of Simon the leper,	
A Supper is Made in His Honor		(SATURDAY) as he sat at table,	2 There they made him a supper; Martha served, but Laz´a-rus was one of those at table with him.
Mary Anoints Jesus	7 a woman came up to him with an alabaster jar of very expensive ointment,	a woman came with an alabaster jar of ointment of pure nard, very costly,	3 Mary took a pound[b] of costly ointment of pure nard
His Head and His feet	and she poured it on his head, as he sat at table.	and she broke the jar and poured it over his head.	and anointed the feet of Jesus and wiped his feet with her hair; and the house was filled with the fragrance of the ointment.
	8 But when the disciples saw it,	4 But there were some who said	4 But Judas Iscariot, one of his disciples, (he who was to betray him),
Judas Misunderstands and Criticizes Mary	they were indignant, saying, "Why this waste?	to themselves indignantly, "Why was the ointment thus wasted?	said,
He Accuses Her of Sinful Extravagance	9 For this ointment might have been sold for a large sum, and given to the poor."	5 For this ointment might have been sold for more than three hundred denarii,[a] and given to the poor."	5 "Why was this ointment not sold for three hundred denarii,[a] and given to the poor?"
The Rest Fall for It		And they reproached her.	
What Judas' Motive Is			6 This he said, not that he cared for the poor, but because he was a thief and as he had the money box, he used to take what was put into it.
Jesus Defends Mary and Explains Her Deed and Commends Her	10 But Jesus, aware of this, said to them, "Why do you trouble the woman? For she has done a beautiful thing to me.	6 But Jesus said, "Let her alone; why do you trouble her? She has done a beautiful thing to me.	7 Jesus said, "Let her alone, let her keep it for the day of my burial.
He Refutes Their Argument	11 For you always have the poor with you, but you will not always have me.	7 "For you always have the poor with you, and whenever you will, you can do good to them; but you will not always have me.	8 "The poor you always have with you, but you do not always have me."
She has Anointed Him for Burial	12 "In pouring this ointment on my body she has done it to prepare me for burial.	8 "She has done what she could; she has anointed my body beforehand for burying.	
A Great Promise Is Made to Her	13 "Truly, I say to you, wherever this gospel is preached in the whole world, what this woman has done will be told in memory of her."	9 "And truly, I say to you, wherever the gospel is preached in the whole world, what she has done will be told in memory of her."	(e.g. Jn.11:2, p.160)

[a] See on Matthew 18:28. [three hundred days' wages] [b] Greek litra. *For Mk.14:1,2 see § 194, p.207.

(2) The Crowds Hear the News of Jesus' Arrival at Bethany. § 162

Jn. 12:9-11

When The People Hear that Jesus is at Bethany They Go to See Both Jesus and Lazarus

9When the great crowd of the Jews
learned that he was there, *(SATURDAY)*
they came, not only on account of Jesus
but also to see Laz'a-rus,
whom he had raised from the dead.

The Jewish Officials Plot to Kill Lazarus Also

10So the chief priests planned
to put Laz'a-rus also to death,
11because on account of him
many of the Jews were going away
and believing in Jesus.

C. THE CONSUMMATION

I. CONTROVERSIES AND PROPHETIC WARNINGS *(pp. 179-205)*
(Sunday to Tuesday of Passion Week)

(I) THE FINAL APPEALS (§§ 163-173) pp.178-189.

1. THREE DRAMATIZED PARABLES (§§ 163-166) pp.178-182.

(1) The Triumphal Entry (Mt. 21:1-11; Mk. 11:1-11; Lk. 19:29-44; Jn. 12:12-19) *(Sunday)*

(2) The Withering of The Fig Tree (Mt. 21:18-19; Mk. 11:12-14) *(Monday)*

(3) The Cleansing of the Temple (Mt. 21:12-17; Mk. 11:15-19; Lk. 19:45-48) *(Monday)*

(4) Christ's Lesson from the Withered Fig Tree (Mt. 21:20-22; Mk. 11:20-26) *(Tuesday)*

2. THREE PARABLES OF WARNING (§§ 167-170) pp.183-186. *(Tuesday)*

(1) The Two Sons (Mt. 21:23-32; Mk.11:27-33; Lk.20:1-8)

(2) The Wicked Husbandmen (Mt. 21:33-46; Mk. 12:1-12; Lk. 20:9-19)

(3) The Marriage of the King's Son (Mt. 22:1-14)

3. THREE CATCH QUESTIONS (§§ 171-173) pp.187-189. *(Tuesday)*

(1) About Giving Tribute to Caesar (Mt. 22:15-22; Mk. 12:13-17; Lk. 20:20-26)

(2) About The Resurrection (Mt. 22:23-33; Mk.12:18-27; Lk.20:27-39)

(3) About the Greatest Commandment (Mt. 22:34-40; Mk. 12:28-34; Lk.20:40)

4. CHRIST'S UNANSWERED QUESTION (§ 174) p.189.

About the Messiah Being the Son of David (Mt. 22:41-46; Mk. 12:35-37; Lk. 20:41-44)

[(II) THE FINAL DEPARTURE *(see p. 190)*] *(Tuesday)*

[II. SUFFERINGS AND DEATH *(see p. 206)*

(I) THE PREPARATIONS FOR HIS DEATH *(see p. 206)*

(II) THE EVENTS LEADING TO HIS DEATH *(see p. 223)*]

[III. TRIUMPH AND GLORY *(see p. 247)*

(I) THE RESURRECTION AND APPEARANCES

(II) THE FINAL COMMISSION AND ASCENSION

(III) THE GLORIFICATION OF JESUS
and
THE COMING OF THE HOLY SPIRIT]

(I) THE FINAL APPEALS

1. Three Dramatized Parables

(1) The Triumphal Entry.* §163 *(SUNDAY**)*

Mt. 21:1-11 — Mk.11:1-11 — Lk. 19:29-44 — Jn.12:12-19

In Jerusalem The Crowds Hear That Jesus Has Come To Bethany

Jn.

12The next day *(See Jn.12:1-11, and Footnote, p.245)*
a great crowd who had come to the feast
heard that Jesus was coming to Jerusalem.

They Set Out For Bethany To Meet Him

13So they took branches of palm trees
and went out to meet him, crying,
"Hosanna! Blessed be he who comes in the name of the Lord,
even the King of Israel!"

Meanwhile at Bethany

Mt.

1And when they drew near
to Jerusalem
and came to Bethphage,
to the Mount of Olives,

Mk.

1And when they drew near
to Jerusalem,
to Bethphage and Bethany,
at the Mount of Olives,

Lk.

29When he drew near
to Bethphage and Bethany,
at the Mount that is called Olivet,

Jesus Sends Two Disciples to Bring a Donkey

Mt.

then Jesus sent two disciples,
2saying to them,
"Go into the village
opposite you,
and immediately

Mk.

he sent two of his disciples,
2and said to them,
"Go into the village
opposite you,
and immediately
as you enter it

Lk.

he sent two of the disciples,
30saying,
"Go into the village
opposite,
where on entering

He Tells Them What They Are to Find And Do

Mt.

you will find an ass tied,
and a colt with her;
untie them
and bring them to me.

Mk.

you will find
a colt tied,
on which no one has ever sat;
untie it
and bring it.

Lk.

you will find
a colt tied,
on which no one has ever yet sat;
untie it
and bring it here.

and What They Are To Say

Mt.

3"If anyone says
anything to you,
you shall say,
'The Lord has need of them.'
And he will send them immediately."

Mk.

3"If anyone says to you,
'Why are you doing this?'
say,
'The Lord has need of it,
and he will send it back
here immediately.'"

Lk.

31"If anyone asks you,
'Why are you untying it?'
you shall say this,
'The Lord has need of it.'"

*In This Way Jesus Dramatizes A Messianic Prophecy**

Mt.

4This took place to fulfill
what was spoken by the prophet,* saying, *(Zech.9:9-10)*
5"Tell the daughter of Zion,
Behold, your king is coming to you,
humble, and mounted on an ass,
and on a colt, the foal of an ass."

(Jn.12:15)

The Disciples Go and Do As Jesus Had Instructed Them

Mt.

6The disciples went
and did
as Jesus had directed them;

Mk.

4And they went away,
and found a colt tied at the door,
out in the open street;
and they untied it.
5And those who stood there said,
"What are you doing, untying the colt?"
6And they told them
what Jesus had said.
And they let them go.

Lk.

32So those who were sent went away,
and found it as he had told them.
33And as they were untying the colt,
its owners said to them,
"Why are you untying the colt?"
34And they said,
"The Lord has need of it."

They Bring The Donkey. Jesus Sits on It

Mt.

7They brought the ass
and the colt,
and put their
clothes on them
and he sat thereon.

Mk.

7And they brought
the colt to Jesus.
And threw their
clothes on it;
and he sat upon it.

Lk.

35And they brought
it to Jesus,
and throwing their
garments on the colt
they set Jesus upon it.

Jn.

14And Jesus found
a young ass
and sat upon it;

A Prophecy Comes True

Mt. *(v.4-5)*

Jn.

as it is written, *(Zech.9:9-10)*
15"Fear not, daughter of Zion;
behold thy king is coming,
sitting on an ass's colt!"

His Disciples Did Not Remember Then But After Jesus Was Glorified

....

16His disciples did not understand
this at first;
but when Jesus was glorified,
then they remembered
that this had been written of him
and had been done to him.

*Jesus here dramatizes Zechariah's prophecy about the Messiah. And while he claims to be the Messiah King, He also demonstrates what kind of a king the Messiah will be. (See Zech. 9:9-10). **See Footnotes on pages 205 and 245.

The Procession gets started

Mt.

8 Most of the crowd spread their
garments on the road,
and others cut branches from the trees
and spread them

on the road.

Mk.

8 And many spread their
garments on the road,

and others spread leafy branches
which they had cut from the fields.

Lk.

36 And as he rode along,
they spread their
garments on the road.

The Bethany Crowd Tells of Lazarus

Jn.

17 The crowd that had been with him*
when he called Lazarus out of the tomb
and raised him from the dead bore witness.

The Jerusalem Crowd Had Heard About Lazarus

18 The reason why the crowd** went to meet him
was that they heard he had done this sign.

One Crowd Goes Before The Other Follows Jesus

They Cheer and Shout Hosannas

Mt.

9 And the crowds that went before him**
and that followed him
shouted, "Hosanna to the Son of David!
Blessed be he who comes
in the name of the Lord!"

Hosanna in the highest!"

Mk.

9 And those who went before**
and those who followed *
cried out; "Hosanna!
Blessed be he who comes
in the name of the Lord!
10 Blessed be the kingdom of our father David
that is coming!
Hosanna in the highest!"

As They Reach The Top of The Mountain, and get a First Glimpse of Jerusalem Cheering Breaks Out Again

Lk.

37 As he was now drawing near,
at the descent of the Mount of Olives,
the whole multitude of the disciples began to rejoice
and praise God with a loud voice
for all the mighty works that they had seen, 38 saying,
"Blessed be the King who comes in the name of the Lord!
Peace in heaven and glory in the highest!"

39 And some of the Pharisees in the multitude said to him,
"Teacher, rebuke your disciples."

At This Some Pharisees Object. Jesus Answers Them. They Grumble Among Themselves

40 He answered,
"I tell you, if these were silent,
the very stones would cry out."

Jn.

19 The Pharisees then said to one another,
"You see that you can do nothing;
Look, the world has gone after him."

When, At a sudden Turn In the Road Jerusalem Comes Into Full View Jesus Breaks Out Weeping Over Jerusalem

Lk.

41 And when he drew near and saw the city
he wept over it, 42 saying,
"Would that even today
you knew the things that make for peace!

*(Cf. Mt. 23:37-39, p. 193
Lk. 13:34-35, p. 153)*

But now they are hid from your eyes.
43 For the days shall come upon you,
when your enemies
will cast up a bank about you and surround you,
and hem you in on every side,
44 and dash you to the ground,
you and your children within you,
and they will not leave one stone upon another in you;

because you did not know the time of your visitation."

Then They Reach Jerusalem

They Enter All The City Is Stirred.

Mt.

10 And when he entered Jerusalem,

all the city was stirred, saying,
"Who is this?"
11 And the crowds said,
"This is the prophet Jesus
from Nazareth of Galilee."

Mk.

11 And he entered Jerusalem.

Jesus Enters The Temple, Sees Corrupt Conditions; Then Retires to Bethany.

And he went into the temple.

And when he had looked round at everything,
as it was already late,
he went out to Bethany with the twelve.

**The crowd at Bethany.*

***This was the crowd coming out from Jerusalem to see Jesus (See v. 9).*

(2) The Withering of The Fig-Tree. § 164 *(MONDAY)*

	Mt. 21:18-19	*Mk. 11:12-14*
Next Morning	18In the morning, as he was returning to the city,	12On the following day, [*MONDAY*] when they came from Bethany,
Jesus is Hungry	he was hungry.	he was hungry.
He Seeks Fruit	19And seeing a fig tree by the wayside he went to it.	13And seeing in the distance a fig tree in leaf, he went to see if he could find anything on it.
He Finds only Leaves	and found nothing on it but leaves only.	When he came to it, he found nothing but leaves, for it was not the season for figs.
He Pronounces Judgment	And he said to it, "May no fruit ever come from you again!"	14And he said to it, "May no one ever eat fruit from you again." And his disciples heard it.
The Fig Tree Withers.	And the fig tree withered at once.	

(3) The Cleansing of the Temple.* § 165 *(MONDAY)*

	Mt. 21:12-17	*Mk. 11:15-19*	*Lk. 19:45-48*
Jesus Enters the Temple.	12And Jesus entered the temple of God.[a]	15And they came to Jerusalem. And he entered the temple	45And he entered into the temple
He Drives the Traffickers Out of The Temple.*	And drove out* all who sold and bought in the temple. And he overturned the tables of the money-changers and the seats of those who sold pigeons.	and began to drive out those who sold and those who bought in the temple, and he overturned the tables of the money changers and the seats of those who sold pigeons; 16and he would not allow anyone to carry anything through the temple.	and began to drive out those who sold, *(See Jn.2:13-22,p.31)*
He Explains His Reason.	13He said to them, "It is written, 'My house shall be called a house of prayer;' but you make it a den of robbers."	17And he taught, and said to them, "Is it not written, 'My house shall be called a house of prayer for all the nations'? But you have made it a den of robbers."	46saying to them, "It is written, 'My house shall be *(Isa.56:7)* a house of prayer;' but you have made it a den of robbers."
The Rulers Are Infuriated.		18And the chief priests and the scribes heard it,	
Jesus Teaches and Heals Daily In The Temple.	14And the blind and the lame came to him in the temple, and he healed them.	[*This healing and teaching continued all day long. cf. Mt. 21:18 and Mk. 11:12 and 19*]	47aAnd he was teaching daily in the temple.
The Rulers Object to The Children's Praise.	15But when the chief priests and the scribes saw the wonderful things that he did, and the children crying out in the temple, "Hosanna to the Son of David!" they were indignant; 16and they said to him, "Do you hear what these are saying?"		

....

[a]*Some ancient authorities omit* of God.

**See §26,p.31 and footnote there. Jesus struck here at a monstrous perversion of temple worship for the sake of graft. Annas and the "Chief Priests" "got a corner on the market" by making a rule that since every sacrifice had to be perfect, the priests had to inspect them; but that at passover time it was impossible, so they preinspected a great number of animals and kept them in the temple courts for sale. This gave them a monopoly. Then they boosted the price outrageously (Talmud says as much as 15 times). In this way they were robbing the people. Think what this would do to the would be worshippers.*

Jesus Defends Them

Mt.

And Jesus said to them,
"Yes; have you never read, *(Ps.8:2)*
'Out of the mouth of babes and sucklings
thou hast brought perfect praise'?"

*From now on The Rulers Keep Seeking * A Way To Destroy Him,*

Mk.

and sought* a way to destroy him;
for they feared him,

Lk.

47b
The chief priests and the scribes and
the principal men of the people
sought* to destroy him; *(Cf. § 58, Mk.3:6 and Note)*
48but they did not find anything they could do,

But The People "Hang on His Words" until evening came; then

Mk.

because all the multitude
was astonished at his teaching.

Lk.

for all the people *(Lk.4:22,p.38;Mk.1:22,p.42)*
hung upon his words. *(Mk.12:37,p.189)*

Jesus and The Twelve Go Out to Bethany, On Olivet for The Night

Mt.

17And
leaving them,
he went out of the city
to Bethany,
and lodged there.

Mk.

19And when evening came,
they[a] went out of the city.

Cf. Lk.21:37-38, as on p.205

(4) Christ's Lesson from The Withered Fig Tree. § 166 *(TUESDAY)***

Mt. 21:20-22 — *Mk. 11: 20-26*

Next Morning On the Way Back to the Temple

Mk.

20As they passed by in the morning,**
they saw the fig tree withered away to its roots.

The Disciples Marvel At The Withered Fig-Tree

Mt.

20When the disciples saw it
they marveled, saying,
"How did the fig-tree wither at once?"

Mk.

21And Peter remembered and said to him,
"Master,[b] look!
The fig-tree which you cursed has withered."

Jesus Teaches A Lesson From It on Faith and Prayer

Mt.

21And Jesus answered them,
"Truly, I say to you,
if you have faith
and never doubt,
you will not only do
what has been done to the fig tree,
but even if you say to this mountain,
'Be taken up and cast into the sea,'
(Cf.Mt.17:20,p.113, Lk.17:5-6,p.159)
it will be done.

Mk.

22And Jesus answered them,
"Have faith in God.
23Truly, I say to you,
'Whoever says to this mountain, *(Mt. of Olives)*
'Be taken up and cast into the sea,'
and does not doubt in his heart,
but believes
that what he says will come to pass,
it will be done for him.

Mountains of Difficulty In the Way of Duty Can Be Removed (See Isa.41:15-16; Zech.4:7-9 Here the Seemingly Impossible Task of rebuilding The Temple)

True Faith, and Assurance of Answered Prayer.

Mt.

22"And whatever you ask in prayer,
you will receive,
if you have faith."

Mk.

24"Therefore I tell you, *(Mk.9:23,p.112)*
whatever you ask in prayer, *I Jn.5:13-15*
believe that you receive it,
and you will.

Forgiveness and Prayer

(Cf.Mt.6:12,14,15, and references)

25"And whenever you stand praying,
forgive, if you have anything against any one;
so that your Father also who is in heaven
may forgive you your trespasses."[c]

....

**Or* kept seeking *(from this time on)*. ***See Footnotes pages 179,205,245 and cf. Mk.11:12,19,20.*
[a]*Some ancient authorities read* he. [b]*Or* Rabbi. [c]*Many ancient authorities add verse 26.* "But if you do not forgive, neither will your Father who is in heaven forgive your trespasses."

(1) The Occasion:

Jesus Authority Challenged. § 167

	Mt. 21:23-27	Mk. 11:27-33	Lk. 20:1-8
Jesus Is Teaching In The Temple	23 And when he entered the temple,	27 And they came again to Jerusalem. And as he was walking in the temple,	1 One day, as he was teaching the people in the temple and preaching the gospel,
The Jewish Officials Accost Him	the chief priests and the elders of the people came up to him as he was teaching,	the chief priests and the scribes and the elders came to him.	the chief priests and the scribes with the elders came up
They Question His Authority	and said, "By what authority are you doing these things, and who gave you this authority?"	28 And they said to him, "By what authority are you doing these things, or who gave you this authority to do them?"	2 and said to him, "Tell us by what authority you do these things, or who is it that gave you this authority."
Jesus Replies With a Question	24 Jesus answered them, "I also will ask you a question; and if you tell me the answer, then I also will tell you by what authority I do these things.	29 Jesus said to them, "I will ask you a question; answer me, and I will tell you by what authority I do these things.	3 He answered them, "I also will ask you a question; now tell me,
What His Question Is	25 "The baptism of John, whence was it? From heaven or from men?"*	30 "Was the baptism of John from heaven or from men? Answer me."	4 "Was the baptism of John from heaven or from men?"
They Argue Among Them-selves Before Answering	And they argued with one another, "If we say, 'From heaven,' he will say to us, 'Why then did you not believe him?' 26 But if we say, 'From men,' we are afraid of the multitude; for all hold that John was a prophet."	31 And they argued with one another, "If we say, 'From heaven,' he will say, 'Why then did you not believe him?' 32 But shall we say, 'From men?'" -- They were afraid of the people; for all held that John was a real prophet.	5 And they discussed it with one another, saying, "If we say, 'From heaven,' he will say, 'Why did you not believe him?' 6 But if we say, 'From men', all the people will stone us; for they are convinced that John was a prophet."
They Reply to Jesus	27 So they answered Jesus, "We do not know."	33 So they answered Jesus, "We do not know."	7 So they answered that they did not know whence it was.
He Answers And then Tells Them A Story	And he said to them, "Neither will I tell you by what authority I do these things."	And Jesus said to them, "Neither will I tell you by what authority I do these things."	8 And Jesus said to them, "Neither will I tell you by what authority I do these things."

(2) The Parable of the Two Sons. § 168

	Mt. 21:28-32	Mk. 12:1a
		1 And he began to speak to them in parables.
A Father's Request of His First Son	28 "What do you think? A man had two sons; and he went to the first and said, 'Son, go and work in the vineyard today.'	
His Refusal	29 "And he answered, 'I will not';	
His Repentance	But afterward he repented and went.	

**If they had really answered His question they would have had the answer to their own. For this answer study John's testimony about Jesus on p.27, all of it, but especially vv.31-34.*

The Second Son Is Asked	30" And he went to the second and said the same;
His Promise and Failure.	and he answered, 'I go, sir,' but did not go.
Jesus' Query	31" Which of the two did the will of his father?"
Their Answer,	They said, " The first."
Jesus' Interpretation	Jesus said to them, " Truly, I say to you, the tax collectors and the harlots go into the kingdom of God before you. *(Lk.7:29-30,p.69)*
His Accusation of the Jewish Rulers,	32" For John came to you in the way of righteousness, and you did not believe him, but the tax collectors and the harlots believed him;
Their Failure.	" and even when you saw it, you did not afterwards repent and believe him."

(3) The Parable of the Wicked Husbandmen. § 169

	Mt. 21:33-46	*Mk. 12:1-12*	*Lk. 20:9-19*
The Vineyard Is Built Up Painstakingly	33" Hear another parable. There was a householder whc planted a vineyard, and set a hedge around it, and dug a wine press in it, and built a tower,	1b" A man planted a vineyard, and set a hedge around it, and dug a pit for the wine press, and built a tower,	9And he began to tell the people this parable: " A man planted a vineyard,
Then It Is Rented Out The Owner Leaves	and let it out to tenants, and went into another country.	and let it out to tenants and went into another country.	and let it out to tenants and went into another country for a long while.
In Harvest He Sends His Agents To Get His Share	34" And when the season of fruit drew near, he sent his servants to the tenants, to get his fruits;	2" When the time came, he sent a servant, to the tenants, to get from them some of the fruit of the vineyard.	10" When the time came, he sent a servant to the tenants, that they should give him some of the fruit of the vineyard;
They Are Mistreated	35" and the tenants took his servants and beat one, and killed another, and stoned another.	3" And they took him and beat him, and sent him away empty handed.	but the tenants beat him, and sent him away empty handed.
Other Servants Also Are Rejected In Various Ways	36" Again, he sent other servants, more than the first; and they did the same to them.	4" Again he sent to them another servant, and they wounded him in the head, and treated him shamefully. 5" And he sent another, and him they killed; and so with many others, some they beat and some they killed.	11" And he sent another servant; him also they beat and treated shamefully, and sent him away empty handed. 12" And he sent yet a third; this one they wounded, and cast out.
The Son Is Sent	37" Afterward		13" Then the owner of the vineyard said, 'What shall I do?

As a Last Resort	he sent his son to them, saying, 'They will respect my son.'	6 "He had still one other, a beloved son; finally he sent him to them, saying, 'They will respect my son.'	'I will send my beloved son; it may be they will respect him.'
He Is Plotted Against.	38 But when the tenants saw the son, they said to themselves, 'This is the heir; come, let us kill him and have his inheritance.'	7 "But those tenants said to one another, 'This is the heir; come, let us kill him, and the inheritance will be ours.'	14 "But when the tenants saw him, they said to themselves, 'This is the heir; let us kill him, that the inheritance may be ours.'
And Killed.	39 And they took him and cast him out of the vineyard, and killed him.	8 "And they took him and killed him, and cast him out of the vineyard.	15 "And they cast him out of the vineyard and killed him.
The Reckoning *Jesus' Question*	40 "When therefore the owner of the vineyard comes, what will he do to those tenants?"	9 "What will the owner of the vineyard do?	"What then will the owner of the vineyard do to them?
Their Answer.	41 They said to him, "He will put those wretches to a miserable death, and let out the vineyard to other tenants who will give him the fruits in their seasons."	"He will come and destroy the tenants, and give the vineyard to others.	16 "He will come and destroy those tenants, and give the vineyard to others." When they heard this, they said, "God forbid!"
A Parabolic Scripture. *(Ps.108:22f.)*	42 Jesus said to them, "Have you never read in the scriptures: 'The very stone which the builders rejected has become the head of the corner; this was the Lord's doing, and it is marvelous in our eyes?	10 "Have you not read this scripture: 'The very stone which the builders rejected has become the head of the corner? 11 This was the Lord's doing, and it is marvelous in our eyes'?"	17 But he looked at them and said, "What then is this that is written: 'The very stone which the builders rejected has become the head of the corner'?
Jesus Makes the Application *(a) Of the Parable* *(b) Of the Scripture.*	43 Therefore I tell you, the kingdom of God will be taken away from you and given to a nation producing the fruits of it." [a]		18 "Everyone who falls on that stone will be broken to pieces; but when it falls on any one, it will crush him."
They See His Meaning *And Then*	45 When the chief priests and the Pharisees heard his parables, they perceived that he was speaking about them.	*(Cf. v. 12 below)*	19 The scribes and the chief priests *(Cf. v. 19b below)*
They Seek to Arrest Him, but are Afraid	46 But when they tried to arrest him, they feared the multitudes, because they held him to be a prophet. *(Cf. v.45 above)*	12 And they tried to arrest him, but feared the multitude, for they perceived that he had told the parable against them;	tried to lay hands on him at that very hour, but they feared the people; for they perceived that he had told this parable against them.
They Give Up the Attempt.		so they left him, and went away.	

[a] *Some ancient authorities add verse 44*, "And he who falls on this stone will be broken to pieces; but when it falls on anyone, it will crush him."

Mt. 22:1-14

The Feast Is Ready	[1]And again Jesus spoke to them in parables, saying,
The First Notice to the Invited Guests Is Refused	[2]" The kingdom of heaven may be compared to a king who gave a marriage feast for his son, *(Cf.Lk.14:15-24,p.154)* [3]and sent his servants to call those who were invited to the marriage feast; but they would not come.
A Second Notice Is Sent	[4]" Again he sent other servants, saying, 'Tell those who are invited, Behold, I have made ready my dinner, my oxen and my fat calves are killed, and everything is ready; come to the marriage feast.' *(Lk.14:17)*
This Also Is Spurned	[5]" But they made light of it and went off, one to his farm, another to his business, [6]while the rest seized his servants, treated them shamefully, and killed them.
The King Wreaks Vengeance	[7]" The king was angry, and he sent his troops and destroyed those murderers and burned their city.
Other Guests Are Invited	[8]" Then he said to his servants, 'The wedding is ready, but those invited were not worthy. [9]Go therefore to the thoroughfares, and invite to the marriage feast as many as you find.'
They Come	[10]" And those servants went out into the streets and gathered all whom they found, both bad and good; so the wedding hall was filled with guests.
One Man Is There Without A Wedding Garment	[11]" But when the king came in to look at the guests, he saw there a man who had no wedding-garment.
He Is Questioned	[12]" and he said to him, 'Friend, how did you get in here without a wedding-garment?' " And he was speechless.
He Is Rejected	[13]" Then the king said to the attendants 'Bind him hand and foot, and cast him into the outer darkness; there men will weep and gnash their teeth.'
Jesus States The General Truth	[14]" For many are called but few chosen."

(1) About Giving Tribute to Caesar. § 171

(The Pharisees' Question)

	Mt. 22:15-22	*Mk. 12:13-17*	*Lk. 20:20-26*
The Plot of The Rulers	15 Then the Pharisees went and took counsel *(Cf.Mk.3:6, p.55)* *(v.16)* how to entangle him in his talk.	13 And they sent to him some of the Pharisees and some of the Herodians, to entrap him in his talk.	20 So they watched him, and sent spies, who pretended to be sincere, that they might take hold of what he said,
Their Purpose			so as to deliver him up to the authority and jurisdiction of the governor.
Their Emissaries	16 And they sent their disciples to him, along with the He-ro´di-ans,	*(v.13)*	
Their Flattering Address	saying, "Teacher, we know that you are true, and teach the way of God truthfully, and care for no man; for you do not regard the position of men.	14 And they came and said to him, "Teacher, we know that you are true, and care for no man; for you do not regard the position of men, but truly teach the way of God.	21 They asked him, "Teacher, we know that you speak and teach rightly, and show no partiality, but truly teach the way of God.
Their Question	17 "Tell us, then, what you think. Is it lawful to pay taxes to Caesar, or not?"	"Is it lawful to pay taxes to Caesar, or not? 15 Should we pay them, or should we not?"	22 "Is it lawful for us to give tribute to Caesar, or not?"
Christ's Discerning Reply and Request	18 But Jesus aware of their malice, said, "Why put me to the test, you hypocrites? 19 Show me the money for the tax."	But knowing their hypocrisy, he said to them, 'Why put me to the test? Bring me a coin,[a] and let me look at it."	23 But he perceived their craftiness, and said to them, 24 "Show me a coin.[a]
Their Ready Response	And they brought him a coin.[a]	16 And they brought one.	
*His * Question*	20 And Jesus said to them, "Whose likeness and** inscription is this?"	And he said to them, "Whose likeness and** inscription is this?"	"Whose likeness and inscription has it?"
Their Reply	21 They said, "Caesar's."	They said to him, "Caesar's."	They said, "Caesar's."
His Answer to The Problem,- "Pay Taxes. Worship God"	Then he said to them, "Render therefore to Caesar the things that are Caesar's, and to God the things that are God's."	17 Jesus said to them, "Render to Caesar the things that are Caesar's, and to God the things that are God's."	25 He said to them, "Then render to Caesar the things that are Caesar's, and to God the things that are God's."
They Are Baffled in Their Trick			26 And they were not able in the presence of the people to catch him by what he said;
They Marvel at His Reply, and Walk away.	22 When they heard it, they marveled; and they left him, and went away.	And they were amazed at him.	but marveling at his answer they were silent.

[a]*Greek* denarius. **See footnotes pages 179, 205, 245.*

***It is said that the "likeness" was Caesar's, on a throne with some one kneeling to him, pouring out a drink-offering in worship to him. The "inscription" called him "divine Augustus." Some rabbis said, "whoever pays his taxes acknowledges the truth of this." Such idolatry was abhorrent to all Jews.*

(2) About the Marriage Tie in the Resurrection. § 172

(The Sadducees' Question)

	Mt. 22:23-33	Mk. 12:18-27	Lk. 20:27-39
		Their Query	
The Belief of The Sadducees	23The same day Sad'du-cees came to him, who say that there is no resurrection;	18And Sad'du-cees came to him, who say that there is no resurrection;	27There came to him some Sad'du-cees, those who say that there is no resurrection,
The Problem Is Posed (Dt.25:5-10)	and they asked him a question, 24saying, "Teacher, Moses said, 'If a man dies, having no children, his brother must marry the widow, and raise up children for his brother.'	and they asked him a question, saying, 19"Teacher, Moses wrote for us that if a man's brother dies and leaves a wife, but leaves no child, the man[a] must take the wife, and raise up children for his brother.	28and they asked him a question, saying, "Teacher, Moses wrote for us that if a man's brother dies, having a wife but no children, the man[a] must take the wife and raise up children for his brother.
A Test Case Is Framed	25"Now there were seven brothers among us; the first married, and died, and having no children left his wife to his brother. 26So too the second and the third, down to the seventh. 27"And after them all, the woman died.	20"There were seven brothers; the first took a wife, and when he died left no children; 21"and the second took her, and died, leaving no children; and the third likewise; 22and the seven left no children. "Last of all the woman also died.	29"Now there were seven brothers; the first took a wife and died without children; 30and the second 31and the third took her and likewise all seven left no children and died. 32Afterward the woman also died.
The Question They Ask Jesus	28"In the resurrection, therefore, to which of the seven will she be wife? For they all had her."	23"In the resurrection whose wife will she be? For the seven had her as wife."	33"In the resurrection, therefore, whose wife will the woman be? For the seven had her as wife."
		The Reply of Jesus	
His Reply *The Basis of Their Error*	29But Jesus answered them, "You are wrong, because you know neither the scriptures nor the power of God.	24Jesus said to them, "Is not this why you are wrong, that you know neither the scriptures nor the power of God?	34And Jesus said to them,
The State of Men and Women in the Resurrection	30"For in the resurrection they neither marry nor are given in marriage, but are like angels[b] in heaven.	25"For when they rise from the dead, they neither marry nor are given in marriage, but are like angels in heaven.	"The sons of this age marry and are given in marriage; 35but those who are accounted worthy to attain to that age and to the resurrection from the dead neither marry nor are given in marriage, 36for they cannot die anymore, because they are equal to angels and are sons of God, being sons of the resurrection.
Their More Fundamental Error Corrected	31"And as for the resurrection of the dead, have you not read (Ex.3:6) what was said to you by God,	26"And as for the dead being raised, have you not read in the book of Moses, in the passage about the bush, how God said to him,	37"But that the dead are raised, even Moses showed, in the passage about the bush, where he calls the Lord
What The Scripture Says	32'I am the God of Abraham, and the God of Isaac, and the God of Jacob?' He is not God of the dead, but of the living."	'I am the God of Abraham, and the God of Isaac, and the God of Jacob'? 27He is not the God of the dead, but of the living; you are quite wrong."	'the God of Abraham and the God of Isaac, and the God of Jacob.' 38Now he is not Cod of the dead, but of the living; for all live to him."
The Effect on the Multitudes and on the Scribes	33And when the crowd heard it they were astonished at his teaching.		39And some of the scribes answered, "Teacher, you have spoken well."

[a] *Greek* his brother. [b] *Many ancient authorities add* of God.

(3) About Which is the Greatest Commandment. § 173

(A Lawyer's Question)

	Mt. 22:34-40	Mk. 12:28-34	Lk. 20:40
The Pharisees Rally, and Venture Another Encounter	34But when the Pharisees heard that he had silenced the Sadducees, they came together. 35And one of them, a lawyer, asked him a question, to test him.	Mk. 28And one of the scribes came up and heard them disputing with one another, and seeing that he answered them well, asked him,	
Their Query	36"Teacher, which is the great commandment in the law?"	"Which commandment is the first of all?"	
Jesus' Answer	37And he said to him,	29Jesus answered, "The first is, 'Hear, O Israel: The Lord our God, the Lord is one;	
Christ's Summary of The Old Testament	"You shall love the Lord your God with all your heart, *(Dt.6:5)* and with all your soul, and with all your mind.	30and you shall love the Lord your God with all your heart, and with all your soul, and with all your mind, and with all your strength.'	
(Lev.19:18)	38"This is the great and first commandment. 39And a second is like it. You shall love your neighbor as yourself.	31"The second is this, 'You shall love your neighbor as yourself.' "There is no other commandment greater than these.	
(Mt.7:12)	40On these two commandments depend all the law and the prophets."		
The Lawyer's Rejoinder		Mk. 32And the scribe said to him, "You are right, Teacher; you have truly said that he is one, and there is no other but he; 33and to love him with all the heart, and with all the understanding, and with all the strength, and to love one's neighbor as oneself, is much more than all whole burnt-offerings and sacrifices."	
Our Lord's Commendation		34And when Jesus saw that he answered wisely, he said to him, "You are not far from the kingdom of God."	
All Are Silenced	*(Cf. 22:46b)*	Mk. And after that no one dared to ask him any question.	Lk. 40For they no longer dared to ask him any question.

4. CHRIST'S UNANSWERED QUESTION. § 174
ABOUT THE MESSIAH BEING THE SON OF DAVID

	Mt. 22:41-46	Mk. 12:35-37	Lk. 20:41-44
The Occasion	41Now while the Pharisees were gathered together,	35And as Jesus taught in the temple,	
The Question	Jesus asked them a question, 42saying, "What do you think of the Christ? Whose son is he?"	he said,	41But he said to them,
Their Ready Answer	They said to him, "The son of David."	"How can the scribes say that the Christ is the son of David?	"How can they say that the Christ is David's son?
Jesus Points Out The Difficulty	43He said to them, "How is it then that David, inspired by the Spirit,[a] calls him Lord, saying, 44'The Lord said to my Lord, Sit at my right hand, till I put thy enemies under thy feet?'	36David himself inspired by[a] the Holy Spirit[b] declared, *(Ps.110:1)* 'The Lord said to my Lord, Sit at my right hand, till I put thy enemies under thy feet.'	42For David himself says, in the book of Psalms, 'The Lord said to my Lord, Sit thou at my right hand, 43till I make thy enemies a stool for thy feet.'
	45"If David thus calls him Lord, how is he his son?"	37"David himself calls him Lord, so how is he his son?"	44"David thus calls him Lord; so how is he his son?"
They Are Not Able to Answer	46And no one was able to answer him a word, nor from that day did any one dare to ask him any more questions.	*(Cf. 12:34b)*	*(Cf. 20:40)*
		And the great throng heard him gladly. *(See Lk.19:47,p.182)*	

---

[a] Or in the Spirit. [b] Or himself, in.

[For General Outline, see p. 178]

[(I) See page 179]

(II) THE FINAL DEPARTURE [In Detailed Outline § 175-193½] pp.190-205.

1. *LEAVING THE TEMPLE FOR THE LAST TIME* pp.190-195 *(Tuesday)*
(Some Last Minute Happenings)

(1) Warning His Disciples Against the Example of the Jewish Rulers § 175 p.191
(Mt. 23:1-12; Mk. 12:38-40; Lk. 20:45-47)
(2) A Seven-Fold Warning Against the Scribes and Pharisees (Mt. 23:13-36) § 176 p.192-193.
(3) Lamenting Over Jerusalem (Mt. 23:37-39) § 177 p.193
(4) Commending a Poor Widow's Gift (Mk. 12;41-44; Lk. 21:1-4) § 178 p.193
(5) Reflecting about the Coming of the Greeks (Jn. 12:20-36a) § 179 p.194
(6) The Sinful Unbelief of the Jews (Jn. 12:36b-43) § 180 p.195
(7) Jesus Summarizes His Own Message and Mission. (Jn. 12:44-50) § 181 p.195
(8) On Leaving The Temple Christ Makes An Astonishing Prediction. (§ 182)

2. *LOOKING BACK FROM THE MT. OF OLIVES* pp.196-205 *(Tuesday Evening)*
(Prophecies About (a) The Destruction of Jerusalem and (b) the Coming Again of the Christ
Mt. 24,25; Mk. 13:1-37; Lk. 21:5-36)

(1) The Apostles' Questions (Mt. 24:1-3; Mk.13:1-4; Lk.21:5-7) § 182 p.196
a. When Shall These Things be?
b. What Shall Be the Sign of Thy Coming?
c. What Shall Be the Sign of The End of the Age?

(2) Christ's Answers. Our Lord's Prophetic Discourse (Mt.24:4-25; Mk.13:5-37: Lk.21:8-36) pp.197-205
a. General *WARNINGS*, - Against False Alarms (Mt. 24:4-14; Mk. 13:5-13; Lk. 21:8-19) § 183 pp.197-8
b. Specific *PROPHECIES*, - About The True Signs (Mt. 24:15-31; Mk. 13:14-27; Lk. 21:20-28) § 184 pp.199-200

(a) About the Destruction of Jerusalem and The Times of the Gentiles
(Cf. The Apostles' Question) (Mt. 24:15-22; Mk. 13:14-20; Lk. 21:20-24) p.199
a¹ The Destruction of Jerusalem and The End of the Jewish Nation
(Mt. 24:15-22; Mk. 13:14-20; Lk. 21:20-24a)
b¹ "The Times of the Gentiles" (Lk. 21:24b)

(b) About the Coming Again of The Messiah and The Consummation of the Age
(Cf. the Apostles' Question) (Mt. 24:23-31; Mk. 13:21-27; Lk. 21:25-28) p.200

c. Illustrative *PARABLES* About, - First, The Uncertainty of the Time; pp.201-205
and Second, The Consequent Necessity of Being Always Ready (Mt. 24:32-25:46; Mk. 13:28-37; Lk. 21:29-36)

(a) *Specific Predictions About THE DESTRUCTION OF JERUSALEM and the End of The Jewish Nation*
The Parable of the Fig Tree (Mt.24:32-34;Mk.13:28-30;Lk.21:29-32. § 185 p.201.

(b) *Definite Prophecies About THE PASSING AWAY OF HEAVEN AND EARTH and The End of the Age*
(Mt. 24:35-25:46; Mk. 13:31-37; Lk. 21:33-36) pp.201-205

a¹ General Statement (Mt.24:35-36; Mk.13:31-32; Lk.21:33) § 186 p.201
b¹ The Parable of the Days of Noah - or
The Uncertainty of the Time (Mt. 24:37-42; Mk.13:33; Lk.21:34-36) § 187 pp.201-202
c¹ The Parable of The Householder on a Journey (Mk. 13:34-37) § 188 p.202
d¹ The Parable of The Thief at Night - or
The Importance of Being Always Ready (Mt. 24:43-44) § 189 p.202
e¹ The Double Parable of The Wise and The Evil Servants - or
Faithfulness to Duties Assigned Is The Method of "Watching" (Mt.24:45-51) § 190 p.202
f¹ The Parable of The Ten Virgins - or
The Necessity and Sufficiency of the Grace of God to Enable Us to be Faithful (Mt. 25:1-13) § 191 p.203
g¹ The Parable of The Talents - or
Our Duties and Responsibilities are Commensurate With Our Abilities (Mt. 25:14-30) § 192 p.203
h¹ The Parable of The Sheep and The Goats - or
The General Nature of Our Duties Is Like That of the Ordinary Everyday Duties of Life
(Mt. 25:31-46) § 193 pp.204-205

3. *GENERAL STATEMENTS BY THE GOSPELS ABOUT THIS JUNCTURE OF EVENTS* p.205

(1) ABOUT THE MOVEMENTS OF JESUS DURING PASSOVER WEEK
(2) ABOUT THE APPROACHING PASSOVER.
(3) ABOUT THE LOVE OF JESUS FOR HIS OWN EVER SINCE HE KNEW THAT HIS HOUR HAD COME, AND THAT HE MUST LEAVE THEM.

(1) Warning His Disciples Against the Example of the Jewish Rulers. § 175

	Mt. 23:1-12	Mk. 12:38-40	Lk. 20:45-47
Follow the Rulers' Teachings,	1 Then said Jesus to the crowds and to his disciples,	38 And in his teaching he said,	45 And in the hearing of all the people he said to his disciples,
	2 "The scribes and the Pharisees sit on Moses' seat; 3 so practice and observe		
But Not Their Practices	whatever they tell you, but not what they do; for they preach, but do not practice.	"Beware of the scribes,	46 "Beware of the scribes,
They Are Tyrannical	4 "They bind heavy burdens, hard to bear,[a] and lay them on men's shoulders; but they themselves will not move them with their finger.		*(Lk.11:46,p.141)*
Hypocritical	5 They do all their deeds to be seen of men; for they make their phylacteries broad and their fringes long,		
		Mk.	*Lk.*
		who like to go about in long robes,	who like to go about in long robes, *(Cf. Lk.11:43,p.141)*
Vain-glorious	6 and they love	and to have salutations in the marketplaces, 39 and the best seats in the synagogues	and love salutations in the marketplaces and the best seats in the synagogues
	(Cf. v. 6 below) the place of honor at feasts,	and the places of honor at feasts,	and the places of honor at feasts,
	and the best seats in the synagogues, 7 and salutations in the marketplaces, and being called rabbi by men.	*(Cf. v.39 above)* *(Cf. v. 38)*	*(Cf. v. 46 above)*
		40 who devour widows' houses, and for a pretense make long prayers. They will receive the greater condemnation."	47 who devour widows' houses and for a pretense make long prayers. They will receive the greater condemnation."
We Should not Seek Praise From Men	8 "But you are not to be called rabbi, for you have one teacher, and you are all brethren. 9 "And call no man your father on earth, for you have one Father, who is in heaven. 10 Neither be called masters, for you have one master, the Christ.		
True Greatness Is in Humility and Service	11 "He who is greatest among you *(Mt.18:4,p.114;20:26,p.173)* shall be your servant; 12 "whoever exalts himself shall be humbled, and whoever humbles himself shall be exalted. *(Lk.14:11,p.153;Lk.18:14,p. 167)*		

[a] *Some ancient authorities omit* hard to bear.

*See Footnotes, pages 179,205,245.

Mt. 23:13-36

The Rulers Are Condemned:	13 "But woe to you, scribes and Pharisees, hypocrites!
(a) For Hindering Believers; E.G. Jn. 9:13-34; & 11:45-53; 12:10,	because you shut the kingdom of heaven against men; for you neither enter yourselves, nor allow those who would enter to go in.[a] *(Jn. 9:22,34, p.130)*
(b) For Corrupting Proselytes.	15 "Woe to you, scribes and Pharisees, hypocrites! for you traverse sea and land to make a single proselyte, and when he becomes a proselyte, you make him twice as much a child of hell[b] as yourselves.
(c) For Perverting the Law, By "The Traditions of The Elders," E.G. The Sabbath, (See Note p.55 and references there). And Also in the constant practices and teachings of The Rabbis.	16 "Woe to you, blind guides, who say, *(v.24)* 'If any one swears by the temple, it is nothing; but if any one swears by the gold of the temple, he is bound by his oath.' 17 "You blind fools! For which is greater, *(Mt. 5:33-37, p.60)* the gold or the temple that has made the gold sacred? 18 And you say, 'If any one swears by the altar, it is nothing; but if any one swears by the gift that is on the altar, he is bound by his oath.' 19 "You blind men! For which is greater, the gift or the altar that makes the gift sacred? 20 "So he who swears by the altar, swears by it and by everything on it; 21 and he who swears by the temple, swears by it and by him who dwells in it; 22 and he who swears by heaven, swears by the throne of God and by him who sits upon it.
(d) For Neglecting Mercy and Justice.	23 "Woe to you, scribes and Pharisees, hypocrites! for you tithe mint and dill and cummin, *(Lk. 11:42, p.141)* and have neglected the weightier matters of the law, justice and mercy and faith; these you ought to have done, without neglecting the others. 24 "You blind guides, *(v.16,19,26; Mt. 15:14, p.103)* straining out a gnat and swallowing a camel!
(e) For Inner Neglect and Outward Ceremonialism.	25 "Woe to you, scribes and Pharisees, hypocrites! for you cleanse the outside of the cup and of the plate, *(Lk. 11:39, p.141)* but inside they are full of extortion and rapacity. 26 "You blind Pharisee! *(v.24)* first cleanse the inside of the cup and of the plate, that the outside also may be clean.
(f) For Inner Corruption With Outward Smugness	27 "Woe to you, scribes and Pharisees, hypocrites! for you are like whitewashed tombs, which outwardly appear beautiful, but within they are full of dead men's bones and all uncleanness. 28 So you also outwardly appear righteous to men, but within you are full of hypocrisy and iniquity.
(g) For Murdering God's Messengers	29 "Woe to you, scribes and Pharisees, *(Lk. 11:47-51, p.141)* hypocrites! for you build the tombs of the prophets and adorn the monuments of the righteous, 30 saying, 'If we had lived in the days of our fathers, we would not have taken part with them in shedding the blood of the prophets.'

[a] *Some authorities add here (or after verse 12) verse 14,* Woe to you, scribes and Pharisees, hypocrites! for you devour widows' houses, and for a pretence you make long prayers; therefore you will receive greater condemnation. [b] *Greek* Gehenna.

31 " Thus you witness against yourselves,
that you are sons of those who murdered the prophets.

Their Consequent Doom

32 " Fill up, then, the measure of your fathers.
33 You serpents, you brood of vipers,
how are you to escape being sentenced to hell?[a]

In Spite of Many Warnings Instead of Heeding They Will Persecute Them But Judgment Will Strike

34 " Therefore I send you *(Lk.11:49,p.141)*
prophets
and wise men
and scribes,
some of whom you will kill and crucify,
and some you will scourge in your synagogues
and persecute from town to town,

35 " that upon you may come *(Lk.11:50-51,p.141)*
all the righteous blood shed on earth,
from the blood of innocent Abel* to the blood of Zech-a-ri´ah* the son of Bar-a-chi´ah,
whom you murdered between the sanctuary and the altar.

It Is Imminent

36 Truly, I say to you,
all this will come upon this generation.

(3) Lamenting over Jerusalem. § 177

Mt. 23:37-39

(The Supreme Patriot Bewails His Nation's Destruction)

(a) Jerusalem is the Killer of the Prophets

37 " O Jerusalem, Jerusalem, *(Cf.Lk.19:41-44,p.180)* *(Also Lk.13:34,p.153)*
killing the prophets
and stoning those who are sent to you!

(b) Jesus' Yearning to Deliver Her Is Rejected

" How often would I have gathered your children together
as a hen gathers her brood under her wings,

And you would not!

(c) Her Doom and Desolation are Sure

38 " Behold, your house is forsaken and desolate.[b]
39 For I tell you,
you will not see me again until you say,
'Blessed be he who comes in the name of the Lord.' "

(4) Commending a Poor Widow's Gift. § 178

	Mk. 12:41-44	*Lk. 21:1-4*
Jesus Is Watching the Contributors	41 And he sat down opposite the treasury, and watched the multitude putting money into the treasury.	
(a) The Rich	Many rich people put in large sums.	1 He looked up and saw the rich putting their gifts into the treasury;
(b) The Poor Widow	42 And a poor widow came, and put in two copper coins, which make a penny.	2 and he saw a poor widow put in two copper coins.
Calling His Disciples	43 And he called his disciples to him, and said to them,	3 And he said,
He Commends the Widow	" Truly I say to you, this poor widow has put in more than all those who are contributing to the treasury.	" Truly I tell you, this poor widow has put in more than all of them;
He Explains Why	44 " For they all contributed out of their abundance; but she out of her poverty has put in everything she had, her whole living."	4 " for they all contributed out of their abundance, but she out of her poverty put in all the living that she had."

....

[a] *Greek* Gehenna.
[b] *Some ancient authorities omit* and desolate.

**In the Hebrew Old Testament the last book of the O.T. is II.Chronicles. So the first murder of a righteous man in their Bible was Abel (Gen.4:1-15) and the last one was Zechariah (II Chron.24:20-22). The expression amounts to our saying, " From Genesis to Revelation."*

(5) Reflecting About the Coming of the Greeks.* § 179

Jn. 12:20-36

Some Greeks Ask Philip to See Jesus

20Now among those who went up to worship at the feast
were some Greeks.
21So these came to Philip, who was from Beth-sa′i-da in Galilee,
and said to him,
"Sir, we wish to see Jesus."

Philip and Andrew Tell Jesus

22Philip went and told Andrew;
Andrew went with Philip
and they told Jesus.

Jesus Is Deeply Moved

23And Jesus answered them,
"The hour has come for the Son of man to be glorified.

He Announces A Profound Principle, and Applies It To All His Followers

24Truly, truly, I say to you,
unless a grain of wheat falls into the earth and dies,
it remains alone;
but if it dies, it bears much fruit.
25He who loves his life loses it,
and he who hates his life in this world will keep it for eternal life.

26If any one serves me, he must follow me;
and where I am, there shall my servant be also;
if any one serves me, the Father will honor him.

He Prays, Expressing His Inward Profound Struggle

27"Now is my soul troubled.
And what shall I say?
'Father, save me from this hour'?
No, for this purpose I have come to this hour.
28Father, glorify thy name."

A Voice Answers from Heaven

Then a voice came from heaven,
"I have glorified it,
and I will glorify it again."

The Crowd Call It Thunder or The Voice Of an Angel

29The crowd standing by heard it
and said that it had thundered.
Others said,
"An angel has spoken to him."

Jesus Explains The Meaning of the Voice

30Jesus answered,
"This voice has come for your sake, not for mine.
31Now is the judgment of this world,
now shall the ruler of this world be cast out;
32and I, when I am lifted up from the earth,
will draw all men to myself."
33He said this to show by what death he was to die.

The Crowd Inquires Further

34The crowd answered him,
"We have heard from the law
that the Christ remains forever.
How can you say
that the Son of man must be lifted up?
Who is this Son of man?"

Jesus Answers Them

35Jesus said to them,
"The light is with you for a little longer.
Walk while you have the light,
lest the darkness overtake you;
he who walks in the darkness does not know where he goes.
36While you have the light, believe in the light,
that you may become sons of light."

*Jesus Leaves * Them.*

When Jesus had said this,
he departed and hid himself from them. [*Tuesday evening. See footnotes, pp.179,205,245*]

....

**This is His very last Public Appearance and Final Appeal, and so in verses 44-50, He sums up the essential significance of His whole Message and Mission. Hence the title of this book (See p.I).*

Jn. 12:37-43

The Author Sums Up The Results of Jesus' Ministry Among the Rulers

(a) The Unbelief of the Jews

37Though he had done so many signs before them,
yet they did not believe in him;
38it was that the word spoken by the prophet Isaiah might be fulfilled:
"Lord, who has believed our report,
and to whom has the arm of the Lord been revealed?"
39Therefore they could not believe.
For Isaiah again said,

(b) A Prophecy Comes True,

40"He has blinded their eyes and hardened their hearts,
lest they should see with their eyes and perceive with their hearts,
and turn for me to heal them." *(Isa.6:9-10; Cf. Matthew's interpretation, Mt.13:13-18,p.75)*
41Isaiah said this, because he saw his glory
and spoke of him.

(c) Many Rulers Believe, but Do not Confess,

42Nevertheless many even of the authorities believed in him,
but for fear of the Pharisees they did not confess it,

(d) The Reason,

lest they should be put out of the synagogue;
43for they loved the praise of men
more than the praise of God.

(The setting is that of v.36b. verses 37-43 are parenthetical)

(7) Jesus Himself Summarizes His Own Message and Mission. § 181

(How appropriate this is as His very last public appeal!)

Jn. 12:44-50

Jesus is the Revealer of the Father (Cf. 1:18)

44And Jesus cried out and said,
"He who believes in me, believes not in me but in him who sent me.
45And he who sees me sees him who sent me.
46I have come as light into the world, *(vs.35-36; Jn.8:12; 9:5; 1:4,5,8,9)*
that whoever believes in me may not remain in darkness.

Men Are Judged by His Word for Rejecting Him

47"If any one hears my sayings and does not keep them,
I do not judge him;
for I did not come to judge the world
but to save the world.
48He who rejects me and does not receive my sayings
has a judge; *(Jn.3:16-24; 5:22-24,27; Ac.17:31)*
the word that I have spoken will be his judge on the last day.

Because It Is the Father's Message

49"For I have not spoken on my own authority;
the Father who sent me has himself given me commandment
what to say and what to speak. *(Jn.7:16-18; 17:6-8,p.220)*
50And I know that his commandment is eternal life.
What I say, therefore,
I say as the Father has bidden me."

Special Outline for the Study of

CHRIST'S PROPHETIC DISCOURSE *(pages 196-205, immediately following)*

(Complete Outline on p.190)

I. Christ Makes an Astounding Prediction
II. The Apostles Ask Three Confused Questions
III. Christ Answers These Questions Clearly

(I) GENERAL WARNINGS

Against False Alarms

(II) SPECIFIC PROPHECIES

1. About The End of The Jewish Nation
2. About The End of The Age

(III) ILLUSTRATIVE PARABLES

(About The Uncertainty of The Time; and The Consequent Necessity of Being Always Ready)

1. A Parable About The End of The Jewish Nation
2. Many Parables About The End of The Age

(PROPHETIC DISCOURSE TO THE DISCIPLES)

Mt. 24,25; Mk. 13; Lk. 21:5-36

PROPHECIES ABOUT THE DESTRUCTION OF JERUSALEM

AND THE COMING AGAIN OF JESUS

(1) The Apostles' Questions. § 182

Mt. 24:1-3; Mk. 13:1-4; Lk 21:5-7

Jesus Solemnly Predicts the Destruction of the Temple

	Matthew	Mark	Luke
Jesus and His Disciples Are Leaving the Temple	1 Jesus left the temple and was going away,	1 And as he came out of the temple,	
His Disciples Speak of the Buildings	when his disciples came to point out to him the buildings of the temple.	one of his disciples said to him, "Look, Teacher, what wonderful stones and what wonderful buildings!"	5 And as some spoke of the temple, how it was adorned with noble stones and offerings,
Christ Astonishes Them In His Reply	2 But he answered them, "You see all these, do you not? Truly, I say to you,	2 And Jesus said to him, "Do you see these great buildings?"	he said, 6 "As for these things which you see, the days will come when
They Go On to the Mt. of Olives In Silence	there will not be left here one stone upon another, that will not be thrown down."	there will not be left here one stone upon another, that will not be thrown down."	there shall not be left here one stone upon another that will not be thrown down."

The Journey to the Mount of Olives (in astonished silence) Intervenes

The Disciples Ask Three Questions*

	Matthew	Mark	Luke
Then As They Are Seated on Olivet	3 As he sat on the Mount of Olives,	3 And as he sat on the Mount of Olives opposite the temple,	
The Disciples Question Jesus	the disciples came to him privately, saying,	Peter and James and John and Andrew asked him privately,	7 And they asked him,** "Teacher,
(1) When will it be?	"Tell us,**	4 "Tell us, **	
(2) What Will Be The Signs Of the Destruction Of Jerusalem? (See Mark) →	when will this be?	when will this be? And what will be the sign when these things are all to be accomplished?"	when will this be? And what will be the sign when this is about to take place?"
(3) What Will Be The Signs Of Christ's Coming? Of The Close Of The Age?	And what will be the sign of your coming and of the close of the age?"		

*See footnotes, pp.179,205,245.

**They confusedly asked three distinct questions, requiring three distinct answers. They were confused; Jesus was not. In studying this passage, constantly consult "special outline", footnote page 195, and the complete outline of the section on p.190.

(2) Christ's Answers.

Our Lord's Prophetic Discourse

(Mt. 24:4-25; Mk. 13:5-37; Lk. 21:8-36)

*a. GENERAL WARNINGS.**

[*b. Specific Prophecies, §184, p.199, 200*]
[*c. Illustrative Parables, pp.201ff*]

Against False Alarms.* § 183

[*Contrast "About True Signs, § 184, pp.199, 200*]

	Mt. 24:4-14	*Mk. 13:5-13*	*Lk. 21:8-19*
In His Answer Jesus Begins With Warnings Against False Alarms	4 And Jesus answered them, "Take heed that no one leads you astray.	5 And Jesus began to say to them, "Take heed that no one leads you astray.	8 And he said, "Take heed that you are not led astray;
(a) False Messiahs, (Are Not The Sign)	5 For many will come in my name saying, 'I am the Christ,' and they will lead many astray.	6 "Many will come in my name, saying, 'I am he!' *(See Mk.13:21, p.200)* and they will lead many astray.	"for many will come in my name, saying, 'I am he!' and 'The time is at hand!' Do not go after them.
(b) Wars and Rumors of Wars, (Are Not The Sign)	6 "And you will hear of wars and rumors of wars; see that you are not alarmed; for this must take place, but the end is not yet.	7 "And when you hear of wars and rumors of wars, do not be alarmed; this must take place, but the end is not yet.	9 "And when you hear of wars and tumults, do not be terrified; for this must first take place, but the end will not be at once." 10 Then he said to them,
(c) National Upheavals, (Are Not The Sign)	7 "For nation will rise against nation, and kingdom against kingdom,	8 "For nation will rise against nation, and kingdom against kingdom;	"Nation will rise against nation, and kingdom against kingdom;
(d) Natures' Disturbances (Are Not The Sign)	and there will be famines and earthquakes in various places:	there will be earthquakes in various places, there will be famines;	11 there will be great earthquakes, and in various places famines and pestilences; and there will be terrors and great signs from heaven.
	8 "all this is but the beginning of the sufferings.	this is but the beginning of the sufferings.	
(e) Persecutions, (Are Not The Sign)		9 "But take heed to yourselves; for they will deliver you up to councils;	12 "But before all this they will lay their hands on you, and persecute you, delivering you up
By Jews,		and you will be beaten in synagogues;	to the synagogues and prisons,
By Gentiles, And How They Shall Meet Them. *(Mt.10:18, p.89)*		and you will stand before governors and kings for my sake,	and you will be brought before kings and governors for my name's sake. 13 This will be a time
The Disciples Must Testify (e.g. See Ac.3,4;5:17-26)		to bear testimony before them.	for you to bear testimony.
And Preach Everywhere (Ac.1:8).		10 "And the gospel must first be preached to all nations.	

....

*See footnote on next page.

	Matthew	Mark	Luke
How To Meet Persecution		11 And when they bring you to trial and deliver you up,	14 " Settle it therefore in your minds,
Don't Worry beforehand, *Say What Is Given You,* *The Holy Spirit Will Help You.*		do not be anxious beforehand what you are to say; but say whatever is given you in that hour,	not to meditate beforehand how to answer; *(Cf.Lk.12:11-12,p.142)*
Such Divine Wisdom Will Be Irresistable		for it is not you who speak, but the Holy Spirit.	15 " for I will give a mouth and wisdom which none of your adversaries will be able to withstand or contradict.
They Will Be Betrayed By Friends and Relatives	9 Then they will deliver you up to tribulation, *(Mt.10:21-22,p.89)* and put you to death;	12 " And brother will deliver up brother to death, and the father his child, and children will rise against parents and have them put to death;	16 " You will be delivered up even by parents and brothers and kinsmen and friends, " and some of you they will put to death;
They Will Be Hated By All Nations	and you will be hated by all nations for my name's sake.	13 " and you will be hated by all for my name's sake.	17 " you will be hated by all for my name's sake. 18 " But not a hair of your head will perish.
Many Will Fall Away	10 " And then many will fall away,[a] and betray one another, and hate one another.		
Many False Teachers Will Arise	11 " And many false prophets will arise and lead many astray. *(Mt.7:15-19,p.65)*		
Many Will Grow Cold	12 " And because wickedness is multiplied, most men's love will grow cold.	*(The Two Essentials)*	
They Must Have Fortitude	13 " But he who endures to the end will be saved.	" But he who endures to the end will be saved.	19 " By your endurance you will gain your lives.
They Must Preach the Gospel Everywhere	14 " And this gospel of the kingdom will be preached throughout the whole world, as a testimony to all nations.		
The End Will Come When God Wills	And then the end will come.* *(See Ac.1:6-8, and also Mt.24:35-36, §186, p.201)*		

....

[a] *Or* stumble.

* *So far, only General Warnings, Against False Alarms have been considered; and they apply, practically, to both " The End of The Jewish Nation," and " The End of The Age."*
Note how very different and how very specific His prophecies are from here on.

b. SPECIFIC PROPHECIES

About The True Signs. § 184

Mt. 24:15-31; Mk. 13:14-27; Lk. 21:20-28

(a) Prophecies Concerning The Destruction of Jerusalem

	Mt. 24: 15-22	Mk. 13:14-20	Lk. 21: 20-24
Specific Prophecies:-	15" So when	14" But	20" But when you see Jerusalem surrounded by armies,
(1) Concerning the Destruction of Jerusalem and the Jewish Nation	you see the desolating sacrilege spoken of by the prophet Daniel, *(Dan.9:27;11:31;12:11)* standing in the holy place (let the reader understand),	when you see the desolating sacrilege set up where it ought not to be (let the reader understand),	
(a) The Sure Sign,			then know that its desolation has come near.
(b) Precipitate Flight the Only Safety	16then let those who are in Judea flee to the mountains;	then let those who are in Judea flee to the mountains;	21Then let those who are in Judea flee to the mountains, and let those who are inside the city depart,
Any Delay for any Reason Will Be Disastrous,	17let him who is on the housetop not go down to take what is in his house; 18and let him who is in the field not turn back to take his mantle.	15let him who is on the housetop not go down, nor enter his house, to take anything away; 16and let him who is in the field not turn back to take his mantle.	and let not those who are out in the country enter it; 22" for these are days of vengeance, to fulfill all that is written.
(c) Hindrances to Fleeing,	19" And alas for those who are with child and for those who give suck in those days!	17" And alas for those who are with child and for those who give suck in those days!	23" Alas for those who are with child and for those who give suck in those days!
Prayer to Escape,	20Pray that your flight may not be in winter or on a sabbath.	18Pray that it may not happen in winter.	
(d) The Unprecedented Greatness of the Distress, (Consult Josepheus' History of the Destruction of Jerusalem)	21" For then there will be great tribulation, such as has not been from the beginning of the world until now, no, and never will be. 22" And if those days had not been shortened, no human being would be saved; but for the sake of the elect those days will be shortened.	19" For in those days there will be such tribulation as has not been from the beginning of the creation which God created until now, and never will be. 20" And if the Lord had not shortened the days, no human being would be saved; but for the sake of the elect, whom he chose, he shortened the days.	" For great distress shall be upon the earth and wrath upon this people.
*(e) The Completeness of the Desolation Some Killed, The Rest Led Captive,***			Lk. 24" They will fall by the edge of the sword, and be led captive among all nations;
(f) The Duration of Jewish Humiliation,			and Jerusalem will be trodden down by the Gentiles, until* *(See Ac. 1:7)* the times of the Gentiles are fulfilled."

....

**This "until" is perhaps the longest word in the New Testament; it covers all the time from A.D. 70, when Jerusalem and the Jewish nation were destroyed until now; and how much longer " it is not for us to know" (Ac. 1:7)*

***Christians, however, history tells us, did escape, by heeding Jesus' Warnings.*

(b) Prophecies Concerning The Coming Again of Christ

False Alarms

(2) Specific Prophecies Concerning the Coming of Christ

	Mt.	*Mk.*
(2) Specific Prophecies Concerning the Coming of Christ	23" Then if any one says to you, 'Lo, here is the Christ!' or 'There he is!' do not believe it.	21" And then if any one says to you, 'Look, here is the Christ!' *(Lk.21:8,p.197)* or, 'Look, there he is!' do not believe it.
a. Warning Against False Alarms (a) Great Signs	24" For false Christs and false prophets will arise and show great signs and wonders, so as to lead astray, if possible, even the elect.	22" False Christs and false prophets will arise and show signs and wonders, to lead astray, if possible, the elect.
(b) Urgent Pleas	25" Lo, I have told you beforehand.	23" But take heed; I have told you all things beforehand.
All Must Be Disregarded	26 " So, if they say to you, 'Lo, he is in the wilderness,' do not go out; if they say 'Lo, he is in the inner rooms,' do not believe it.	*(Cf.Lk.17:23-24,p.165)*
b. The True Signs Will Be Unmistakeable	27" For as the lightning comes from the east and shines as far as the west, *(Lk.17:24)* so will be the coming of the Son of man.	
Where Corruption Is Judgment Will Fall	28" Wherever the body is, there the eagles[a] *(Lk.17:37,p.166)* will be gathered together.	

The True signs

	Mt.	*Mk.*	*Lk.*
There Will Be Signs in Heaven	29" Immediately after the tribulation of those days the sun will be darkened, and the moon will not give its light, and the stars will fall from heaven,	24" But in those days, after that tribulation, the sun will be darkened, and the moon will not give its light, 25and the stars will be falling from heaven,	25" And there will be signs in sun and moon and stars,
and Signs upon Earth			and upon the earth distress of nations in perplexity at the roaring of the sea and the waves,
Nature's Powers Will Be Shaken	and the powers of the heavens will be shaken;	and the powers in the heavens will be shaken.	26men fainting with fear and with foreboding of what is coming on the world; for the powers of the heavens will be shaken.
Then Will Be The Coming of Christ " in Glory"	30" then will appear the sign of the Son of man in heaven, and then all the tribes of the earth will mourn,		

The Coming Itself

	Mt.	*Mk.*	*Lk.*
On The Clouds	" and they will see the Son of man coming on the clouds of heaven with power and great glory.	26" And then they will see the Son of man coming in clouds with great power and glory.	27" And then they will see the Son of man coming in a cloud with power and great glory.
With The Angels As His Reapers Of The Whole Earth	31" And he will send out his angels with a loud trumpet call, and they will gather his elect from the four winds, from one end of heaven to the other.	*Mk.* 27" And then he will send out the angels, and gather his elect from the four winds, from the ends of the earth to the ends of heaven.	*(Mt.13:36-43,p.78)* *(Rev.14:17-20)*
The Christian's Triumphant Hope			*Lk.* 28" Now when these things begin to take place, look up and raise your heads, because your redemption is drawing near."

[a]Or vultures.

c. ILLUSTRATIVE PARABLES* About the Uncertainty of the Time, And the Consequent Necessity of Being Always Ready

Mt.24:32-25:46; Mk.13:28-37; Lk.21:29-36

(a) A Parable* Concerning The Destruction of Jerusalem and the End of The Jewish Nation. § 185

	Mt. 24: 32-34	*Mk. 13:28-30*	*Lk. 21:29-32*
The Parable of the Fig Tree	32" From the fig tree learn its lesson: as soon as its branch becomes tender and puts forth its leaves, you know that summer is near.	28" From the fig tree learn its lesson: as soon as its branch becomes tender and puts forth its leaves, you know that summer is near.	29And he told them a parable: " Look at the fig tree, and all the trees; 30as soon as they come out in leaf, you see for yourselves and know that the summer is already near.
The Coming of the Kingdom of God*	33" So also, when you see all these things you know that he* *(See Lk.* is near, at the very gates.	29" So also, when you see these things taking place, you know that he* *(See Lk.* is near, at the very gates.	31" So also, when you see these things taking place, you know that the kingdom* of God is near.
To Be Fulfilled in That Generation	34" Truly, I say to you, this generation will not pass away [place till all these things take **	30" Truly, I say to you this generation will not pass away, before all these things take place. **	32" Truly, I say to you, this generation *(Cf.Mk.9:1,p.109)* will not pass away till all has taken place.

(b) Parables Concerning The End of The Age, and The Coming Again of Christ. *(Mt.24:35-25:46; Mk.13:31-37; Lk.21:33-36)*

a[1] General Statement. § 186

	Mt. 24:35-36	*Mk. 13:31-32*	*Lk. 21:33*
(a) The Certainty of the Event	35" Heaven and earth ** will pass away, but my words will not pass away.	31" Heaven and earth ** will pass away, but my words will not pass away.	33" Heaven and earth ** will pass away, *(See Mt.5:18)* but my words will not pass away."
(b) The Time Absolutely Unknown (See Ac.1:7)	36" But of that day and hour no one knows, not even the angels of heaven, nor the Son, but the Father only."	32" But of that day or that hour no one knows, not even the angels in heaven, nor the Son, but only the Father."	*(Ac.1:6-8)*

b[1] The Parable of the Days of Noah, or Life Going On As Usual. § 187

	Mt. 24:37-42	*Mk. 13:33*	*Lk. 21:34-36*
	37" As were the days of Noah, so will be the coming of the Son of man. *(Cf.Lk.17:25-37)* 38For as in those days before the flood they were eating and drinking, marrying and giving in marriage, until the day when Noah entered the Ark. 39And they did not know until the flood came and swept them all away, so will be the coming of the Son of man. 40" Then two men will be in the field; one is taken and one is left. 41Two women will be grinding at the mill; one is taken and one is left."		

***Note very carefully that verses 35 and 36 of Mathew change the subject from " The End of the Jewish Nation", to " The End of Heaven and Earth." Note also how emphactically verses 34 and 36 of Mt. are Contrasted with each other*

....

**Should be translated, "it;" the kingdom of God is not properly alluded to as " he" , but it. See Luke's specific statement (Lk. 21:31-32); also the next verse in Matthew's and Mark's accounts. Here it is exceptionally important to study the analytic outline of this whole section: (page 195) note especially the three main divisions:*

a. General WARNINGS against False Alarms.
b. Specific PROPHECIES About the True Signs.
c. Illustrative PARABLES About the Uncertainty of the Times, and watching.

How Always to Be Ready Take Heed, Watch, and Pray.

Mk.

33 "Take heed,

Lk.

34 "But take heed to yourselves
lest your hearts be weighed down
with dissipation and drunkenness
and cares of this life,
and that day come upon you suddenly like a snare;
35 for it will come upon all
who dwell upon the face of the whole earth.

Mt.

42 "Watch therefore,
for you do not know on what day
your Lord is coming."

Mk.

watch and pray;[a]
for you do not know
when the time will come."

Lk.

36 "But
watch at all times,

praying that you may have strength
to escape all these things that will take place,
and to stand before the Son of man."

c' The Parable of the Householder on a Journey, or Always Watching, because We Can't Know When. § 188

Mk. 13:34-37

The Parable

34 "It is like a man going on a journey,
when he leaves home and puts his servants in charge,
each with his work,
and commands the doorkeeper to be on the watch.

(Cf. Mt. v.42 above and 43 below)

Its Application The Time Is Uncertain

35 "Watch therefore--
for you do not know when the master of the house will come,
in the evening, or at midnight, or at cockcrow, or in the morning--
36 lest he come suddenly and find you asleep.

Therefore It Is Necessary for Everyone To Watch

37 "And what I say to you I say to all:
Watch."

d' The Parable of the Thief, or the Unexpectedness of the Time. § 189

Mt. 24:43-44

The Parable. Be Always Ready, for The Time Will Be Unexpected

43 "But know this,
that if the householder had known in what part of the night the thief was coming,
he would have watched and would not have let his house be broken into.

44 "Therefore you also must be ready;
for the Son of man is coming at an hour you do not expect."

e' The Parable of the Wise and the Evil Servants, or Faithfulness is the Essential Virtue. § 190

Mt. 24:45-51

Responsibilities Assigned

45 "Who then is the faithful and wise servant, *(Lk. 12:35-38, p. 144)*
whom his master has set over his household,
to give them their food at the proper time?

The Reward of the Good Servant

46 "Blessed is that servant whom his master when he comes
shall find so doing.
47 Truly, I say to you, he will set him over all his possessions.

The Punishment of the Evil Servant

48 "But if that wicked servant says to himself, *(Lk. 12:45-46, p. 144)*
'My master is delayed',
49 and begins to beat his fellow servants,
and eats and drinks with the drunken,

50 the master of that servant will come on a day when he does not expect him
and at an hour he does not know, *(See Mk. v.35 above)*

51 and he will punish[b] him and put him with the hypocrites;
there men will weep and gnash their teeth."

---

[a] *Some ancient authorities omit* and pray.
[b] *Or* cut him in pieces.

f[1] The Parable of the Ten Virgins, or The Grace of God Is Necessary in Order that We May be Faithful. § 191

Mt. 25:1-13

An Illustration of The Kingdom

1 "Then the kingdom of heaven shall be compared to ten maidens,
who took their lamps, and went to meet the bridegroom.[a]

Foolish and Wise Bridesmaids

2 "Five of them were foolish,
and five were wise.

3 "For when the foolish took their lamps they took no oil with them; *
4 but the wise took flasks of oil with their lamps.

Meet Unexpected Delay

5 "As the bridegroom was delayed, they all slumbered and slept.

6 "But at midnight there was a cry,
'Behold, the bridegroom!
Come out to meet him.'

The Wedding Procession

Arouses Excitement and Dismay and Hurried Efforts;

7 "Then all those maidens rose and trimmed their lamps.

8 And the foolish said to the wise,
'Give us some of your oil, for our lamps are going out.'

9 "But the wise replied,
'Perhaps there will not be enough for us and for you;
go rather to the dealers and buy for yourselves.'

But Careless Neglect Brings Disappointment,

10 "And while they went to buy,
the bridegroom came;
and those who were ready went in with him to the marriage feast;
and the door was shut.

Frantic Pleas Are Rejected.

11 "Afterward the other maidens came also, saying,
'Lord, Lord, open to us.'
12 "But he replied,
'Truly, I say to you, I do not know you.'

The Meaning of The Parable Faithful Watching Is Necessary

13 "Watch therefore,
for you know neither the day nor the hour."

g[1] The Parable of the Talents, or God Assigns Work According to Each One's Abilities But These Abilities Must Be Diligently Used. § 192 [*Contrast* § 159]

Mt. 25:14-30

A Lord Assigns Work to His Servants

14 "For it will be as when a man going on a journey,
called his servants and entrusted to them his property.

15 "To one he gave five talents,[b]
to another two,
to another one,
to each according to his ability.

He Goes Away;

"Then he went away.

The Servants Get Busy

16 "He who had received the five talents went at once and traded with them; **
and he made five talents more.

17 "So too, he who had the two talents
made two talents more.

All But One

18 "But he who had received the one talent,
went and dug in the ground and hid his master's money.

The Lord Returns

19 "Now after a long time
the master of those servants came and settled accounts with them.

His Faithful Servants Report to Him and Are Rewarded

20 "And he who had received the five talents[b]
came forward, bringing five talents more,
saying,
'Master, you delivered to me five talents;[b]
here I have made five talents more.'

---

[a] *Some ancient authorities add* and the bride. [b] *See note on Mt. 18:24. A talent equals about $1,000.*
**The " foolish virgins" were not prepared to wait long enough. (See Lk.18:8)*
***Contrast v.16 and Lk.19:13b, p.174, " trade herewith.*

21 "His master said to him,
'Well done, good and faithful servant;
you have been faithful over a little, I will set you over much;
enter into the joy of your master.'

22 "And he also who had the two talents came forward saying,
'Master, you delivered to me two talents;
here I have gained two talents more.'

23 "His master said to him,
'Well done, good and faithful servant;
you have been faithful over a little, I will set you over much;
enter into the joy of your master.'

An Unfaithful Servant Reports

24 "He also who had received the one talent came forward, saying,
'Master, I knew you to be a hard man,
reaping where you did not sow, and gathering where you did not winnow;
25 so I was afraid,
and I went and hid your talent in the ground. *(cf.Lk.19:21,p.175)*
Here you have what is yours.'

He Is Judged

26 "But his master answered him,
'You wicked and slothful servant!
You knew that I reap where I have not sowed and gather where I have not winnowed?
27 Then you ought to have invested my money with the bankers,
and at my coming I should have received what was my own with interest.
28 So take the talent from him,
and give it to him who has the ten talents.

He Is Punished.

29 'For to every one who has will more be given, and he will have abundance;
but from him who has not, even what he has will be taken away.

30 'And cast the worthless servant into the outer darkness;
there men will weep and gnash their teeth.'"

h[1] The Parable of the Sheep and the Goats, or The Work Assigned to Each One of Us Is Every Day Duties. § 193

Mt. 25:31-46

An Illustration of Judgment

31 "When the Son of man comes in his glory, *(cf.Lk.9:26,p.109)*
and all the angels with him,
then he will sit on his glorious throne.

32 "Before him will be gathered all the nations,

The Separation

and he will separate them one from another
as a shepherd separates the sheep from the goats,
33 and he will place the sheep at his right hand, but the goats at the left.

The Sentence: *The Reward to Those on the Right*

34 "Then the King will say to those at his right hand,
'Come, O blessed of my Father,
inherit the kingdom prepared for you from the foundation of the world;
35 for I was hungry and you gave me food,
I was thirsty and you gave me drink,
I was a stranger and you welcomed me,
36 I was naked and you clothed me,
I was sick and you visited me,
I was in prison and you came to me.'

Their Reply

37 "Then the righteous will answer him,
'Lord, when did we see thee hungry and feed thee?
or thirsty and give thee drink?
38 And when did we see thee a stranger and welcome thee?
or naked and clothe thee?
39 And when did we see thee sick or in prison and visit thee?'

The King's Answer

40 "And the King will answer them, *(v.45;cf.Mt.10:42,p.90)*
'Truly, I say to you,
as you did it to one of the least of these my brethren, you did it to me.'

The Fate of Those on the Left

41 "Then he will say to those at his left hand,
'Depart from me, you cursed,
into the eternal fire prepared for the devil and his angels;

42 'for I was hungry and you gave me no food,
I was thirsty and you gave me no drink,
43 I was a stranger and you did not welcome me,
naked and you did not clothe me,
sick and in prison and you did not visit me.'

Their Reply

44 "Then they also will answer,
'Lord, when did we see thee hungry or thirsty
or a stranger or naked or sick or in prison,
and did not minister to thee?'

The King's Answer

45 "Then he will answer them,.
'Truly, I say to you,
as you did it not to one of the least of these, you did it not to me.' *(v.40)*

The Final Destiny of Each.

46 "And they will go away into eternal punishment,
but the righteous into eternal life."

3. General Statements By The Gospels Concerning This Juncture of Events. § 193½

(1) About the Movements of Jesus During this Week

Lk. 21:37-38

In the Temple By Day, On Olivet By Night

37 And every day he was teaching in the temple,
but at night he went out and lodged on the mount called Olivet.
38 And early in the morning
all the people came to him in the temple to hear him.
(Cf. Mk.11:19: Mt.21:17)

(2) About The Approaching Passover

Mt.26:1-2	Mk.14:1	Lk.22:1
	[*1 It was now two days before* the Passover and the feast of Unleavened Bread.*]	[*1 Now the feast of Unleavened Bread drew near, which is called the Passover.*]

Late On Tuesday

On Leaving Olivet Jesus Predicts His Arrest and Crucifixion on the Approaching Passover

1 When Jesus had finished these
sayings, *(Ch.25)*
he said to his disciples,
2 "You know that after two days*
the Passover is coming,
and the Son of man will be
delivered up to be crucified."

(3) About the Love of Jesus for His Own Ever Since He Knew His Hour Had Come and That He Must Leave Them. *(See* §§ 103,106,155)

Jn. 13:1

Jesus' love for His own grows steadily in intensity as He sees the end approaching.

1 Now before the feast of the Passover,
when Jesus knew that his hour had come
to depart out of this world to the Father,
having loved his own who were in the world,
he loved them to the end. [*i.e.*'to the limit']

**i.e., as we should say, "day after tomorrow". This then was Tuesday P.M. and so this passage combined with Mk. 15:42 (Where see footnote, p.245) definitely fixes the day of Crucifixion.*

We have no record of what happened on Wednesday; however, it is not hard to guess that the Jewish rulers were completing their plots to arrest and kill him; and that Jesus on His part was preparing His disciples for the event's which He here speaks of as sure to follow.

Judas also arranged for the betrayal. (§§194,195,p.207).

II. SUFFERINGS AND DEATH pp.206-246.

(Wednesday to Saturday of Passion Week)

(In Detailed Outline)

(I) THE PREPARATIONS FOR HIS DEATH § 194-206, pp. 207-222

1. *BY THE JEWS. -- PLOTTING WITH JUDAS -- MALICE TO THE LIMIT* p.207 *(Wednesday night)*

(1) The Conspiracy of the Rulers (Mt. 26:3-5; Mk.14:1-2; Lk.22:1-2) § 194
(2) The Treason of Judas (Lk. 22:3) § 195
(3) The Changed Plans (Mt. 26:14-16; Mk. 14:10-11 ; Lk. 22:4-6) § 195

2. *BY JESUS. -- WORSHIPPING WITH THE TWELVE -- "LOVE TO THE UTTERMOST."* pp.208-223 *(Thursda*

(1) The Passover Prepared (Mt. 26:17-19; Mk. 14:12-16; Lk. 22:7-13) § 196 p.208
(2) The Passover Transformed (Mt. 26:20-29; Mk. 14:17-25; Lk. 22:14-30; Jn. 13:1-32) p.209-212

- *a. The Opening Prayers* § 197
- *b. The Foot Washing* § 198
- *c. The Supper* § 199
- *d. The Eucharist* § 200

(3) The Farewell Discourses p.213-219

- *a. The Introduction* § 201
- *b. The First Discourse - Concerning His going Away and the Coming of Another Helper to Take His Place (Jn. 14:1-31 ; Mt. 26:31-35; Mk. 14:17-31; Lk. 22:31-38)* § 202
- *c. The Second Discourse - Concerning the Unity of All True Believers (in Spite of His Going Away), in the Holy Spirit, With Him and with the Father (Jn. 15:1-16:3)* § 203
- *d. The Third Discourse - Concerning His Going Away, Again (Jn. 16: 4-33)* § 204

(4) The Intercessory Prayer (Jn. 17) § 205 pp.220-221
(5) The Prayer in Gethsemane (Mt. 26:30,36-46; Mk.14:26,32-42; Lk.22:39-46; Jn. 18:1) § 206 pp.221-222

(II) EVENTS LEADING TO HIS DEATH. pp. 223-

1. THE PREPARATIONS BY THE JEWS
"MALICE TO THE UTTERMOST"

(1) The Secret Plot of Jewish Officials Against Jesus. § 194 (WEDNESDAY P.M.)*

	Mt. 26:3-5	Mk. 14:1-2	Lk. 22:1-2 Cf. Jn. 13:1
The Time Exactly. The Approaching Feast	[When Jesus had finished these sayings, He said to his disciples, "You know that after two days The Passover is coming, and the Son of Man will be delivered up to be crucified."] (Ch.26:20)	1 It was now* two days before** the Passover and the feast of Unleavened Bread.	1 Now the feast of Unleavened Bread drew near which is called the Passover.
The Jewish Rulers Assemble,	3 Then the chief priests and the elders of the people gathered in the palace of the high priest, who was called Ca´ia-phas,	And the chief priests and the scribes	2 And the chief priests and the scribes
To Plot the Death of Jesus;	4 and took counsel together in order to arrest Jesus by stealth and kill him.	were seeking how to arrest him by stealth, and kill him;	were seeking how to put him to death;
They Agree To Defer Action,	5 But they said, "Not during the feast, lest there be a tumult among the people."	2 for they said, "Not during the feast, lest there be a tumult of the people.."	for they feared the people.
	* (See § 161, page 176)	(For vs.6-13 see page 176) *	

(2) The Conspiracy With Judas. § 195 (WEDNESDAY NIGHT)*
Their Plans are Changed

	Mt. 26:14-16	Mk. 14:10-11	Lk. 22:3-6
Then Satan Takes Possession of Judas;	14 Then one of the twelve, who was called Judas Iscariot,	10 Then Judas Iscariot, who was one of the twelve,	3 Then Satan entered into Judas called Iscariot, who was of the number of the twelve.
He Seeks Out The Top Officials;	went to the chief priests	went to the chief priests in order to betray him to them.	4 He went away and conferred with the chief priests and captains how he might betray him to them.
He Plots With Them,	15 and said, "What will you give me if I deliver him to you?"		
They Bribe Him,		11 And when they heard it they were glad, and promised to give him money.	5 And they were glad, and engaged to give him money.
He Agrees, They Pay Him;	And they paid him thirty pieces of silver.		6 So he agreed,
He Keeps Seeking Opportunity.	16 And from that moment he sought*** an opportunity to betray him.	And he sought*** an opportunity to betray him.	and sought*** an opportunity to betray him to them in the absence of the multitude.

*See § 193½ on preceding page. For Mt.26:6-13 and Mk.14:3-9 see § 161, page 176. The historical order of Luke and John are here followed, rather than the logical arrangements of Matthew and Mark.
**i.e. as we should say, "day after tomorrow." Cf. footnotes on pages 179, 205, 245.
***Or kept seeking.

2. *PREPARATIONS BY JESUS, or " LOVE TO THE UTTERMOST "*

(1) The Passover Prepared. § 196

(Thursday Forenoon)

	Mt. 26:17-19	*Mk. 14:12-16*	*Lk. 22:7-13*
The Day Comes To Kill The Passover Lamb	17 Now on the first day of Unleavened Bread	12 And on the first day of Unleavened Bread, when they sacrificed the passover lamb,	7 Then came the day of Unleavened Bread, on which *(Exodus 12:6-8)* the passover lamb had to be sacrificed.
Jesus tells Peter and John To Prepare The Passover.	the disciples came to Jesus	*(v.13)*	8 So Jesus[a] sent Peter and John, saying, " Go and prepare the passover for us, that we may eat it."
They Ask Where?	saying, " Where will you have us prepare for you to eat the passover?"	his disciples said to him, " Where will you have us go and prepare for you to eat the passover?"	9 They said to him, " Where will you have us prepare it?"
He Tells Them How to Find The Place	18 He said, " Go into the city	13 And he sent two of his disciples, and said to them, " Go into the city,	*(v.8)* 10 He said to them, " Behold, when you have entered the city
	to such a one,	and a man carrying a jar of water will meet you; follow him,	a man carrying a jar of water will meet you; follow him
		14 and wherever he enters,	into the house which he enters,
And What To Say to the House-holder	and say to him, 'The Teacher says, My time is at hand; I will keep the passover at your house	say to the householder, 'The Teacher says,	11 and tell the householder, 'The Teacher says to you,
		Where is my guest room, where I am to eat the passover	Where is the guest room, where I am to eat the passover
And What Response To Expect.	with my disciples.'"	with my disciples?'	with my disciples?'
What They Are To Do Then.		15 " And he will show you a large upper room furnished and ready; there prepare for us."	12 And he will show you a large upper room furnished; there make ready."
They Go and	19 And the disciples did as Jesus had directed them,	16 And the disciples set out, and went to the city,	13 And they went,
Find Things As He Had Said		and found it as he had told them;	and found it as he had told them;
(Thursday Afternoon) *They Prepare the Supper.*	and they prepared the passover.	and they prepared the passover.	and they prepared the passover.*

[a]*Greek* he. **According to Jewish traditional regulations, they went and got the selected lamb, took it to the temple to pour out its blood at the brazen altar; then took it to the place Jesus directed.*

(2) The Passover Transformed. § 197

Mt. 26:20-29 — *Mk. 14:17-25* — *Lk. 22:14-30*

(Thursday evening. See footnotes, pp. 179,205,245)

A. Introduction

At Even They Come To The Passover.

Mt. 26:20-29	Mk. 14:17-25	Lk. 22:14-30
20When it was evening,	17And when it was evening he came with the twelve.	14And when the hour came,
he sat at table with the twelve disciples.[a]		he sat at table, and the apostles with him.

*a. The Opening Prayers**

Lk.

*The First Blessing * For The Day*

15And he said to them,
"I have earnestly desired
to eat this passover with you
before I suffer;
16for I tell you
I shall never eat it again[b]
until it is fulfilled in the kingdom of God."

*The Second Blessing * For The Food*

17And he took a cup,*
and when he had given thanks he said,
"Take this, and divide it among yourselves;

Jesus Interprets The Passover. (cf. v. 28-30)

18for I tell you that from now on
I shall not drink of the fruit of the vine
until the kingdom of God comes."

[*For verses 19-20 see* § 200 *and footnote; for verses 21-23 see* § 199]

*b. The Contention Among the Disciples***

Lk.

*Ambition Rebuked*** *(§ 108, p.114; § 156, p.172)*

24A dispute also arose among them,
which of them was to be regarded as the greatest.

Wrong Ideals of Greatness

25And he said to them,
"The kings of the Gentiles exercise lordship over them;
and those in authority over them are called benefactors.

The True Secret of Greatness

26"But not so with you;
rather let the greatest among you become as the youngest,
and the leader as one who serves.

Christ Is The True Example

27"For which is the greater,
one who sits at table, or one who serves?
Is it not the one who sits at table?

"But I am among you as one who serves.

The True Greatness The Apostles Shall Achieve *(Cf. Mt. 19:28, p.170)*

28"You are those who have continued with me in my trials;
29as my Father appointed a kingdom for me,
so do I appoint for you
30that you may eat and drink at my table in my kingdom,
and sit on thrones judging the twelve tribes of Israel.

B. The Foot Washing*** § 198

Jn. 13:1-17

(a) Introductory Notes by the Author

(1) As The Coming of The Passover Forewarns Jesus of His Death, His Love Intensifies.

[1Now before the feast of the Passover,
when Jesus knew that his hour had come
to depart out of this world to the Father,
having loved his own who were in the world,
he loved them to the end.]****

[*See p.205,* § 193½]

[a]*Many authorities omit* disciples. [b]*Some ancient authorities omit* again.

**According to Edersheim (the Great Jewish-Christian Commentator) the Passover, in the time of Christ, was opened with a two-fold blessing (one for the* day, *and one for the* food), *accompanied by the passing of a first cup.* ***According to Oriental custom this strife about rank and place of honor at table would occur when they took their places round the table. So as soon as the opening blessings were said, Jesus rebukes such a spirit.*
****The Passover as kept by the Jews in the time of Jesus had a hand-washing, near the beginning,* by the leader; *and another, later,* by all *(See Edersheim: "Life and Times of Jesus the Messiah"). Jesus combines the two and transforms The Ceremony into a* foot-washing.
*****Or* to the uttermost.

(2) During The Passover Itself (While Judas Meditates Betrayal)

2 And during supper,
when the devil had already put it into the heart of Judas Iscariot,
Simon's son, to betray him, *(Lk.22:3,p.207)*

a. Jesus Is Thinking of His Own Divine Power, His Divine Origin, and Divine Destiny.

3 Jesus,
knowing that the Father had given all things into his hands,
and that he had come from God *(Jn.16:28,p.219;17:11)*
and was going to God,

(b) The Ceremony

b. Then Jesus gives Expression of His Thoughts, Sacramentally

4 rose from supper,

laid aside his garments,
and girded himself with a towel.

5 Then he poured water into a basin,

He Begins to Wash the Disciples' Feet

and began to wash the disciples' feet,
and to wipe them with the towel with which he was girded.

(c) The Explanation to Peter In the Midst of The Service

6 He came to Simon Peter;

Peter Raises Strenuous Objection

and Peter said to him,
"Lord, do you wash my feet?"

Jesus Prefers to Explain later

7 Jesus answered him,
"What I am doing you do not know now,
but afterward you will understand."

Peter Refuses Emphatically.

8 Peter said to him,
"You shall never wash my feet."

Cleansing Necessary to Fellowship.

Jesus answered him,
"If I do not wash you, you have no part in me."

Jesus Persuades Him and Explains Further.

9 Simon Peter said to him,
"Lord, not my feet only but also my hands and my head!"

It is a Symbol of Continuous Cleansing, or Sanctification.

10 Jesus said to him,
"He who has bathed does not need to wash, except for his feet,[a]
but he is clean all over;
and you are clean,
but not all of you."

The One Who Was Not Clean

11 For he knew who was to betray him;
that was why he said,
"You are not all clean."

(d) The Explanation Afterwards

12 When he had washed their feet,
and taken his garments,
and resumed his place,
he said to them,
"Do you know what I have done to you?

It Is Also a Symbol of Love and of Service.

13 "You call me Teacher and Lord;
and you are right, for so I am.

14 "If I then, your Lord and Teacher, have washed your feet,
you also ought to wash one another's feet.
15 For I have given you an example,
that you also should do as I have done to you. [*See Lk.22:24-26,27-30*]

It Is Also a Symbol of Humility and Obedience.

16 Truly, truly, I say to you,
a servant[b] is not greater than his master; *(16:20)*
nor is he who is sent greater than he who sent him.
17 If you know these things, blessed are you if you do them."

[a] *Some ancient authorities omit* except for his feet. [b] *Or* slave.

c. The Supper. § 199

Mt. 26:21-25 *Mk. 14:18-21* *Lk. 22:21-23* *Jn. 13:18-30*

Then, as They Eat The Supper, The Soul of Jesus Is Stirred

Jn.
18 " I am not speaking of you all;
I know whom I have chosen;
it is that the scripture may be fulfilled,
'He who ate my bread has lifted his heel against me.' [Ps.41:9]

19 " I tell you this now, before it takes place,
that when it does take place you may believe that I am he.

20 " Truly, truly, I say to you,
he who receives any one whom I send receives me;
and he who receives me receives him who sent me."

Then He Makes

Mt. 21 And as they were eating, he said,

Mk. 18 And as they were at table eating, Jesus said,

Jn. 21 When Jesus had thus spoken, he was troubled in spirit, and testified,

A Startling Announcement

Lk. 21 " But behold the hand of him who betrays me is with me on the table."

One of Them Will Betray Him

Mt.: " Truly, I say to you, one of you will betray me."

Mk.: " Truly, I say to you, one of you will betray me, one who is eating with me."

Jn.: " Truly, truly, I say to you, one of you will betray me."

Lk. 22 " For the Son of man goes as it has been determined; but woe to that man by whom he is betrayed!"

Mt.: (Cf.v.24) *Mk.:* (Cf.v.21)

They Are Greatly Moved by Sorrow And They Question Who It is

Mt. 22 And they were very sorrowful,

Mk. 19 They began to be sorrowful

Jn. 22 The disciples looked at one another, uncertain of whom he spoke.

Lk. 23 And they began to question one another, which of them it was that would do this.

Then Each One Asks "Is It I?"

Mt. and began to say to him one after another, " Is it I, Lord?"

Mk. and to say to him one after another, " Is it I?"

Jesus Replies

(a)" It is One of the Twelve"

(b)"One dipping in the same dish".

Mt. 23 He answered, " He who has dipped his [hand in the dish with me, will betray me.

Mk. 20 He said to them, " It is one of the twelve, one who is dipping bread in the same dish with me.

(c)The awfulness of the Deed

Mt. 24 " The Son of man goes, as it is written of him, but woe to that man by whom the Son of man is betrayed! It would have been better for that man if he had not been born."

Mk. 21 " For the Son of man goes as it is written of him, but woe to that man by whom the Son of man is betrayed! It would have been better for that man if he had not been born."

(d)Peter Appeals Through John

Jn.
23 One of his disciples, whom Jesus loved,
was lying close to the breast of Jesus;
24 so Simon Peter beckoned to him and said,
" Tell us who it is of whom he speaks."

John Asks Jesus

25 So lying thus, close to the breast of Jesus, he said to him,
" Lord, who is it?"

*(e)Jesus Answers Enigmatically **

26 Jesus answered,
" It is he to whom I shall give this morsel
when I have dipped it."

**If it is asked,"Why all these mysterious references to Judas' treachery?" It is enough to reply, " Consider what would have happened to Judas if the rest of those stalwart men had known,Two of them carried daggers in their belts"(Lk.22:38,p.214). Jesus spoke so that Judas alone would understand and repent;--but in vain.*

He Gives the Sop to Judas

Jn.
So when he had dipped the morsel,
he gave it to Judas, the son of Simon Iscariot.

27Then after the morsel,
Satan entered into him.

(f) Judas Asks, "Is It I?"

Mt.
25Judas, who betrayed him, said,
"Is it I, Master?" [a]
He said to him,
"You have said so."

(g) Judas, Having Resisted Every Appeal, Even This Last One, Is Possessed by Satan; and Is Sternly Dismissed by Jesus. The Others Do Not Understand.

Jesus said to him,
"What you are going to do, do quickly."

28Now no one at the table knew why he said this to him.
29Some thought that,
because Judas had the money box,
Jesus was telling him,
"Buy what we need for the feast";
or, that he should give something to the poor.

(h) Judas Goes Out.

30So, after receiving the morsel,
he immediately went out;
and it was night.

D. The Eucharist. § 200

Mt. 26:26-29 Mk.14:22-25 Lk.22:19-20 Jn. 13:31-32

Introductory Thoughts About His Glorification: Through Death, (a) It is Already an Accomplished Fact in Spiritual Reality (b) It Will Become Manifest soon.

Jn.
31When he had gone out,
Jesus said,
"Now is the Son of man glorified, *(Cf.17:1;p.220)*
and in him God is glorified;
if God is glorified in him,
32God will also glorify him in himself,
and glorify him at once."

The Bread Is Blessed and Broken and Given to Them

Mt.
26Now as they were eating,
Jesus took bread,
and blessed,
and broke it,
and gave it to the disciples
and said,
"Take, eat;
this is my body."

Mk.
22And as they were eating,
he took bread,
and blessed,
and broke it,
and gave it to them,
and said,
"Take;
this is my body."

Lk.
19And
he took bread,
and when he had given thanks
he broke it
and gave it to them,
saying,
"This is my body. [b] *(Cf.I.Cor.11:24-25)*
[which is given for you.
Do this in remembrance of me."

Its Significance

Then The Cup Is Blessed and Given

Mt.
27And he took a cup,
and when he had given thanks
he gave it to them,
saying,
"Drink of it, all of you;

Mk.
23And he took a cup,
and when he had given thanks
he gave it to them,
And they all drank of it.

Lk.
20And likewise the cup after supper,
saying,

Its Symbolic Meaning

Mt.
for this is my blood
of the[c] covenant,
which is poured out for many
for the forgiveness of sins.

Mk.
24And he said to them,
"This is my blood
of the[c] covenant,
which is poured out for many.

Lk.
"This cup
which is poured out for you
is the new covenant in my blood.

Its Final Fulfilment

Mt.
29"I tell you
I shall not drink again of this fruit of the vine
until that day when I drink it new with you
in my Father's kingdom."

Mk.
25"Truly, I say to you, *(For vs.21-23 see p.211)*
I shall not drink again of the fruit of the vine
until that day when I drink it new *(See vs.14-18,p.2*
in the kingdom of God."

[a] *Or* Rabbi.

[b] *Many ancient authorities add [bracketed lines above.]*

[c] *Many ancient authorities insert* new.

(*Jn. 13:33-16:33*)

a. Introduction to All the Discourses. § 201

Mt. 26:31-35 *Mk. 14:27-31* *Lk. 22:31-38* *Jn. 13:33-38*

(a) A Startling Announcement

The Occasion: When the Ceremonies are Over Jesus Announces His Going Away

Jn.

33 " Little children,
yet a little while I am with you.
You will seek me;
and as I said to the Jews
so now I say to you,
'Where I am going you cannot come.'

(b) A New Commandment

And Commands Them To Love One Another When He Is Gone.

(15:12,p.216)

34 " A new commandment I give to you,
that you love one another;
even as I have loved you,
that you also love one another.
35 By this all men will know
that you are my disciples,
if you have love for one another."

(c) Panic Among the Disciples

Peter Asks Where He Is Going

36 Simon Peter said to him,
" Lord, where are you going?"

Jesus Answers They Cannot Now Follow Him.

Jesus answered,
" Where I am going
you cannot follow me now;
but you shall follow afterward."

Jesus Forewarns Them All.

Mt.
(For v. 30 see below, before 26:36)
31 Then Jesus said to them,
" You will all fall away
because of me this night;
for it is written,
'I will strike the shepherd,
and the sheep of the flock
will be scattered.'

Mk.
(For v. 26 see below, before 14:32)
27 And Jesus said to them,
" You will all fall away;
for it is written,
'I will strike the shepherd,
and the sheep
will be scattered.'

(Mt.26:56b)

He Promises To Return (After The Resurrection).

Mt.
32 " But
after I am raised up,
I will go before you to Galilee."

Mk.
28 " But
after I am raised up,
I will go before you to Galilee."

(Mt.28:16,p.258) *(Mk.16:7,p.250)*

Peter Explodes Again

Mt.
33 Peter
declared to him
" Though they all fall away
because of you,
I will never fall away."

Mk.
29 Peter
said to him,
" Even though they all fall away,
I will not."

Jesus Specially Warns Peter, but also Comforts Him.

Lk.
31 " Simon, Simon,
behold, Satan demanded to have you,[a]
that he might sift you[a] like wheat,
32 but I have prayed for you
that your faith may not fail;
and when you have turned again,
strengthen your brethren."

Peter Again Vows Faithfulness at all Hazards Even Prison or Death

Lk.
33 And he said to him,
" Lord,
I am ready to go with you
to prison
and to death."

Jn.
37 Peter said to him,
" Lord,
Why cannot I follow you now?
I will lay down my life for you."

---

[a] *The Greek word for* you *here is plural; in verse 32 it is singular.*

* *Cf. footnotes, pp.179, 205, 245.*

	Mt.	*Mk.*	*Lk.*	*Jn.*
Jesus Predicts Peter's Failure Before the Night Is Over	34 Jesus said to him, "Truly, I say to you, this very night, before the cock crows, you will deny me three times."	30 And Jesus said to him, "Truly, I say to you, this very night, before the cock crows twice, you will deny me three times."	34 He said, "I tell you, Peter, The cock will not crow this day until you three times deny that you know me."	38 Jesus answered, "Will you lay down your life for me? Truly, truly, I say to you, the cock will not crow, till you have denied me three times."
Peter's Exceeding Vehemence.	35 Peter said to him, "Even if I must die with you, I will not deny you."	31 But he said vehemently, "If I must die with you, I will not deny you"		
They All Protest	And so said all the disciples.	And they all said the same.		

(For the outcome see § 212)

Jesus Further Forewarns Them of the Stern Trials Just Ahead

Lk. 35 And he said to them,
"When I sent you out with no purse or bag or sandals,
did you lack anything?"
They said,
"Nothing."
36 He said to them,
"But now, let him who has a purse take it,
and likewise a bag.
And let him who has no sword sell his mantle and buy one.
37 For I tell you that this scripture must be fulfilled in me,
'And he was reckoned with transgressors';
For what is written about me has its fulfillment."

Their Blind Rejoinder, and His Answer (No Use Arguing Further)

38 And they said,
"Look, Lord, here are two swords."

And he said to them,
"It is enough."

b. The First Discourse. § 202

Jn. 14:1-31

(His Continued Presence with Them, and Their Access to the Father and Him, Through the Holy Spirit)

Jn.

(a) Coming to the Father, Through Following Jesus

Don't Worry Trust God Trust Me Too

1 "Let not your hearts be troubled; *(Cf.v.27)*
believe in God,
believe also in me.

The Father's Home Has Many Staying Places;

2 "In my Father's house are many rooms;
if it were not so, would I have told you that
I go to prepare a place for you?

I am Going There

3 "And when I go and prepare a place for you, I will come again
and will take you to myself, *(Jn.13:36,p.213;12:26,p.194;17:24,p.221)*
that where I am you may be also.

And You Know The Way There

4 "And you know the way where I am going." [a]

You too Will Come, If You Follow Me

5 Thomas said to him,
"Lord, we do not know where you are going;
how can we know the way?"
6 Jesus said to him,
"I am the way, and the truth, and the life;*
no one comes to the Father, but by me.

(b) Knowing the Father, Through Knowing Jesus

Christ's Statement

7 "If you had known me, you would have known my Father also;
henceforth you know him and have seen him."

Philip's Reply

8 Philip said to him,
"Lord, show us the Father, and we shall be satisfied."

[a] *Some ancient authorities read* where I am going you know, and the way you know.
* *I prefer to translate,* "I am the way, both the truth and the life."

Jesus' Answer: Seeing Jesus Means Seeing the Father For The Father Dwells In Him As His Deeds Testify

9 Jesus said to him,
"Have I been with you so long, and yet you do not know me, Philip?
He who has seen me has seen the Father; how can you say, 'Show us the Father'?
10 Do you not believe that I am in the Father and the Father in me? *(Mt.10:40,p.90;*
The words that I say to you I do not speak on my own authority; *Jn.12:44,p.195)*
but the Father who dwells in me does his works.
11 Believe me that I am in the Father and the Father in me;
or else believe me for the sake of the works themselves. *(Jn.10:38,p.149)*

(c) Working for the Father, Through Believing in Jesus

Works and Faith

12 "Truly, truly, I say to you,
he who believes in me will also do the works that I do;
and greater works than these will he do, because I go to the Father.

Works and Glorifying God, Prayer and Works

13 "Whatever you ask in my name, I will do it, *(15:7; 15:16; 16:23)*
that the Father may be glorified in the Son;
14 if you ask[a] anything in my name, I will do it.

(d) Living with the Father Through Loving and Obeying Jesus

Through Love and Obedience The Helper Will Be Given Why The World Cannot Receive Him

15 "If you love me, you will keep my commandments.
16 And I will pray the Father, and he will give you another Counselor,*
to be with you forever,
17 even the Spirit of truth, whom the world cannot receive,
because it neither sees him nor knows him;
you know him, for he dwells with you,
and will be in you. *(15:26)*

But He Will Not Leave His Own As Helpless Orphans They Will Have His Continual Presence

18 "I will not leave you desolate; I will come to you. *(v.21,23)*
19 Yet a little while, and the world will see me no more,
but you will see me; because I live, you will live also.

Experiential Knowledge of God

20 "In that day you will know that I am in my Father,
and you in me, and I in you. *(Jn.10:38;14:10f.;15:1-11;17:20-23,pp.215-220)*

Will Come to Them; Christ Will Manifest Himself To Them.

21 "He who has my commandments and keeps them, he it is who loves me;
and he who loves me will be loved by my Father,
and I will love him and manifest myself to him." *(18,23)*

How Can This Be?

22 Judas (not Iscariot) said to him,
"Lord, how is it that you will manifest yourself to us, and not to the world?"

If Anyone Loves Christ And Obeys Him, He and The Father Will Make Their Home With Him

23 Jesus answered him,
"If a man loves me, he will keep my word,
and my Father will love him, *(Jn.8:29,p.127)*
and we will come to him and make our home with him. *(18,21)*
24 He who does not love me does not keep my words;
and the word which you hear is not mine but the Father's who sent me.

(e) Conclusion of the First Discourse**

Through Such Spiritual Presence They Will Remember And Understand

25 "These things I have spoken to you, while I am still with you.
26 But the Counselor,* the Holy Spirit, whom the Father will send in my name,
he will teach you all things, *(16:12-14, p.218; I Jn.2:27)*
and bring to your remembrance all that I have said to you.

And They Will Have The Peace Of Christ

27 "Peace I leave with you; my peace I give to you; *(Jn.16:33,p.219)*
not as the world gives do I give to you.
Let not your hearts be troubled, neither let them be afraid. *(Cf.v.1)*

Jesus Is Going To The Father They Should Rejoice Because That Is Best (Cf.16:7f)

28 "You heard me say to you,
'I go away, and I will come to you.' *(13:3)*
If you loved me, you would have rejoiced, because I go to the Father;
for the Father is greater than I.

He Forewarns Them So That They May Know What To Expect

29 "And now I have told you before it takes place,
so that when it does take place, you may believe.

How He Meets Satan's Attack Doing As The Father Commands Him Adjournment Proposed,

30 "I will no longer talk much with you,
for the ruler of this world is coming.
He has no power over me; 31 but I do as the Father has commanded me, *(12:49-50)*
so that the world may know that I love the Father.
"Rise, let us go hence."

---

[a] *Many ancient authorities add* me. **Or* Helper.

*** *What such spiritual presence of the Indwelling Christ will mean to them, and why He is talking thus with them just now, at this most critical transition moment--from His bodily to His Spiritual presence, from outward to inward presence.*

c. The Second Discourse. § 203

Jn. 15:1-16:3

(Still They Linger In the Upper Room See Jn.18:1, p.221)

(The Unity, Through the Holy Spirit, of All True Believers with the Son and with the Father)

1 " I am the true vine, and my Father is the vine-dresser. *(14:10f;15:20-23)*

Continuance, or "Abiding" Is Necessary for Cleansing

2 " Every branch of mine that bears no fruit, he takes away,
and every branch that does bear fruit he prunes,
that it may bear more fruit.
3 You are already made clean by the word which I have spoken to you.
4 *Abide in me, and I in you. *(v.10)*

Abiding Is Also The Condition For Fruit-bearing—

" As the branch cannot bear fruit by itself, unless it abides in the vine,
neither can you unless you abide in me.
5 I am the vine, you are the branches.
He who abides in me and I in him, he it is that bears much fruit.

In Fact, For Everything

" For apart from me you can do nothing.

Also To Escape Self-Destruction,

6 " If a man does not abide in me, he is cast forth as a branch and withers;
and the branches are gathered, thrown into the fire and burned.

For Answered Prayer.

7 " If you abide in me, and my words abide in you, *(v.10)*
ask whatever you will, and it shall be done for you. *(14:13;6:23)*
8 By this my Father is glorified, that you bear much fruit,
and so prove to be my disciples.

We "Abide" As He Does. Abiding In His Love Means "Keeping His Commandments"

9 " As the Father has loved me, so have I loved you; *(17:26)*
abide in my love.
10 If you keep my commandments, you will abide in my love, *(v.4)*
just as I have kept my Father's commandments and abide in his love.

The Purpose of This Plea to Abide, Is Fulness Of Joy

11 " These things I have spoken to you, that my joy may be in you,
and that your joy may be full."

The Relation of Christians to Each Other

Love One Another As Christ Has Loved

12 " This is my commandment,
that you love one another *(13:34-35,p.213)*
as I have loved you.

The Measure of The Greatest Love

13 " Greater love has no man than this,
that a man lay down his life for his friends. *(Romans 5:7-8)*
14 You are my friends if you do what I command you.

Loved Not as Servants But as Friends

15 " No longer do I call you servants,[a]
for the servant[b] does not know what his master is doing;
but I have called you friends,
for all that I have heard from my Father I have made known to you. *(12:44-50,p.195)*

How We Become Friends of Christ and Why

16 " You did not choose me, but I chose you and appointed you *(14:13,15:7)*
that you should go and bear fruit
and that your fruit should abide;
so that whatever you ask the Father in my name, he may give it to you.

The Command To Love Reiterated

17 " This I command you, to love one another." *(v.12)*

---

* *This verb "abide" in Greek means* stay, *or* remain. In fact our English word *"remain" is derived from it. The noun form of this word is "abode", which means* lodging place, *or* staying place, *or* home. *That is its meaning in Jn. 1:38-39.*

[a]Or slaves. [b]Or slave.

The Relation of the Christian to the World

(a) The World's Attitude to The Christian — It is Inevitable

18"If the world hates you,
know that it has hated me before it hated you. *(Jn.7:7,p.121;Mt.5: 10-12,p.59)*
19If you were of the world, the world would love its own;
but because you are not of the world, but I chose you out of the world,
therefore the world hates you.
20Remember the word that I said to you,
'A servant[a] is not greater than his master.' *(13:16)*

They Will Hate Us

If they persecuted me, they will persecute you;
if they kept my word, they will keep yours also.

Because They Hate Christ

21"But all this they will do to you on my account, *(Mt.5:10,p.59)*
because they do not know him who sent me.
22If I had not come and spoken to them, they would not have sin; *(v.24)*
but now they have no excuse for their sin. *(Jn.7:7,p.121)*

And The Father As Revealed in Christ

23"He who hates me hates my Father also.
24If I had not done among them the works which no one else did,
they would not have sin; *(v.22)*
but now they have seen and hated both me and my Father.
25It is to fulfill the word that is written in their law,
'They hated me without a cause.' *(Ps.35:19;69:4)*

(b) The Christian's Attitude to the World

We must Witness, Because The Holy Spirit Does

26"But when the Counselor* comes,
whom I shall send to you from the Father, *(Jn.14:15-17)*
even the Spirit of truth, who proceeds from the Father,
he will bear witness to me;
27and you also are witnesses, *(Ac.1:8)*
because you have been with me from the beginning.

Jn. 16:1-3

Concluding Paragraph: Why He Is Forewarning Them

1"I have said all this to you
to keep you from falling away.

To Prevent Apostacy Because of Persecution

2"They will put you out of the synagogues;
indeed, the hour is coming when whoever kills you
will think he is offering service to God.
3And they will do this
because they have not known the Father, nor me. *(Jn.9:22,34,p.131)*

....
* Helper.
[a]Or slave.

MAIN STREET
OF
BETHLEHEM

d. The Third Discourse. § 204

(His Going Away, Discussed More Fully)

Jn. 16:4-33

Introductory Transition Paragraph (Vs. 4-5)

4 " But I have said these things to you,
that when their hour comes
you may remember that I told you of them.
I did not say these things to you from the beginning,
because I was with you.

Why He Is Telling Them This Now.

5 " But now I am going to him who sent me; *(v.17,28)*
yet none of you asks me,
'Where are you going?'

The Reason for His Going Away

Their Mistaken Sorrow

6 " But because I have said these things to you,
sorrow has filled your hearts. *(13:33-14:1f;p.213,214)*

Christ's Going Is Essential for the Spirit's Coming.

7 " Nevertheless I tell you the truth:
it is to your advantage that I go away,
for if I do not go away, the Counselor* will not come to you;
but if I go, I will send him to you."

The Result of His Going

The Holy Spirit Will Conquer the World

8 " And when he comes, he will convince the world *(See Jn.6:44-45,p.99)*
of sin and of righteousness and of judgment:
9 of sin, because they do not believe in me;
10 of righteousness, because I go to the Father, and you will see me no more;
11 of judgment, because the ruler of this world is judged.

12 " I have yet many things to say to you, but you cannot bear them now.

And Guide Believers For He Will Teach About Christ,

13 " When the Spirit of truth comes,
he will guide you into all the truth; *(14:26,p.215;1 Jn.2:27)*
for he will not speak on his own authority,
but whatever he hears he will speak,
and he will declare to you the things that are to come.

He Will Glorify Christ In This Way.

14 " He will glorify me,
for he will take what is mine and declare it to you. *(14:26)*
15 All that the Father has is mine;
therefore I said that
he will take what is mine
and declare it to you.

Christ's Own Going Away (Bodily, by Death)
And His Coming Back (Spiritually, by Resurrection)

His Statement

16 " A little while, and you will see me no more;
again a little while, and you will see me."

Their Questioning: What Does He Mean?

17 Some of his disciples said to one another,
" What is this that he says to us,
'A little while, and you will not see me,
and again a little while, and you will see me';
and
'Because I go to the Father?'" *(13:3,33;14:2-6;16:5,10,28)*

....

* Helper.

18They said,
" What does he mean by
'A little while'?
We do not know what he means."

His Explanation: Foretelling His Resurrection After His Death

19Jesus knew that they wanted to ask him;
so he said to them,
" Is this what you are asking yourselves,
what I meant by saying,
'A little while, and you will not see me,
and again a little while, and you will see me'?

20" Truly, truly, I say to you,
you will weep and lament,
but the world will rejoice;
you will be sorrowful,
but your sorrow will turn into joy. *(v.22)*

His Illustration

A Mother's Experience In Child-Birth

21" When a woman is in travail she has sorrow,
because her hour has come;
but when she is delivered of the child,
she no longer remembers the anguish,
for joy that a child[a] is born into the world.

Its Application To Them

22" So you have sorrow now,
but I will see you again
and your hearts will rejoice, *(Jn.20:20b.,p.254)*
and no one will take your joy from you.

Their Access to the Father " In His Name"

They Will Have Access No Longer Through Conversation With Christ, but now Through Prayer " In Christ's Name"

23" On that day you will ask me no questions.
Truly, truly, I say to you,
if you ask anything of the Father, *(14:13;15:7)*
he will give it to you in my name.

24" Hitherto you have asked nothing in my name;
ask, and you will receive,
that your joy may be full.

It All Seems Dark Now, But Then All Will Be Plain. For They Will Have Direct Access to the Father, In Christ's Name

25" I have said this to you in figures; *(Mt.13:35,p.78)*
the hour is coming when I shall no longer speak to you in figures,
but tell you plainly of the Father.
26In that day you will ask in my name;
and I do not say to you that I shall pray the Father for you;
27for the Father himself loves you, because you have loved me
and have believed that I came from the Father.

A Final Word About His Coming out from the Father, and His Going Back to the Father

His Explicit Statement

28I came from the Father and have come into the world; *(Jn.13:3,p.210;16:10,17)*
again, I am leaving the world and going to the Father."

The Disciples' Optimistic Comment

29His disciples said,
" Ah, now you are speaking plainly, not in any figure!
30Now we know that you know all things, and need none to question you;
by this we believe that you came from God." *(Jn.7:28-29;13:3)*

His Foreboding Reply

31Jesus answered them,
" Do you now believe?
32The hour is coming, indeed it has come,
when you will be scattered, every man to his home,
and will leave me alone; *(Mt.26:31,p.213;26:56b)*

" yet I am not alone,
for the Father is with me. *(8:29,p.127)*

The General Conclusion to All the Discourses: In Christ We Have The Answer To Every Human Problem

33" I have said this to you,
that in me you may have peace. *(14:27,p.215)*
In the world you have tribulation;
but be of good cheer, *(Jn.15:18-27,p.217)*
I have overcome the world."

[a]*Greek*, a human being.

Jn. 17:1-26

The Occasion

1When Jesus had spoken these words, (Chs.14-16)
he lifted up his eyes to heaven and said,

a. His Prayer for Himself

His Hour
His Request.
His Purpose Is To Glorify God By Giving Life Eternal.

"Father, the hour has come;
glorify thy Son that the Son may glorify thee,
2since thou hast given him power over all flesh, (Jn.3:35;5:20;Mt.11:25;28:18)
so that he might give eternal life
to all whom thou hast given him.

Life Eternal Is Personal Acquaintance With Christ and God

3"And this is eternal life,
that they know thee the only true God,
and Jesus Christ whom thou hast sent.

Since His Work Here Is Finished He Asks To Be Glorified

4"I glorified thee on earth, (v.1)
having accomplished the work which thou gavest me to do;

5"and now, Father, glorify thou me in thy own presence
with the glory which I had with thee before the world was made! (v.24;Heb.1;2,3)

b. His Prayer for the Apostles

He Gave Them God's Word
They Have Kept It And So They Know It Is From God
They Received The Word As From God And So They Know That He Is From God

6"I have manifested thy name to the men whom thou gavest me out of the world;
thine they were, and thou gavest them to me, (12:44-50,p.195)
and they have kept thy word.
7Now they know that everything that thou hast given me is from thee;
8for I have given them the words which thou gavest me,
and they have received them
and know in truth that I came from thee;
and they have believed that thou didst send me. (v.25;16:30,p.219)

He Prays for Them
(a) Because They Belong to God

9"I am praying for them;
I am not praying for the world but for those whom thou hast given me,
for they are thine;
10all mine are thine, and thine are mine
and I am glorified in them.

He Is Leaving Them, and They Are in the World, but not of It

11"And now I am no more in the world,
but they are in the world,
and I am coming to thee. (v.13;13:3,p.210)

Therefore Keep Them In Union With God

"Holy Father, keep them in thy name which thou hast given me,
that they may be one, even as we are one.

His New Relation to Them (See Ch. 14)

12"While I was with them I kept them in thy name which thou hast given me;
I have guarded them, and none of them is lost but the son of perdition,
that the scripture might be fulfilled.

But Now He Is Coming To The Father; He Wants Their Joy To Be Like His And The World Hates Them.

13"But now I am coming to thee; (v.11)
and these things I speak in the world,
that they may have my joy fulfilled in themselves.
14I have given them thy word; (v.8)
and the world has hated them (15:18-26)
because they are not of the world, even as I am not of the world.

(b) The Petitions: Keep Them in His Name, and out of all Evil;

15"I do not pray that thou shouldst take them out of the world,
but that thou shouldst keep them from the evil one.[a]

16"They are not of the world, even as I am not of the world. (v.14)

Consecrate Them by the Truth

17"Consecrate them in the truth; thy word is truth.

In order To Save the World

18"As thou didst send me into the world, so I have sent them into the world.
19And for their sakes I consecrate myself,
that they also may be consecrated in truth.

c. His Prayer for All Future Believers

Their Present and Future Salvation:

20"I do not pray for these only,
but also for those who are to believe in me through their word,

(a) That They May Be One with God and Christ Now

21"that they may all be one;
even as thou, Father, art in me, and I in thee, (Jn.10:38,p.149; 14:10f.,20-23,p.215;
that they also may be in us, 15:1-11;17:22-23,pp.215-221)
so that the world may believe that thou hast sent me.

[a]Or from evil.

Jn.

This Was Christ's Glorious Privilege On Earth It May Be Theirs	22 "The glory which thou hast given me I have given to them, that they may be one even as we are one, 23 I in them and thou in me, *(v.26)*
Then The World Will Know.	"that they may become perfectly one, so that the world may know that thou hast sent me and hast loved them even as thou hast loved me.
(b) That They May Share His Eternal Glory Forever	24 "Father, I desire that they also, whom thou hast given me, may be with me where I am, *(14:2-3 and ref. p.214)* to behold my glory which thou hast given me in thy love for me before the foundation of the world. *(v.5)*
and the Father's Love,	25 "O righteous Father, the world has not known thee, but I have known thee; and these know that thou hast sent me. *(v.8)* 26 I made known to them thy name, and I will make it known,
Through Spiritual Unity With Christ.	that the love with which thou hast loved me may be in them, *(15:9)* and I in them." *(v.23)*

(5) The Prayer in Gethsemane. § 206

	Mt. 26:30,36-46	*Mk. 14:26, 32-42*	*Lk. 22:39-46*	*Jn. 18:1*
a. Introduction				
Going out to the Mount of Olives	30 And when they had sung a hymn, they went out	26 And when they had sung a hymn, they went out	39 And he came out,*	1 When Jesus had spoken these words, *(Ch.17)* he went forth* with his disciples
	(For vv.31-35 and Mk.27-31, see p.213)		and went, as was his custom,	across the Kidron valley,
	to the Mount of Olives.	to the Mount of Olives.	to the Mount of Olives; and the disciples followed him.	
Coming to Gethsemane	36 Then Jesus went with them to a place called Geth-sem´a-ne,	32 And they went to a place which was called Geth-sem´a-ne;		where there was a garden, which he and his disciples entered. *(Jn. 18:2 f., p.224)*
Leaving Them, He Goes to Pray,	And he said to his disciples, "Sit here, *(Cf. vs. 41 below)* while I go yonder and pray."	and he said to his disciples, "Sit here, *(Cf. v. 38 below)* while I pray."	40 And when he came to the place he said to them, "Pray that you may not enter into temptation.	
Selecting Three They Withdraw,	37 And taking with him Peter and the two sons of Zeb´e-dee,	33 And he took with him Peter and James and John,		
His Great Burden of Sorrow.	he began to be sorrowful and troubled.	and began to be greatly distressed and troubled.		
He Leaves the Three to Watch	38 Then he said to them, "My soul is very sorrowful, even to death; remain here, and watch[a] with me."	34 And he said to them, "My soul is very sorrowful even to death; remain here, and watch."[a]		
b. His First Prayer				
He Withdraws He Kneels Then Bows His Face To The Ground	39 And going a little farther he fell on his face	35 And going a little farther, he fell on the ground	41 And he withdrew from them about a stone's throw, and knelt down	

....

[a] Or keep awake.

*He went out. *Until now they were still in the upper room. According to the last words of Ch.14, "Rise, let us be going," they probably were standing, ready to go, but still lingering. At 18:1 they actually go out.*

	Mt.	Mk.	Lk.
Then He Prays First, "If It Be Possible"	and prayed, "My Father, if it be possible,	and prayed that, if it were possible, the hour might pass from him.	and prayed,
But All Things Are Possible To God		36 And he said, "Abba, Father, all things are possible to thee;	42 "Father, if thou art willing,
Then, "If Thou Wilt"	let this cup pass from me; nevertheless, not as I will, but as thou wilt."	remove this cup from me; yet not what I will, but what thou wilt."	remove this cup from me; nevertheless not my will, but thine, be done."
An Angel Strengthens Him			43 And there appeared to him an angel from heaven, *(Jn.12:29,p.194* strengthening him. *(Jn.1:51,p.28)*
He Prays More Earnestly			44 And being in an agony he prayed more earnestly; and his sweat became like great drops of blood falling down upon the ground.[a]
He Rises He Returns To The Three He Rebukes Them for Sleeping	40 And he came to the disciples and found them sleeping; and he said to Peter, "So, could you not watch[b] with me one hour?	37 And he came and found them sleeping, and he said to Peter, "Simon, are you asleep? Could you not watch one hour?"	45 And when he rose from prayer, he came to the disciples and found them sleeping for sorrow. 46 And he said to them, "Why do you sleep?
He Exhorts Them To Be Vigilant and Pray To Overcome Temptation	41 Watch[b] and pray, that you may not enter into temptation; the spirit indeed is willing, but the flesh is weak."	38 Watch[b] and pray that you may not enter into temptation; the spirit indeed is willing, but the flesh is weak."	Rise and pray that you may not enter into temptation."

c. His Second Prayer

	Mt.	Mk.
He Prays Again the Same Words	42 Again, for the second time, he went away and prayed, "My Father, if this cannot pass unless I drink it, thy will be done." *(Mt.6:10, p.62)*	39 And again he went away and prayed, saying the same words.
Returning, Again He Finds Them Asleep	43 And again he came and found them sleeping, for their eyes were heavy.	40 And again he came and found them sleeping, for their eyes were very heavy; and they did not know what to answer him

d. His Third Prayer

	Mt.	Mk.
Once Again He Prays The Same Words	44 So, leaving them again, he went away and prayed for the third time, saying the same words.	
For a Third Time He Finds Them Sleeping	45 Then he came to the disciples and said to them, "Are you still sleeping and taking your rest? Behold the hour is at hand, and the Son of man is betrayed into the hands of sinners.	41 And he came the third time, and said to them, "Are you still sleeping and taking your rest? It is enough; the hour has come; *(Jn. 2:4; 7:6,8,30,p.121-123)* the Son of man is betrayed into the hands of sinners.
He Goes to Meet the Traitor and His Mob	46 "Rise, let us be going; see, my betrayer is at hand."	42 "Rise, let us be going; see, my betrayer is at hand."

[a] *Many ancient authorities omit verses 43-44.* [b] Or keep awake.

(II) THE EVENTS LEADING TO HIS DEATH § 207-226 pp.223-246.

1. *THE BETRAYAL AND ARREST* (Mt.26:47-56; Mk.14:43-52; Lk.22:47-54; Jn.18:2-12) § 207 pp.223-226.

(1) The Coming of Judas and the Mob p.223 *(THURSDAY NIGHT)*

(2) The Betrayal p.223

(3) The Arrest pp.224-226

2. *THE CONDEMNATION AND CRUCIFIXION* pp.227-242 *(THURSDAY NIGHT)*

(1) The "Trials" and Mockings By the Jewish (Religious) Authorities pp.227-232

a. Jesus Is brought to the Palace of The High Priest § 208 pp.227-228
b. The Inquisition and Mocking Before Annas (Jn. 18:19-23) § 209 p.228
c. The "Trial" Before Caiaphas (Mt. 26:59-75; Mk. 14:55-72; Jn.18:24-27) § 210 p.229
d. The Mocking Afterwards § 211 p.229
e. The Denials By Peter § 212 pp.230-231
f. The Condemnation By the Sanhedrin (Mt. 27:1 ; Mk. 15:1; Lk. 22:66-71) *(FRIDAY MORNING)* § 213 p.231
g. The Suicide of Judas § 214 p.232

(2) The "Trials" and Mockings By the Roman (Civil) Authorities pp.233-238

a. The First "Trial" Before Pilate (Mt. 27:2,11-14; Mk.15:1-5; Lk. 23:1-6 Jn.18:28-38) § 215 pp.233-234
(a) The Jewish Rulers Send Jesus Into Pilate's Court Room, But they remain Outside.
(b) Pilate Brings Jesus Out to The Jews in the Court-Yard.
(c) Pilate Sends Jesus to Herod

b. The "Trial" By Herod (Lk. 23:7-12) § 216 p.234
(a) Herod Questions Jesus
(b) He Mocks Him
(c) He Sends Jesus Back to Pilate

c. The "Trial" By Pilate Resumed and Concluded (Mt. 27:15-26; Mk. 15:6-20; Lk. 23:13-25; Jn. 18:39-19:16) § 217 pp.235-238
(a) Pilate Again Brings Jesus Out on to the Porch Facing The Court Yard, Where The Jews Are Waiting
(b) The Trial Is Interrupted By a Messenger From Pilate's Wife
(c) Pilate Resumes The Trial
(d) Pilate Takes Jesus Inside and Has Him Scourged
(e) Pilate Comes Out, Followed By Jesus
(f) Pilate Takes Jesus Inside To Examine Him Privately
(g) Pilate Comes Out Alone and Continues The Trial
(h) Pilate Has Jesus Brought Out to Be Sentenced
(i) Pilate Makes a Final Appeal, As He "Washes His Hands" of This Affair
(j) Then Pilate Gives Formal Sentence
(k) He Releases Barabbas
(l) He Delivers Jesus To the Soldiers for Execution

d. The Soldiers Mock Jesus (Mt. 27:27-31; Mk.15:16-20) § 218 p.238

(3) The Crucifixion pp.239-242

a. Jesus is Led Away to Calvary (Mt. 27:31-32; Mk. 15:20-21; Lk. 23:26-32; Jn. 19:17) [§ 219
b. Jesus is Crucified (Mt.27:33-44; Mk. 15:22-32; Lk. 23:33-43; Jn. 19:18-27) § 220
c. He Is Mocked By the Rulers and the Multitudes § 221
d. Jesus Provides for His Mother § 222
e. Darkness Overwhelms the Whole Land (Mt. 27:45; Mk. 15:33; Lk. 23:44-45) § 223

3. *THE DEATH AND BURIAL* pp.243-246

(1) The Death (Mt. 27:46-56; Mk. 15:34-41; Lk. 23:46-49; Jn. 19:28-30) § 224 pp.243-244

(2) The Proof of His Death (Jn. 19:31-37) § 225 p.245

(3) The Burial (Mt. 27:57-60; Mk. 15:42-46; Lk. 23:50-54; Jn. 19:38-42) § 226 pp.245-246

1. The Betrayal and Arrest. § 207

Mt. 26:47-56 *Mk. 14:43-52* *Lk. 22:47-54* *Jn. 18:2-12*

(1) The Coming of Judas and the Mob

Judas (Not Finding Jesus in the Upper Room) Knows Where to Look for Him.

Jn.
2Now Judas, who betrayed him, also knew the place;
for Jesus often met there with his disciples.

3So Judas, procuring a band of soldiers**
and some officers from the chief priests and the Pharisees,
went there with lanterns and torches and weapons.

*A Big Mob** Comes to Gethsemane Soldiers, Police, Priests, Pharisees, and the rabble*

Mt.
47While he* was still speaking,
Judas came,
one of the twelve,
and with him a great crowd
with swords and clubs,**
from the chief priests
and the elders of the people.

Mk.
43And immediately,
while he* was still speaking,
Judas came,
one of the twelve,
and with him a crowd
with swords and clubs,
from the chief priests and the
scribes and the elders.

Lk.
47While he* was still speaking
there came
a crowd,
and the man called Judas,
one of the twelve,
was leading them.

Judas is Leading Them

(2) The Betrayal

Jn. 18:4-9

Jesus Goes to Meet The Mob

4Then Jesus,
knowing all that was to befall him,
came forward and said to them,
"Whom do you seek?"

5They answered him,
"Jesus of Nazareth."

Jesus said to them,
"I am he."

Judas Is With Them

Judas, who betrayed him,
was standing with them.

Jesus Offers Himself

6When he said to them,
"I am he,"

They Are Terrified and Stagger Backward. When They Recover Their Poise

they drew back
and fell to the ground.

Jesus Again Offers Himself.

7Again he asked them,
"Whom do you seek?"

And they said,
"Jesus of Nazareth."

He Saves The Apostles From Arrest

8Jesus answered,
"I told you that I am he;
so, if you seek me,
let these men go."

As He Had Foretold

9This was to fulfill the word which he had spoken,
"Of those whom thou gavest me
I lost not one."

Judas Had Given Them a Sign

Mt.
48Now the betrayer had given them a sign,
saying,
"The one I shall kiss is the man;
seize him."

Mk.
44Now the betrayer had given them a sign,
saying,
"The one I shall kiss is the man;
seize him
and lead him away safely."

....

**That is, Jesus. As in last verses on page 222.*

***The "soldiers" were from the Roman garrison, the "officers" were Jewish temple police. The "torches" belonged to the Roman soldiers and the "lanterns" to the Jewish police. So also the "swords" were carried by the soldiers, and the clubs by the police.*

	Mt.	Mk.	Lk.	Jn.
Judas Betrays Jesus	49 And he came up to Jesus at once and said, "Hail, Master!" [a] And he kissed him.	45 And when he came, he went up to him, at once and said, "Master!" [a] And he kissed him.	He drew near to Jesus to kiss him;	
Jesus Rebukes Him			48 but Jesus said to him, "Judas, would you betray the Son of man with a kiss?"	
and Commands Him to Do the Deed. [b]	50 Jesus said to him, "Friend, why are you here?" [b]*			

(3) The Arrest

	Mt.	Mk.	Lk.	Jn.
Jesus Is Seized and Held Fast	Then they came up and laid hands on Jesus and seized him.	46 And they laid hands on him, and seized him.	*(Cf. v.54)*	*(Cf. v.12)*
(As Yet He Is Not Bound See Jn. 18:12) The Apostles Ask Whether They Should Fight			49 And when those who were about him saw what would follow, they said, "Lord, shall we strike with the sword?"	
They Do Not Wait for an Answer. Peter Drawing a Sword Strikes a Hasty Blow	51 And behold, one of those who were with Jesus stretched out his hand and drew his sword, and struck the slave of the high priest, and cut off his ear.	47 But one of those who stood by drew his sword, and struck the slave of the high priest and cut off his ear.	50 And one of them struck the slave of the high priest and cut off his right ear.	10 Then Simon Peter, having a sword, drew it and struck the high priest's slave and cut off his right ear. The slave's name was Malchus.
Jesus Sternly Rebukes Him And So Prevents a Fight.	52 Then Jesus said to him, "Put your sword back into its place; for all who take the sword will perish by the sword.		51 But Jesus said,	11 Jesus said to Peter, "Put your sword into its sheath;"
Jesus Could Get Protection	53 "Do you think that I cannot appeal to my Father, and he will at once send me more than twelve legions of angels?			
Why He Does Not Command It	54 "But how then should the scriptures be fulfilled, that it must be so?"			
Jesus Accepts The Cup as From The Father's Hand.				"Shall I not drink the cup which the Father has given me?"
He Heals Malchus' Ear			"No more of this!" ** And he touched his ear and healed him.	
Jesus Rebukes the Mob	55 At that hour Jesus said to the crowds,	48 And Jesus said to them,	52 Then Jesus said to the chief priests and captains of the temple and elders, who had come out against him,	

[a] *Or* Rabbi. [b] *Or* Do that for which you have come. [**This reading is preferable*]

** Suffer ye thus far *is the literal translation and probably means "Let me reach far enough to touch his ear."*

	Mt.	Mk.	Lk.	Jn.
Their Injustice and	"Have you come out as against a robber with swords and clubs to capture me?	"Have you come out, as against a robber, with swords and clubs to capture me?	"Have you come out as against a robber, with swords and clubs?	
Unfairness	"Day after day I sat in the temple teaching, and you did not seize me.	49 "Day after day I was with you in the temple teaching, and you did not seize me.	53 "When I was with you day after day in the temple, you did not lay hands on me.	
But His Hour Has Come, and He Surrenders Himself to Them Being Guided By The Scriptures	56 "But all this has taken place, that the scriptures of the prophets might be fulfilled." *(Cf. v.50)*	"But let the scriptures be fulfilled." *(Cf. v.46)*	"But this is your hour, and the power of darkness." *(Cf. Jn.7:30;8:20,p.124,126)* *(Cf.Lk.24:25-27,p.253)*	
			Lk.	*Jn.*
			54 Then they	12 So the band of soldiers and their chief captain and the officers of the Jews
They Grab Him and Bind Him			seized him.	seized Jesus and bound him.
The Disciples Flee	Then all the disciples forsook him, and fled.	50 And they all forsook him, and fled.		

*(4) A Footnote By The Author**

	Mk.
John Mark Narrowly Escapes*	51 And a young man followed him, with nothing but a linen cloth about his body; and they seized him, 52 but he left the linen cloth and ran away naked.

**Since Mark alone records this detail, it is generally believed that this young man was Mark.*

(1) The Trials and Mockings Before the Jewish Religious Authorities

a. Jesus is Brought to the Palace of the High Priest.* § 208 *(THURSDAY NIGHT)*

*(a) He is Turned Over to Annas***

	Mt. 26:57-58	*Mk. 14:53-54*	*Lk. 22:54-55*	*Jn. 18:13-18*
Jesus is Led Away From Gethsemane,	57 Then those who had seized Jesus led him	53 And they led Jesus	and led him away,	13 First they led him
*to the High Priest's Palace**	to Ca´ia-phas the high priest,*	to the high priest;*	bringing him into the high priest's house.*	to Annas,** for he was the father-in-law of Ca´ia-phas, who was high priest that year.
*They Take Him First to the Apartments of Annas***				*Jn.* 14 It was Ca´ia-phas *(See Jn. 11:47-53)* who had given counsel to the Jews that it was expedient that one man should die for the people.

(b) Meanwhile Caiaphas Summons The Sanhedrin

	Mt.	*Mk.*
Meanwhile The Members of the Sanhedrin Are Coming in one by one to the Court Room of Caiaphas.	where the scribes and the elders had gathered	and all the chief priests. and the elders and the scribes were assembled.

(c) John and Peter Also Join The Crowds in the Palace Court-Yard

	Mt.	*Mk.*	*Lk.*	*Jn.*
The Two Disciples Follow Jesus	58 But Peter followed him at a distance, as far as the court-yard*** of the high priest.	54 And Peter had followed him at a distance,	Peter followed at a distance;	15 Simon Peter followed Jesus,
John Enters With the Crowd				*Jn.* and so did another disciple. As this disciple was known to the high priest, he entered the court*** of the high priest along with Jesus,
Peter, Following at A Distance, Is Left Outside The Gates. Then John Brings Him in.				16 while Peter stood outside at the door. So the other disciple, who was known to the high priest, went out and spoke to the maid who kept the door, and brought Peter in.
	Mt. And going inside,	*Mk.* right into the courtyard of the high priest;		
The Maid at the Door Innocently Asked Peter if He, too, is a Disciple of Jesus				17 The maid who kept the door said to Peter, "Are not you also one of this man's disciples?" He said, "I am not."

The Palace of the High Priest, or "the High Priest's House," was an elaborate building with many apartments, built round a central court-yard, (aule´ in Greek, usually translated "court", but meaning "court-yard").
Annas and Caiaphas probably both lived in this "Palace of the High Priest," although in separate apartments. Jesus is brought first to the apartments of ANNAS.

***ANNAS was the "big boss" among "the chief priests." He had been High Priest from A.D. 6 to 15. According to the Mosaic Law he should have continued to hold that office until his death. But the Roman governor deposed him, and gave the office to the one who paid the most money for it. Annas was astute politician enough to so maneuver as to get five of his sons appointed to the High Priesthood. And after that he got his son-in-law appointed, Caiaphas, who holds the office at the time of the trial of Jesus.*

****A court-yard is a paved house-yard surrounded with buildings.*

(d) The Crowd Kindles a Fire and Gathers Round It.

	Mt.	Mk.	Lk.	Jn.
The Servants and the Officers Kindle a Fire In The Courtyard			55 and when they had kindled a fire in the middle of the court-yard	18 Now the servants[a] and the officers had made a charcoal fire
And Warm Themselves				because it was cold, and they were standing and warmi themselves; Peter also was with them, standing and warming himself.
They Sit Down By The Fire			and sat down together,	
Peter Also Sits Down Awaiting The Outcome	he sat with the guards to see the end.	And he was sitting with the guards, and warming himself, at the fire.	Peter sat among them.	

b. Jesus Is Cross-questioned by Annas.* § 209 *(THURSDAY NIGHT)*

Jn. 18:19-23

Inside, Annas Questions Jesus, Hoping to Extract some Incriminating Evidence.

19 The high priest *(Annas cf. v.24)*
then questioned Jesus
about his disciples and his teaching.

Jesus Replies Factually,

20 Jesus answered him,
"I have spoken openly to the world;
I have always taught in synagogues
and in the temple,
where all Jews come together;
I have said nothing secretly.

but in Stern Rebuke.

21 "Why do you ask me?
Ask those who have heard me,
what I said to them;
they know what I said."

A Temple-Police Officer 'slaps Jesus on the Mouth

22 When he had said this,
one of the officers standing by
struck Jesus with his hand,
saying,
"Is that how you answer the high priest?"

Jesus Rebukes Him

23 Jesus answered him,
"If I have spoken wrongly,
bear witness to the wrong;
but if I have spoken rightly,
why do you strike me?

[a] Or slaves.

While Caiaphas is preoccupied in assembling the Sanhedrin, in special emergency session, in the late hours of the night, Jesus is brought first to Annas (Jn. 18:13). That astute old political boss seizes the opportunity to cross-question Jesus personally, probably in order to get Him, if possible, to incriminate Himself.

c. Jesus is Condemned by Caiaphas. § 210 *(THURSDAY NIGHT)*

Mt. 26:59-66 — *Mk. 14:55-64* — *Jn. 18:24*

*Jesus Is Brought to Caiaphas In His Own Court Room **

Jn.
24Annas then sent him bound
to Ca'ia-phas the High Priest.*

(a) They Seek Vainly for Witnesses

They Seek False Witnesses

Mt.
59Now the chief priest and the whole council
sought false witness against Jesus,
that they might put him to death,

60but they found none,
though many witnesses came forward.

Mk.
55Now the chief priests and the whole council
sought testimony against Jesus,
to put him to death;

but they found none.
56For many bore false witness against him,

and their witness did not agree.

Two Come Forward,

Mt.
At last two came forward

Mk.
57And

some stood up and bore false witness against him,
saying,

Distorting One of His Sayings

Mt.
61and said,
"This fellow said,
'I am able to destroy the temple of God,

and to build it in three days.'"

(Cf.Jn.2:18-21,p.31)

Mk.
58"We heard him say,
'I will destroy this temple that is made with hands,
and in three days I will build another,
not made with hands.'"

But They Don't Agree.

Mk.
59Yet not even so did their testimony agree.

(b) The High Priest Questions Jesus.

The High Priest Is Exasperated He Cross-questions Jesus,

Mt.
62And the high priest stood up
and said,
"Have you no answer to make?
What is it that these men testify against you?"

Mk.
60And the high priest stood up in the midst,
and asked Jesus,
"Have you no answer to make?
What is it that these men testify against you?"

Jesus Remains Quiet.

Mt.
63But Jesus was silent.

Mk.
61But he was silent and made no answer.

Caiaphas Attempts to Put Jesus on Oath

Mt.
And the High priest said to him,
"I adjure you by the living God,
tell us if you are the Christ, the Son of God."

Mk.
Again the high priest asked him,

"Are you the Christ, the Son of the Blessed?"

*He Declines to Swear, but Answers Simply That He Is The Messiah in Power.** (Rom.1:4)*

Mt.
64Jesus said to him,
"You have said so. But I tell you,
hereafter you will see the Son of man
seated at the right hand of Power,**

and coming on the clouds of heaven."

Mk.
62And Jesus said,
"I am; and (Cf.Lk.22:69-71,p.231;Jn.19:7,p.236)
you will see the Son of man
sitting at the right hand of Power,**

and coming with the clouds of heaven."

(c) They Condemn Jesus to Death for Blasphemy

Jesus Is Falsely Condemned for Blasphemy,

Mt.
65Then the high priest tore his robes, and said,
"He has uttered blasphemy.
Why do we still need witnesses?
You have now heard his blasphemy.
66What is your judgment?"

Mk.
63And the high priest tore his mantle, and said,

"Why do we still need witnesses?
64You have heard his blasphemy.
What is your decision?"

And Sentenced to Death

Mt.
They answered,
"He deserves death."

Mk.
And they all condemned him
as deserving death.

After the Condemnation by Caiaphas and While Waiting for Daylight to Come

d. Jesus is Mocked by the Jews. § 211

Mt. 26:67-68 — *Mk.14:65* — *Lk.22:63-65*

He is Shamefully Treated: They Spit on Him, Strike Him, Slap Him, Blind-fold and Bid Him Prophesy.

Mt.
67Then They

spat in his face

and struck him:
and some slapped him,

68saying,
"Prophesy to us, you Christ!
Who was it that struck you?"

Mk.
65And some began

to spit on him, and
to cover his face,
and to strike him,

saying to him,
"Prophesy!"

Lk.
63 Now the men who were holding Jesus
mocked him

and beat him;

64 they also blindfolded him
and asked him,
"Prophesy!
Who was it that struck you?"

The Temple Police Also Strike Him

Mk.
And the guards***
received him with blows.

Lk.
65
And they spoke many words against him,
[reviling him.

*To his courtroom, where the Sanhedrin had now been assembled. **Jesus here speaks of two things,- first, of his exaltation to the right hand of God, immediately after His ascension; and second, of His final coming again at the end of the age. ***The Jewish temple police.

[Also during this Time of Waiting for Daylight]

e. Jesus is Denied by Peter. § 212 *(THURSDAY NIGHT)*

	Mt.26:69-75	*Mk.14:66-72*	*Lk.22:56-62*	*Jn.18:25-27*
(a) The First Group of Denials.*				
While Peter Is Sitting By the Fire	[69]Now Peter was sitting outside in the courtyard.	[66]And as Peter was below in the courtyard,		
The Door-Maid Approaches and Sees Peter	And a maid	one of the maids of the high priest came; [67]and seeing Peter warming himself,	[56]Then a maid, seeing him as he sat in the light	
She Comes up to Him	came up to him,			
She Stares At Him; She Accuses Him.	and said, "You also were with Jesus the Galilean."	she looked at him, and said, "You also were with the Nazarene, Jesus."	and gazing at him, said, "This man also was with him."	
But He denies Emphatically.	[70]But he denied it before them all, saying, "I do not know what you mean."	[68]But he denied it, saying, "I neither know nor understand what you mean."	[57]But he denied it, saying, "Woman, I do not know him."	
Then He Gets Up and Goes Out to the Porch. There A Cock Crows		And he went out into the gateway.[a]		
(b) The Second Round of Denials	*Mt.*	*Mk.*	*Lk.*	
When He Comes Back	[71]And when he went out to the porch,	[69]And	[58]And a little later	
Another Maid Accuses Him	another maid saw him, and she said to the bystanders, "This man was with Jesus of Nazareth."	the maid saw him, and began again to say to the bystanders, "This man is one of them."	some one else ** saw him and said, "You also are one of them."	
He Denies Again, With an Oath This Time.	[72]And again he denied it with an oath, "I do not know the man."	[70]But again he denied it.	But Peter said, "Man, I am not."	
(c) The Third Round of Denials				*Jn.*
An Hour Later the Men by the Fire Accuse Peter,	[73]After a little while the bystanders came up and said to Peter,	And after a little while again the bystanders said to Peter,	[59]And after an interval of about an hour still another insisted, saying,	[25]Now Simon Peter was standing and warming himself. They said to him,
They Ask Him He Denies.				"Are not you also one of his disciples He denied it and said, "I am not."
They Are Sure For He Is A Galilean	"Certainly you are also one of them, for your accent betrays you."	"Certainly you are one of them; for you are a Galilean."	"Certainly this man also was with him; for he is a Galilean."	
A Kinsman of Malchus (whose ear Peter had cut off) Confirms It Personally				*Jn.* [26]One of the servants[b] of the high priest, a kinsman of the man whose ear Peter had cut off, asked, "Did I not see you in the garden with him?
Peter, Now Completely Dismayed			*Lk.* [60]But Peter said, "Man, I do not know what you are saying."	[27]Peter again denied it;

**The many denials by Peter naturally arrange themselves into three groups (not counting the one to the portress Jn. 18:17) (1) After the* First *round, Peter goes out into the porch. (2) After an interval he is again accosted by another maid, and comes back to the group at the fire, only to have them, too, join in the accusations. (3) After another interval--an hour later--the men again take up the question. Others joins in the fray, and Peter ends by cursing. His Galilean brogue betrays him. Then Jesus in passing looks on Peter. Peter ends it all by going out and weeping bitterly.*

***A man.*

[a]*Or,* forecourt. *Some ancient authorities add* and the cock crowed. [b]*Or* slaves.

<table>
<tr><th></th><th>Mt.</th><th>Mk.</th><th>Lk.</th><th>Jn.</th></tr>
<tr><td>Begins to Curse and He Swears That He Never Knew Jesus</td><td>74 Then he began to invoke a curse on himself and to swear,
"I do not know the man."</td><td>71 But he began to invoke a curse on himself, and to swear,
"I do not know this man of whom you speak."</td><td></td><td></td></tr>
<tr><td>Just Then The Cock Crows</td><td>And immediately
the cock crowed.</td><td>72 And immediately
the cock crowed a second time.</td><td>And immediately, while he was still speaking, the cock crowed.</td><td>and at once
the cock crowed.
[Continued in § 215]</td></tr>
<tr><td>Jesus Turns and Looks at Peter; Peter Recalls Jesus' Words of Warning</td><td>75 And Peter remembered the saying of Jesus,
"Before the cock crows, you will deny me three times."</td><td>And Peter remembered how Jesus had said to him,
"Before the cock crows twice you will deny me three times."</td><td>61 And the Lord turned and looked at Peter.
And Peter remembered the word of the Lord, how he had said to him,
"Before the cock crows today, you will deny me three times."</td><td></td></tr>
<tr><td>He Goes Out and Weeps Heartbreakingly.</td><td>And he went out and wept bitterly.</td><td>And he broke down and wept.</td><td>62 And he went out, and wept bitterly.</td><td></td></tr>
</table>

Jesus Is Condemned By the Sanhedrin. § 213 *(FRIDAY AT SUNRISE)*

<table>
<tr><th></th><th>Mt. 27:1</th><th>Mk. 15:1</th><th>Lk. 22:66-71</th></tr>
<tr><td>After Daylight***
A Formal Meeting of the Sanhedrin Condemns Jesus As Guilty of Blasphemy</td><td>1 When morning came,
all the chief priests and the elders of the people</td><td>1 And as soon as it was morning
the chief priests with the elders and scribes,</td><td>66 When day came, the assembly of the elders of the people gathered together, both chief priests
and scribes;</td></tr>
<tr><td>(This Meeting Is Held in "The Hall of Hewn Stone," On the Temple Area, The Official Meeting-place of the Sanhedrin)</td><td>took counsel</td><td>and the whole council held a consultation.</td><td>and they led him away, to their council.</td></tr>
<tr><td>And As Deserving Death</td><td>against Jesus
to put him to death;</td><td></td><td></td></tr>
<tr><td>They Ask Whether He is The Messiah.</td><td></td><td></td><td>And they said,
67 "If you are the Christ, tell us.</td></tr>
<tr><td>He Despairs of Justice or Fair Play</td><td></td><td></td><td>But he said to them,
"If I tell you, you will not believe;
68 and if I ask you*, you will not answer.</td></tr>
<tr><td>But He Bears Witness Officially That He Is The Messiah</td><td></td><td></td><td>69 "But from now on the Son of man shall be seated at the right hand of the power of God."</td></tr>
<tr><td>Then They Ask Him, Are You The Son of God? He Affirms A second time that He Is (See §210)</td><td></td><td></td><td>70 And they all said,
"Are you the Son of God, then?"
And he said to them,
"You say that I am."</td></tr>
<tr><td>On This Count, Then, They Formally Condemn Him.</td><td></td><td></td><td>71 And they said,
"What further testimony do we need?**
We have heard it ourselves from his own lips."</td></tr>
</table>

**i.e., Ask you questions.*

***So Jesus was condemned to die because He officially and voluntarily claimed to be, 1st. The Son of Man, i.e., The Messiah (vs.67-69). 2nd. The Son of God. (v.70-71).*

This repeats and ratifies officially, by a legally called daylight meeting in the official temple court-room, the same sentence voted at the previous illegal night session held at the High Priest's House (§ 210).

It was illegal by Sanhedrin rules to condemn a man to death at night, as they had done (§ 210). This formal meeting after daylight, makes it legally correct.

g. The Suicide of Judas. § 214 [*cf.* § 195, *p.205*]

Mt. 27:3-10

(1) What Judas Did

a. The Remorse of Judas **

He Sees that Jesus Is Condemned

3 When Judas,
his betrayer,
saw that he was condemned,
he repented.

He Returns The Blood Money

And brought back the thirty pieces of silver
to the chief priests and elders,
4 saying,
"I have sinned in betraying innocent blood."

[*Jn.18:28. Then they led Jesus from Caiaphas ("the sanhedrin"), to Pilate*

The Priests Are Cynical

They said,
"What is that to us?
See to it yourself."

b. The Despair of Judas

*He Flings The Accursed Money Into the Holy Place**

5 And throwing down the pieces of silver
in the temple,*
he departed;

c. The Suicide Of Judas

and he went and hanged himself.

(2) What the Chief Priests Did

The Dilemma of the Priests

6 But the chief priests, taking the pieces of silver,
said,
"It is not lawful to put them into the treasury,
since they are blood money."

Their Decision

7 So they took counsel,
and bought with them the potter's field,
to bury strangers in.
8 Therefore that field has been called
the Field of Blood to this day.

A Prophecy Comes True

9 Then was fulfilled
what had been spoken by the prophet Jeremiah,
saying,
"And they took the thirty pieces of silver,
the price of him on whom a price had been set
by some of the sons of Israel,
10 and they gave them for the potter's field,
as the Lord directed me."

....

**Or*, into the sanctuary; *Gk.* eis ton naon.

In Gethsemane they seized Jesus (Lk.54a), then "led him away" (54b) and brought him to "the palace of the high priest", a huge pile of buildings, in which was also the high priest's own court-room. (See notes p.227).

From the Palace of the high priest, they brought Jesus, "as soon as it was day," to "the official court room of "the Sanhedrin", what Josephus calls "the hall of hewn stone," just south of the temple. Here the final official sentence of the Jewish supreme court was passed upon Jesus. Luke contrasts accurately "the palace of the high priest"(Lk.22:54) with "their Sanhedrin"(Lk.22:66

From this official courtroom of the sanhedrin, just south *of the temple, they are (now that He has been officially condemned) conducting Jesus to deliver him to Pilate's judgment hall, the Pretorium, just* north *of "the temple area. In doing so they must pass directly in front of the "holy place", "the* naon."

This gives Judas his chance to do this spiteful thing, and he flings the now hated money into the holy place, ("the sanctuary.")

***Remorse differs from repentance in that it lacks faith in the forgiving love of God, and so Judas despairs instead of repenting.*

a. The First "Trial" Before Pilate. § 215 *(FRIDAY AFTER SUNRISE. See footnotes; pp.179,205,245.)*

*(a) Jesus Is Delivered to the Governor (in "the Pretorium")]**

*Jesus Is Is Bound And Led **From the Jewish Courtroom "The Sanhedrin" into Pilate's Courtroom, "The Pretorium" Turned Over To Pilate, The Governor.*

Mt. 27:2, 11-14	Mk. 15: 1b-5	Lk. 23:1-6	Jn. 18:28-38
		1Then the whole company of them arose,	28Then they
2And they bound* him and led him away,	1band they bound* Jesus and led him away		led Jesus from [the house of]** Caiaphas to the Praetorium.
and delivered him to Pilate the governor.	and delivered him to Pilate.	and brought him before Pilate.	It was early. [About 6 a.m.]
(vs.3-10 § 214)			

(b) The Jews Remain Outside in The Court Yard

The Jews Stay Outside in the Court-yard;

Jn. 28b
They themselves did not enter the Praetorium,
so that they might not be defiled,
but might eat the passover.

(c) Pilate Comes Out To Inquire What Jesus Is Accused Of

Outside Pilate's Courtroom There was a Porch Facing the Yard So Pilate Comes Out On This Porch To Ask What The Charges Are. They Seek to Dodge the Issue.

Jn.18:29-32
29So Pilate went out to them*** and said,
"What accusation do you bring against this man?"

30They answered him,
"If this man were not an evildoer,
we would not have handed him over."

Pilate Forces Them to Come Out in the Open. They Seek Death by Crucifixion

31Pilate said to them,
"Take him yourselves and judge him by your own law."

The Jews said to him,
"It is not lawful for us to put any man to death."

So Christ's Prophecy Comes True

32This was to fulfill the word which Jesus had spoken,
to show by what death he was to die. *(Mt.20:17-19,p.172)*

Then They Accuse Jesus Specifically of Treason on three Counts

Lk.
2And they began to accuse him, saying,
"We found this man perverting our nation,
and forbidding us to give tribute to Caesar,
and saying that he himself is Christ a king." *(Cf.Jn.18:36 below; Jn.6:15,p.95)* *(See v.14-15,p.235)*

(d) Pilate Goes In to Examine Jesus Personally

Pilate Enters the Court-Room, Calling Jesus, He Examines Him Personally

Mt.	Mk.	Lk.	Jn.
			33Pilate entered the Praetorium again and called Jesus,
11Now Jesus stood before the governor; and the governor asked Him, "Are you the King of the Jews?"	2And Pilate asked him, "Are you the King of the Jews?"	3And Pilate asked him, "Are you the King of the Jews?"	and said to him, "Are you the King of the Jews?"

Jesus Inquires Why He Asks This — For He did not Hear The Charges made outside

Jn.
34Jesus answered,
"Do you say this of your own accord,
or did others say it to you about me?"

Pilate Says the Jews had Accused Him of Wanting To Be King

35Pilate answered
"Am I a Jew?
Your own nation
and the chief priests
have handed you over to me;
what have you done?"

....

*He was first bound, when arrested, in the Garden (Jn. 18:12); later He was unbound during the trial; and now he is bound again, before being led away to the Roman governor.

**The words, "the house of" are not in the Greek text, and should be omitted; for it was from the official trial by the Sanhedrin in their official court room, near the temple. Luke contrasts accurately "the high priests house" (22:54) with "their council" (22:66).

***The Governor came out of the Courtroom, onto the porch, facing the Court-yard.

Then Jesus Explains The Spiritual Nature Of His Kingdom

Jn.
36Jesus answered,
"My kingship is not of this world;
if my kingship were of this world,
my servants would fight,
that I might not be handed over to the [Jews;
but my kingship is not from the world."

Pilate Persists

37Pilate said to him,
"So you are a king?"

Jesus Says He Is King Of Truth

Mt.
Jesus said to him,
"You have said so."

Mk.
And he answered him,
"You have said so."

Lk.
And he answered him,
"You have said so."

Jn.
Jesus answered,
"You say that I am a king.
For this I was born,
And for this I have come into the [world
to bear witness to the truth.
Every one who is of the truth
hears my voice."

38Pilate said to him,
"What is truth?"

(e) Pilate Brings Jesus Out to the Jews, Intending to Free Him

Then Pilate Goes Outside, Taking Jesus Along, saying, He had Found no Crime In Jesus.

Lk.
4And Pilate said to the chief
priests and the multitudes,
"I find no crime in this man."

Jn.
After he had said this,
he went out to the Jews again,
and told them,
"I find no crime in him."

Then The Jews Accuse Him of Many Things

Mk.
3And the chief priests
accused him of many things.

Jesus Keeps Silent.

Mt.
12But when he was accused
by the chief priests and elders
he made no answer.

Pilate Urges Him To Reply,

Mt.
13Then Pilate said to him,
"Do you not hear
how many things they testify
against you?"

Mk.
4And Pilate again asked him,
"Have you no answer to make?
See how many charges they bring against you."

But Jesus Keeps Still

Mt.
14But he gave him no answer,
not even to a single charge;
so that the governor wondered
greatly.

Mk.
5But Jesus made no further answer,
so that Pilate wondered.

The Jews are More Urgent They Speak of Jesus' Work In Galilee;

Lk.
5But they were urgent, saying,
"He stirs up the people,
teaching throughout all Judea,
from Galilee even to this place."

6When Pilate heard this,
he asked whether the man was a Galilean.

But Galilee Is Ruled by Herod.

b. The "Trial" Before Herod. § 216 *(FRIDAY MORNING).*

Lk. 23:7-12

(a) Pilate Sends Jesus to Herod

So Pilate Shifts Responsibility To Herod.

7And when he learned that he belonged to Herod's jurisdiction,
he sent him over to Herod, who was himself in Jerusalem at that time.

Pilate Sends Jesus to Herod

8When Herod saw Jesus, he was very glad,
for he had long desired to see him, because he had heard about him,
and he was hoping to see some sign done by him.

(See § 85, p.91,Lk.9 and footnote

Herod Is Gratified

9So he questioned him at some length;
but he made no answer.

He Questions Jesus

10The chief priests and the scribes stood by, vehemently accusing him.

The Jews Accuse Him.

11And Herod with his soldiers treated him with contempt and mocked him;

(Cf. § 211, and Lk.22:63-65, p.231 Jn. 19:2,31; § 21

(b) Herod Sends Jesus Back to Pilate

Herod and His Courtiers Mock Jesus.

then, arraying him in gorgeous apparel, he sent him back to Pilate.

Herod Sends Him Back to Pilate

12And Herod and Pilate became friends with each other that very day,
for before this they had been at enmity with each other.

Mt. 27:15-26 Mk. 15:6-20 Lk. 23:13-25 Jn. 18:39-19:16

[Herod sends Jesus Back to Pilate, v.11]

(a) Pilate Again Brings Jesus Out On the Porch Facing the Courtyard Where the Jews are Waiting.

Pilate Comes Out and Calls the Jews Together Again

Lk.
13Pilate then called together the chief priests and the rulers and the people,
14and said to them,
"You brought me this man as one who was perverting the people;
and after examining him before you,
behold, (Jn.18:38
I did not find this man guilty of any of your charges against him;
15neither did Herod, for he sent him back to us. (Cf. Lk.23:2, p.233 and
Behold, nothing deserving death has been done by him." Jn.18:38f)

He Sums Up The Trial, Up to This Moment

(b) Pilate Proposes a Compromise

Then, According to an Ancient Custom,

Mt.
15Now at the feast the governor was accustomed
to release for the crowd any one prisoner
whom they wanted.

Mk.
6Now at the feast he used
to release for them any one prisoner
whom they asked.

Jn.
39But you have a custom
That I should release one man for you
at the passover;

Pilate Proposes to Release Jesus, After Scourging Him,

Lk.
16"I will therefore chastise him and release him.[b]
(Cf. Mt.27:26) (Cf. Mk.15:15) (See v.22f. and Jn.19:1)

But there is Another Prisoner, an Assassin, Jesus-Barabbas;

Mt.
16And they had then
a notorious prisoner,
called Bar-ab'bas.[a*]

Mk.
7And among the rebels in prison,
who had committed murder in the insurrection,
there was a man called Bar-ab'bas. (Lk.23:19,25; Jn.18:40)

The Crowds Ask For The Usual Favor.

Mt.
17So when they had gathered,

Mk.
8And the crowd came up
and began to ask Pilate
to do as he was wont to do for them.

Pilate Appeals to the Mob, to Demand Jesus-Christ

Mt.
Pilate said to them,
"Whom do you want
me to release for you,
Bar-ab'bas[a*] or
Jesus who is called Christ?"

Mk.
9And he answered them,
"Do you want me
to release for you
the King of the Jews?"

Jn.
"Will you
have me release for you
the King of the Jews?"

In Spite of the Priests' Purpose To Kill Jesus.

Mt.
18For he knew
that it was out of envy
that they had delivered him up.

Mk.
10For he perceived
that it was out of envy
that the chief priests had delivered him up.

(c) The Trial Is Interrupted by a Messenger

Just Then Pilate Is Interrupted by a Messenger from His Wife.

Mt.
19Besides, while he was sitting on the judgment-seat,
his wife sent word to him,
"Have nothing to do with that righteous man, (See Jn.18:38)
for I have suffered much over him today in a dream."

While Pilate Is Thus Occupied, the Jewish Rulers Incite the Mob to Demand Barabbas

Mt.
20Now the chief priests
and the elders
persuaded the people
to ask for Bar-ab'bas,
and destroy Jesus.

Mk.
11But the chief priests
stirred up the crowd
to have him release for them Bar-ab'bas instead. (v.7)

....

[a*] Some ancient authorities read Jesus Barabbas.

[b] Here, or after verse 19, some ancient authorities add verse 17. Now he was obliged to release one man to them at the festival.

(d) Pilate Continues The Trial

Mt.

Pilate Again Asks Which One

21The governor again said to them,
"Which of the two do you want me to release for you?"

They Answer Fiercely

Mt.	Lk.	Jn.
And they said,	18But they all cried out together,	40They cried out again, "Not this man,
	"Away with this man and release to us	but
"Bar-ab'bas."	Bar-ab'bas" --	Bar-ab'bas."

"Barabas!"

The Character of Barabbas

(Cf.Mk.15:7,p.235) Now Bar-ab bas was a robber.

A Robber And Insurrectionist A Murderer.

(cf. v.16) (cf. v.7)

19a man who
had been thrown into prison for an insurrection
started in the city,
and for murder.

Then Pilate Asks, what Then Shall I Do with Jesus-The-Christ?

Mt.	Mk.	Lk.
22Pilate said to them, "Then what shall I do with Jesus who is called Christ?"	12And Pilate again said to them, "Then what shall I do with the man whom you call the King of the Jews?"	20Pilate addressed them once more, desiring to release Jesus;

They Shout, Crucify! Crucify Him!

Mt.	Mk.	Lk.
They all said, "Let him be crucified."	13And they cried out again, "Crucify him!"	21but they shouted out, "Crucify, crucify him!"
23And he said, "Why, what evil has he done?"	14And Pilate said to them, "Why, what evil has he done?"	22A third time he said to them, "Why, what evil has he done?

Next Pilate Proposes Scourging, Instead of Crucifixion.

(Jn.18:38;19:6)

I have found in him no crime deserving [death;
I will therefore chastise him
and release him." *(See v.16)*

(e) Pilate Takes Jesus Inside, and Has Him Scourged

Jn. 19

So Jesus Is Scourged:

1Then Pilate took Jesus [*inside. See v. 4*]
and scourged him. *(Cf. Mt. 27:26b; Mk. 15:15b; Lk. 23:16)*

Then The Soldiers Mockingly Array Him as a King and Hail Him.

2And the soldiers plaited a crown of thorns, [*cf.* § 211,212,216,218,221]
and put it on his head,
and arrayed him in a purple robe;

3they came up to him, saying,
"Hail, King of the Jews!"
and struck him with their hands.

(f) Pilate Brings Jesus Out Mockingly Arrayed Like a King

Pilate Comes Out

4Pilate went out again, and said to them,
"Behold, I am bringing him out to you,
that you may know that I find no crime in him." *(v.6)*

Followed by Jesus.

5So Jesus came out, wearing the crown of thorns and the purple robe.

Pilate Presents Jesus to Them;

Pilate said to them,
"Here is the man!"

They Demand Crucifixion

6When the chief priests and the officers saw him, they cried out,
"Crucify him, Crucify him!"

Pilate Asserts Jesus' Innocence

Pilate said to them,
"Take him yourselves and crucify him, *(v.4, Mt.27:24)*
for I find no crime in him."

The Jews Accuse Him of Claiming to Be The Son of God

7The Jews answered him,
"We have a law, and by that law he ought to die,
because he has made himself the Son of God." *(Mk.14:61-64,p.229; Lk.22:70,p.231 and Note)*

The Governor Becomes Superstitious,

8When Pilate heard these words,
he was the more afraid;

(g) Pilate Takes Jesus Inside, to Examine Him Privately About This Charge;

He Goes Inside

Jn.

He Questions Jesus Privately.

9He entered the praetorium again
and said to Jesus,
"Where are you from?"

Jesus Gives No Answer.

But Jesus gave no answer.

Pilate Demands to Know Why

10Pilate therefore said to him,
"You will not speak to me?
Do you not know that I have power to release you,
and power to crucify you?"

Jesus Avows His Sublime Faith in God.

11Jesus answered him,
"You would have no power over me
unless it had been given you from above; *(Jn.3:27,p.33)*
therefore he who delivered me to you has the greater sin."

(h) Pilate Comes Out Alone and Resumes Trial

Pilate Comes Out Alone, and Again attempts to Release Jesus

12Upon this, Pilate sought [*again*] to release him,

The Jews Threaten to Accuse The Governor of Treason Against Caesar

but the Jews cried out,
"If you release this man, you are not Caesar's friend;
everyone who makes himself a king sets himself against Caesar."

(i) Pilate Has Jesus Brought Out Again; This Time to Be Sentenced

Pilate Is Afraid. So He Has Jesus Brought out to Be Sentenced.

13When Pilate heard these words,
he brought Jesus out

and sat down on the judgment seat,
at a place called The Pavement, and in Hebrew, Gab'ba-tha.

14Now it was the [day of] Preparation for the Passover;*
it was about the sixth hour.

Pilate Taunts the Jews

He said to the Jews,
"Here is your King!"

	Mt.	*Mk.*	*Lk.*	*Jn.*
They Become Furious	23bBut they shouted all the more,	14bBut they shouted all the more,	23But they were urgent, demanding with loud cries	15They cried out, "Away with him, away with him,
and Demand Crucifixion.	"Let him be crucified!"	"Crucify him!"	that he should be crucified.	crucify him!"

Jn.

He Retorts

Pilate said to them,
"Shall I crucify your king?"

They Make a Final Thrust.

The chief priests answered,
"We have no king but Caesar."

(j) Pilate Makes a Final Appeal, As He Washes His Hands of This Matter

Mt.

Pilate Tries a Final Alibi

24So when Pilate saw that he was gaining nothing,
but rather that a riot was beginning,
he took water and washed his hands before the crowd,
saying,
"I am innocent of this man's blood;[a]
see to it yourselves."

They Accept His Challenge and Cry Out for His Blood

25And all the people answered,
"His blood be on us
and on our children!"

They Win. ....

Lk.

And their voices prevailed.

*Should be "The Preparation" *of* the Passover. *See footnote to* § 226, p. 245.
[a]*Some authorities read* this righteous blood, *or* this righteous man's blood.

(k) Then Pilate Gives Sentence

	Lk.
Pilate Gives Formal Sentence of Death by Crucifixion	24So Pilate gave sentence that their demands should be granted.

(l) Then He Releases Barabbas

	Mt.	Mk.	Lk.
He Releases a Murderer, To The Jews.	26Then	15So Pilate, wishing to satisfy the crowd,	
	he released for them Bar-ab´bas,	released for them Bar-ab´bas;	25He released the man who had been thrown into prison,-- for insurrection and murder, *(v.19)* whom they asked for;
		(Mk.15:7; Jn.18:40,p.236)	

(m) He Delivers Jesus to The Soldiers for Execution

	Mt.	Mk.	Lk.	Jn.
He Turns Jesus Over to The Soldiers	and having scourged Jesus,	and having scourged Jesus,	but Jesus *(cf. 23:16)*	16Then *(cf. 19:1)*
	delivered him	he delivered him	he delivered up	he handed him over to them
			to their will.	
for Execution.	to be crucified.	to be crucified.		to be crucified.

d. The Soldiers Mock Jesus. § 218 [*cf.* § 211,212,216,221]

	Mt. 27:27-31	Mk. 15:16-20
The Soldiers	27Then the soldiers of the governor	16And the soldiers
Take Jesus Inside,	took Jesus	led him away inside the palace
	into the Praetorium,	(that is, the Praetorium);
They All Gather.	and gathered the whole battalion before him.	and they called together the whole battalion.
The Purple Robe	28And they stripped him, and put a scarlet robe on him.	17And they clothed him in a purple cloak,
A Mock Crown	29And plaiting a crown of thorns they put it on his head,	and plaiting a crown of thorns they put it on him.
A Mock Scepter	and put a reed in his right hand.	
		(v.19)
Mock Homage	And kneeling before him they mocked him, saying, "Hail, King of the Jews!"	18And they began to salute him, "Hail, King of the Jews!" 19And they struck his head with a reed,
Insults They Spit on Him and Strike Him	30And they spat upon him, and took the reed and struck him on the head. *(v.19c)*	and spat upon him, and they knelt down in homage to him.
They Reclothe Him	31And when they had mocked him, they stripped him of the robe, and put his own clothes on him.	20And when they had mocked him, they stripped him of the purple cloak, and put his own clothes on him.

	Mt. 27:31b-45.	*Mk. 15:20b-41*	*. 23:26-49*	*Jn. 19:17-30*

a. Jesus Is Led Away to Be Crucified. § 219

(a) They Set Out for Calvary

	Mt.	Mk.	Lk.	Jn.
They Lead Jesus Away Bearing His Own Cross	31b And led him away to crucify him.	20b And they led him out to crucify him.		17 So they took Jesus, and he went out, bearing his own cross,
Later Simon	32 As they were marching out, they came upon a man of Cy-re´ne,		26 And as they led him away, they seized one	
Is Compelled to Bear the Cross	Simon by name;	21 And they compelled a passer-by Simon of Cy-re´ne, who was coming in from the country, the father of Alexander and Rufus,	Simon of Cy-re´ne, [*In N.Africa*] who was coming in from the country,	
	this man they compelled to carry his cross.	to carry his cross.	and laid on him the cross, to carry it behind Jesus.	

(b) A Great Multitude Follows

	Lk.
A Great Crowd Including Women Bewail Jesus	27 And there followed him a great multitude of the people, and of women who bewailed and lamented him.
Jesus Warns the Women	28 But Jesus turning to them said, "Daughters of Jerusalem, do not weep for me, . but weep for yourselves and for your children.
He Prophesies Of Future Calamities for Jerusalem	29 "For behold, the days are coming when they will say, 'Blessed are the barren, and the wombs that never bore, and the breasts that never gave suck!' 30 "Then they will begin to say to the mountains, 'Fall on us'; and to the hills, 'Cover us.' 31 "For if they do this when the wood is green, what will happen when it is dry?"
Jesus Is A Companion of Criminals	32 Two others also, who were criminals, were led away to be put to death with him.

(c) They Arrive At Calvary

	Mt.	Mk.	Lk.	Jn.
They Come To Calvary	33 And when they came to a place called Gol´go-tha,* (which means the place of a skull),	22 And they brought him to the place called Gol´go-tha * (which means the place of a skull).	33 And when they came to the place which is called The Skull ,	to the place called the place of a skull, which is called in Hebrew Gol´go-tha.*
They Offer Jesus A Sedative	34 they offered him wine to drink, mingled with gall; but when he tasted it, he would not drink it.	23 And they offered him wine mingled with myrrh: but he did not take it.		

....

**According to the Latin,* Calvary, *which has the same meaning. "Gordon's Calvary" is the only spot perfectly fitting every scriptural allusion. It is a small hill north of the city, just outside the "Damascus gate," in the middle of the north wall. As one comes out of this gate, directly in front of him, one sees, across the road running outside the north wall, a precipice, about as high as a house, forming the south side of the hill called "Gordon's Calvary." In that wall of rock one sees at once three large holes somewhat resembling the eye-sockets and mouth holes in a human skull. Hence the nickname, "Skull Hill," or in Latin Calvary, or in Hebrew "Golgotha". To ascend the hill, the procession turned east a few rods and then to the left a few rods more, and then again left, so as to ascend the gentle eastern slope to the top of the ridge. This is the place of Crucifixion.* *(See also note, p. 246).*

b. Jesus Is Crucified. § 220

	Mt. 27: 35-36	*Mk. 15: 24-25*	*Lk. 23:33b-34*	*Jn. 19: 18-25*
Here Jesus Is Crucified	*(Cf.v.38 below)*	24 And they crucified him, *(Cf. v.27 below)*	There they crucified him,	18 There they crucified him,
Also Two Criminals.			and the criminals one on the right and one on the left.	and with him two others, one on either side, and Jesus between them.
Jesus Prays Forgiveness As the Nails Are Driven.			34 And Jesus said, "Father, forgive them; for they know not what they do."[a]	
The Title Is Placed On the Cross.	*(v.37)*	*(v.26)*		19 Pilate also wrote a title and put it on the cross; It read, "Jesus of Nazareth, the King of the Jews." 20 Many of the Jews read this title, for the place where Jesus was crucified was near the city; and it was written in Hebrew, in Latin, and in Greek.
The Jews Protest				21 The chief priests of the Jews then said to Pilate, "Do not write, 'The King of the Jews', but, 'This man said, 'I am King of the Jews.'"
Pilate Is Stubborn				22 Pilate answered, "What I have written I have written."

	Mt.	*Mk.*	*Lk.*	*Jn.*
	35 And when they had crucified him,			23 When the soldiers had crucified Jesus they took his garments
The Soldiers Divide His Garments As Their Own Loot.	they divided his garments among them	and divided his garments among them,	And they cast lots to divide his garments.	and made four parts, one for each soldier.
For His Coat They Gamble	by casting lots;	casting lots for them, to decide what each should take.		But his tunic was without seam, woven from top to bottom; 24 So they said to one another, "Let us not tear it, but cast lots for it to see whose it shall be." This was to fulfill the scripture, "They parted my garments among them, and for my clothing they cast lots." 25 So the soldiers did this.
It is Nine O'clock.		25 And it was the third hour,* when they crucified him.		
Then The Soldiers Keep Guard.	36 then they sat down and kept watch over him there.			

....

[a] *Some ancient authorities omit the sentence* And Jesus said,----what they do.

* *Nine o'clock A.M. reckoned according to Jewish time.*

c. Jesus Is Mocked By the Rulers and the Multitudes. § 221

	Mt. 27:37-44	*Mk. 15:26-32*	*Lk. 23:35-43* [*Cf.* §§ *211,212,216,218*]
The People Gaze			35 And the people stood by, watching;
The Rulers Scoff	*(Cf. v.41 below)*	*(Cf. v.31 below)* *(Cf. v.32 below)*	but the rulers scoffed at him, saying, "He saved others; let him save himself, if he is the Christ of God, his Chosen One!"
The Soldiers Mock			36 The soldiers also mocked him, coming up and offering him vinegar, 37 and saying, "If you are the King of the Jews, save yourself!"
His Title Accuses Him	37 And over his head they put the charge against him, which read, "This is Jesus the King of the Jews."	26 And the inscription of the charge against him read, "The King of the Jews."	38 There was also an inscription over him[a] *(Cf.Jn.19:10-22)* "This is the King of the Jews."
	38 Then two robbers were crucified with him, one on the right and one on the left.	27 And with him they crucified two robbers, one on his right and one on his left.[b]	*(Cf. vs.32,33b above)*
The Crowds Rail At Him	39 And those who passed by derided him, wagging their heads 40 and saying, "You who would destroy the temple and build it in three days, save yourself! If you are the Son of God, come down from the cross."	29 And those who passed by derided him, wagging their heads, and saying, "Aha! You who would destroy the temple and build it in three days, 30 save yourself, and come down from the cross!"	 *(Cf. v.37 above)*
Even the Priests and Scribes Join The Tirade of Mockery	41 So also the chief priests, with the scribes and elders, mocked him, saying, 42 "He saved others; he cannot save himself. "He is the King of Israel; let him come down now from the cross, and we will believe in him. 43 "He trusts in God; let God deliver him now, if he desires him; for he said, 'I am the Son of God.'"	31 So also the chief priests mocked him to one another with the scribes, saying, "He saved others; he cannot save himself. 32 "Let the Christ, the King of Israel, come down now from the cross, that we may see and believe."	*(Cf. v. 35 above)* *(Cf. v.35 above)*
The Robbers Too Reproach Him	44 And the robbers who were crucified with him also reviled him in the same way.	Those who were crucified with him also reviled him.	

....

[a]*Many ancient authorities add,* in letters of Greek and Latin and Hebrew. [b]*Many ancient authorities insert verse 28* And the scripture was fulfilled, which says, "He was reckoned among the transgressors."

Lk. 23:35-43

Then One of Them Repents

39One of the criminals who were hanged
railed at him, saying,
"Are you not the Christ?
Save yourself and us!"

40But the other rebuked him, saying,
"Do you not fear God,
since you are under the same sentence of condemnation?
41And we indeed justly;
for we are receiving the due reward of our deeds;
but this man has done nothing wrong."

And Begs For Mercy

42And he said,
"Jesus, remember me
when you come in your kingly power."[a]

He Is Forgiven

43And he said to him,
"Truly, I say to you,
today you will be with me in Paradise."

d. Jesus Provides for His Mother. § 222

Jn. 19:25-27

Christ Makes Final Provision for His Mother

25bBut standing by the cross of Jesus were
his mother,
and his mother's sister,
Mary the wife of Clo'pas,
and Mary Mag'da-lene.

Entrusting Her To The Beloved Disciple

26When Jesus saw his mother,
and the disciple whom he loved standing near,
he said to his mother,
"Woman, behold your son!"

27Then he said to the disciple,
"Behold your mother!"

He Accepts The Charge

And from that hour
the disciple took her to his own home.

e. Darkness Overwhelms the Whole Land. § 223

Darkness Prevails

Mt. 27:45	*Mk. 15:33*	*Lk. 23:44-45*
45Now from the sixth hour* there was darkness over all the land[b] until the ninth hour.	33And when the sixth hour had come,* there was darkness over the whole land[b] until the ninth hour.	44It was now about the sixth hour,* and there was darkness over the whole land[b] until the ninth hour, 45while the sun's light failed;[c] and the curtain of the temple was torn in two.
(Mt. 27:51)	*(Mk. 15:38)*	

---

[a] *Greek* kingdom.
[b] *Or* earth.
[c] *Or* the sun was eclipsed. *Many ancient authorities read* the sun was darkened.
**6th hour is 12 o'clock noon, by our reckoning.*

(1) The Death. § 224

(a) The End Approaches

	Mt. 27:46-56	Mk. 15:34-41	Lk. 23:46-49	Jn. 19:28-30
Jesus Prays To The Father	46And about the ninth hour* Jesus cried with a loud voice, "Eli, Eli, la'ma sa-bach-tha'ni?" that is, "My God, my God, why hast thou forsaken me?"	34And at the ninth hour* Jesus cried with a loud voice, "E'lo-i, E'lo-i, la'ma sa-bach-tha'ni?" which means, 'My God, my God, why hast thou forsaken me?"		
What The People Said	47And some of the bystanders hearing it said, "This man is calling Elijah."	35And some of the bystanders hearing it said, "Behold, he is calling Elijah."		
				Jn. 19:28 28After this Jesus, knowing that all was now finished, said (to fulfill the scripture), "I thirst." 29A bowl full of vinegar stood there;
They Gave Him vinegar to Drink	48And one of them at once ran and took a sponge, filled it with vinegar, and put it on a reed, and gave it to him to drink.	36And one ran and, filling a sponge full of vinegar, put it on a reed and gave it to him to drink,		so they put a sponge full of the wine on hyssop and held it to his mouth.
Some Object	49But the others said, "Wait, let us see whether Elijah will come to save him." a	saying, "Wait, let us see whether Elijah will come to take him down."		

(b) Jesus Dies

	Mt.	Mk.	Lk.	Jn.
				30When Jesus had received the vinegar,
Jesus Cries Out, He Prays	50And Jesus cried again with a loud voice	37And Jesus uttered a loud cry,	46Then Jesus, crying with a loud voice, said, "Father, into thy hands I commit my spirit!"	he said, "It is finished."
He Gives Up His Life	and yielded up his spirit.	and breathed his last.	And having said this he breathed his last.	And he bowed his head (Cf. Jn.10:18) and gave up his spirit.

....

[a]Many ancient authorities insert And, another took a spear and pierced his side, and out came water and blood.. *Three P.M.

(c) Nature Shudders

	Mt.	Mk.	Lk.
The Veil of the Temple Is Torn	51And behold, the curtain of the temple was torn in two, from top to bottom;	38And the curtain of the temple was torn in two, from top to bottom.	*(Lk. 23:45)*
The Earth Quakes	and the earth shook, and the rocks were split;		
Tombs Are Torn Open Some Dead Are Raised	52the tombs also were opened, and many bodies of the saints who had fallen asleep were raised, 53and coming out of the tombs after his resurrection they went into the holy city and appeared to many.		

(d) The People Tremble

	Mt.	Mk.	Lk.
A Soldier Testifies	54When the centurion	39And when the centurion, who stood facing him,	47Now when the centurion,
The Guards Are Filled With Awe	and those who were with him, keeping watch over Jesus,		
By What They Saw	saw the earthquake and what took place,	saw	saw what had taken place,
		that he thus[a] breathed his last,	
	they were filled with awe,		he praised God,
And Make Various Remarks	and said, "Truly this was a Son of God!"	he said, "Truly this man was a Son of God."	and said, "Certainly this man was innocent!"
The Crowd Are Awe-Stricken			48And all the multitudes who assembled to see the sight, when they saw what had taken place, returned home beating their breasts.
Jesus' Friends His Mother, and Other Women Witness His Death	55There were also many women there looking on from afar, who had followed Jesus from Galilee, ministering to him;	40There were also women looking on from afar,	49And all his acquaintances and the women who had followed him from Galilee stood at a distance and saw these things.
Some Are Named	56among whom were Mary Mag´da-lene, and Mary the mother of James and Joseph, and the mother of the sons of Zeb´e-dee.	among whom were Mary Mag´da-lene, and Mary the mother of James the younger and of Joses, and Sa-lo´me,	
		41who, when he was in Galilee, followed him, and ministered to him; and also many other women who came up with him to Jerusalem.	*(cf. v.49)*

[a]*Many ancient authorities insert* cried out and.

(2) The Proof of His Death. § 225

Jn. 19:31-37

The Jews Request The Removal of the Bodies

31Since it was the[day of] Preparation,* [*i.e., for the Sabbath, Hence Friday**]
in order to prevent the bodies from remaining on the cross on the sabbath
(for that sabbath was a high day),
the Jews asked Pilate that their legs might be broken,
and that they might be taken away.

Soldiers, Breaking the Legs of the Two

32So the soldiers came
and broke the legs of the first,
and of the other who had been crucified with him;

See That Jesus is Already Dead But They Pierce His Heart.

33but when they came to Jesus
and saw that he was already dead,
they did not brake his legs.
34But one of the soldiers pierced his side with a spear,
and at once there came out blood and water.

John Explains What He Saw

35He who saw it has borne witness--
his testimony is true,
and he knows that he tells the truth--
that you also may believe.

Messianic Prophecies Come True

36For these things took place
that the scripture might be fulfilled,
"Not a bone of him shall be broken."
37And again another scripture says,
"They shall look on him whom they have pierced."

(3) The Burial. § 226 *(FRIDAY EVENING)*

a. Joseph Gets Permission to Bury

	Mt. 27:57-60	*Mk. 15:42-46*	*Lk. 23:50-54*	*Jn. 19:38-42*
Joseph Begs the Body	57When it was evening	42And when evening had come, since it was the day of Preparation,* that is, the day before the sabbath,		38After this
Who Joseph Is	there came a rich man from Ar-i-ma-the´a, named Joseph,	43Joseph of Ar-i-ma-the´a,	50Now there was a man named Joseph from the Jewish town of Ar-i-ma-the´a.	Joseph of Ar-i-ma-the´a,
		a respected member of the council,	He was a member of the council, a good and righteous man, 51who had not consented to their purpose and deed,	
		who was also himself look-[ing for the kingdom of God,	and he was looking for the kingdom of God.	
	who also was a disciple of Jesus.			who was a disciple of Jesus, but secretly, for fear of the Jews
He Petitions the Governor	58He went to Pilate and asked for the body of Jesus.	took courage and went to Pilate, and asked for the body of Jesus.	52This man went to Pilate and asked for the body of Jesus.	asked Pilate that he might take away the body of Jesus;

....

**Greek* "the Preparation." Consider *A.T. Robertson's note (d) (Harmony of the Gospels, p.283). Harper Brothers, New York.*

"(d) John 19:14, "Now it was the Preparation of the Passover." This is claimed to mean the day preceding the Passover festival. Hence Christ was crucified on the 14th Nisan, in opposition to the Synoptists. The afternoon before the Passover was used as a preparation, but it was not technically so called. This phrase "Preparation" was really the name of a day in the week, the day before the Sabbath, our Friday. We are not left to conjecture about this question. The Evangelists all use it in this sense alone. Matthew uses it for Friday (27:62), Mark expressly says that the Preparation was the day before the Sabbath (15:42), Luke says that it was the day of the Preparation, because the Sabbath was at hand. The New Testament usage is conclusive, therefore, on this point. This, then, was the Friday of Passover week. And this agrees with the Synoptists. Besides, the term "Preparation" has long been the regular name for Friday in the Greek language, caused by the New Testament usage. It is so in the Modern Greek today. It was the Sabbath eve, just as the Germans have Sonnabend for Sunday eve, i.e., Saturday afternoon. So this passage also becomes a positive argument for the agreement between John and the Synoptists." (Used by permission)

See especially Lk.23:54, p.246 and recall that the Jewish sabbath began at sunset on Friday.

	Mt.	Mk.	Lk.	Jn.
Pilate Is Surprised		44And Pilate wondered if he were already dead;		
He Investigates		and summoning the centurion, he asked him whether he was already dead.[a]		
The Centurian Certifies To the Fact		45And when he learned from the centurion that he was dead,		and Pilate
Pilate Grants Joseph's Request	Then Pilate ordered it to be given to him.	he granted the body to Joseph.		gave him leave.

b. The Body Is Taken Down

	Mt.	Mk.	Lk.	Jn.
They Take Down The Body	59And Joseph took the body,	46And he bought a linen shroud, and taking him down,	53Then he took it down	So he came and took away his body.
Nicodemus gives His Tribute				39Nicodemus also, *(Jn.3:1;7.* who had at first come to him by night, came bringing a mixture of myrrh and aloes, about a hundred pounds[b] weight.
They Prepare The Body For Burial	and wrapped it in a clean linen shroud,	wrapped him in the linen shroud, *(Mk.16:1,p.248)*	and wrapped it in a linen shroud,	40They took the body of Jesus, and bound it in linen cloths with the spices, as is the burial custom of the Jews.

c. It Is Laid in The Tomb

	Mt.	Mk.	Lk.	Jn.
The Place of Burial Is Described				41Now in the place where he was crucified there was a garden, and in the garden
The Body of Jesus Is Laid in the Tomb	60and laid it in his own new tomb, which he had hewn in the rock;**	and laid him in a tomb which had been hewn out of the rock;**	and laid him in a rock-hewn tomb, where no one had ever yet been laid.	a new tomb where no one had ever been laid.
	and he rolled a great stone to the entrance of the tomb, and departed.	and he rolled a stone against the door of the tomb.		
*It Is Friday * Just Before Sunset, When the Jewish Sabbath Begins*			54And it was the [day of] Preparation*, and the sabbath was beginning.[c]	42So because of the Jewish [day of] Preparation* as the tomb was close at hand ** they laid Jesus there.

* "The Preparation," *see footnote on preceding page.*

[a] *Some ancient authorities read* whether he had been sometime dead. [b] *Greek* litras. [c] *Greek* was dawning.

*** Just down the west slope of "Gordon's Calvary" is "a garden." It is a small level yard, with a few fruit trees, flower beds, and a vegetable garden bed. At the north end, the rock of the hill is cut perpendicular, like a wall as high as a house. In this rock wall is an opening into the rock. One must stoop to enter. A runway is cut there in front of the stone face of the rock wall, for a large stone, in wheellike form, to be rolled over so as to close the opening into the rock wall of the hill-side. Within, there is a room some 9 or 10 feet square. On the east side there is a ledge or bench of rock as high as a seat, on which to lay the body of the dead. Many believe this is the true sepulcher of our Lord. At least it fits, in every particular, the scriptural account. (See also note, p. 239)*

III. TRIUMPH AND GLORY pp.247-258
(Friday Evening of Passion Week to Pentecost)

(I) THE RESURRECTION AND APPEARANCES *(The Specific Order of Events)* pp.247-258

1. *BETWEEN THE BURIAL AND THE RESURRECTION* *(Jerusalem and Bethany)* p.248

(1) The Women, Sitting Over Against the Sepulchre,
See Where He is Buried (Mt. 27:61; Mk.15:47; Lk.23:55) *(Friday p.m.)* § 227
(2) They Returned and Prepared Spices (Lk. 23:56a) § 228
(3) They Rest on the Sabbath (Lk. 23:56b) *(Friday 6p.m. to Saturday 6p.m.)* § 229
(4) A Guard Is Stationed Before The Tomb (Mt. 27:62-66) § 230
(5) A While Before Sunset, Saturday evening,
the Women go to see the Tomb (Mt. 28:1) § 231
(6) Then, after Sunset, They go to Buy Additional Spices (Mk. 16:1) § 232
(7) After that, they go Home for the Night § 233

2. *THE RESURRECTION MORNING* *(Jerusalem and Bethany)* pp.249-252

(1) Before Sun-up on Sunday, They Start for the Tomb (Mk.16:2; Jn.20:1) § 234
(2) At sunrise, Jesus is resurrected
(3) Then an Angel Comes and Rolls Back the Stone and Sits on it (Mt. 28:2-4) § 235
(4) The Women are Coming to the Tomb Wondering,
"Who shall roll away the stone."(Mk. 16:2-3; Lk.24:1; Jn.20:1a) § 236
(5) They See the Tomb Already Open (Jn. 20:1: Mk.16:4; Lk.24:2) § 237
(6) Then Mary Magdalene Runs to tell Peter and John (Jn. 20:2) § 238 p.249
(7) The Angel Takes the Other Women Inside -
Where They see a Second Angel Seated
He Shows the Place Where the Body of Jesus Had Lain
Then He Bids Them, "Go and Tell the Apostles;"
They run to tell the news (Mt. 28:5-8; Mk.16:5-8; Lk.24:3-8a) § 239
(8) Peter and John Come to the Tomb to Investigate,
and Then Go Home (Jn. 20:3-10; Lk.24:12) § 240
(9) Mary Magdalene Returns to the Tomb -
and Looking in She Sees The Two Angels Seated (Jn. 20:11-13; Mk.16:9-11) § 241
Jesus Manifests Himself to Mary Magdalene (Jn. 20:14-18) p.251
(10) Jesus Meets the Other Women (Mt. 28:9-10; Lk.24:9-11) § 242
(11) The Women Report to The Other Disciples § 242½
(12) The Report of The Guard (Mt.28:11-15) § 243.

3. *THE RESURRECTION AFTERNOON* *(Jerusalem and Emmaus)* pp.253-254

(1) Later Jesus Appears to Peter (Lk. 24:33b-34; 1 Cor. 15:5) § 244 p.253
(2) Jesus Appears to Cleopas and Another,
On the Way to Emmaus (Mk. 16:12-13; Lk. 24:13-32) § 245 p.253

4. *THE RESURRECTION EVENING* *(Jerusalem)* pp.254-255

(1) In the Evening He Appears to the Ten (Mk.16:13-14; Lk.24:33b-43; Jn.20:19-20) § 246
(2) He Commissions and Equips Them. (Jn.20:21-25) § 247

5. *THE NEXT LORD'S DAY* *(Jerusalem)* p.255

A Week Later He Appears to the Eleven (Jn. 20:26-29; 1 Cor. 15:5) § 248 p.255

6. *SOME TIME LATER (Galilee)* pp. 256-257

(1) Jesus Appears to the Fishermen at the Lake of Galilee. (Jn.21:1-14) §250 p.256
(2) After Breakfast Jesus Reinstates Peter. (Jn.21:15-23) § 251 p.257
[(3) (A Final Explanatory Note) (Jn.21:24-25)] § 252 p.257

(II) THE FINAL COMMISSION AND ASCENSION (Mk.16:16, 19-20; Lk.24:50-53; Acts 1:4-12) p.258

STILL LATER

1. Jesus Appears on A Mountain in Galilee. (Mt.28:16-20; Mk.16:15-18) § 253 p.258

FINALLY ON ASCENSION DAY

2. Jesus Appears for The Last Time (Lk.24:44-49; cf.Ac.1:4-5)
   (1) In Jerusalem (Lk.24:44-49; cf. Ac.1:4-5) § 254 p.258
   (2) On Mt. Olivet
   Jesus Ascends Into Heaven (Mk.16:19-20; Lk.24:50-53) § 255 p.258

(III) THE GLORIFICATION OF JESUS, AND THE COMING OF THE HOLY SPIRIT *(Jerusalem)* p.258

1. *THE PROMISES (Jn. 14:15-23,2 5,26; 16:15; 20:23; Lk. 24:49; Mt. 28: 19-20)*
2. *THEIR FULFILMENT (Acts 1:8; 2:1-36, 38, 39)*
3. *THE DISCIPLES GO AND PREACH EVERYWHERE (Mk. 16:20)*

(I) THE RESURRECTION AND APPEARANCE *(Glorious Victory Desolate Suspense)*

1. BETWEEN THE BURIAL AND THE RESURRECTION

(1) The Women See Where He is Buried. § 227

(Friday Afternoon)

Mt. 27:61 — *Mk. 15:47* — *Lk. 23:55*

The Women Attend The Burial

Lk.: [55]The women who had come with him from Galilee followed, *(See Lk.8:1-3, § 67)*

Mt.: [61]Mary Mag´da-lene lene
and the other Mary
were there,
sitting opposite the tomb.

Mk.: [47]Mary Mag´da-lene
and Mary the mother of Joses
saw where he was laid.

Lk.: and saw the tomb,
and how his body was laid;

(2) They Prepare Spices. § 228

(Friday Evening)

Then They Return Home

Lk. 23:56a

[56]then they returned, and prepared spices
and ointments.

(3) They Rest on the Sabbath. § 229

(Friday After Sunset, and Saturday Up to Sunset)

They Rest Until Late Afternoon

Lk. 23:56b

On the sabbath they rested according to the commandment.

(4) The Jewish Officials Place a Guard Before the Tomb. § 230

(Saturday forenoon)

Mt. 27:62-66

The Jews Request a Guard for the Tomb

[62]Next day, [*Saturday*]
that is, the day after the day of Preparation,* [*i.e.* the day after Friday.]
the chief priests and the Pharisees gathered before Pilate [63]and said,
"Sir, we remember how that impostor said, while he was still alive,
'After three days I will rise again.' *(See Mt.16:21,p.109)*

To Guard Against Fraud and False Rumors

[64]"Therefore order the tomb to be made secure until the third day,
lest his disciples go and steal him away,
and tell the people,
'He has risen from the dead,'
and the last fraud will be worse than the first."

Pilate Grants The Request

[65]Pilate said to them,
"You have a guard[a] of soldiers;
go, make it as secure as you can." [b]

The Entrance Is Sealed a Guard Is Placed

[66]So they went, and made the tomb secure
by sealing the stone and setting a guard. *(Sequel in § 234 and 243)*

(5) The Women Go to See the Tomb. § 231

(Saturday before Sunset)

Mt. 28:1

Late Saturday Afternoon Before Sunset The Women Come to See the Tomb

[1]Now after** the sabbath, [*i.e. just before sunset, on Saturday; See note***]
toward the dawn of the first day of the week,
Mary Mag´da-lene and the other Mary went to see the tomb.
[*Note the purpose of their coming was "to see" the tomb.*]

(6) They Buy Additional Spices. § 232

(Saturday After Sunset)

Mk. 16:1

Saturday Evening After Sunset They Go to Buy Additional Spices

[1]And when the sabbath was past, [*i.e. just after sunset Saturday*]
Mary Mag´da-lene, and Mary the mother of James, and Sa-lo´me,
bought spices,*** so that they might go and anoint him. *(Cf.Jn.19:40,p.246)*

(7) They Go Home for the Night. § 233

(And Then Go Home for the Night) .... *(Not definitely Stated but Necessarily Implied)*

*"The Preparation" was an idiomatic expression (or "technical term") among the Jews. It meant "the day before the sabbath." --and hence in our terminology it was Friday. (See note, p.245).

** ASV reads , Now late on the sabbath day; and so avoids contradicting Mk.16:1, and also adds a new touch to the story." See Thayer, Liddel and Scott ,A.T.Robertson, and note carefully the above outline and explanatory notes.

***On Saturday evening, just after sunset, the stores were opened, because the Sabbath was now past.

[a]Or Take a guard. [b]Greek know.

(1) Before Sunup on Sunday The Women Start for The Tomb § 234

(Mk. 16:2; Jn. 20:1)

(2) At Sunrise Jesus Is Resurrected.

(No Record of the Exact Moment or Manner of Christ's Raising)

Jesus Is Raised From The Tomb.

(3) An Angel Comes and Opens the Tomb. § 235

Mt. 28:2-4

An Angel Exhibits The Empty Tomb.

2And behold, there was a great earthquake;
for an angel of the Lord descended from heaven
and came and rolled back the stone,
and sat upon it.

The Angel Is Radiant. The Guards Are Scared Stiff

3His appearance was like lightning,
and his raiment white as snow. (Cf. § 230 and 243)
4And for fear of him the guards trembled
and became like dead men.

(4) Just After Sunrise The Women Arrive at the Tomb. § 236

Before Sunrise, Sunday Morning, the Women Set Out for the Tomb.*

Mk. 16:2-3

2And
very early on the first
day of the week

Lk. 24:1

1But
on the first day of the week,
at early dawn,
they went to the tomb,
taking the spices
which they had prepared.

Jn. 20:1a

1Now
on the first day of the week
Mary Magdalene
* came to the tomb
early, while it was still dark,*

After Sunrise They Arrive at the Tomb

they went* to the tomb
when the sun had risen.*

They Are Wondering About Opening The Tomb

3And they were saying to one another,
"Who will roll away the stone for us from the door of the tomb?"

(5) They See The Tomb Already Opened. § 237

Suddenly They See that It Has Been Opened,

Mk. 16:4

4And looking up, they saw
that the stone was rolled back;
for it was very large.

Lk. 24:2

2And they found
the stone rolled away
from the tomb,

Jn. 20:1b

and saw that
the stone had been taken away
from the tomb.

(6) Mary Magdalene Runs to Tell Peter and John. § 238

Seeing that the Tomb Had Been Opened,

Mary Magdalene Runs Away to Tell Peter and John

Jn. 20:2

2So she ran, and went to Simon Peter
and the other disciple,
the one whom Jesus loved,
and said to them,
"They have taken the Lord out of the tomb,
and we do not know where they have laid him."

(7) The Other Women Enter the Tomb. § 239

Mt. 28:5-8 Mk. 16:5-8 Lk. 24:3-8a

The Other Women Remain

The First Angel Invites Them Into the Tomb

5But the angel said to the women,
"Do not be afraid;
for I know that you seek Jesus who was crucified.
6He is not here;
for he has risen, as he said.
Come, see the place where he lay."

They Enter, and Do Not Find the Body

Mk.

5And entering the tomb,

Lk.

3But when they went in,
they did not find the body.[a]

But They See A Second Angel, Inside, Seated He Rises as They Enter So Now There Are Two Angels Standing The Women Are Frightened.

Mk.

they saw a young man sitting on the right side,
dressed in a white robe;
and they were amazed.

Lk.

4While they were perplexed about this,
behold, two men stood by them
in dazzling apparel;
5and as they were frightened
and bowed down their faces to the ground,

---

*The Greek word here translated "went" in Mk.16:2, and "came" in Jn.20:1, is the Gk. word erchomai; it means either go ("went"), or come ("came"), according to the context. If these two translations here in Mark and in John were exactly reversed, all seeming contradiction in the stories would be removed. Plainly the women set out from Bethany (2miles from the tomb) "while it was yet dark", and arrived at the tomb "when the sun had risen."

[a]Some ancient authorities add of the Lord Jesus.

Mt. 28:5-8 | Mk. 16:5-8 | Lk. 24:3-8a

The Angels Explain To Them

Mk.
6And he said to them,
"Do not be amazed;
you seek Jesus of Nazareth, who was crucified.

Lk.
the men said to them,

Why Jesus Is Not There

Lk.
"Why do you seek the living among the dead?" [a]

Mk.
"He has risen,
he is not here;

They Show The Empty Place

Mk.
"see the place where they laid him!"

They Remind Them of the Master's Words;

(Cf. § 103, p.109)

Lk.
6"Remember how he told you, while he was still in Galilee,
7that the Son of man must be delivered
into the hands of sinful men,
and be crucified,
and on the third day rise."

8And they remembered his words,

And Command Them To Go Tell The Disciples

Mt.
7"Then go quickly and tell his disciples,
that he has risen from the dead;
and behold he is going before you to Galilee:
there you will see him.

Lo, I have told you." (Mt.26:32,p.213)

Mk.
7"But go, tell his disciples
and Peter
that he is going before you to Galilee;
there you will see him,
as he told you."

The Women Go With All Speed.

Mt.
8So they departed quickly from the tomb,
with fear and great joy,

and ran to tell his disciples.

[Mt.v.9,p.252]

Mk.
8And they went out and fled from the tomb;

for trembling and astonishment had come upon them;
and they said nothing to any one, for they were afraid. [b]

(8) Peter and John Visit the Tomb. § 240

Lk. 24:12 | Jn. 20:3-10

Informed By Mary Magdalene

Peter and John Run to the Tomb

Lk.
[*12But Peter rose
and ran to the tomb;

Jn.
3Peter then came out
with the other disciple,
and they went toward the tomb.

4They both ran,

John Arrives First;

but the other disciple outran Peter
and reached the tomb first;

He stoops and Looks In;

5and stooping to look in,
he saw the linen cloths lying there, (Jn.19:40,p.246)

But He Does Not Enter.

but he did not go in.

Then Comes Peter

6Then Simon Peter came
following him,

He too, Looks In

Lk.
stooping and looking in,
he saw the linen cloths
by themselves;

Then He Enters to Inspect Conditions.

Jn.
and he went into the tomb;
he saw the linen cloths lying, (v.5)
7and the napkin, which had been on his head,
not lying with the linen cloths
but rolled up in a place by itself.

Then John also Enters. They Are Convinced But in a Maze.

8Then the other disciple, who reached the tomb first,
also went in,
and he saw,
and believed;

9for as yet they did not know the scripture,
that he must rise from the dead.

Pondering, They Return to Their Lodgings.

Lk.
and he went home
wondering at what had happened.]

Jn.
10Then the disciples went back to their homes.

---

[a] *Some ancient authorities add* He is not here, but has risen.

[b] *Some texts and versions add verses 9-20. In the present parallel arrangement these verses will be placed in the chronological sequence of the events they record.*

* *The Revised Standard Version places verse 12 in the margin.*

(9) Jesus Appears to Mary Magdalene. § 241

Mk. 16:9 | *Jn. 20:11-18*

Jesus appears First to Mary Magdalene

[[9]Now when he rose
early on the first day of the week,
he appeared first to Mary Magdalene,
from whom he had cast out seven demons.

Mary Magdalene Returns To The Tomb, She Stands Weeping Outside the Tomb Then Looking in, She Sees Two Angels Seated Inside

[11]But Mary stood weeping outside the tomb,
and as she wept she stooped to look into the tomb;

[12]and she saw two angels in white,
sitting where the body of Jesus had lain,
one at the head
and one at the feet.

They Ask Why She Is Weeping

[13]They said to her,
"Woman, why are you weeping?"

She Tells Why

She said to them,
"Because they have taken away my Lord,
and I do not know where they have laid him."

Then, Turning About, She Sees Jesus

[14]Saying this,
she turned round
and saw Jesus standing,
but she did not know that it was Jesus. *(Lk.24:16,31)*

He Also Asks Why She Weeps and What She Seeks

[15]Jesus said to her,
"Woman, why are you weeping?
Whom do you seek?"

She Replies, Thinking He Is The Gardener,

Supposing him to be the gardener,
she said to him,
"Sir, if you have carried him away,
tell me where you have laid him,
and I will take him away."

Then Jesus Calls Her Name;

[16]Jesus said to her,
"Mary."

She Recognizes His Voice, Then Addresses Him Adoringly

She turned
and said to him in Hebrew,
"Rab-bo´ni!"
(which means Teacher).

He Commands Her Go and Tell Others

(Mt.28:9,p.252) [17]Jesus said to her,
"Do not hold me,
for I have not yet ascended to the Father;

That He Is About To Ascend To The Father

But go to my brethren
and say to them,
'I am ascending to my Father
and your Father,
to my God
and your God.'"

(10) Jesus Appears to the Other Women Returning to the City. § 242

Mt. 28:9-10 | *Lk. 24:9 11*

Jesus Meets The Other Women

[9]And behold, Jesus met them [*For v.8 See p.250*]
and said,
"Hail!"

They Worship Him

And they came up and took hold of his feet
and worshipped him.

He Asks Them to Dismiss their Fears, But To Tell Others To Meet Him In Galilee

[10]Then Jesus said to them,
"Do not be afraid;
go and tell my brethren
to go to Galilee,
and there they will see me."

....

*See note at close of Mk. 16:8, § 239.

(11) The Women Report to The Other Disciples § 242½

Mary Magdalene And the Other Women Tell What They Have Seen To The Other Disciples

Who They Were

The Other Disciples Are Skeptical They Stubbornly Disbelieve

Mk.16:10-11*	Lk.24:9-11	Jn.20:18
	9 And returning from the tomb	
10 She went	they	Mary Magdalene went
and told those who had been with him,	told all this to the eleven	and said to the disciples,
	and to all the rest.	
as they mourned and wept.		
		"I have seen the Lord", and she told them that he had said these things to her.
	10 Now it was Mary Magdalene and Jo-an′na and Mary the mother of James and the other women with them who told this to the apostles;	
11 But when they heard that he was alive and had been seen by her,	11 But	
	these words seemed to them an idle tale,	
They would not believe it.]	and they did not believe them.[a]	

(12) The Guard Reports to the Jewish Officials. § 243 (cf. §§ 230, 234)

Mt. 28:11-15

While The Women Are Going The Guards Report the Facts.

11 While they were going,
behold, some of the guard went into the city
and told the chief priests
all that had taken place.

The Soldiers Are Given a Bribe, and Told What to Say

12 And when they had assembled with the elders
and taken counsel,
they gave a sum of money** to the soldiers 13 and said,
"Tell people,
'His disciples came by night
and stole him away while we were asleep.'

*Pilate Also Is Quieted****

14 "And if this comes to the governor's ears,
we will satisfy him ***
and keep you out of trouble."

So That Report Continues Among The Jews.

15 So they took the money
and did as they were directed;
and this story has been spread among the Jews to this day.

....

*For verse 12, see §240, p.250.
**A Bribe; ***Probably with a huge bribe.

(1) Jesus Appears to Peter. (See Lk. 24:34; I Cor. 15:5) § 244

(2) Jesus Appears to the Two On the Way to Emmaus. § 245

	Mk. 16:12*	Lk. 24:13-33a
Two Disciples Are Going To Emmaus	[12And after this he appeared in another form to two of them, as they were walking into the country.]	13That very day two of them were going to a village named Em-ma´us, about seven miles[a] from Jerusalem,

They Are Discussing Events

14and talking with each other about all these things that had happened.

Jesus Joins Them

15While they were talking and discussing together,
Jesus himself drew near and went with them.

They Do Not Recognize Him.

16But their eyes were kept from recognizing him. *(v.31;Jn.20:14;21:4)*

He Inquires About Their Trouble

17And he said to them,
"What is this conversation which you are holding with each other
as you walk?"

They Are Astonished at His Question

And they stood still, looking sad.

18Then one of them, named Cle´o-pas, answered him,
"Are you the only visitor to Jerusalem
who does not know the things that have happened there in these days?"

He Makes Further Inquiry.

19And he said to them,
"What things?"

They Reveal Their Lost Hope and Their Despair

And they said to him,
"Concerning Jesus of Nazareth,
who was a prophet mighty in deed and word
before God and all the people,

20"and how our chief priests and rulers delivered him up
to be condemned to death and crucified him.

21"But we had hoped that he was the one to redeem Israel.

They Tell about

"Yes, and besides all this, it is now the third day since this happened.

The Incredible Reports of the Women,

22"Moreover, some women of our company amazed us.
They were at the tomb early in the morning 23and did not find his body;
and they came back saying that they had even seen a vision of angels,
who said that he was alive.

And of Some Apostles.

24"Some of those who were with us went to the tomb,
and found it just as the women had said;

but him they did not see."

He Chides Them For Their Unbelief, and Raises a Question

25And he said to them,
"O foolish men, and slow of heart to believe
all that the prophets have spoken!
26Was it not necessary that the Christ should suffer these things
and enter into his glory?"

He Expounds The Prophecies of Scripture.

27And beginning with Moses and all the prophets,
he interpreted to them in all the scriptures **
the things concerning himself.

When They Arrive at Home,

28So they drew near to the village to which they were going;
and he made as though he would go further,

They Invite Him to Stay With Them, and

29but they constrained him, saying,
"Stay with us,
for it is toward evening and the day is now far spent."

He Goes In With Them

So he went in to stay with them.

[a]Greek, sixty stadia. *See note at close of Mk. 16:8, § 239.

**What would we not give to have this interpretation by Jesus Himself of the Old Testament prophecies of the Messiah! Is it not likely that at least some of the New Testament interpretations have their roots here?*

Lk. 24:13-33[a]

While They are Eating,

30When he was at table with them,
he took the bread and blessed, and broke it, and gave it to them.

They Recognize Him

31And their eyes were opened *(v.16; See II Kings 6:14-16)*
and they recognized him;

Then He Vanishes.

and he vanished out of their sight.

They Describe Their Feelings and Immediately

32They said to each other,
"Did not our hearts burn within us while he talked to us on the road,
while he opened to us the scriptures?"

They Return to Jerusalem To Report To the Rest,

33And they rose that same hour and returned to Jerusalem;

4. THE RESURRECTION EVENING

(1) Jesus Appears in the Evening to Ten Apostles and Others. § 246

*Mk. 16:13-14** *Lk. 24:33b-43* *Jn. 20:19-20*

The Disciples Are in Hiding (Cf. I Cor. 15:5b)

Jn. 19On the evening of that day, the first day of the week,
the doors being shut where the disciples were,
for fear of the Jews,

But They Find Them

Lk. 33b and they found the eleven gathered together
and those who were with them, 34who said,
"The Lord has risen indeed, and has appeared to Simon!"

And Report Their Experiences;

Mk. [13And they went back
and told the rest

Lk. 35Then they
told what had happened on the road,
and how he was known to them in the breaking of the bread.

The Others Disbelieve,

Mk. but they did not believe them.

Then Jesus Appears To Them

Mk. 14Afterward
he appeard
to the eleven themselves
as they sat at table;

Lk. 36As they were saying this,
Jesus himself
stood among them.[a]

Jn. Jesus came
and stood among them
and said to them,
"Peace be with you."

They are Frightened

Lk. 37But they were startled and frightened,
and supposed that they saw a spirit.

Jesus Upbraids Them

Mk. and he upbraided them for their unbelief
and hardness of heart,
because they had not believed
those who saw him after he had risen.]

He Appeals for Belief,

Lk. 38And he said to them,
"Why are you troubled,
and why do questionings rise in your hearts?
39See my hands and my feet, that it is I myself;
handle me, and see;
for a spirit has not flesh and bones
as you see that I have."[b]

He Proves Himself to Them;

Lk. [40 And when he had said this,
he showed them his hands
and his feet.]

Jn. 20When he had said this
he showed them his hands
and his side.

They Still Disbelieve

Lk. 41And while
they still disbelieved for joy,
and wondered,

So He Gives Them Additional Proof

he said to them,
"Have you anything here to eat?"**

42They gave him a piece of broiled fish,
43and he took it and ate before them.

They Believe and Rejoice,

Jn. Then the disciples were glad
when they saw the Lord. *(16:22)*

[a] *Some ancient authorities add* and saith unto them, "Peace to you." [b] *Some ancient authorities add verse 40,* And when he had said this he showed them his hands and his feet. **See note at close of Mk.16:8.*
***See Ac. 10:41, "chosen witnesses, who ate and drank with him after he rose from the dead." Cf. Lk.24:30,41-43; Jn.21:9,12,15.*

(2) He Commissions and Equips Them. § 247

Jn. 20:21-25

Jesus sends Them As God Had Sent Him.

21Jesus said to them again,
"Peace be with you.
As the Father has sent me, even so I send you."

He Bids Them Receive The Holy Spirit, Telling Them There Is No Other Way of Salvation.

22And when he had said this,
he breathed on them, and said to them,
"Receive the Holy Spirit.

23"If you forgive the sins of any, they are forgiven;
if you retain the sins of any, they are retained."

Thomas Is Absent, and Misses All This The Rest Report to Him,

24Now Thomas, one of the twelve, called the Twin,
was not with them when Jesus came.

25So the other disciples told him,
"We have seen the Lord."

He Disbelieves Obstinately.

But he said to them,
"Unless I see in his hands the print of the nails,
and place my finger in the mark of the nails,
and place my hand in his side,
I will not believe."

5. ONE WEEK LATER

Jesus Appears to the Apostles with Thomas. § 248

Jn. 20:26-29

A week later Jesus Appears Again

26Eight days later,
his disciples were again in the house,
and Thomas was with them.

Again He Greets Them

The doors were shut,
but Jesus came and stood among them,
and said,
"Peace be with you."

Then He Appeals to Thomas

27Then he said to Thomas,
"Put your finger here, and see my hands;
and put out your hand, and place it in my side;
do not be faithless, but believing."

Thomas Is Overwhelmed

28Thomas answered him,
"My Lord and my God!"

Jesus Speaks of the Blessing of Faith

29Jesus said to him,
"Have you believed because you have seen me?
Blessed are those who have not seen and yet believe."

Explanatory Note. § 249

Jn. 20:30-31

John Tells His Purpose In Writing His Gospel, And What His Principle of Selection Has Been In Writing His Book

30Now Jesus did many other signs in the presence of the disciples,
which are not written in this book;

31but these are written
that you may believe that Jesus is the Christ,
the Son of God,
and that believing you may have life in his name.

6. SOME TIME LATER

(I) Jesus Appears to the Fishermen at the Lake of Galilee. § 250

Jn. 21:1-14

Another Manifestation

1 After this
Jesus revealed himself again to the disciples
by the Sea of Ti-be´ri-as;
and he revealed himself in this way.

The Circumstances

2 Simon Peter, Thomas called the Twin, Na´than-a-el of Cana in Galilee,
the sons of Zeb´e-dee,
and two others of his disciples were together.

They Fish All Night

3 Simon Peter said to them,
"I am going fishing."
They said to him,
"We will go with you."
They went out and got into the boat;

But in Vain.

but that night they caught nothing.

In the Morning Jesus Stands on the Shore

4 Just as day was breaking, Jesus stood on the beach;
yet the disciples did not know that it was Jesus. *(Jn.20:14; Lk.24:16,31)*

His Inquiry and Their Answer

5 Jesus said to them,
"Children, have you any fish?"

They answered him,
"No."

His Suggestion and the Result

6 He said to them,
"Cast the net on the right side of the boat,
and you will find some."

So they cast it,
and now they were not able to haul it in, for the quantity of fish.

John Recognizes Jesus and tells Peter

7 That disciple whom Jesus loved said to Peter,
"It is the Lord!"
When Simon Peter heard that it was the Lord,
he put on his clothes, for he was stripped for work,
and sprang into the sea.

They Come to Shore

8 But the other disciples came in the boat,
dragging the net full of fish,
for they were not far from the land, but about a hundred yards[a] off.

A Bonfire Is There

9 When they got out on land,
they saw a charcoal fire there,
with fish lying on it, and bread.

Jesus speaks To Them

10 Jesus said to them,
"Bring some of the fish that you have just caught."

They Pull The Net on Shore

11 So Simon Peter went aboard, and hauled the net ashore,
full of large fish, a hundred and fifty-three of them;
and although there were so many, the net was not torn.

They Breakfast With Jesus

12 Jesus said to them,
"Come and have breakfast."

They All Know That It Is Jesus

Now none of the disciples dared ask him,
"Who are you?"
They knew it was the Lord.

He Serves Them

13 Jesus came and took the bread and gave it to them,
and so with the fish.

This Is The Third Time Jesus Met Them In a Group

14 This was now the third time that Jesus was revealed to the disciples
after he was raised from the dead.

---

[a] *Greek* two hundred cubits.

(2) After Breakfast Jesus Reinstates Peter. § 251

Jn. 21:15-23

Jesus Questions Peter: The First Time

Question

Answer

15When they had finished breakfast,
Jesus said to Simon Peter,
"Simon, son of John, do you love me more than these?"

He said to him,
"Yes, Lord; you know that I love you."

Charge

16He said to him,
"Feed my lambs."

A Second Time

A second time he said to him,
"Simon, son of John, do you love me?"
He said to him,
"Yes, Lord; you know that I love you."
He said to him,
"Tend my sheep."

A Third Time

17He said to him the third time,
"Simon, son of John, do you love me?"

Peter Is A Bit Irritated

Peter was grieved because he said to him the third time,
"Do you love me?"

And he said to him,
"Lord, you know everything; you know that I love you."

Jesus said to him,
"Feed my sheep."

Jesus Forecasts Peter's Death

18Truly, truly, I say to you,
when you were young, you girded yourself and walked where you would;
but when you are old, you will stretch out your hands,
and another will gird you and carry you where you do not wish to go."

19(This he said to show by what death he was to glorify God.)

Then They Walk Away Together

And after this, he said to him,
"Follow me." *

Peter Asks About John

20Peter turned and saw following them the disciple whom Jesus loved,
who had lain close to his breast at the supper and had said,
"Lord, who is it that is going to betray you?"

Jesus Replies Reproachfully

21When Peter saw him, he said to Jesus,
"Lord, what about this man?"
22Jesus said to him,
"If it is my will that he remain until I come, what is that to you?
Follow me!"

The Author Corrects a Misunderstanding

23The saying spread abroad among the brethren
that the disciple was not to die;
yet Jesus did not say to him that he was not to die, but,
"If it is my will that he remain until I come, what is that to you?"

(A Final Explanatory Note in John). § 252

Jn. 21:24-25

The Author Is Certified

24This is the disciple who is bearing witness to these things,
and who has written these things;
and we know that his testimony is true.

Why Not More Is Written

25But there are also many other things which Jesus did;
were every one of them to be written,
I suppose that the world itself could not contain the books
that would be written.

Perhaps meaning, Come with me.

FOOTNOTES TO FOLLOWING PAGE

**See note following Mk. 16:8,* § 239.
***Literally,* all the days.
[a]*Or* nations. Beginning from Jerusalem you are witnesses.
[b]*Many ancient authorities add* and was carried up into heaven.
[c]*Many ancient authorities add* worshipped him, and.

STILL LATER

1. Jesus Appears on A Mountain in Galilee. § 253

Mt. 28:16-20 — *Mk. 16:15-18 ** *(Cf. Mk. 14:28, p. 213)*

The Disciples Go to Meet Jesus by Appointment

16Now the eleven disciples went to Galilee,
to the mountain which Jesus had directed them.

They See Him.

17And when they saw him they worshipped him; but some doubted.

His Message Is "The Great Commission": They are To Go And Preach in All the world and Make Disciples and baptize them; and When They are Enrolled as Pupils, Then Teach Them All Things. In This He Will Work With Them

18And Jesus came and said to them,
"All authority in heaven and on earth
has been given to me.

Mk.
[15*And he said to them,*
"Go into all the world
and preach the gospel to the whole creation."

19Go therefore
"and make disciples of all nations,
baptizing them
in the name of the Father
and of the Son
and of the Holy Spirit,
20"teaching them to observe all that I have commanded you;
"and lo, I am with you always,**
to the close of the age."

Believers Will Be saved

Mk.
16*"He who believes and is baptized will be saved;*
but he who does not believe will be condemned.

Signs Will Follow

17*"And these signs will accompany those who believe:*
in my name they will cast out demons;
they will speak in new tongues;
18*"they will pick up serpents,*
and if they drink any deadly thing, it will not hurt them;
they will lay their hands on the sick, and they will recover."]

FINALLY ON ASCENSION DAY

2. Jesus Appears for the Last Time

Lk. 24:44-51; Cf. Ac. 1:4-5

(1) In Jerusalem. § 254

Lk. 24:44-49; Cf. Ac. 1:4-5

Jesus Meets The Apostles in Jerusalem.

44Then he said to them,

Jesus Reminds Them Of His Testimony to Messianic Prophecy,

"These are my words which I spoke to you, while I was still with you, [*See Lk. 18:31-33; 9:22, 44; 22:37; Mt. 26:54; etc.*]
that everything written about me
in the law of Moses and the prophets and the psalms
must be fulfilled."

He Opens Their Minds to the Meaning of the Scriptures About His Death and Resurrection,

45Then he opened their minds to understand the scriptures,
46and said to them,
"Thus it is written, that the Christ should suffer
and on the third day rise from the dead,

and The Great Salvation,

47"and that repentance and forgiveness of sins
should be preached in his name
to all nations,[a] beginning from Jerusalem.

They Are His Witnesses;

48"You are witnesses of these things.

He Will Empower Them;

49"And behold, I send the promise of my Father upon you;

They Are to Wait For This Equipment.

"but stay in the city, until you are clothed with power from on high."

[*Ac. 1:4-5*
4*And while staying*[a] *with them he charged them*
not to depart from Jerusalem,
but to wait for the promise
of the Father, which, he said,
"you heard from me,
5*for John baptized with*
water, but before many days
you shall be baptized
with the Holy Spirit."]

[a]Or eating.

(2) On Mt. Olivet — Jesus Ascends Into Heaven. § 255

*Mk. 16:19-20** — *Lk. 24:50-53*

Jesus Leads to Olivet;

50Then he led them out as far as Bethany,

There He Blesses the Apostles;

and lifting up his hands he blessed them.
51While he blessed them, he parted from them.[b]

Then Ascends.

[19*So then the Lord Jesus,*
after he had spoken to them,
was taken up into heaven,
and sat down at the right hand of God.

They Go Out and Preach Everywhere.

20*And they went forth and preached everywhere,*
while the Lord worked with them
and confirmed the message
by the signs that attended it. Amen.]

52And they[c] returned to Jerusalem with great joy,
53and were continually in the temple blessing God.

FOOTNOTES AT THE BOTTOM OF PRECEDING PAGE

ORDER OF EVENTS AND MAIN DIVISIONS OF THE LIFE OF CHRIST

(Continued from page 3)

The epoch making events introducing the ministry of Jesus begin when John the Baptist suddenly startles the whole nation with the good-news that the great Messiah is about to come.

Jesus begins his own *PRELIMINARY MINISTRY* at the capital of the nation at the great Passover festival by dramatically driving the traders out of the temple. It ends when He is driven from Nazareth.

The *SETTLED MINISTRY* begins when Jesus moves His base of operations to Capernaum. It is divided into two periods. The *FIRST PERIOD* ends when Jesus goes to the Passover at Jerusalem.

The *SECOND PERIOD* of the *SETTLED MINISTRY* extends from feast to feast. While Jesus himself did not attend the Passover of John 6, still His ministry in Galilee was more or less interrupted because of the absence of the people from Galilee attending the Passover at Jerusalem. This period, again, ends in a crisis, "The Great Galilean Crisis."

The *SPECIALIZED MINISTRY* is characterized by Jesus being a fugative and a wanderer, because he is forsaken by most of his disciples; because of the danger of a political revolution; and because of Herod's hostility and treachery. (He had just foulley murdered John the Baptist) All through this special period, Jesus avoids the territory of Herod Antipas; avoids crowds as much as possible; and avoids the Jewish blood-hounds who are dogging his footsteps. Meanwhile Jesus devotes himself to specially preparing his apostles for the time when he will be taken from them.

It is only at the beginning of the end of the *SPECIALIZED MINISTRY* that Jesus returns to Herod's territory (at Capernaum), and then only long enough to take permanent leave of Galilee, so as to spend the remaining six months before the end evangelizing in Judea and Perea.

The *CONCLUDING MINISTRY* also begins at a Feast in Jerusalem. It is forced to a break when the Jewish Rulers for the first time break out in open violence and he must flee to the *COUNTRY* for three months or more. Then again after the Feast of Dedication, mob violence breaks out once more; and Jesus escapes to *PEREA* and evangelizes there for the remaining time up to the end.

The "*EVANGELIZING IN PEREA*", too, is brought to an abrupt close by the death of Lazarus and the plea of His beloved friends of Bethany. But after only a few days of his presence at Bethany the Sanhedrin officially votes his death. They now contemplate official execution instead of mob violence, such as occurred at the last two feasts.

So with a price on his head, Jesus flees to *EPHRAIM* and remains in hiding until Passover time arrives.

Even then Jesus does not risk going privately to Jerusalem by the direct road, but goes north, through Samaria, to join the great Pilgrim crowds thronging the highways near the boundary between Samaria and Galilee. Jesus crosses the Jordan with the vast throngs, so seeking safety, until "his hour should come." Surely this is the simplest, most logical solution of that puzzling text where Luke says that Jesus went "through the (midst) of Samaria and Galilee;" it certainly should be translated, "*ALONG THE BOUNDARY BETWEEN* Samaria and Galilee." Any other hypothesis is so difficult and complicated that it breaks down and is unconvincing.

If now you will turn to page 9 and look at the diagram of the main divisions of the Life of Christ, you will see at the bottom of each column a crisis event indicated: these separate the main divisions of the Life of Christ. The Passovers and the other feasts, named by John, fit in with this. Only one major division is otherwise indicated. That is, by Jesus moving his headquarters from Nazareth to Capernaum, and the settlement there, which move is precipitated by the threat on His life by his hometown friends in Nazareth.

If we should ask why Jesus spent thirty years in private life, and only so brief a period in public ministry, is it not a sufficient answer that during those thirty years he was learning his message by meeting, under the Father's guidance, the everyday cares and trials and duties of life in the midst of men? Did He not also learn to know human nature and man's needs and find out how to meet those needs and so receive from the Father the message which he afterwards preached? All his later teaching has its roots here. Furthermore, *(Heb.5:8)* it is almost universally believed that his foster father Joseph had died shortly after Jesus was twelve years of age, leaving a widowed mother of at least seven children. Jesus was the oldest child and therefore on him lay the heaviest responsibility to help his mother support and rear the family. It was only when these children were grown and settled that he could honorably leave home and devote himself so utterly to public life.

COMPOSITE PORTRAIT OF CHRIST IN THE GOSPELS

The *DOCTRINE OF CHRIST* as given in the Gospels has been summed up in the following outline:

I. HIS DIVINE PRE-EXISTENCE
II. HIS HUMAN INCARNATION
III. HIS PERFECT LIFE
IV. HIS ATONING DEATH
V. HIS VICTORIOUS RESURRECTION
VI. HIS GLORIOUS EXALTATION
VII. HIS COMING AGAIN TO CONSUMMATE ALL THINGS

His "Perfect Life" implies not only Perfect Maturity, Perfect character and Perfect Conduct; but also a Perfect Ideal to aspire to, a Perfect Standard to be judged by, and that He worked out for us under human conditions the only perfect solutions of all human problems--"The Way of Salvatiin."

In a word, Jesus, the Son of God, demonstrated in His earthly life the kind of a human life that would be perfectly satisfactory to God, because it was lived in perfect harmony with the will and nature of God, and so a life lived wholly true to the eternal nature of the universe.

THE BASIC LITERARY STRUCTURE OF EACH OF THE GOSPELS

As to the structure of the four gospels themselves, only Mark and Luke are primarily historical. They have very little literary organization except the logic of the events themselves, and it is very difficult to form an outline of them except the sequences of the narrative itself. Moreover they rather closely coincide, in so far as Mark relates the dramatic happenings.

MARK, or Peter if he be the real author of the narrative, begins to tell the story of the Messiah's coming exactly where that generation itself became acquainted with Jesus, that is with the beginning of the *GOOD NEWS* as it was heralded by the forerunner John. He tells what he knew, and probably experienced, in a straightforward and realistic way, and very briefly, but most dynamically. Virtually the Gospel of Mark is just a string of stories following along in rapid sequences. He seldom stops for special teachings unless indeed they are interwoven with his story itself and are an integral part of the incident he is relating.

Here is a Diagram of the Thought-Structure of Mark.

Division	Subdivision	Chapter	Contents
THE PREPARATION	YOUNG MANHOOD OF JESUS	1	THE PREACHING OF JOHN; THE BAPTISM OF JESUS; THE TEMPTATION OF JESUS
THE SETTLED MINISTRY IN GALILEE — JESUS GOES THRUOUT GALILEE TEACHING AND HEALING	FIRST PERIOD	1[14] 2	AT CAPERNAUM; THRUOUT GALILEE; BACK AT CAPERNAUM
			2ND PASSOVER (JN. 5:1)
	SECOND PERIOD	3 4 5 6	IN AND ABOUT CAPERNAUM; TO MT. OF BEATITUDES & RETURN; PARABLES BY THE SEA; TO GERASENES AND RETURN; TO NAZARETH AND SENDS 12 THRUOUT ALL GALILEE; HEROD KILLS JN. & SEEKS JESUS; TO BETHSAIDA AND RETURN THROUGH GENNESARET
			3RD PASSOVER (JN. 6:4)
THE SPECIALIZED MINISTRY	MOSTLY OUTSIDE GALILEE — AVOIDS HEROD AND CROWDS, TEACHES APOSTLES	7 8 9	TO TYRE AND SIDON; THRU DECAPOLIS; TO DALMANUTHA; TO BETHSAIDA; TO CESAREA-PHILIPPI; THRU GALILEE TO CAPERNAUM
			FEAST OF TABERNACLES (JN. 7)
THE CONCLUDING MINISTRY	IN PEREA EVANGELIZING ON WAY TO PASSOVER	10	APPROACHING PEREA; THRU PEREA; AT JERICHO; ON UP TO BETHANY
			THE LAST PASSOVER
THE CONSUMMATION AT JERUSALEM	CONTROVERSIES AND WARNINGS	11 12	FINAL APPEALS; FINAL DEPARTURE
	SUFFERINGS AND DEATH	13 14	PREPARATIONS FOR HIS DEATH; EVENTS LEADING TO HIS DEATH
	TRIUMPH AND GLORY	15 16	RESURRECTION AND APPEARANCES; FINAL COMMISSION; GLORIFICATION; THE ASCENSION

THE ORDER AND STRUCTURE OF LUKE ARE SHOWN IN THE FOLLOWING DIAGRAM.

LUKE by his own confession was not an original disciple. And not having lived through these revolutionary events himself but coming in from the outside, being a Greek, he sees things in a larger perspective. In his prolonged and intensive researches (probably while he was attending Paul during his imprisonment at Caeserea for two years) discovered many records and traditions. See his own account of it in his preface, Luke 1:1-4. Having the instinct of the greatest historian of ancient times as Sir William Ramsay so stoutly contends, he evaluated and sifted events, and wove them together in the finest account we have of the Gospel times. In his searchings he certainly discovered the Gospel of Mark and evidently followed its main thread of events paralleling and retelling many of them with delicious original touches of color and literary art.

But he also discovered some most important records not otherwise preserved to us. This is our immeasurable debt to him. Following his historical genius he probed into the antecedents and consequences. In all this he had full and free access through two years, to personal help of the Apostle Paul whom Borden P. Bowne calls " the greatest thinker of all time," and who wrote and influenced nearly one-half of the New Testament. Who knows, it may have been at his suggestion that Luke wrote. Surely we should give this great historic genius the liberty to tell his own story in his own way, without mutilating it too much just to force it to fit in to what others have said.

Division	Subdivision	Chapter	Contents
THE PREPARATION	INFANCY	1	ANNUNCIATIONS
	CHILDHOOD	2	BIRTHS OF JOHN & JESUS; NAMING; CONSECRATION; TO PASSOVER; TO NAZARETH
	YOUTH	3	JOHN IS PREACHING; JESUS IS BAPTIZED
	YOUNG MANHOOD	4[13]	JESUS IS TEMPTED
			REMOVAL TO CAPERNAUM (MT. 4:12-LK. 4:31)
THE SETTLED MINISTRY IN GALILEE — JESUS GOES THRU GALILEE TEACHING AND PREACHING	FIRST PERIOD	4[14] 5	JESUS LEAVES NAZARETH; AT CAPERNAUM; THRUOUT GALILEE; AT CAPERNAUM AGAIN
			2ND PASSOVER (JN. 5)
	SECOND PERIOD	6 7 8 9[17]	OPPOSITION GROWS; ORDAINS APOSTLES; SERMON ON MT.; THRU SO. GALILEE AND RETURN; PARABLES AT CAPERNAUM; TO GERASENES AND RETURN; 12 THRUOUT ALL GALILEE; AND RETIRES TO BETHSAIDA
			3RD PASSOVER (JN. 6:4)
THE SPECIALIZED MINISTRY		9[18-50]	TO CAESSAREA PHILIPPI; RETURN TO CAPERNAUM
			FEAST OF TABERNACLES (JN. 7-2)
THE CONCLUDING MINISTRY	EVANGELIZING IN JUDEA	9[51] 10 11 12 13[21]	GOES TO JERUSALEM; 70 SENT THRUOUT JUDEA; A LAWYER QUESTIONS HIM; PHARISEES ACCUSE HIM; DINING WITH A PHARISEE; CONTROVERSIES AND TEACHINGS
			FEAST OF DEDICATION (JN. 10:22)
	EVANGELIZING IN PEREA — 1ST PART OF THE PEREAN MINISTRY	13[22] 14 15 16 17[10]	JESUS ANSWERS AND WARNS THE PHARISEES; HE TEACHES AND WARNS THE MULTITUDE; HE TEACHES AND WARNS HIS DISCIPLES
			RAISING LAZURUS (JN. 11)
	2ND PART OF THE PEREAN MINISTRY	17[11] 18 19[28]	APPROACHING PEREA; JOURNEYING THRU PEREA; PASSING THRU JERICHO; NEARING JERUSALEM; ARRIVING AT BETHANY
			FOURTH PASSOVER
THE CONSUMMATION	CONTROVERSIES AND WARNINGS	19[29] 20	FINAL APPEALS; FINAL DEPARTURE
	SUFFERINGS AND DEATH	21 22	PREPARATIONS FOR THE DEATH; EVENTS LEADING TO HIS DEATH
	TRIUMPH AND GLORY	23 24	RESURRECTION AND APPEARANCES; THE GREAT COMMISSION; THE GLORIFICATION; THE ASCENSION

MATTHEW

As for *MATTHEW* the structure of his book is not primarily historical sequence but predominately logical and topical relationship. I remember hearing a college President who was very fond of Plato say that Matthew's logical method reminded him very much of Plato's philosophy and life of Socrates.

Matthew's Gospel is primarily a series of great doctrinal discourses. These are strung together by groups of historical incidents to give something of realism and graphic background to the Master's teachings. Several of the reports of the incidents are almost pure discourse, with only a meager historical introduction. Others are hot debates in which great teachings are brought out. The Literary structure of Matthew is as simple as that. A series of discourses connected by groups of intervening incidents; but even these incidents are logically, not chronologically, grouped according to their doctrinal implications, as for example, Chapter's 8-9, where the incidents related demonstrate Jesus' supreme power, over men, over all diseases of body and mind, over demons, nature, sin and death.

Here is a Diagram of the Thought-Structure of *MATTHEW*

GENEALOGY; INFANCY AND CHILDHOOD; YOUNG MANHOOD; SERMON ON THE MOUNT; INCIDENTS SHOWING THE POWER OF JESUS; THE APOSTLES SENT OUT; JESUS HEALING AND TEACHING; WHERE CHRIST'S POWER COMES FROM; PARABLES; EVANGELIZING IN GALILEE; FORETELLING DEATH; TRANSFIGURATION AND HEALING; RELATION OF GREAT AND LITTLE IN THE KINGDOM; EVANGELIZING IN PEREA; FINAL CONTROVERSIES WITH JEWISH RULERS; CHRIST LAMENTING THE FATE OF RULERS AND CITY; PROPHESYING THE END OF NATION AND WORLD; EVENTS OF CHRIST'S DEATH; EVENTS OF RESURRECTION

1 2 3 4 5 6 7 8 9 10 11 12 13 14 15 16 17 18 19 20 21 22 23 24 25 26 27 28

GENEALOGY; INCIDENTS; DISCOURSE; INCIDENTS; DISCOURSE; INCIDENTS; TEACHINGS; HOT DEBATE; DISCOURSE; INCIDENTS; DISCOURSE; INCIDENTS; DISCOURSE; INCIDENTS; DEBATE; DISCOURSE; DISCOURSE; INCIDENTS; INCIDENTS

JOHN

As for the Gospel of *JOHN* the structure of the book is still perhaps most simply explained by the earliest suggestion coming from the church fathers: it was written to supplement what other evangelists had written, especially to bring into bold perspective Christ's ceaseless conflicts with the Jewish rulers; which resulted, John 5, in their purpose to kill him; in John 8 and 10, in mob violence; in John 11, in an official vote by the Sanhedrin to execute him, and in verse 55, led them to set a price on his head. In addition to this the logic of his procedure is almost completely dominated by the author's essential purpose, to inspire saving faith in Jesus, as set forth by himself in John 20:30 and 31.

As to historical background, it is probable, too, that John had in mind refuting the false teachings of docetism and incipient gnosticism, that are also reflected in parts of Ephesians Colossians and Revelation.

Evident it is that the author of the fourth Gospel, whoever he was, had before him the other Gospels, essentially as we know them, when he wrote.

PROLOG; BEGINNINGS OF THE MINISTRY; AT THE FEAST (JN. 5:1) "RULERS PERSECUTE JESUS"; PASSOVER (6:4) GREAT CRISIS IN GALILEE; AT THE FEAST OF TABERNACLES; (OPEN VIOLENCE BREAKS OUT); FEAST OF DEDICATION (THEY TRY TO STONE JESUS); LAZARUS RAISED (SANHEDRIN VOTES TO KILL JESUS); LAST APPEALS (FINAL BREAK WITH RULERS); THE LAST SUPPER (LOVE TO THE UTTERMOST); CHRIST'S PRAYER; SUFFERINGS AND DEATH (MALICE TO THE UTTERMOST); RESURRECTION; EPILOG

1:1-18 1:19 2 3 4 5 6 7 8 9 10:1-21 10:21-42 11 12 13 14 15 16 17 18 19 20 21

INTRODUCTION; PUBLIC MINISTRY; POPULAR ACCLAIM; JESUS GATHERS OUT "HIS OWN" (13:1) TRUE BELIEVERS (6:34-45); "THERE AROSE A DIVISION AMONG THEM" (cf. 5:16-18; 6:66; 7:43; 9:16, etc.) (10:20-21); CONFLICTS WITH THE JEWS; SIFTINGS; DISCIPLES IN FOREGROUND; ENEMIES PLOTTING SECRETLY; THE END; DISCIPLES IN HIDING; ENEMIES TRIUMPHANT; VICTORY; NEW BEGINNING

Diagram of Thought-Structure of John

HOW TO STUDY THE BIBLE (Discussion Continued from page. 5)

When the principles of Psychology and the Methods of Pedagogy are seriously applied to Bible study, there emerge the following elements of Scientific Method of Interpretation:

I. IMPRESSIONIST METHOD — *POINTS I to III deal with* FACTS
II. ANALYTIC METHOD
  1. Literary Analysis
  2. Grammatical Analysis
III. HISTORICAL METHOD
IV. DOCTRINAL (Philosophical) METHOD — *IV Deduces* PRINCIPLES, *or* UNIVERSAL SPIRITUAL LAWS
V. PRACTICAL (Psychological) METHOD — *V and VI work out the* APPLICATION *to ourselves and others*
VI. DEVOTIONAL (Spiritual) METHOD

These procedures come most naturally in this order, though not necessarily nor usually so. Most of the time we mix them up, because none of our minds work altogether logically. Sometimes one or two of these elements are most emphasized: sometimes others, -- according to our purpose. But no passage of scripture has been completely studied or fully understood until all these techniques have been used in so far as they are applicable to the case in hand.

The IMPRESSIONIST METHOD is the one our grandmothers used when they read their Bibles every day, and would just "think what comes," and be thrilled by the impressions that came to their minds. In fact this is everybody's method in beginning the study of any new passage of scripture, just because it is the natural movement of the mind. We begin thinking about any new thing by first, overall impressions, before we come to closer grips. When, however, this naive Method is formulated into a scientific instrument of interpretation it gives us not merely our first general impressions, but also the whole sequence of thought, or the literary context, or the psychological movement of the author's mind from point to point.

As for the scientific technique of this method, it begins with the fact that the essential literary units of the Bible are individual books, or in the case of the Psalms, a complete poem. Each literary unit, therefore, should be studied first as a whole. This means the book or poem should be read through rapidly from beginning to end, without interupting our movement of thought to solve individual difficulties. Then,read through again and again.

But as one proceeds in such rapid readings and re-readings of the literary unit as a whole, one begins to discern the main points in the movement of the author's thought from point to point. That is to say the unit as a whole begins to analyze itself or break up into its main points. This is LITERARY ANALYSIS.

LITERARY ANALYSIS then proceeds until, not only the main points are discovered, but the main points themselves break up into sub-divisions. And this process goes on until the essential paragraphs are reached.

The same method is then applied in reference to each PARAGRAPH. This is GRAMMATICAL ANALYSIS. It begins by analyzing a paragraph into sentences, -- declarative, interrogative, imperative, exclamatory.

GRAMMATICAL ANALYSIS then proceeds further to analyze sentences into clauses, clauses into phrases, phrases into words and their relation to each other. This leads on to word study,-- orthography, etymology, inflections, etc.

Such LITERARY and GRAMMATICAL ANALYSIS constitute the main part of what is ordinarily called EXEGESIS.

However, Exegesis also emphasizes another element of method, and that is, HISTORICAL METHOD, which gives us the background, foreground, atmosphere,out of which the literary work was created. It furnishes the graphic details of geography, topography, place, time, persons, etc. In this the following questions are answered: What? Who? When? Where? Why? How?

The next method is DOCTRINAL METHOD. This is really the objective goal of our intellectual study: truths or laws of spiritual life are deduced, or the message which the Bible means to bring us, or which Christ came to reveal. There remain the ethical and practical studies.

For DOCTRINES *will do us no good unless they are translated into* DUTIES: *truth must be translated into virtue; theory must become practice. We must become doers of what we find in the perfect law of liberty. This is the practical or psychological phase of method. The general truth, which our study has given us and which inductive method has formulated into law or principle, must be thought out in our lives today in life-situations we meet, face to face with the every day sins, temptations, stresses, strains, from which we "must be saved."*

But even such practical application of eternal truth will do nobody any good unless we not only think it but live by it. We must not only recognize our duties and privileges but by repeated doing build them into habits of character. Here is where we must be saved. The "blessing" as James reminds us comes only "in the doing". But such doing or living of the Gospel is first of all an inward transaction between the individual soul and the infinite God. It is an utter yielding, in the depths of one's being, to the Spirit of God. This is inward obedience. *But "inward obedience" must now become outwardly expressed, executed in the objective world about us. And no truth of God, however sound the doctrine may be, ever bears fruit until such transaction between the soul and God takes place. This is the* devotional climax of Bible study. *This is the REAL GOAL OF BIBLE STUDY, its ultimate objective.*

Scientific Method applied to the study of the Life of Christ, would mean, if you are studying any one section or incident: First you would read it through repeatedly until you get the thought-sequence. Then you would analyze the story into its "scenes", by noting changes of time, place, persons, event, etc. Then visualize each scene by adding every graphic detail of color. Then note the connection of each scene with the next, and make your outline. Then you would find the "central truth" of the story as intended by the writer. Then think out the application of this spiritual law to life today. Finally, you would have a personal transaction with God about this truth and your life and that of those you teach, in vital prayer for yourself and for them. Here is where the word bears fruit, where truth becomes virtue, where religion becomes objective reality.

Everybody knows how "crazy" people are about the movies and the theater, i.e. all kinds of drama. You know that teachers and preachers and story tellers are popular according to their ability to be graphic, to VISUALIZE with dramatic realism. It is true of all great literature from Homer to Whitcomb Riley; from the comic strips and magazines up to the greatest artists and illustrators; of great orators from Demosthenes and Cicero to Patrick Henry and Daniel Webster; of all great preachers from St. Paul to Philips Brooks and D. L. Moody.

But Why?

For one big reason: VISUALIZATION and dramatization make your message seem real and life-like, they bring the truth "close home", where you can understand and appreciate it, and know how to translate the truths into virtues of character; so that they "become a part of you", and you can "live" them.

Jesus knew this art perfectly, and used it to perfection, that's why He demonstrated what God can do thru one who is wholly obedient. And that is why Jesus used so many stories; and His stories are the best in the world, both as to content and as to literary form.

That is why God sent Him to live among us. And when you and I as teachers visualize the stories of His life, people feel they have seen Him, and have heard Him tell His own stories. How often students have said, "Why, I just feel as if I have been back there and seen those things happen."

That's why this book was prepared with such endless pains, so as to give you every possible help to visualize His life and teachings.

SCENIC ANALYSIS

But all great dramas and stories are a series of successive pictures, moving in rapid succession to a dramatic climax and conclusion.

These successive scenes we must analyze out and see, as separate pictures, before we can vivify them. Every story in the Gospels is here so analyzed. The "marginal titles" are really "moving pictures". Study every event with this in mind, and your teaching, and story telling, and dramatization, and expository preaching, will improve a hundred per cent over night. First analyze your story into its scenes; then visualize each scene with life-like realism.

Each "scene" of a story is distinguished from those before and those that follow by changes in, (1) the place, (2) the time, (3) the persons, (4) the event that happens. Pick out your favorite story and try this technique and see for yourself.

THE PSYCHOLOGY OF REALIZATION

The Problem

How do the teachings, the doctrines, the ideals, the example of Christ, the perfect life which He demonstrated under human limitations and conditions *(Phil.2:6-8)* become Christian virtues and Christian character in us?

How does one become a "partaker of the divine nature?" and "escape the corruption that is in the world" - "through the knowledge of Him who called us," by his own glory and virtue? (II Peter 1:4).

How does an idea become a reality? How is a thought turned into action?

How does an abstract truth become a concrete and habitual virtue of character?

How can one "put foundations under one's air castles", as Hawthorne says?

How does one proceed to "realize one's ideals?" Or to make "one's dreams come true?"

And turn theory into practice? and how can we guide others to "practice what we preach?"

In other words, what are the steps of faith in the process of the Psychology of Realization?

The Solution

The method of procedure has been slowly and laboriously wrought out by Psychologists, Educationists, and Efficiency engineers. In brief outline it will be summed up here, for it is of extreme importance and significance to the religionist. (See diagram at bottom of page).

Before a thought or an idea can become objectively realized it must first become an ideal; it must be visualized in concrete, lifelike form. This requires a process of imagination. The abstract mental image must become concrete, i.e. realistic. "The real is always 100% concrete." And we cannot fully evaluate and so motivate an idea until it can be envisaged in lifelike realistic form. We evaluate and so motivate an ideal, until it becomes a dominant desire; then we choose it, i.e., we judge it valuable to the self; we desire and approve it, and so it becomes dominant desire; we identify ourselves with it, and decide to strive to make it come true, i.e., become a fact of experience in objective reality.

The next step, then, after motivation, will be to form a definite whole-hearted Purpose or Choice. Then, after having definitely chosen an ideal as our objective, we project a plan of action so that what we have thought, and idealized, and chosen or wholeheartedly purposed, may become objectively realized in experience.

But General Plans are not enough. They are important, absolutely essential in fact, but not enough; but now the General Plan must be supplemented with a blue print and specifications; it must now become a Schedule. We must consider time, place, materials, equipment, personnel, operations--before it can be objectively realized in experience.

This is true in the simplest affairs, and in the most complicated--in making a chair, or in building a Cathedral; in cooking breakfast, or in commanding an army.

It is likewise true in all spiritual realization; in making prayers come true; in winning a soul to Christ; in administering a church program or in personal counseling.

But Ideas and Ideals, Choices and Purposes, Plans and Schedules, are not enough; there must then be fulness of Fa Obedience, and Action. There must be the fiat, or definite act of will to "cast the die", -- to begin the operation of the machine or equipment, upon the material, in the definite place and definite time, putting the Plan into action, to realize the choice of the ideal which is the concrete form of the idea or thought.

Fullness of Faith is necessary to Action. No action ever takes place without FAITH. This is the PSYCHOLOGY OF REALIZATION. In this way then the truths Jesus taught and the ideals he gave us become Christian virtues in people, and institutions in society. This "faith" process is so very important because without faith no action takes place. There must be strong, dynamic faith in the Idea, the Ideal, the Plan, etc, -- and all the way through the process, until the thought is actually realized in experience.

Ideas and Ideals, Choices and Purposes, Plans and Schedules, Despatching and Action equal Objective Realization in experience.

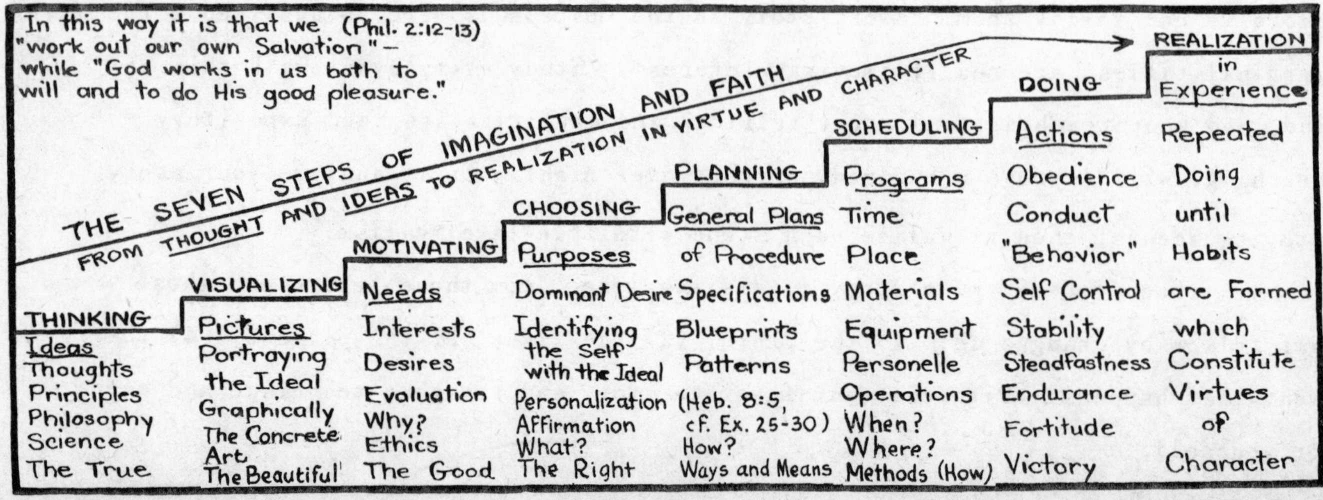

INDEX

3. THE SPECIALIZED MINISTRY

4. THE CONCLUDING MINISTRY

PART THREE: THE CONSUMMATION

1. CONFLICTS AND WARNINGS

2. SUFFERINGS AND DEATH

3. TRIUMPH AND GLORY